THE
PUSHCART PRIZE, XX:
BEST OF THE
SMALL PRESSES

AN ANNUAL SMALL PRESS READER

THE PUSHCART PRIZE XX

20th Anniversary

1996

BEST OF THE SMALL PRESSES

*Edited by
Bill Henderson
with the
Pushcart Prize
editors.
Poetry Editors:
Carol Muske,
Dennis Schmitz
Essays Editor:
Anthony Brandt*

PUSHCART PRESS

Note: nominations for this series are invited from any small, independent, literary book press or magazine in the world. Up to six nominations—tear sheets or copies, selected from work published, or about to be published, in the calendar year—are accepted by our December 1 deadline each year. Write to Pushcart Press, P.O. Box 380, Wainscott, N.Y. 11975 for more information.

Distributed by W. W. Norton & Co.
500 Fifth Ave., New York, N.Y. 10110

Library of Congress Card Number:76–58675
ISBN: 0–916366–99–5
     0–916366–63–4 (paperback)
ISSN: 0149–7863

Manufactured in The United States of America
by RAY FREIMAN and COMPANY, Stamford, Connecticut

Acknowledgments

Selections for the Pushcart Prize are reprinted with permission of the authors and the following presses:

The Nearness of the World © 1994 American Short Fiction
The Swing of Things © 1994 Pitt Magazine
The Match © 1994 Ontario Review
The More I Like Flies © 1994 The Kenyon Review
Pity © 1994 ZYZZYVA
Mother-Tongue © 1994 Bamboo Ridge
Milk © 1994 Ploughshares
The End of the World © 1994 The Antioch Review
An Instinct For Bliss © 1994 The Paris Review
The Kingdom of the Sun © 1994 Story
The Late Style © 1994 Mississippi Review
The Women Come and Go © 1994 New England Review
Wilma Bremer's Funeral © 1994 The American Voice
False Water Society © 1994 Conjunctions
A Happy Vacancy © 1994 The Southern Review
Videotape © 1994 Antaeus
My Father's Chinese Wives © 1994 Quarterly West
Closing Out the Visit © 1994 Iowa Review
The Undesirable Table © 1994 Raritan
Super Night © 1994 TriQuarterly
The Ring of Brightest Angels Around Heaven © 1994 The Paris Review
Sex © 1994 ZYZZYVA
Updike and I © 1994 Antaeus
Bad © 1994 Ploughshares
Magic © 1994 The Georgia Review
When Words Became Windows © 1994 Harvard Review; Faber and Faber
Stillborn © 1994 The Iowa Review
Last Things © 1994 Ploughshares
Six Days: Some Rememberings © 1994 Alaska Quarterly Review
Elizabeth Bishop © 1994 Threepenny Review
The Barbarians Are Coming © 1994 Milkweed Review
Film Noir: Train Trip Out of Metropolis © 1994 Antioch Review
The Storm Chasers © 1994 The Gettysburg Review
The Era of the Vari-Vue © 1994 Oxford Magazine
Seizure © 1994 Field
Theories of Illusion © 1994 The Missouri Review
Phlox Diffusa © 1994 The Yale Review
Elizabeth, Listening © 1994 Faultline
Chinese Food In The Fifties © 1994 Pequod
In The Pasture of Dead Horses © 1994 The Journal
A Little Thing Like That © 1994 Chelsea
Something Like Happiness © 1994 Antaeus

*IN CELEBRATION OF
OUR TWENTIETH ANNIVERSARY
THIS EDITION IS DEDICATED TO
THE FOUNDING EDITORS
OF THE PUSHCART PRIZE SERIES
AND TO THE HUNDREDS OF CONTRIBUTING
EDITORS WHO HAVE SUSTAINED US
THROUGH THE YEARS*

INTRODUCTION

by BILL HENDERSON

I APPROACHED THIS 20th Anniversary Introduction with two tentative outlines: a long piece detailing the history of *The Pushcart Prize* series from its inception at the Mediterranean coffee house in Berkeley, California (a note I jotted on a pad in June, 1975 "a best of the small presses? so little read, so much good out there"); or a brief intro honoring the idea that an introduction is meant to get the reader moving smartly into the book. I chose the latter.

What else could be said at length here that hasn't been said many times about *The Pushcart Prize* in this space by guest introducers Gail Godwin, Jane Anne Phillips, George Plimpton, Cynthia Ozick, Frank Conroy, Richard Ford, Russell Banks, Edward Hoagland and myself? Not much. We live in a spiritual vacuum created by our society's compulsive hunger for money and only money, whatever the real cost. Once magazine and book publishers were at least partially immune to this disease; not so today. Commercial publishers now chase the buck with total concentration. The life of literature—of our dreaming, longing and thoughtful selves—is left to noncommercial journals and presses. Said before, said again here for our 20th, and to be repeated for our 30th if necessary.

My special thanks here to Carol Muske and Dennis Schmitz for reading hundreds of poems with diligence; to Tony Brandt for plugging through stacks of essays; and to Lee Smith and Rick Moody my co-fiction editors. My appreciation also to Hannah Turner who has kept the records straight at Pushcart for many years.

A sad note: Dan Halpern's *Antaeus* folded last year. *Antaeus* was simply one of the best of the best. Dan is a Founding Editor of this se-

11

ries, and a good friend. His Ecco press continues, and several selections from the last *Antaeus* follow.

Finally, my thanks to the Founding Editors and the thousands of editors and writers who have contributed to this project over the past two decades. You are the soul of our culture. Please never forget that—or we are all goners.

As always, you will find much to appreciate in our Twentieth, and perhaps some things not to your taste. I leave you with a quote from Marvin Bell: "There is no one way and no right way to write; there is no one way and no right way to talk about writing, either. No one knows enough. Those who say they know—run from them, run from them."

THE PEOPLE WHO HELPED

FOUNDING EDITORS—*Anaïs Nin (1903–1977) Buckminster Fuller (1895–1983), Charles Newman, Daniel Halpern, Gordon Lish, Harry Smith, Hugh Fox, Ishmael Reed, Joyce Carol Oates, Len Fulton, Leonard Randolph, Leslie Fiedler, Nona Balakian (1918–1991), Paul Bowles, Paul Engle (1908–1991), Ralph Ellison (1914–1994) Reynolds Price, Rhoda Schwartz, Richard Morris, Ted Wilentz, Tom Montag, William Phillips, H. L. Van Brunt*

CONTRIBUTING EDITORS FOR THIS EDITION—*John Allman, Ralph Angel, A. Manette Ansay, Antler, Philip Appleman, Tony Ardizzone, Jennifer Atkinson, David Baker, Will Baker, Steve Barthelme, Rick Bass, Marvin Bell, Joe David Bellamy, Karen Bender, Michael Bendzela, André Bernard, Linda Bierds, Philip Booth, Marianne Boruch, Michael Bowden, Rosellen Brown, Michael Dennis Browne, Bliss Broyard, Christopher Buckley, Richard Burgin, Kathy Callaway, Gillian Conoley, Henry Carlile, Judith Ortiz Cofer, Henri Cole, Michael Collier, Jane Cooper, Stephen Corey, Mark Cox, Philip Dacey, John Daniel, Jim Daniels, Carl Dennis, Stuart Dischell, Stephen Dixon, Rita Dove, John Drury, Stuart Dybek, Kim Edwards, Raymond Federman, Edward Field, Maria Flook, H. E. Francis, Alice Fulton, Kenneth Gangemi, Timothy Geiger, Reginald Gibbons, Gary Gildner, Molly Giles, C. S. Giscombe, Marilyn Hacker, James Harms, Ehud Havazelet, Robin Hemley, Patricia Henley, DeWitt Henry, Edward Hirsch, Jane Hirshfield, Edward Hoagland, Tony Hoagland, Andrew Hudgins, Lawson Fusao Inada, Colette Inez, Elizabeth Inness-Brown, Mark Irwin, Richard Jackson, Mark Jarman, David Jauss, Ha Jin, Laura Kasischke, Edmund*

13

Keeley, George Keithley, Brigit P. Kelly, Thomas E. Kennedy, William Kennedy, Carolyn Kizer, Richard Kostelanetz, Maxine Kumin, JoEllen Kwiatek, Wally Lamb, Norman Lavers, David Lehman, Brenda Hillman, Mark Levine, Philip Levine, Lisa Lewis, Fatima Lim-Wilson, Stanley Lindberg, James Linville, Gordon Lish, Gerry Locklin, Adrian C. Louis, D. R. MacDonald, David Madden, Clarence Major, Melissa Malouf, Jack Marshall, Michael Martone, Carole Maso, Dan Masterson, Susan Onthank Mates, Lou Mathews, Cleopatra Mathis, Khaled Mattawa, William Matthews, Gail Mazur, Robert McBrearty, Rebecca McClanahan, Lynne McFall, Campbell McGrath, Kristina McGrath, Sandra McPherson, Jay Meek, Leonard Michaels, Brenda Miller, Jane Miller, Steven Millhauser, Susan Mitchell, Jewel Mogan, Lisel Mueller, Joan Murray, Kent Nelson, Josip Novakovich, Sigrid Nunez, Naomi Shihab Nye, Joyce Carol Oates, Ed Orchester, Sharon Olds, Frankie Paino, Walter Pavlich, Mary Peterson, Robert Phillips, Robert Pinsky, Eileen Pollack, Joe Ashby Porter, C. E. Poverman, Tony Quagliano, Donald Revell, Alberto Alvaro Rios, David Rivard, Len Roberts, Pattiann Rogers, David Romtvedt, Ken Rosen, Gibbons Ruark, Sharman Apt Russell, Vern Rutsala, Lisa Sandlin, Sherod Santos, Dean Schabner, Lloyd Schwartz, Joanna Scott, Barbara Selfridge, Laurie Sheck, Diann Blakely Shoaf, Jim Simmerman, Arthur Smith, Carol Snow, James Solheim, Elizabeth Spires, Maura Stanton, Eugene Stein, Dan Stern, Pamela Stewart, Pat Strachan, David St. John, Ron Tanner, Jean Thompson, Lee Upton, Lloyd Van Brunt, Dennis Vannatta, Sam Vaughan, Arthur Vogelsang, David Foster Wallace, Michael Waters, Gordon Weaver, Roger Weingarten, Susan Wheeler, Ellen Wilbur, Theodore Wilentz, George Williams, Joy Williams, David Wojahn, Robert Wrigley, Lois Ann Yamanaka, Christina Zawadiwsky, Paul Zimmer

ROVING EDITOR—*Lily Frances Henderson*

EUROPEAN EDITORS—*Liz and Kirby Williams, Genie Chipps*

MANAGING EDITOR—*Hannah Turner*

AT LARGE—*Marvin Bell*

FICTION EDITORS—*Bill Henderson with Rick Moody, Lee Smith*

POETRY EDITORS—*Carol Muske, Dennis Schmitz*

ESSAYS EDITOR—*Anthony Brandt*

EDITOR AND PUBLISHER—*Bill Henderson*

CONTENTS

THE
PUSHCART PRIZE, XX:
BEST OF THE
SMALL PRESSES

PITY

fiction by AVNER MANDELMAN

from ZYZZYVA

WE'VE BEEN watching him for two weeks, Léon and I, from inside a shop across the avenue Foch. It belonged to a local Jew who helped the *Mossad* every now and then, and didn't ask any questions. This time he closed his shop for us—I didn't ask how much it was costing him. It was a posh boutique, with chinchilla and astrakhan coats hanging under Tiffany lamps, and mink jackets in the corners, and Léon and I made ourselves at home, taking turns at the Zeiss monoscope behind the curtain. We watched the second floor apartment across the avenue, where the man who called himself Charles LeGrand now lived.

Until the month before we weren't even sure it was he; but then the local Mossad *katsa* broke into the office of LeGrand's dentist in Neuilly, made copies of his x-rays and sent them to the archive of *Yad VaShem,* and after weeks the answer came back that it was indeed he, Karl Joachim Gross, The Smiler himself. In '43, he had personally supervised the killing of five, maybe six thousand Jews in the Lodz ghetto, two thousand of them children, and who knows how many more in Maidanek. Not a very big fish, compared with Eichmann and Mengele, but a fish just the same. Took us five years to locate him, once it was decided to go one level down, since we had gotten all the ones above him already. The funny thing is, the HQ for catching Nazi fugitives was in Paris, and Gross was number three on our list, yet it took us that long to find him. We had looked for him in Rio, and La Paz, even in Santiago, and here he was all the time in avenue Foch, right between our legs, 400 meters away from our own consul's apartment.

This Gross, he now owned a little newspaper by the name of *Vents Neufs*, New Winds, a liberal paper, supportive of Israel, culture art, shit like that. Most probably as camouflage, because fuckers like him never change. It's in the blood, whatever it is. He was old now, more than 70, though he carried himself as erect as if he were De Gaulle, or something, and he lived on the second floor of a gray apartment building on the good side of the avenue, the north side, with two poodles, a little girl (his granddaughter, maybe, or a niece), and a blond Swedish nurse or a nanny, whatever she was, that took care of the girl, maybe of him, too. We didn't care about her, or the girl. Only him. I especially. My grandparents went in the Lodz ghetto, also two uncles, three aunts, and all my cousins. Only my father escaped.

At first, after I had tracked Gross down in Paris, the *Memuneh*, the Mossad's chief, got cold feet and wanted to take me off the case. But then my father intervened and said I was a pro, he had trained me himself, I could handle it, they shouldn't insult me, this and that. So they let me continue, but they glued Léon Aboulafia to me, a Moroccan Jew from Casablanca, who knew Nazis only from the movies, from Tach'kemoni High School, and maybe also from *Yad VaShem*, but that's it. Eichmann, too, they had let only Moroccan Jews guard him. I mean, we are all good soldiers and obey orders, but why take chances.

So we had been watching this Gross for two weeks, pigging out on *boeuf en croûte* and *croissants* and fancy cheeses that the local shadowers who kept a back-up team in a café nearby left us every morning at the back door, when we finally got the go-ahead, straight from the *Midrasha* in Tel Aviv. The embassy *bodel*, a short fat woman by the name of Varda, came by one evening and slid an envelope into the mail slot in the front door, just like that, with the code words *Sun in Giv'on*, which meant we could take him, and it was up to us how to do it.

The orders, when we had left Tel Aviv, were to take Gross alive, bring him to Yerushalayim for a trial, but if anything went wrong, not to think twice, to take him down immediately, silent or noisy, then scram to London via Calais, where two DST border guards were on our payroll.

It went without saying that taking down Gross would look bad for me, what with my father's intervention, and the Memuneh breaking the rules for me, and everything. "But better this than headlines," my father said, when right after Léon and I had landed in Paris, I called him from a hookers' café in Pigalle, going through one of our Zurich lines. "If you got to take him down, do it."

"No, I'll bring him alive, don't worry," I said.

"But don't take chances. I don't want to see you with *tzitzes* on your back." Which meant, "I don't want to see you on the front cover of *Ha'Olam HaZeh*."

Ha'Olam HaZeh is the yellow rag of Israel. The back pages show women with exposed tzitzes, the front cover exposes the political scandal of the day.

"Oh, don't worry," I said, "I'll bring him. Nobody'll know anything, until he's in the glass booth."

The glass booth was where Eichmann had sat for his trial, so a crazed survivor of some camp couldn't shoot him or something.

There was a little pause. All around me were hookers, cackling in argot.

"Don't worry," I said again. "He'll be there soon."

"With God's help," my father said. (He had become religious in his old age, after he had retired.) "With God's help."

"With, without, you get the cage ready," I said, "he'll be there."

This was two weeks before. Now it was Friday night. I had been watching the literary program *Apostrophes* on the small television, using the earphones, and Léon was at the 'scope, when the envelope slid in. We both knew what it was, even before Léon clicked open his katsa knife and slit it open.

It took him two minutes to decipher the message with his *Tzadi-Aleph*.

"Mother's cunt," Léon said to me in Hebrew, after finishing the computation. "We go."

Usually we spoke French, in case someone heard voices inside. But I guess he got excited. Take-downs he had done already, two, maybe three, but this was his first abduction, and a Nazi, too.

I myself had done three abductions before, two of them in Europe, one in Cairo. None was a Nazi, but so what. Nazis, Arabs, they are all the same to me. Haters of Yisrael, destroyers of Ya'acov, as the Bible said, it is a *mitzvah* to persecute them, to exterminate them to the tenth generation, like King Shaul was supposed to do to the Amalekite, by the order of God, when he foolishly took pity on his enemy and so lost his kingship. We learned about this, in the Midrasha, in the katsa course; about the dangers of having a soft heart. No pity or compassion for these fuckers. None.

Not that I had any fear, now, of this. If anything, it was just the opposite. I knew the stories as well as anyone, what the old hands said, that there was nothing like catching a Nazi—it's better than sex, getting your hands on one of them, a real live one, being part of God's own Sword of Vengeance, so to speak. Even experienced katsas sometimes went crazy, when they saw a Nazi up close. Six years ago in Buenos Aires, two katsas from *Eytanim* department, the Russian shadowers, with 15 years service between them, slit the throat of an old hag they were supposed to bring in, some Austrian nurse who was said to have helped Mengele do selections. Her trial in Yerushalayim was ready to begin, with documents stacked a meter high, Golda's speech to the Knesset already printed in large type, so she could read it to the TV cameras without glasses, the editor's committee already briefed, everything, when suddenly, the night before shipment, the Nazi hag said a few words to one of them, maybe spit in his face, something, and they slit her throat. Just like that, both of them, one after the other. They were not even Ashkenazi Jews, or anything. One a Moroccan, like Léon, the other a Jerusalemite, his parents originally from Turkey, both sets of grandparents still living, even; still they did her, not a second thought. Go learn why. Maybe it's in the genes, now, this hatred. Like men and snakes, forever and ever, with no forgiveness possible.

Later the two were demoted, of course, but after less than six months they both got their ranks back, after Golda personally intervened on their behalf with my father, who was the Memuneh then. Because who can say he would have behaved differently? she said. Who can say he would have stayed his hand? Orders are orders, but sometimes there's a limit.

A week in that furrier boutique, still waiting for the go-ahead, that's exactly what I had begun to feel. Ten days, and still nothing. By then I was really beginning to worry, because you never know, someone might have gotten it into his head to cancel. Who knows what goes on in the corridors in the *Q'irya*, in Tel Aviv, or in the Knesset committees, in Yerushalayim, with all these soft-hearted kibbutzniks. I even suggested to Léon, once, to do it before any orders arrived, then tell the Midrasha we were faced with F.C.R.I., field-circumstances-requiring-initiative. But Léon said no. It was too this, it was too that, and I didn't argue with him too much, because, let's face it, I didn't want to make more of a mess than we had to, and also because of my father, and the Memuneh, and everything. But with every day that passed, my obedience was weakening, because I was getting sicker and sicker of seeing this Gross strolling down the avenue with the poodle leash in one hand, the little girl's hand in the other, the nurse behind. Every time I saw him ambling by, happy and smiling and pink, not more than five meters away, I had to stop myself from rushing out to stick a tape over his white smile, throw him in the VW van, then drive the parcel to the Israeli embassy and let the resident katsa take care of the rest. I mean, the consul would have plotzed, since it would have made him directly involved. But what the hell, we could, if we had to. In such matters we outranked him and he knew it.

Anyway, the orders came, so the only thing left to do, beside the actual job, was decide when and how to do it, and how to ship him over. Finally (it took three hours of arguing), we decided to bag Gross on Sunday. (Sunday mornings he went with his little granddaughter, or niece, or whatever she was, to La Madeleine, without the nurse.) We would then ship him out to Israel the very same night, no delay.

Now, normally, shipping him would have been an Aleph-Aleph problem, because after Switzerland, which is a complete police state, where the SSHD always knows when every foreigner farts, France is the worst place in Europe. In Switzerland they are at least polite to you, and also are honest and stay bribed, once you pay them off. But these French fuckers—everybody, *flics,* DST, SDECE, CRS—they'll all happily take whatever you slip them, stick it in their ass-pocket, then go and haul you in anyway and divide the loot with the boss. That's the national character. Whores from birth, is what they are. No wonder they all collaborated with the Nazis in the forties, helped them ship the Jews to the camps, also managed some of the local camps for them, from Vichy. Fucking bastards, the Nazis and the French both. I once saw the train station on the outskirts of Paris, near the Porte de Clignancourt, from where they had sent the Jews east—a crumbling structure and rusty rails, not even a sign of what had once happened there. Not a plaque, not a note, nothing. Sometimes I wish I had been born then, so I could fight the fuckers when they were still young, like my father did, after he got out of the Polish forests and roamed all over Europe with a pair of knives and a Luger, and a little notebook where he kept score in *Rashi* Hebrew script. But we can't all be lucky.

This time, though, it seemed we were: two of our missile boats were docked in Marseille, for installation of these new CW radars from Dassault, and Thomson CSF digital sonar, that Peres had bribed out of Giscard, and by chance I knew the captain of one of them—also a Tel Aviv boy, by the name of Amirav Feiglin, who had once been with me in Young Maccabi, and also later, in Flight Course, which we both flunked. Years before, in Wormaiza Street, he had once stolen my bike, and when I caught him I of course beat him up, but I also let him beat me back a little, and we remained friends. Saturday morning, Varda arrived for last-minute instructions. I asked her to send Ami a message in *Tzadi-Tzadi*, regular I.D.F. MilCode, bypassing the embassy katsa, and ask him if he would take a live package with him on the boat to Haifa, in a large box, and also us, Léon and me, without passports.

Varda made a face when I asked her to bypass the embassy katsa, but she agreed, as I knew she would. I used to fuck her, two years before, when she was new in the Paris station and not yet so fat from all this Parisian butter. I was stationed in Paris then for a series of take-downs of some local PLO *shawishes*, who had helped blow up two El Al offices, and she was the decoy, masquerading as a hooker. Old business, this, doesn't matter. The main thing is, she agreed to give Ami the message, and also help drive the van.

"You need anything else?" she asked, after I had finished telling her what I wanted.

She had entered the boutique via the side door, and now sat in the purple armchair of the furrier's customers, rubbing her cheek on a white astrakhan coat that cost maybe 200,000 francs, maybe more. Her freckled face, under the thick make-up, was still pretty, also her tits were still upright; only her flanks had begun to go flabby and her ankles had thickened, maybe from all this walking, trailing people, eating on the run. Also, two years ago, she was told to put on weight, because Arabs like them fat, and now it was probably hard to take it off. It's not the healthiest thing, being a junior embassy katsa. But what do you want, there are worse things than giving your youth to your people. At least there's still a people to give it to.

"Yes," said Léon, "syringes, tapes, sack, everything."

He, too, had fucked her once or twice, I am sure, for form's sake, when he had arrived in Paris. But of course it was no big deal. In the Mossad, fucking is like a handshake. It's a greeting to a colleague. It's even sort of encouraged, so you don't have people falling in love with each other, screwing up the operational chain of command. If everyone screws everyone, it doesn't matter anymore, and you can direct your mind to more important stuff. Anyway, that's the theory. I re-member how after fucking Varda exclusively for more than a year, I was told several times to look around, there were more women in the Mossad, a new crop every year coming from the Midrasha, what did I get stuck on this fat broad for. (She wasn't fat, then.) Finally, I got the hint and stopped it; or maybe she did, I can't remember. Maybe she got the hint, too. This was just after the business with the PLO shaw-ishes. Anyway, it was a long while back.

She said now, "Maybe you need more people?"

I saw she was eager to get in on the thing, not just to drive. Catch-ing a live Nazi, it doesn't come up every day.

"No," I said. "Léon and I are enough, for this."

"Sure," Léon said. "It's a small job."

His first abduction, already an expert.

"No, I can help, too," Varda said. "Really."

I saw she didn't get it, so I said, "You are also a Polack, a Bilavsky, they won't let you."

Couldn't she see it? The orders were to bring him alive, that's why there were only two of us, in a job that required four at least. To min-imize the chances of a repeat of the Buenos Aires fuck-up.

"Only on my father's side," Varda said. "My mother was from Greece."

"Same thing."

The Nazis had also killed half the Jews of Greece, and sent the other half to Auschwitz. I was once in Salonika with a small back-up team from *Kardomm*, on a take-down job of a PLO mechanic. On my day off I went to the local Jewish cemetery. It was so full of headstones, you could hardly walk. If Tito hadn't stopped them in Yugoslavia, and Montgomery in El Alamein, these fuckers would have done the same in Tel Aviv, brought down the Third Temple. Touch and go, it was. Touch and go.

Varda said, "No, I got my Authorization last month. Really."

"Congratulations," Léon drawled. "Commander."

The Authorization is a permission to kill without having your life or the life of a colleague threatened, based on F.C.R.I. It's roughly equiv-alent to an officer's commission in the Army.

Varda's nose turned red. "No, really. So if you need someone."

I began to say it was O.K. by me, but Léon said quickly it was not something he wanted to take on. Maybe because she was half a Polack, or maybe because he did not want a woman on the job.

Moroccans are like that. Women for them are good only for one thing, babies. Maybe for fucking, too, but even for this they prefer each other.

"Authorization, shmauthorization," Léon said. "You want to help drive, fine, drive, but this thing, Mickey and I do it."

He said it as if he was giving the order all of a sudden, and I got mad. I said if she wanted to help, let her help, why not? Maybe we could use a woman.

"Like how, use?" Léon said. "We don't need anybody else. Two is enough, for this, mother's cunt, an old man and a little girl!"

I said, "But if, I don't know, the little girl shouts, or something."

"So what? Mother's cunt! She shouts, he shouts, anyone shouts, it's the same thing. Anything goes wrong, we take him down, ten seconds, we are gone."

"You or me?" I said. "Who will do him? If we have to."

Léon got all red in the neck. He knew very well that the one who took down Gross would have it on his file forever. The Panicker, the one who had screwed up The Smiler's trial. But if he now said I should do it, if we had to, it would be like admitting he didn't have the stomach for it.

Varda looked at me with professional admiration, at how I had hemmed Léon in. But I didn't give a shit about that, now. "So who would do him?" I asked again.

"We won't have to," Léon said at last, his voice sandy.

"And if he fights?"

I don't know why I was so mad at Léon, all of a sudden.

"So he fights!" Léon snarled. "So he fights! Lift some weights tonight, so you can bend his arm!"

Varda said pacifically, "This Swedish nurse, she could make trouble, if she comes, or the girl, what do I know."

Léon snapped at her that he would ask for her opinion if he wanted it.

"Fuck you," Varda snapped back at him. "Fuck you, ya Aboulafia, you speak nicely or I'll take off your left ball."

I liked her again, now. That's the way.

"It's too big for you," Léon said.

"An olive, I bet," Varda said, which was nice of her, too, implying she had never seen it.

There was a short silence while we regrouped, so to speak, picking at the cheese, pouring Chambertin, passing napkins.

Finally, Léon said the nurse never came on Sundays. The shadowers had told us so.

I said nothing. Both he and I knew that this did not mean a thing. The shadowers fucked up half the time. A bunch of Yemenite boys good for nothing. Only because of the coalition agreement did they take them in at all.

"Yeah," I said at last, not wishing to restart anything. It would all go on our report anyway, every word of this, from the tape recorder, which we had to leave open by standing orders.

"But I can take care of her," Varda said, not making clear whether she had meant the nurse, if she came, or the girl.

"No, no," Léon said. "Mickey and I will do it. It'll be a breeze."

"So anyway, if you need me."

"Fine, fine," Léon snapped. "We heard you."

But of course it wasn't a breeze.

I had the first inkling of this the next morning, when we parked the VW van on rue Blé, a quiet side street forking off the north end of avenue Foch, waiting for Gross to appear.

Half an hour and he hadn't come yet.

"Abort," I said to Léon. "He's late. Late! Something is wrong. Abort, Léon, abort!"

Taking down Gross, each one of us could decide on his own, and justify later. But aborting on lateness, for this we needed a consensus.

"Nah," Léon said. "Don't be a *yachne*. He had a diarrhea, from too much cheese, or maybe a hangover. Something."

Fifteen minutes more. Still nothing.

"Abort!" I said.

"You want to veto?" Léon said. "On your head."

I thought about it. Aborting on a hunch was permissible, but if it came out later it was nothing, I would be a yachne forever. An old woman. Not in my file, but where it counts. In the Midrasha's cafeteria, in the Sayeret's summer camp, in the hotel safe rooms.

"It's a Nazi," Varda said. Her face had become puffy, as if air was blowing through it, from within. "A fucking Nazi. You won't wait for him a half hour?"

"All right," I said at last. "For a Nazi I'll wait."

Ten minutes more. Fifty minutes late.

"Relax," Léon said to me. "It's still quiet."

29

Indeed, rue Blé was deserted. Even avenue Foch had almost no cars. Maybe a cab or two going to Neuilly.

"Yeah," I said, grudgingly. "It's quiet."

Maybe it would still be all right.

But when Gross finally came around the corner, embalmed in a black suit and sporting a dark Tyrolean hat, it was plain for all to see that it was an Aleph-Aleph fuck-up.

He was holding the girl in one hand, the Swedish nurse in the other, and behind the nurse, all holding hands, were a bunch of little girls all dressed in black, squeaking and chirping like blackbirds. (Later we learned it was the niece's birthday, and her school friends had all come along, for church.)

"Shit in yogurt!" Varda said in Hebrew.

I said nothing, but it was obviously a disaster.

Without looking at me, Léon said we should abort. "Just let him go, we'll come back next week."

But now I, all of a sudden, was hot to trot. Maybe because, I don't know, I saw him now before me. The bright smile, the upturned old nose, the soft white hands.

"No," I said to Léon. "Let's get him."

Léon, crouching near his own eyehole, at the van's door, shook his head, so I grabbed his shoulders and said the missile boats were leaving Marseille the next day. If we postponed, we'd have to wait another week, dump Gross in the embassy, to be sent on El Al as diplomatic cargo, in a box, then he might die en route, there'd be no trial, nothing, only bureaucratic shit forever and ever. "You want Bleiman telexing Glilot for the next hundred years?"

Yoram Bleiman was our consul in Paris—his daughter was married to the PM's younger son, the one who avoided military service by going to a yeshiva. I knew for a fact the PM could stand neither one of the three; but did I want my fuck-ups coming up at Friday evening meals at the PM's table for the next five years? Also, I could see my own father giving me that pained look, across our own Friday table. (After my mother died I went to live with him, in our old apartment, on Wormaiza Street.)

"So he'll telex," Léon said. "Let him telex."

"All right, sure," I said. "Let's go back, have one more croissant, wait another week, maybe they'll send another team, an experienced one. Maybe a bunch of Yemenites they'd pull off some tail-job, in Cyprus."

30

Léon got all white around the nose. For a brief moment I thought he would punch me. Then he got up from the floor. "All right, fuck it, let's go."

Even this late on a Sunday morning, perhaps ten o'clock already, rue Blé was still deserted as a lane in Yerushalayim on Yom Kippur. The café-tabacs were all shuttered, the lottery office closed, not even pigeons on the sidewalks. Aside from the squealing little girls, it was calm and quiet. We might even have had the required 30 seconds to do it—rush out when he was passing the *pâtisserie*, grab him, inject him, and throw him in, all in one movement (a dozen times we had practiced this, before we left Tel Aviv), but because we had hesitated and argued, Gross had already passed us by. So when we finally jumped out, clanging the van's door open in our haste, he turned, and stared at us. His cheeks got all tight and military—he knew on the instant—and then his face fell apart and he screamed. It was a scream the likes of which I had never heard before, worse than if someone had slit his throat open.

And then everything got fucked up all to hell.

The Swedish nurse, as if she had practiced this before, bashed Léon on the back of the head with both fists, twice, and he fell as if he was made of wood, straight forward, mashing his nose on the pavement: there was a loud crack, like a piece of lumber breaking, and blood squirted out of his face as though a faucet had burst.

All the little girls began to scream, the whole lot of them, and scurry about like crazed mice, and by that time Gross was running down rue Blé—72 years old, but loping ahead like a deer towards avenue Foch. Then the Swedish nurse threw herself on me, tugging at the roots of my hair, spitting and hissing, in Swedish and German and French.

For a full minute I battled with her, first punching her ample solar plexus, then between her legs, all the while trying to inject her in various parts, when all at once she tore away from me and threw herself upon Varda, who was for some reason struggling with the little girl.

"My angel!" the nurse screeched in German. "No one is going to take you if I—"

Varda let go of the girl and grabbed the nurse by the hair, and in a second had her on the sidewalk in a reverse nelson. I wanted to shout at her, to tell her to go easy, but I had no time to talk, because right then two little girls in lace-trimmed black dresses raced past me, screeching, and as one tripped, both of them fell upon each other and

31

somehow got tangled between my legs, just as I was trying to hoist Léon on my shoulder.

I was knocked down again, with Léon on top of me; and as I kept trying to peer from between the skinny white socks dancing and scampering before my eyes, with Léon's blood dripping on my eyebrows, I saw the nurse lying on the sidewalk, like a large blonde chicken with her neck bent sideways, oddly elongated.

Varda's pink face swam into my view. "I had to!" she screeched. "I had to!"

"Get into the van and let's go!" I said, struggling again to my feet, feeling Léon's blood dripping on my neck.

But Varda was already gone, racing toward avenue Foch, Gross's little girl dragging behind her, legs akimbo.

"Mathilde!" I hollered. (This was Varda's codename.) "Mathilde! Let's go!"

But she kept running, dragging the little girl behind her.

"*Halt!*" she shouted at Gross in German, and I saw that she had grabbed his little niece by the throat, with her own katsa knife under the little ear. "Come back, you fucker!"

Madness!

Through Léon's blood I saw Varda jerking the little girl's head back, the white neck arching upwards.

Madness! Madness! One look at the Nazi, and we forgot everything. Everything!

Then, as in a slow dream, I saw that the girl was not Gross's niece at all, but one of the other girls Varda had grabbed by mistake. The girl's eyes, frozen with terror, looked up into Varda's chin, as if something was growing out of it.

I wanted to shout, to tell Varda that she had got the wrong girl, that she had made a dreadful error, that the Smiler would never come back for a stranger, that the flics would be upon us in a second, but an invisible fist seemed to have been rammed down my throat and not a word came out.

"Halt!" Varda screamed across the Avenue. "*Ha-a-lt!*"

Then, to my dull astonishment, as in a silent movie, I saw Gross halt in mid stride.

He turned around, honking cars flowing to his right and left, like water unfurling before a reed growing in the Yarkon River, and for a brief second he looked at Varda, then at me, smiling crookedly.

"*Haalt!*" Varda howled, in a voice like an animal's "Come heeere!"

Madness!

As I tugged my Beretta out of its plastic holster at the small of my back and hoisted it up, Gross kept staring at me with that peculiar little smile. Then his smile widened and softened and turned radiant. And as Varda's knife began to move, I felt my bladder loosen; and all at once, with my index finger already searching for the soft trigger-spot, I found myself hoping that the man floating in the V of my gunsight would dash away from me, hoping beyond hope.

Nominated by ZYZZYVA

ANNA LIFFEY

by EAVAN BOLAND

from AMERICAN POETRY REVIEW

Life, the story goes,
Was the daughter of Cannan,
And came to the plain of Kildare.
She loved the flat-lands and the ditches
And the unreachable horizon.
She asked that it be named for her.
The river took its name from the land.
The land took its name from a woman.

A woman in the doorway of a house.
A river in the city of her birth.

There, in the hills above my house,
The river Liffey rises, is a source.
It rises in rush and ling heather and
Black peat and bracken and strengthens
To claim the city it narrated.
Swans. Steep falls. Small towns.
The smudged air and bridges of Dublin.

Dusk is coming.
Rain is moving east from the hills.

If I could see myself
I would see
A woman in a doorway

Wearing the colors that go with red hair.
Although my hair is no longer red.

I praise
The gifts of the river.
Its shiftless and glittering
Re-telling of a city,
Its clarity as it flows,
In the company of runt flowers and herons,
Around a bend at Islandbridge
And under thirteen bridges to the sea.
Its patience at twilight—
Swans nesting by it,
Neon wincing into it.

Maker of
Places, remembrances,
Narrate such fragments for me:

One body. One spirit.
One place. One name.
The city where I was born.
The river that runs through it.
The nation which eludes me.

Fractions of a life
It has taken me a lifetime
To claim.

I came here in a cold winter.

I had no children. No country.
I did not know the name for my own life.

My country took hold of me.
My children were born.

I walked out in a summer dusk
To call them in.

One name. Then the other one.
The beautiful vowels sounding out home.

Make of a nation what you will
Make of the past
What you can—

There is now
A woman in a doorway.

It has taken me
All my strength to do this.

Becoming a figure in a poem.

Usurping a name and a theme.

A river is not a woman.
        Although the names it finds
                The history it makes
And suffers—
        The Viking blades beside it.
                The muskets of the Redcoats,
                        the flames of the Four Courts
Blazing into it
        Are a sign.
                    Any more than
A woman is a river.
        Although the course it takes.
                Through swans courting and distraught willows.
Its patience
        Which is also its powerlessness,
                From Callary to Islandbridge,
                    And from source to mouth,
Is another one.
                        And in my late forties
Past believing
        Love will heal
                What language fails to know
And needs to say—
        What the body means—
                I take this sign
And I make this mark:
        A woman in the doorway of her house.
                A river in the city of her birth.

The truth of a suffered life.
    The mouth of it.

The seabirds come in from the coast.
The city wisdom is they bring rain.
I watch them from my doorway.
I see them as arguments of origin—
Leaving a harsh force on the horizon
Only to find it
Slanting and falling elsewhere.

Which water—
The one they leave or the one they pronounce—
Remembers the other?

I am sure
The body of an aging woman
Is a memory
And to find a language for it
Is as hard
As weeping and requiring
These birds to cry out as if they could
Recognize their element
Remembered and diminished in
A single tear.

An aging woman
Finds no shelter in language.
She finds instead
Single words she once loved
Such as "summer" and "yellow"
And "sexual" and "ready"
Have suddenly become dwellings
For someone else—
Rooms and a roof under which someone else
Is welcome, not her. Tell me,
Anna Liffey,
Spirit of water,
Spirit of place,
How is it on this
Rainy Autumn night

As the Irish sea takes
The names you made, the names
You bestowed, and gives you back
only wordlessness?

Autumn rain is
Scattering and dripping
From car-ports
And clipped hedges.
The gutters are full.

When I came here
I had neither
Children nor country.
The trees were arms.
The hills were dreams.

I was free
to imagine a spirit
in the blues and greens,
the hills and fogs
of a small city.

My children were born.
My country took hold of me.
A vision in a brick house.
Is it only love
that makes a place?

I feel it change.
My children are
growing up, getting older.
My country holds on
to its own pain.

I turn off
the harsh yellow
porch light and
stand in the hall
Where is home now?

Follow the rain
out to the Dublin hills.

Let it become the river.
Let the spirit of place be
a lost soul again.

In the end
It will not matter
That I was a woman. I am sure of it.
The body is a source. Nothing more.
There is a time for it. There is a certainty
About the way it seeks its own dissolution.
Consider rivers.
They are always en route to
Their own nothingness. From the first moment
They are going home. And so
when language cannot do it for us,
cannot make us know love will not diminish us,
there are these phrases
of the ocean
to console us.
Particular and unafraid of their completion.
In the end
everything that burdened and distinguished me
will be lost in this:
I was a voice.

Nominated by Pamela Stewart

MAGIC

by ART HOMER

from THE GEORGIA REVIEW and *THE DROWNT BOY: AN OZARK TALE* (UNIVERSITY OF MISSOURI PRESS)

I WASN'T BORN in a log cabin. Friends accuse me of this curiously American origin, but I can't boast the distinction. My birth certificate shows place of birth as Carter's Medical Clinic, Ellington, Missouri. Then, my parents brought me home to a log cabin, twenty miles north on a red dirt road through second-growth oak and hickory mixed with pine.

You can still drive this road—if you can find it—past small frame houses, white, with tin roofs, becoming fewer and farther from the road as you leave the town behind. You can still drive through roadside redbud, sassafras, and dogwood, giving way to oak, maple, juniper, and on certain slopes large stands of yellow pine, unexpectedly cool. Chambers of light open in the wall of trees where former homesteads stood—some of them my relatives'. Turkeys may dart in front of you. Certainly the large box turtles will be out if it is summer. Deer are plentiful, as were half-wild cattle and hogs when I was a child and the hills were open range. Breathe deeply, and the hardwood forest with extensive stands of pine reminds you how John Muir savored the Sierra forests for their variety of aromas and tonics. The Ozarks are home, too, for diverse wildlife. The rivers hold sixty to ninety species of fish, depending upon how many separate minnows you distinguish.

The road evolved from abandoned railroad right-of-way when my father was a young man. Previously, backwoods folks took their mule-drawn wagons on the logging access road across marsh and up steep grades. Traces of it still run through the hills, overgrown now. The

40

"nigh cut" they called any such forest track—even if it were longer than the high road. People still hauled corn and cane to town in wagons when I was a child in the midfifties. The Depression had moved into the Ozarks, liked it, and retired there after World War II, letting the rest of the country go on with the boom times.

For geological ages this place was bypassed. The landscape is part of the Appalachian uplift, separated from its parent by the fault under the Missouri and Mississippi. Rivers running through the broken peneplain are literally older than the hills: they once ran through plains that sank under seas, then lifted, submerged, and rose again. Now the plateau is broken and eroded into hills and steep hollows, the rocks softened and crumbly from erosion. The rivers retain the meanders of plains rivers, though hills have risen and half collapsed around them. The rocks are old: sandstone dissolving around granite knobs, limestone from sea creatures, flinty chips of chert working up through plowed fields with the frost heave. And the forest is old, a crossroads of geology, of plant and animal life from the Eastern woodlands and Western plains. Southern riparian species homestead in the river bottoms. Northern ferns forced south by the Wisconsin ice sheet survive in the mouths of caves and in cool spring branches hundreds of miles from their current range.

This is a crossroads of peoples too. Here, the unimposing Bluff Dweller looked down on the Hopewell—Mississippian city-states, along the river. Centuries later, guerrilla conflicts of the Civil War brought first one side and then the other ferrying their wounded to Hospital Cave in jonboats. The James gang rode through, leaving a bullet hole in one of the log uprights of the Centerville post office—a legendary opening which, by the time I saw it, was worn smooth and round from generations of boys sticking their fingers into it.

What I have to say about the place is no truer than the claim my friends make for my birth. "You'd argue with a signpost and go the wrong way," my mother says. A combination of childhood memory, history, and wishful thinking, my research has been haphazard. The bullet hole, for instance, could be a clerk's joke at the expense of small boys. The post office is absent from current guidebooks of the place. No one remembers it. I may be remembering the wrong town.

Then again, no one else remembers the old tram road past my folks' place. Visiting Ellington for the first time in thirty years, I asked directions at a supermarket. A country gospel group performed from a flatbed trailer in the parking lot. I remembered clearly where the

41

curving low-water bridge used to sit under two feet of water at flood. My uncle, the bus driver, traversed it in low gear, water climbing the bus steps, he finding the curve by memory. The clerk had lived in the town all her life yet didn't remember the bridge or the road. She knew the half-surviving town of Corridon, a forty-mile drive by the state highway instead of twenty over the old right-of-way. But the stock boy, she said, had "taken that hotrod of his over all the back roads in the country." He could tell me where to find it if anybody could.

He did.

The low-water bridge was gone, the road now reached by a turn-off the other side of county bridge sixteen. I didn't recognize the first three miles of the tram road under its curious paving. The calico asphalt of varying age and composition looked like excess from highway projects rolled out when the heavy equipment operators got around to it. Soon, however, it turned to red rock and clay, leveled monthly by the county grader—down in the morning, back twenty miles that afternoon. Across these same ridges the school bus had carried me, a backwoods kid, into a town of sophisticates with running water and electricity. Seventeen miles to Ellington, three and a half to the village of Corridon—towns most kids in the fifties would have considered irredeemably hicksville. And at night I took the road back, way, way back into the woods. Back into the past and into magic.

*

That the woods mean magic I had always taken as personal mythology—finding the submerged road by memory—until I began reading nature writers. Now I can construct a veneer of scientific backing for my beliefs. Most chroniclers of natural history portray the plains as the place where progress happens, and magic has nothing to do with progress. In "How Flowers Changed the World," Loren Eiseley explains that evolving plants and insects of the plains literally prepared the ground for increasingly sophisticated animals, some of which crept back into the forests. Ecologist Paul Shepard, in his *Thinking Animals* gives a riveting account of the evolution of intelligence, important segments of which process happened in the plains. As Shepard describes it, "The intelligence of mammals and insects and birds is the mind of the grassland . . . ," whereas "trees are comparatively shallow beings and the earth beneath them a cool veneer."

42

If progress is necessary to evolution, however, so is escape; if memory, also forgetting. Shepard does credit the forest with a role in the evolution of intelligence: when our mammalian ancestors were driven back under the trees, their vision-centered intelligence was forced to use the hearing centers of the brain to adapt to a limited horizon and nocturnal habits. Out of such marginal forebears and forced connections intelligence arose.

Similarly, marginal peoples retreat to the forest. Theirs is a journey backward in time, be their forest the oak groves of Europe, the rain forest of the Tasaday, or the Appalachian hollows. Abandoned in this journey are not only the rewards of technological progress, but some of the assumptions of postindustrial, postmodern society. These assumptions—for better *and* for worse—are forced into connection with older postulates about the world.

If our rational vision has given us principles with which to control our surroundings—to predict the future and avoid some of the consequences of time's one-way arrow—perhaps some of the older, magical visions better prepare us to accept the present in all of its contradictions. This divination is not a foretelling, but a telling, a way of casting and recasting experience to give it meaning in terms apprehensible to the heart, however painful that may be. We can then accept consequence, can literally be con-sequent—following together. For a moment, time's arrow points toward us, the present, from all directions.

The Ozarks remained, if not retrograde, at least untouched by progress until the census crews, and the lumber and lead-mining companies, took notice at the turn of the century. They discovered people still living the frontier life on old homesteads, hunting, curing with herbs, subsistence farming, and open ranging. Old Scottish tunes retained their original forms. So did the language, as well as various social structures from Scotland, Ireland, England, and (later) Germany and Russia. The church clung to the splintery cross of its early Protestant dourness, but it wasn't standing still. Even Calvinism devolved enough to coexist with root doctors, snake handling, and who-knows-what kinds of African and Southern po'-white, holy-rolling, shout-your-hair-down practices. Secluded as the Vietnam vets in the Olympic rain forest or a forgotten Japanese soldier on his jungle island, the Ozarkians were retreating in time, the forest working its charm on them.

In truth, however, my first memories are not of the Ozarks, but of St. Louis. When my parents went there for work, they alternately left

43

me in my grandmother's care or took me along. Such memories blend with my mother's stories, and both deny the black-and-white photos. The towheads in them could not possibly be my brother and me. We stare moonfaced over a birthday cake, lean against the cabin. Here we are behind the chair in which we got our haircuts, now in front of the Model-T with the crank dangling from the radiator. I remember curbs, a two-year-old's tiredness at the hard sidewalks and new, hard-soled shoes. Mother and Aunt Helen, or Mother and Father, lifted me by my arms up and down the city's curbs—*wheeee!*—trying to make a game of it, but I wasn't buying. This is corroborated by photos of me in an honest-to-God Buster Brown suit, standing between my parents—the archetypal little man fighting to separate mother earth and father sky. They're still happy. I frown like trouble waiting to happen.

We soon came back to the cabin of two rooms—living room and kitchen—and to subsistence farming. Our eighty acres of forest had less than five cleared. Sumac had reclaimed a grazing field on the access road, and a couple of acres surrounded the cabin. The yard sat on a knoll, native grass on the north side, plowed garden on the south. From the gate at the turnaround, ending a mile of access road, a well-defined dusty path ran to the door. Later, the addition on the north of the cabin created a bedroom and a living room with picture windows. Father scythed the grass and raked it by hand, and we fed it to whatever stock happened to be about, either ours or unclaimed. Later, we moved to Ellington twice for my father to find work, but returned—me happily—to the cabin each time.

Fortunately for my personal mythology, reforestation programs and national park expansion have reestablished pine stands and aided the natural succession. The forest has outgrown my memory of it—not an easy thing to do. Living in a log cabin is like living inside a tree. Ours was local pine, crosscut, the knotholes axed down more or less smooth, hand-chiseled notches forming the corner joints. As the logs warped, the gaps between them needed constant chinking. The floor joists rested on rock pilings, so settling and leveling were consanguineous with the land. The house rotated slightly on its foundations in one strong storm—not uncommon in what is still tornado country, despite its relatively high relief. And nature lives with you, for chinking will not keep out animals. I once had to convince my mother the banded snake crawling on the rafters was a coral snake, not its innocuous mimic, the king snake. The encyclopedia was on my side—black and red bands separated by yellow borders. I had sighted a semitropical snake in a temperate climate. No wonder it wanted to move inside; the nights were cold.

My mother had warned me there could be snakes and who-knows-what under the house. I thought it would be safe, however, since my dog made her home down there, and I crawled in after her. I kept a sharp lookout. My mother walked above me in the kitchen. I crawled along on my back, the dirt like lowering sky above my head. The bottom of the floor was all the more alien for being upside down. My mother dropped something and yelled. A pale body washed across the bark of the rough-hewn joist, crossed down into the dirt, and coiled in a scrape the dog had dug to escape the heat. I didn't want to call out. Thankfully, the dog quietly came and ate the white-bellied coil— actually, lapped it up. Like a slide projection suddenly brought into focus, the snake resolved itself into a pool of milk, spilled between the floorboards, along the joist, and into the dirt. While I was busy trying to understand what I had seen, the dog had capitalized on my mother's accident.

Other guests were more a danger to themselves than to us. In the half-finished addition, the picture window gaped unglazed for weeks. Two smaller windows on the side walls had frames and panes. Hummingbirds barreled in the opening and tried to leave through the glass; they buzzed the panes like flies. We had to catch them and rush them outside quickly before they exhausted themselves. If we held them long, fright killed them. Each nearly weightless body was a soft palpitation punctuated with the light scratch of claws as it discharged itself into the air.

Not primeval, the Ozarks, but primal—a first step out of reason's merciless light and back into the liquid motion of shadows under branches. What the nineteenth-century scientists referred to as Nature's profligacy was my affluence. A more directed teacher might have presented the ant as ample demonstration that the six-legged exoskeleton was a viable anatomical design, and then I could have learned the happy word "cooperation" as I watched the social structure of the hive. Instead, I continued to watch bugs willy-nilly: termite; walking stick; the clickbug whose hard, jointed body squirts from your fingers like a watermelon seed when he "clicks" his joint; dungbeetle; ladybug; leafy katydid; praying mantis (the wonderful pun of her pious stance, the body broken before her); a milkweed butterfly emerging from the cocoon; the potato beetle and its soft grub. Also, in no particular sequence: reptiles, amphibians, birds, mammals and, always, the column trees, those first and most universal caryatids. These were my daily companions in the absence of others. Because we subsisted on a nearly equal level with these—our prey, our predators, and our competitors for hard-won food—a part of my experience would be forever strange to my generally urbanized generation, and even to kids from the increasingly domesticated, industrialized farms of more prosperous areas.

We were backward—not anachronistic but antichronistic, half-feral by some standards. Like the novelist's character living a flashback to develop the plot, like the equations of the astrophysicist studying ever more distant and ancient sources of light from the Big Bang, like the computer models linking modern genetic patterns to fossil DNA, we existed with the arrow of time inverted. We were like T. H. White's wonderful conception of Merlin, living reversed in time, whom the young Arthur meets (not coincidentally in the forest) weeping in farewell to his longtime friend from the perspective of the wizard's antichronological progress (egress?) toward birth. Who were his contemporaries? Who are mine?

*

Come here,
Motherless Sparrows
And play
with me.

So wrote Issa, the sixteenth-century Japanese haiku master, at age six. Like him, I sometimes preferred my forest playmates: birds, bugs, and snakes. Lizards were my pets for a day. The tails of the blue bellies detached, flipping like baby snakes to distract the bird or young boy who grasped the tip of one. They rode my shoulder leashed with a string around my top shirt button. They would not be fed; not herbivores, as a few experiments with garden greens showed, they had no interest in dead or stunned flies. They suffered no ill effects from my handling. Once captured they adjusted by sleeping, keeping one double-lidded eye open for escape, and conserving energy. (My frenetic metabolism put out enough heat for both of us.)

At school or church functions, boys dashed lizards against rocks or logs to kill them. I once killed one. It lay on its back, its hands slowly curling up, its gesture seeming less a plea than a question: "Why?" I

46

knew the motion was reflex—like a headless chicken's flapping. I had seen birds drop dead lizards in the dirt at my approach. Even minus a head, their feet curled up in this ineffectual gesture. I was not squeamish about dead things, and would analyze—literally "take apart"—whatever I found inside strange skin. The older boys had no interest in this, had probably seen (as I had) the silvery flesh, the amazingly small amount of blood, the translucent bones. Shrikes, or butcher birds, impale lizards on thorns and barb-wire fences. Even this, the victim alive, impaled and left to age in hot sun, was conceivable.

My parents killed for food—chickens, a pig—but they made my brother hold the house plants he had broken until he could hear them cry. It didn't take long. Subsistence hunters, human or animal, are opportunistic feeders, neither amused nor revolted by the dirty but necessary work of killing. The lizard was a hunter, too. Though I whined about being bored, I must have had a modicum of patience. I remember quietly watching frogs in our small woodland pond catch dragonflies—the impossible speed, the moment of the hit frozen in my mind, a wing or tail protruding oddly from the mouth—and wondering whether the frog's tongue or its bite killed.

With patience, I could also watch other stalkings the world usually allows to remain hidden. Fighting drowse at afternoon nap, one could pretend to sleep, watch the minute hand stalk the hour hand, and contemplate the tortoise and the hare. This would have been on the key-wound captain's clock, for we had no electricity. The hands moved slower even than the praying mantis, a pendulum hypnotizing its prey with its swaying. And the clock hands were like the mantis in another way: when the minute hand got close enough, the last increment of distance disappeared in a quantum lunge. First the two hands were apart by ever so little, then they were not, and then the dragonfly was only parts, prying the frog mouth into a gloating *moue*. The mantis dismantled its struggling catch in small bits, a dainty spinster with corn on the cob, the misdirecting wings folded like a napkin. Then the frog again, a grasshopper leg kicking until it came off and dropped on the ground, still jerking like a lizard tail, like my mother shaking me, chiding me for falling asleep so quickly, my nap over and the sun slanting orange through the south window.

This is how time passed, ample to realize the mysteries of eating and dying. First for young boys is eating. Some troubled children ate dirt, according to my mother. Plants grew from dirt. Perhaps one could cut out the middlemen—the plants, the animals—keep hand-over-handing it down the food chain. Forest dirt was mostly leaf matter mixed with sticks and sand, which feels like boulders in the mouth. Dig below the duff and leaf mold, and mineral dirt will give you a literal taste of the land: the nauseating aftertaste I recognized years later when someone talked me into chewing a zinc tablet as a cold remedy. I found clay bland and palatable. Though aluminum-foil generations would doubt it, good clayey mud is perfect for baking potatoes—keeps the heat in as well, and the moisture better. It crumbles off, and you don't have to pack it out. If you're hungry enough, you can eat it to keep the pangs away.

That's what those children were doing—what many poor children in the rural South did and probably still do: eat clay. There's plenty of it. Certain kinds help fight food poisoning and decrease the bitterness of acorns and other food. Some clays—kaolinites—provide antidiarrhetics and fillers in diet foot. Geophagy and other vices of the poor are acquired tastes but, unlike more sophisticated appetites, are rarely conceived out of boredom.

Despite my protests, a child's ill temper, it was hard to be bored. Afternoons I conducted original research into the nature of time and its relationship to food. I had facilities that would be the envy of many a scientist. Poor we may have been, if not reduced to eating clay for lunch, but we had books. Books and kerosene lights for reading at night, an upright piano, a windup Victrola with records from Caruso to Tin-Pan-Alley songs. A wooden, string-jointed Mr. Tambo attached to the spindle and did a minstrel dance. Our radio lit up with mirror-topped vacuum tubes and had a tone that would drive a blues guitarist crazy. It ran on a wet cell the size of a motorcycle battery. On monthly trips to Ellington, we left it at the service station to be recharged. With rationing, the charge would last all month. Bible readings gave way one night a week to Grand Ole Opry direct from Nashville, now clear as a movie sound track, moments later wavery with distance when storms, chance disturbances of the ionosphere, or a variation in the battery's output disturbed the signal.

Most nights, however, we listened to an Ozark chorus of tree frogs, insects, and birds. Some have names little boys can't understand. (If Katy did, why whip poor Will?) Others have no name. Some call in voices like chainsaws starting up, others in the voices of the aliens in the radio version of *War of the Worlds*. The walk across the pasture to the outhouse resounded with such voices. The background calls of whippoorwills answered more distant wills, and farther yet, till one could hear echoes of infinity, the universe expanding like Dante's Paradise, voice to voice—each voice flying away from the other until both went beyond the range of perception, and silence fell amongst the blackness. Even the insect prey of these whiskery night-jars fell silent at such times. I turned and raced through the head-high milk-weed for home, clutching my crotch. I had heard the wills called natural watchdogs, their silence a sure sign of approaching danger. No amount of reason could convince me they were being silent on my account.

Children who roam the woods understand the food chain early. Lizards ate insects, birds ate lizards, I ate birds, and somewhere, probably out on the way to the outhouse, something would eat me. Every summer, dung beetles rolled their Sisyphean burdens up the dusty path. Though it wasn't our droppings they were neatly bundling up, it may as well have been. Everything recycled. I was proving an axiom: the animals at the top of the food chain are more timid than their prey. The bobcat is more furtive than the squirrel or rabbit, having eaten so many that a complete rodent of fear resides within its heart; the predator understands and uses the prey's fear against it. Like both of them, I sat uneasily in my precarious niche. Such inductive reasoning comes easily to children, however unconsciously. I had thousands of specific instances from which to build a general theory.

What I think of as magic comes from this, I believe: *induction,* in both senses of the word. First, the magical in art or in culture is a way of seeing the world. Sympathetic magic perceives the affinity between two things without looking for cause. "Spunkwater," the tannin-stained water that collects in hollow stumps, nourishes fresh shoots. It is highly recommended by "root doctors" for boils, warts, and skin problems of all sorts. The cure is prescribed and taken without, to quote Keats, an "irritable reaching after fact and reason." Magic happens because trees fall in the forest with no Cartesians to ponder them. By deductive standards, if there is one person in the forest there is still no corroboration—but skepticism stands one in poor stead. *On* the plains the tribe huddles together. *In* the forest, the individual is primary.

Yet one never stands alone. The hypothetical question about the falling tree is flawed by definition. *In the forest,* it is impossible for a tree to fall with no one to hear it because a forest is a community. A forest, Thoreau proved in his address to the farmers of Concord, cannot get on about its business without the squirrels. The same goes for the insects, gastropods, and what have you. Besides, the question betrays an ignorance of the language of trees.

Tree language uses the second kind of *induction*—also essential to magic—the more or less physical business described in *Webster's Ninth New Collegiate Dictionary*:

> the process by which an electrical conductor becomes electrified when near a charged body, by which a magnetizable body becomes magnetized when in a magnetic field or in the magnetic flux set up by a magnetomotive force, or by which an electromotive force is produced. . . .

Asking exactly what that process *is* is likely to leave one as thoroughly flummoxed as asking a shaman about the "forces," "fluxes" and "fields" of spirit power. Let's try another definition of induction:

> the sum of the processes by which the fate of embryonic cells is determined and morphogenetic differentiation brought about.

What happens is that something happens. The cells line up like steel shavings over a magnet. The biologist, the information-science theorist, and the third grader all ask the same question: How do they know to do that? The only answer is in the etymology of the word *induce* [*in* + *ducere* to lead]: they don't "know," they are led to it—induced or "brought forward" (another definition of the word).

So, does the electrical field *know?* Does the forest *hear?*

A blight strikes the edge of the woods. Dying trees produce chemical compounds and electrical pulses, thought to be "messages." Scientists can find no mechanism by which trees on the opposite edge of the woods could receive or understand such messages. Nevertheless, the trees adapt before the blight arrives. Perhaps complex molecules are "inhaled" by the tree's respiratory system, perhaps hair-thin roots pick up magnetoelectric fluxes. "All hear, all hear. Yellow pine felled by blight." This is why trees don't bear philosophical chestnuts.

Likewise, in what was as lively a community as any big-city neighborhood, I was picking up messages, too. The word on the street was a bit more universal than the old saw of a syllogism on Plato's mortality: things die and eat and live and change. Frogs from pollywogs eat insects—either on the wing or as mosquito wigglers—and are eaten by snakes. Lizards become dragons when they eat ants that fly like mayflies, though when the ants walk, lizards seldom bother them. Everything—dung, dead trees and pets, live butterflies and baby birds, acorns on the ground, the dirt—is food for whatever can stomach it.

Living in and of the forest makes it hard not to see the motive force of the universe as magic, a net of reactions which follow their orderly patterns simply because those patterns exist. The universe leads itself along by its bootstraps: induction.

Deduction, on the other hand, promises wealth through the application of easily grasped principles. Wealth—of information, money, food surpluses—gives us power over the world. Without power, the attraction fades, and we are left with the habit of seeing what we expect to see. If we are to attain higher aims—sustenance (hunting-gathering), knowledge (religion/pure science), or celebration (art)—we must overcome this experience-shaping process of deduction. A fat white-tail takes several bounds with the flag of its tail up and the hunter's eye (human? cat?) draws a line connecting the dots of each bound toward where the next dot is expected to appear. But then magic intervenes. The deer tucks its tail, changes direction, fades a few steps into the background pattern of the forest—and, from the hunter's perspective, disappears.

*

Whatever sleight of hand the magician shows us is only prelude to the wonders we will see if we abandon our complacency long enough to reenvision the world, to see it in others of the ways it actually is. Seeing the world anew, no matter how stifling we find our old perspective, is difficult and often requires ridiculous postures. Van Gogh wrote his brother that he could see more clearly through his eyelashes—squinting at the world. Thoreau favored looking backward between his legs to stand the world on its head for a better look. When all else fails, we must steal perspective from children.

"Daddy, how does the moon get inside the clouds?" My daughter must have been about five. (My daughter's name is Willow—I'm serious about this tree business.)

"Well, it just looks like that. See, the moon [I make a fist and hold it over my head] is way up here. OK?"

Willow nods.

"And we're way down here." I point at my feet.

Another nod.

"And the clouds are in between." I wiggle my fingers at waist level, conscious of the violence I'm doing to scale. "So you see that the moon can't really be inside the clouds."

"Sure it is. Look!"

"Okay, you tell me. How does the moon get inside the clouds?"

"It blooms in."

"Blooms? I'm not sure I understand?" Getting cagey here, I employed a bit of Socratic technique.

"Sure, you know how a flower blooms *out*?" Using her hands to demonstrate.

"Uh-huh."

Willow reverses the hand motion. "Well, the moon just sort of blooms *in*."

"Okay, Honey. Daddy's got to go home and write now."

*

In *Zen Mind, Beginner's Mind,* a book by Shunryu Suzuki, the title is the premise. When we wish for a child's vision of the world, we are wishing for the oldest one. When a child sees a forest as a city of animals, isn't he or she simply reversing the process that led to the building of the city? Wouldn't it be natural for city builders who have moved to the floodplains, or cleared the forests for extensive fields, to re-create the lookout trees, sheltering boughs, and the myriad trails of the forest when they built their walls and towers and labyrinths of streets?

Augustine characterized the city of man as motivated by self-love, the city of God by love of God. If "Self-contemplation is a curse/That makes an old confusion worse," as Theodore Roethke says, we may wish to look back to the forest for release. Even those celebrated plains dwellers, the Sioux, recognized the center of their nation's hoop, the intersection between the red and black roads, as a tree. Lured from their ancestral forest by the promise of horse power, they kept much of their Eastern woodland ritual. The horse Indians of the Pampas did the same. In *Voyage of the Beagle,* Darwin reports:

> Shortly after passing the first spring we came in sight of a
> famous tree, which the Indians reverence as the altar of

Walleechu. . . . Being winter, the tree had no leaves, but in their place numberless threads, by which the various offerings, such as cigars, bread, meat, pieces of cloth, &c. had been suspended. Poor Indians, not having anything better, only pull a thread out of their ponchos, and fasten it to the tree. Richer Indians are accustomed to pour spirits and maté into a certain hole, and likewise to smoke upwards, thinking thus to afford all possible gratification to Walleechu.

Darwin, empathetic as always, is a hundred years ahead of his time in anthropology as well, observing that: "The Gauchos think that the Indians consider the tree as the god itself; but it seems far more probable, that they regard it as the altar."

At the center of my Ozark world was a hole where offerings were made. The god of this place was present, for I could see my offerings devoured. I called it doodlebug. Known as an ant lion, it was the larva of a small fly (Myrmeleon) that made a whirlpool of sand or dust by crawling backwards in the loose medium until it had excavated a conical pit with its large jaws at the base. Insects, mostly ants, blunder into the pit and disappear, sifted through into a gateway out of this life. Abandon hope . . .

Behind our cabin, a ten-foot-deep pit in the red clay held frogs and water, sometimes in near-equal proportion. This, I explain to my urban friends, was our cistern—a container or reservoir for capturing rain water. A stringy old man had water-witched the cabin site, the hazel wand writhing in his hands, but my parents were too skeptical to follow his recommendation. Since we had no money to hire a drilling rig, and hand-dug wells are an overwhelming project for a man working alone, we relied on the cistern.

In the red dirt my father had piled on the side of the cistern, the ant lions made their pits, and I my sacrifices—ants, an occasional stunned fly. When I tired of feeding them, I could dig them up easily. Scraping up dirt and doodlebug together, I'd blow the dust out of my hand, leaving the bewildered bug in my palm. Despite the ominous jaws, the larva was just that—larval, grub-pale. Then, in a half whisper I began my incantation:

Doodlebug, doodlebug! Backup, backup!
Doodlebug, doodlebug! Backup, backup!

And it would! Encouraged by the drone of a voice (or frightened by the puffs of breath when I dropped my *p*'s), the bug circled backwards in a closing spiral. If I cupped my palm into a creased depression, it would spin into the crack and disappear. And there I sat—"Happy as if I had good sense," as my mother used to say—the jaws of the underworld enclosed in the crease of my palm, and the heavenly city spreading out around me in all directions.

Nominated by Henry Carlile

THE FIRST DAY

by ELIZABETH SPIRES

from THE PARTISAN REVIEW

The ward is quiet, the mothers delivered,
except in one a woman labors still and calls,
with a sharp cry, that she is dying.
She is not dying but cannot know it now.
Trapped in the birthstorm, I did not cry,
but saw my body as the enemy
I could not accommodate, could not deny.
Morning arrived, and my daughter.
That's how it is in this world, birth, death,
matter-of-fact, happening like that.
The room was warm. The room was full of flowers,
her face all petals and leaves, a flower
resembling such as I had never seen.
All day she slept beside me, eyes darting
beneath bruised blue eyelids, retracing the journey,
dreaming the birth dream over and over
until it held no fear for her.
I dared not wake her. The hours passed.
I rested as her soul poured in her body,
the way clear water, poured from a height,
takes the shape of a flaring vase or glass, or light
fills a room's corners on a brilliant winter morning.
Slowly, she opened her eyes, a second waking,
taking me by surprise, a bright being
peering out from behind dark eyes,
as if she already knew what sights would be seen,

what marvels lay ahead of her, weariness and woe,
the joists and beams, the underpinnings of the world
shifting a little to make room for her.
The first day was over forever. Tranced,
I picked up the pen, the paper, and wrote:
I have had a child. Now I must live with death.

Nominated by Henri Cole and Gibbons Ruark

WILMA BREMER'S FUNERAL

fiction by MARIE SHEPPARD WILLIAMS

from THE AMERICAN VOICE

THERE ARE SO many deaths here, that's the main thing you have to grasp right at the start. It isn't that we get used to it, ever, or that we don't care. We do care. I have cried over all the ones who died, or most of them, and got drunk over a few. We all get drunk over a few. And sometimes we rage and scream and curse God. We have been known to pray.

So we are not calloused to the fact of death; it is more like we get confused: *Which is life and which is death? Who is alive and who is dead?*

Deaths seem to come in threes: we wait for the second, and the third, always. We are a superstitious crew, as well as being odd in a number of other respects.

We are called upon to feel so much. The mind rebels. Refuses for a while. Will grieve tomorrow.

And for what should we grieve? For young life, or old, cut off in the midst of what awful pain? What enormity of despair? Better grieve for the birth of the child, better grieve life than death. But we are just ordinary teachers and social workers and nurses, we take it in the only way we know how—we grieve, when we have the time, the luxury, for the loss of our friends, whom we knew better than we knew our husbands and wives and children, because they were in pain, and

*they told us about it, shared pain, that bitter bread, more nourishing
than any other.*

Tomorrow's grief never comes. By tomorrow, we have something
else to worry about. Bruce's doctor says that Bruce has an inoperable
tumor of the brain; Bruce (who is in the sheltered workshop) is both
deaf and blind; how will we tell him, how will we make him understand
that soon he will not be able to work at all any more? Work here is his
whole life.

Sharon dies. She was (we have heard) very depressed for at least a
month before she died. She wanted to talk to us—we got that message.
We did not call; we are on some level intolerably ashamed that we did
not call.

We loved Sharon, and we did a good job for her. She said she
could not possibly bear to live and be blind; she sobbed through
the whole intake interview. I was the intake worker then, I did the
interview—what a word for such an event: initiation, consecra-
tory rite, invitation to Pinocchio's Pleasure Island, to The Good
Ship Lollipop; but *interview?*—I put my arms around her, I made
her smile; her smile was a marvelous gift to me. I promised her that
if she came to us, we could make her feel better in a month. But it
took us only a week. We are very, very good at the job we do here
in the Rehabilitation Center. By the time Sharon left us, five months
later, she hummed and sang all day long; we always knew where
Sharon was because we could hear her singing. And those of us
who can see (are not blind, that is) could spot her jaunty sun-
shade hat, bobbing happily along on top of fat, short Sharon, indoors
or out.

I guess you could say Sharon was a character, one of our favorites.
"You really are something else, Sharon," I said to her once. "Like what
else?" she said. "A three-legged horse?" "Like something wonderful,
like a unicorn," I said. Every once in a while one of them gets to us just
a little more than the others—it isn't fair, but there it is.

Eighteen months later Sharon is dead, of diabetes, gangrene, and
finally kidney failure. She was just my age, which is forty-seven. I identify with her—this is a mortal sin in my business. She was happily married, which I am not. She had a hundred good reasons for living. I am
hard pressed to list three for myself, unless I list my friends as one reason each. Six of us went to the funeral. I did not go. I came down with
the flu instead.

There are just too many deaths.

II.

Who is this "we," "us," I am talking about? Well, there's me, the author of this story. I am the Manager of Community Services at the local center for the blind, and a social worker. Up to a couple months ago, I did intake, which is how it happened that I did the intake on Sharon Wald, who was happy for seventeen months because of what we did, depressed for one month, and now is dead. Then there is another social worker, Vange Kuhlman—Evangeline Josephine, named after two dead aunts, you have heard about her before in these stories—she is the best and bravest and smartest of us all. Vange is partially sighted because of a birth defect, sixty-one years old now, fat and cheerful. But even she, who (asked) is always "most excellent!," has her moments of crap-out.

Then there are the teachers in the Rehabilitation Center who teach blind people how to walk with white canes, for example (that is a terrifying job, I don't know how the hell they can do it; most of the mobility instructors are—or become—very different from the rest of us, somewhat withdrawn and apart. And they more or less consider themselves the high priests of our remarkable craft, as strange and esoteric and religious in its way as any ancient Egyptian embalmer's trade); other teachers who teach blind people how to read braille, use an abacus; how to cook without burning themselves and everything else up when they can't see the fire; how to type, write checks, use cassette recorders, how to knit, model in clay, crochet, weave, do macrame, play poker, and use the power saw. (You think I am putting you on, I'm not, we do teach blind people to use power machinery, why not? We've even got a blind hockey team, blind archers.)

And there are others of us who teach blind people how to work, do jobs, earn money, support themselves and their families, view themselves as workers—after all, that is where it is at, isn't it? You earn money, you are worth something? You do not, you aren't?

So we teach blind people to work.

III.

I promise I'll get to Wilma's funeral quite soon now; I have to lead up to it like this because if I don't, you won't have the background, you will maybe think it was just awful, grotesque, and it wasn't, it was really nice, like Robin said it was. I am coming to Robin soon too—he is another important person in this story. In fact I have only a few more preliminary remarks. Put up with me, please? I give you my word it is going to be worth it. Listen, have I ever lied to you?—trust me: I say that to all my clients—it seems to me that you are in a way at this moment a client of mine.

So anyway we teach blind people to work. Some of them go into our sheltered workshop more or less permanently; some of them use the shop as a transitional experience and go on to work in "The Community." "The Community" is you, assuming you are free, whatever that means, not necessarily white, any age between eighteen and seventy, and possessed of whatever wit, dexterity, skill, mental ability, education and degree of health are necessary to earn an adequate paycheck in the competitive job market.

Some of the blind people, though, stay in the sheltered workshop more or less forever—for whatever reason, mental or physical, they cannot hack it in the fierce, competitive, unloving, no-quarter arena where you and I earn our livings.

IV.

One of the people in the sheltered workshop is Robin. Robin is totally blind and spent thirty years of his life in a state mental hospital—years ago they put many, many blind children into state hospitals as "untrainable." Evangeline Kuhlman got Robin out, worked with him as his counselor for maybe a year, and now he is in the shop. Vange taught him (what a remarkable accomplishment, think about it) to like himself. Robin has many of what we call in the trade "blindisms": he rocks, rubs his hands together, pokes his fingers into his eyes. Other things, some too obscene to mention, but funny, interesting, human: *alive.* He is not retarded, not at all—but he is very different from you and me: he is kind, considerate, loving and warm, and he knows absolutely that he is a good and worthwhile person. I do not believe he is capable of deliberate cruelty—at least, I have never seen that capacity in him, I suppose he has it, he is after all as human as you or me. His thinking is different from yours and mine too—it is right to the point.

He is, I suppose you could say, damaged beyond any hope of further repair by those thirty years in a state hospital and by being born blind; that is, he will never look like you and me. He will never work in "The Community."

He calls Vange and me "his two lovely ladies." I am honored to be included, I do not really deserve it, but this is Robin's great courtesy. He calls all the women he talks to "hon." He buys roses and gives them away sometimes on the bus on his way home to his apartment downtown. He calls up Social Security once in a while when some problem arises. I have heard these conversations.

Robin: "Hello, hon, I just called, um, called to ask you about the NOTICE I have received . . . "

Phone: "Blup, blup, blup . . . "

Robin: (Pausing, obviously thinking how to do this kindly) " . . . well, yes, hon, I do hear what you are saying. And—hon—I wouldn't want to put you down or anything—*oh, I wouldn't do that for worlds— you know that*—but, hon, if it's all right with you I think I'll just check this out with Mrs. Kuhlman, and see what she has to say."

Phone: "Blup, blup, BLUP. . . . "

Robin: "Oh, hon, I don't want to hurt your feelings, really and truly I don't. I know you do the best you can. But you see the fact of the matter is Mrs. Kuhlman, um, knows more about Social Security than you do."

Phone: "Blup."

They thoroughly dislike Mrs. Kuhlman at Social Security, because Robin is right, she does know more about it than they do. Why shouldn't she, she is certainly some kind of genius, and it certainly takes a genius to understand Social Security.

Robin said: "Oh I'm *glad* you see it that way, I'll just talk to Mrs. Kuhlman then, you know she and I have been friends for many many years, and then I'll call you back."

Phone said: "Blup, blup."

Robin: "Goodbye then, and I do thank you, hon, you've been very helpful to me . . . " There is a long pause, Robin is thinking how to end this with real grace, apparently: "Hon, it isn't that I question your intelligence and good will, it is just that I think a person should get many different opinions in a matter of this, um, *consequence*. DON'T YOU?" Who could argue?

I had a dream a couple of nights ago: I dreamed that our building had been knocked down into bricks and all the bricks and chairs and desks and everything had been auctioned off and after it was all over, the total assets, when all the bills had been paid, amounted to $138.00.

I mean, what good is $138.00 in the face of our task? We were finished—God knows, this is not far from the truth. And Vange Kuhlman was sitting amid all the leftover rubble and she was crying. "Oh what will happen to the people in the workshop?" she was crying.

Robin is one of the people in the workshop.

V.

Wilma Bremer was also one of the people in the workshop. But she was one of the ones who could see. Some of the people in the shop (never over 30%) have to be sighted; there are some parts of certain operations—and how we hate to admit it; but we do try to be a little realistic here; although realism is not our strong suit, hope is more like it, denial is more like it—there are some things that do require sight. There are some things that blind people can't do: brain surgery, flying a plane, and certain tricky operations in the workshop. Wilma was a line supervisor in the shop. That was all I knew about her—I mean, that is all the information that I connected with her name.

You have to understand that there is a great chasm, a barrier, between "Rehab" and "The Shop," so that very few of the people from the shop know the people from the rehab, and vice versa. Essentially, I think rehab is shy and aloof because they are somehow afraid of the workshop. And the workshop is very resentful of what they perceive as rehab's disdainful attitude toward them.

Rehab is the class operation—the showpiece of the agency—it is clean, righteous, haloed, the people in it seem to think of themselves as somehow better. (Confess—in your deepest heart don't *you* think *you* are better than a worker on a factory assembly line?) The workshop is like any other factory—the people who work in it get dirty, greasy, covered with lint, etc. The workshop nurses a terrible anger against rehab; whenever anything goes wrong, especially financially, it is "rehab's fault." And it *is*, too—rehab is expensive, it is the child going to college, it cannot support itself entirely. The workshop is the old mother and father who toil and drudge to support that glittering child—but sometimes they are hurt and angry even when they are proud. Especially if that child won't speak to them, especially if the child seems to be ashamed of them.

Rehab is ashamed of its hardworking parent: the workshop. It is a very uneasy relationship. Apparently it cannot be resolved. So the people in rehab do not know many of the people in the workshop.

There is another thing to be considered—the agency is large, there are just too many people to know them all. And the faces keep changing. And rehab is intense, concentrated upon its difficult task.

Vange, though—an exception to every rule I know—knows everybody, loves everybody. She also remembers everybody. She is becoming a sort of legend here: the phone will ring in her office and a voice will say, Hi, Vange, remember me?, and she will say, I remember your voice, talk some more and your name will come to me, and the person talks some more and by God! from twenty years back the name comes to her. The person on the phone is terribly pleased, of course: but how does she do it? She says it is a matter of paying attention to people all the time, of knowing every minute that each one of them is totally and individually important.

At the very end of this story, I am going to tell you some more about this; don't forget, or at the end you will think my story has no point. *Don't forget. Pay attention.* (I do know how hard it is; I am like you, I have not learned the trick.)

VI.

One Monday morning, I arrived at the agency and Vange told me that Wilma Bremer had died suddenly of a heart attack over the weekend, and her funeral was to be Tuesday morning. A lot of the people from the shop wanted to go to the funeral and there weren't enough sighted guides. Would I go as a sighted guide?

"Sure, Vange," I said. It meant no more than that to me, you see, Sure, Vange, we have an emergency situation and everybody (well, all the good folks anyway, all the real ones) pitches in and helps out, part of the job, part of the day's work. I didn't know Wilma Bremer from Adam.

As usual "not enough sighted guides" turned out to be an understatement. I drove four people over to the church in my car; presumably I was to be their sighted guide too. I think there was Bob Troy and Louisa, both total (totally blind, that is), Rene (total), and maybe one partial (partially sighted, anything from 20/200 visual acuity to bare light perception) but I don't remember any more who it was. I don't even remember for sure that it was Rene and Bob and Lou, I didn't really know them at the time, I have got to get this across to you, I was just an instrument in this situation. I was just doing my job.

I also wanted to go because Evangeline, though she is true blue and goes to all of them, really gets upset by funerals. I wanted to be with her. I mean: I *knew* Vange.

VII.

Now, there is a prescribed technique for sighted guide. There is one sighted guide and one blind person. The blind person holds the arm of the sighted person just above the elbow, four fingers in towards the guide's body, thumb out; the blind person walks half a step behind the sighted person, who then "leads" easily and gracefully and in a way that is perfectly dignified and inconspicuous. There are subtle signals: a slight hesitation before a flight of stairs, for example. A signal meaning: follow behind me single file, we are going through a narrow space.

There are good reasons for every detail of this technique, but this is a story, you don't have to get all of it, for God's sake, if you hold out for all of it we'll never make it to the funeral. I only want you to have enough so that you can understand.

Sighted guide becomes automatic after you've done it a few thousand times. It is a very beautiful thing to see when it is done properly; and it is a very beautiful thing to experience. It is an act of pure service, economical, absolutely appropriate, not too much given, not too little. The blind person (if he's a good sort—there are a few holdouts in any category) receives it as such, and this receiving, acceptance, on his or her part, makes it an interaction, a gift, perfectly offered, perfectly received. How many gifts are that pure? I absolutely love being a sighted guide.

Touch comes into it too: the act of serving as sighted guide is, in this culture in which touch is pretty much forbidden, a sanctioned and permitted way to touch another human being physically. If a blind person comes to us afraid to touch people, we must try to break down that fear. We order up The Treatment: touch, touch, touch. And love. You never saw a place where people hug each other, touch each other, so much.

And when the guide leads his own friends, other signals develop. Peter (Russian, blinded in World War II and our communication skills

64

instructor) is my friend. I squeeze Peter's hand between my arm and my body when I lead him—this means: I love you, Peter, we are friends. Peter grips my arm a little tighter—this means, I love you too, Joan, I agree with you that we are friends. When I lead Vange, on the rare occasions when she may need it, the message is more complex: it is, maybe you need this and maybe you don't, but for the sake of seven years' affection let us pretend that you need it, humor me, dammit, you stubborn old woman, if you trip and fall I will feel bad. So humor me. Love me. Accept from me a gift you do not want.

VIII.

But believe me, none of the subtle stuff, none of this beautiful sighted guide technique, went on at Wilma Bremer's funeral. It was bedlam, it was a real hash out in the lobby or whatever you call that entry part of a church. I can't remember exactly, but I imagine that I took two people in first, one on each arm, and then asked them to wait for me while I went back for the other two.

I do remember saying to someone, "Now stand right here, don't move until I get back . . . " But they didn't stand there, of course—why should they? This was the funeral of one of their own, they did as they damn pleased, as indeed they should. Up to a point. I mean, tripping or poking people with the white cane is strictly out, as is stepping on toes or crashing into people. A certain amount of this is however unavoidable in a crowd situation, unless you've got one-to-one on sighted guide, which somehow never seems to happen in the clutch.

When I got back, the two I had left were gone, someone else had taken them into the church, and I ended up with Robin Lennox. Vange took Geraldine Mattson who is very hard of hearing as well as blind.

I led Robin into the church and we found a far forward pew with Vange and Geraldine. We hadn't sat there a minute when Robin said: "Can we go right up to the casket, Joan? *To pay our respects?*"

"Certainly we can, Robin," I said. So we got out of the pew and joined the line of mourners going up to review the open casket. Vange and Geraldine followed us.

When it was our turn, Robin said, *"Can we go right up to it, Joan?"* It was dumb of me not to know that he wanted that, of course, how else could he see it, but to touch it?

65

The truth is, I was scared. I knew what was coming, and I can take a lot, but the idea of what he had in mind was embarrassing to me. I mean, Christ, it is gauche, who touches a casket, who feels a corpse? A blind person who is really interested in who is in the casket, that's who. I admit it, and I am ashamed of it—Robin was going to be embarrassing to me.

I led Robin right up so that his body touched the casket—good sighted guide technique there, recommended by AFB, which is the American Foundation for the Blind: "*Lead* the blind person to the chair so that he can feel it with his body . . . " Robin reached his hand out and found the satin fabric, very delicately brushed it, rubbed it.

"Satin!" he said.

"*What color is it,*" he said. Sighed.

"Kind of peach-colored, Robin," I told him. Very cool, I was.

"Peach-colored!" he said "*Isn't that nice?* Isn't that *nice* for Wilma, Joan? She was a wonderful, wonderful person, Joan—did you know her?"

"Well, no, I didn't, Robin," I said.

Robin: "Are there flowers on the casket, Joan?" I looked at the roughened, folded hands, hands of a worker, resting at last, lying crossed on exquisite pink and white carnations.

"Yes, Robin, she is holding a really nice bouquet of pink and white carnations."

"Oh!" said Robin. "*Pink and white carnations!*" When Robin gets really excited, he lowers his voice to a level of truly dreadful lugubrious enthusiasm. "Isn't that nice. Isn't that *wonderful.* She will be missed, Joan," he sighed, sobbed, breathed, total pleasure in his voice. "*Yes, she will be missed . . .* "

Then—"Um, Joan, would it be asking too much if I could, um, *touch the flowers?*"

"No, it wouldn't be asking too much, Robin," I said.

Very cool lady here. Fuck them all, I thought, these sighted outsiders, relatives and priests and what-have-you, who will think Robin is inappropriate. Fuck appropriate.

I guided Robin's hand to the flowers. ("*Guide* the blind person's hand to the object . . . " I could hear the AFB movie tape playing in my head.) He touched them with one finger, brushed them, caressed them, as delicately, as gently, as surely, as I imagine an artist would touch an original Rembrandt.

Eventually, of course, he touched her hand. "Oh—that's-her-hand-isn't-it,-Joan? That's-Wilma's-hand," he breathed, terribly excited.

"Yes, Robin," I said. "That's her hand."

"Cold in death," he said. Tears started to his eyes.

"Yes, cold in death . . . " He squeezed Wilma's hand, pressed it again and again, hard, for a long time.

I would like to tell you that I looked calmly around and saw the church so that I could describe for you now what it looked like. As a matter of fact, I would like to stick something in here for what writers call "pace"—every trade has its tricks—but the truth is I can't remember a thing, I was absolutely focused and fixated upon Robin's hand and Wilma's. I could hear my mother's voice in my ear from a long time ago: *What will the neighbors think?*

And behind me, as if from another country, far away, I registered as background a strange discreet roaring whisper, which was Vange trying to tell Geraldine what was going on: ROBIN IS HOLDING WILMA'S HAND, GERALDINE. But in a whisper, pitched just right, it is possible they heard it outside in the street. Vange doesn't worry about the neighbors, nor for the most part about anything else; supervising Vange has its trials at times.

"Joan, what does she look like?" Robin asked. "I mean, her face for example, and have they done her hair nicely for her?"

I looked for the first time at the permed, marcelled head resting on the peach satin pillow in the casket.

And there she lay. A woman I knew, had seen standing by the downstairs door waiting for her ride almost every day, had spoken to almost every day for years. Fragments of conversations slipped and slid into my mind, ricocheted: *Hello. How are you. Fine, thanks. Have you had a good day. Take care. Have a nice weekend. My, that's an awful cold you've got there. I hope you'll feel better soon. Good morning. Goodnight. Goodbye. Goodbye.* I had never known her name. *I had never known her name.* A nice woman, a small woman, friendly in an acerbic way, sort of a beaky, birdlike face, sort of a wiry quality about her, sort of a nasal rasp to her voice: someone I liked. I never knew her name.

Very funny things were going on in my mind. Not shock; no not that; remember, we have a lot of deaths. More like, *well, for heaven's sake, so that's* Wilma Bremer. But I never knew her name. (*Lord, can I ever be forgiven? There are so many, Lord. Answer from Lord: There is only one of each.*)

But I give myself full marks here, after all, I am a pro—and like all of us, proud of it—all this didn't take a second. I didn't miss a stroke. "Yes, Robin," I said, "she looks very nice. They've done very well for her."

"Does she look like, you know, *herself?*" asked Robin. "Does she look, um, *natural?*"

"Oh, yes," I said. "She looks like herself." She didn't. Dead is dead. But I got inspired suddenly. Go for broke. We rehab types are gamblers too, good at long shots. "Why, Robin," I said, "she looks *better* than herself. *She looks much better than natural . . .*"

Robin was utterly delighted.

"Oh that's so *nice,*" he breathed. For a second he forgot the appropriate low tone and his voice squeaked high. *"Oh isn't this nice, Joan?"* (*Isn't this fun* seemed like the next logical step . . .)

"Really, nice, Robin," I said. *"Really* nice."

He rubbed his hands together briskly in his great satisfaction. "I suppose we should go," he said, with regret in his voice. "I suppose we are holding up the line." I had a second of panic, a feeling that he would have liked to stay there more or less permanently, I could see the two of us stuck there through eternity, holding Wilma's hand. (*Would that do it, Lord?—is that what you want from me?*)

"It's all right, Robin," I said. "Nobody minds. Wilma doesn't mind. God doesn't mind." (I frequently take it upon myself to speak for God in my capacity as therapist—yes, I am that too, rehab demands great versatility—well, hell, you know, I feel that anybody alive has the right to speak for God. Or as God.) I glared around at the whole damn church, screw you all, back at Vange too, she was probably aware of the whole thing, she usually is (I am God, but she is Buddha, God is really a lot less effective in many situations), and she was probably laughing at me. Goddamn anybody who knows everything.

But we did go back to the pew, knelt. In an excess of terrific enjoyment, Robin reached out and groped for my hand, found it and pressed it, squeezed it.

"I don't believe I asked you this, Joan," he said: "Did you know her?"

"I knew her," I said. *I just never knew her name. I never asked. Did she know mine? Perhaps; even probably; because I am important, I am a supervisor in rehab. It is now too late. Sometimes it is too late. I can never, never, in all of time, say the thing that would have been right: Hello Wilma.*

Hello Robin. Hello Vange. Hello Lou, hello Bob, hello Geraldine. Hello Sharon, hello Bruce, all you dying sons of bitches, all you dead alive, all you beautiful. Hello. Hello.

IX.

As it mentions in some religion or other; *the ineffable name of God that no one can utter* (the Rumpelstiltskin of religion?): perhaps it is Wilma? or Robin? Danny? Fred? Barbara? even Greg? or—God help us all—Jerry? Some dumb-head at Social Security? How can you know? Be safe—remember all the names. Try. Take note of all the people. Look at the faces, if you can see. Remember. Do your best. It counts. It does count. Maybe nothing else counts.

X.

Vange remembers all the names. Even all the voices. Do you recall that I told you somewhere in the middle of this story that I was going to say more about this? I told you not to forget? If you forgot, you will think this is anti-climax, but I tell you I know what I am doing, trust me.

Don't permit yourself to get side-tracked by all the foregoing religious hysteria, grief, shock, etc. That is not the story. This is the story.

Once I was in a restaurant in New Ulm, Minnesota, with Vange. It was called the Kaiserhoff. A waiter came up, spoke to us, asked what we would like to order. He had a European accent, which I could not place. It wasn't quite like Peter's, it wasn't Russian, but it was a little like that.

Well, suddenly I saw Vange do her thing. It is funny to see, but at the same time it is rather alarming. Her face becomes very flat and smooth and her eyes narrow behind her glasses. A perfectly deadpan expression comes and then a little smile, lips together: totally smug. In fact she really does look like Buddha at these times: she is fat enough for it too.

Vange said: *Why I think I remember you. Weren't you the young man who helped me to find some noodles in a National Tea store one night about fourteen years ago in Devil's Lake North Dakota? I asked you where the noodles were and I told you I was a little blind and couldn't find them myself and you were very nice and took me right*

69

over to the shelf and found the right kind of noodles for me? And your name is—pause—oh God, the suspense was incredible, could she really pull this off?—*George!*

Well you *know* that waiter was absolutely knocked out. He said he did remember, she was right, he remembered her, it was his first night on the job, he was just over from Estonia, and he remembered the blind lady. Of course, of course.

Well, it was like Old Home Week. Nothing was too good for us from then on. They stuffed us like we were a goose for royalty. I will never as long as I live forget the deep-fried sauerkraut balls. Some things I do remember.

You think this cannot be true, but I am telling you it *is* true, this did happen. Well, I told you that Vange was a genius—of some kind.

She is also very hard to take. And she probably set blindness back a hundred years in New Ulm; they probably think she could do that because she is blind. I promise you that these things do not happen because she is blind—they happen because she is Vange.

I tell her that what she has is a gift, a talent, and she can't take any credit for it. She says it is not a gift, it is a matter of paying attention. I do not want to believe her; but I think I do believe her. A little.

Goddammit, I'm like Social Security: I do the best I can. I do try harder though since Wilma's funeral.

(Vange put the clincher on Wilma's funeral. She said, when she read this story, I'll bet you never noticed that Wilma had a hare lip, did you? And what do you suppose I answered? Well. You know me a little by this time, don't you? I am like you. No, I never noticed.)

Nominated by Kristina McGrath and The American Voice

SOMETHING LIKE HAPPINESS

by STEPHEN DUNN

from ANTAEUS

Last night Joan Sutherland was nuancing
the stratosphere on my fine-tuned tape deck,
and there was my dog Buster with a flea rash,
his head in his privates. Even for Buster
this was something like happiness. Elsewhere
I knew what people were doing to other people,
the terrible hurts, the pleasures of hurting.
I repudiated Zen because it doesn't provide
for forgiveness, repudiated my friend X
who had gotten "in touch with his feelings,"
which were spiteful and aggressive. *Repudiate*
felt good in my mouth, like someone else's tongue
during the sweet combat of love.
I said out loud, *I repudiate,* adding words
like *sincerity, correctness, common sense.*
I remembered how tired I'd grown of mountaintops
and their thin, unheavenly air,
had grown tired, really, of how I spoke of them,
the exaggerated glamor, the false equation between
ascent and importance. I looked at the vase
and its one red flower, then the table
which Zennists would say existed
in its *thisness,* and realized how wrong it was

to reject appearances. How much more difficult
to accept them! I repudiated myself, citing my name.
The phone rang. It was my overly serious friend
from Syracuse saying *Foucault, Foucault,*
like some lost prayer of the tenured.
Advocates of revolution, I agreed with him, poor,
screwed for years, angry—who can begrudge them
weapons and victory? But people like us,
Joan Sutherland on our tapes and enough fine time
to enjoy her, I said, let's be careful
how we link thought and action,
careful about deaths we won't experience.
I repudiated him and Foucault, told him
that if Descartes were alive and wildly in love
he himself would repudiate his famous dictum.
I felt something like happiness when he hung up,
and Buster put his head on my lap,
and without admiration stared at me.
I would not repudiate Buster, not even his fleas.
How could I? Once a day, the flea travels
to the eye of the dog for a sip of water.
Imagine! The journey, the delicacy of the arrival.

Nominated by David Jauss

THE MATCH

fiction by MAXINE KUMIN

from ONTARIO REVIEW

AT FIRST HE mistook her for a lost child. Watching the tassel of her knitted cap bob up over the granite ledges as she made her way toward him he gradually revised his image. Even as he was being discovered he could see this was a young woman, slightly built, moving awkwardly across the uneven terrain. Unused, he thought contemptuously, to woods walking. As she came up to him, a little out of breath from the climb, he saw she was no longer young although her face had weathered well with smile crinkles at the corners of her generous mouth. It was the snub nose that helped him mistake her for a child.

His one outing of the season when only antlered deer could be taken, he was none too pleased to be walked up to. From where he crouched on his stand he had an almost unbroken view across the glade and partway down the ledges. A providential dusting of fresh snow had fallen overnight powdering the rocks and pine duff. His own footsteps now barely showed; he had been careful to skirt the clearing and climb to his stand as economically as possible. Now he was ready, as ready as any cougar might have been fifty, a hundred years ago, for the big cats knew how to wait to pounce.

The tree stand was traditionally, not technically, his. The property belonged to an out-of-state flatlander named Walter Chester who had bought up huge tracts during the recession and was still holding them, doubtless waiting for the market to improve. By now he had probably forgotten he owned this east-facing slope of Grimes Peak.

The small person had reached the foot of the tree and called up to him. "Why are you doing this?"

73

"What are you doing out here? Who are you?"

"I live down there." She gestured behind her. "I'm trying to find out why you're doing this, what the purpose of it is."

"Jesus!" He replaced his rifle in the sling and clambered down from the platform. "The purpose is to take a deer, lady. It's hunting season, didn't you know that? Here's my license."

"Of course I know that. I mean, why are you hunting? Why do you want to kill a deer?"

He was baffled but only for a minute. "What are you, one of those animal rights nuts? Don't you know the deer would starve if we didn't thin the herd every fall? Or you, you bleeding heart, would you rather see them starve to death?"

"There's no real scientific evidence for that, you know. It's just a line the gun lobby puts out for propaganda. If the deer weren't hunted to death they wouldn't reproduce so heavily and the population would level off."

"Lady, that's just about the dumbest crock of . . . oh hell. I'm not gonna stand here arguing with you. Just turn around and go back the way you came. You've already ruined the morning for me and prob'ly the afternoon, too."

"Do you do it for food? Do you like to eat deer?"

He didn't especially like venison steak. Ground up it made a passable hamburg and doctored, an even better sausage. But he wasn't crazy about the taste of it straight. He gave most of it away.

"It's none of your damn business if I eat it or stuff it. Now get outta here before you get shot at."

She was persistent. "Does Mr. Chester know you're here?"

"This land's not posted. Chester knows better than to post his land. And besides, he probably doesn't even know where his property lines are."

"What does that mean, 'he knows better'?"

"Lotta things happen on posted land. Soreheads'll chop down trees, shoot up signs. One time a bunch of guys sank a rowboat just by plugging it with shells over on Nonesuch Pond. Absentee landowner puts up all those No Hunting signs, he's just asking for trouble."

"It just so happens Walter Chester is a friend of my family's. He'll be interested to hear this. I'm renting the caretaker cottage from him."

"Wonderful." Wes picked up his 30.30 and began sighting along it.

74

He was determined not to say another word. Sure enough, she turned around and started back toward the ledges. Even in the presence of a raised rifle she walked like a proud cat, never hurrying.

Wes had hunted this area ever since he was old enough to carry a gun. At first he went out with his father, a man not in the habit of saying much, and he watched and crouched beside him and tried not to hiccup or scratch himself. His father brought down a deer every year but one and that one was a hard winter with deep snows. The deer all yarded up in cut-over lots lower down the mountain and it was more like shooting fish in a barrel than a man stalking deer with his rifle and his wiles. He didn't even buy a license that year.

Well, the old man was seven years dead. Wes's sister had left Liston five years ago to marry the music and arts teacher in the next town. There were no other siblings. Wes had an ever-changing population of strays, lost or abandoned dogs he had taken in, black and tan, spotted and splotched damaged dogs that were his family. Everybody in Liston knew he was a sucker for dogs. Also cats, but he was not passionate about cats. They didn't meet you halfway.

Like most people in his part of the country, he was respectful of bears. He believed every bear story he heard. He honored coyotes too, for their quick wits. Maybe they brought down a lamb or two, but mostly they preyed on mice and moles. They ate berries, fish. Once he'd watched a coyote casually stalking grasshoppers and catching them in his mouth in mid-jump. Porcupines were vermin in his book, along with woodchucks; skunk didn't rate much higher. You could club a porcupine, just step on his tail and clonk him with a two by four. Wes had pulled enough quills out of enough dogs to whet his appetite for finishing off any porcupines he came across.

If questioned, he would have said he loved deer, loved their secretive presence, the sense of a whole herd of them fanning out, even as he hunted. Loved finding the flattened wallows where they had bedded down. In tall grasses you could spy out a group, four or five all travelling together, lying down together. Lots of times in late summer he'd put up a doe and her fawn, faced them across a clearing, the fawn's tawny spots making it almost invisible in the dappled sunlight. It was something to see.

The day was ruined, he was sure of it. That woman's footprints were visible little ovals laid out like a lure bisecting the glade he had been at such pains not to sully. Her odor was in them and worse, the scent of

75

her perfume, her hair spray, whatever foreign smells she carried. These would linger for hours. He felt violated by the encounter, unnerved to have his rights questioned, his compact with the land cast in doubt.

He knew those crazies were out there, he had read about them picketing experimental labs—and here he had felt a warm onrush of sympathy thinking of dogs held prisoner in metal cages, tortured and then sacrificed for the advancement of medical science. He had read with an almost gluttonous fury about rabbits having their eyelids sewn open to permit technicians to test for allergic reactions to drugs and even to various cosmetics.

But he had never connected these protests to deer season. Or bird season, for that matter. Though he didn't care for duck, from time to time he hunted grouse and bagged his limit. They made a good small meal, legal and plentiful in October. Kinder, he thought, than supermarket chicken which he privately called concentration-camp chicken, knowing the conditions under which they were raised. Why are you doing this? he kept mimicking her lilting treble calling up to him. Cute little open-faced thing, she'd gotten to him. Yea, Wes, why the fuck?

As it turned out, he got an eight-point buck late that afternoon, not more than thirty minutes before sunset. Wes was honorable about hunting hours and leery, too, of being caught in the woods at twilight. Eighty percent of all hunting accidents happen just at sunrise or when the light is fading; he remembered reading that. It was fully dark by the time he got the buck field-dressed and dragged it, leaving a trail of red on the snow, out to his pickup. Grunting from the effort, he loaded it into the back; he'd take it to Deveraux's Hardware, the official inspection station, in the morning.

He would have to admit he delayed getting into town till midmorning in hopes there'd be people around to admire his take, and he was right. It was a bright crisp day for getting errands done; half the town crowded up to the scales where his buck broke 180 lbs., not quite a record. Dev measured, inspected, then tagged it as it hung swaying a little in death, its glazed eyes open. Several little boys daringly poked and stroked its hide. The wispy woman from the woods, coming out of the store with a package under her arm, locked eyes with him as he glanced around. He looked away first.

Since it was the first Saturday of the month, he stuck around for the EMT drill, which was held at noon in the firehouse, preceded by pizzas and followed by beer and horseshoe pitching, if the weather allowed. Wes had been a member of the emergency medical team and the volunteer fire department ever since he came of age twenty years ago. Joining up was part of turning 21 in Liston; he had never questioned it. It said you were a responsible citizen; if not a family man, at least not a hell-raiser.

He was married, briefly, that same year of his majority. In Liston, New Hampshire you pretty much married your high school sweetheart. His, Mary Ellen Dowd, had gone to college out of state, which was in itself unusual. Wes had signed on at the telephone company with his dad right after high school. Most of his work was laying out new lines, which suited him. He guessed he knew every back road in Liston County by heart. He knew where the wild day lilies flowered and which pond's spring peepers gave earliest voice. Often he could take his latest rescued dogs with him. Desk work was a disaster he chose to avoid whenever possible but Mary Ellen thought he ought to take an administrative job and try to get ahead.

She didn't care for the way he hung out with his rowdy buddies late at the firehouse or went off to the tavern on the highway with them for a few beers. Wives traditionally raised these objections and husbands goodhumoredly placated them with white lies and excuses, but in Wes and Mary Ellen's case, things escalated into pitched battles.

Wes wasn't a fighter by nature. He was a low-key guy, kept his own counsel. He treated women carefully, pretty much watched his language around them, never raised his hand to one. Not like men he knew who just lost it when they drank. Beat up their women, then played this game of a thousand sorries after. Flowers and all that, courting them all over again.

They actually got along a lot better after the divorce. Mary Ellen met an aspiring lawyer down in Concord and eventually they married and started a family. She and Wes still exchanged Christmas cards and every once in a while he'd run into her when she came back to Liston to visit her folks.

Bachelorhood suited him. But he wasn't a recluse. He bought a precut log cabin and assembled it over the summer months on a five-acre lot that bordered the federal wetlands. His nearest neighbor was a mile in any direction. Every June he threw a big bash for summer solstice with kegs of beer and loudspeakers blasting rock music well into the night. And every Sunday after Thanksgiving he spread a buffet with venison meatballs and red wine. Everybody came.

77

The women really let down their hair at Wes's parties. People paired off in the goddamnedest combinations; he was always a little obscurely ashamed the next day reviewing these events. He wasn't in the habit of sleeping around though it sometimes happened. He didn't really want a steady woman, a fact that was generally known in town. Mostly he stayed home and talked to his dogs and watched cable TV, which came in at a discount rate on the telephone lines.

Right into December Wes was out on the Grimes Peak Road overseeing the installation of nine new poles. The Liston phone company was converting some of its old lines that zigzagged through woods on right-of-ways to less maintenance-dependent lines along the roads. The men were hurrying to get poles into the ground before a hard freeze closed them down for the winter.

Going in and out the one-lane road twice or even three times a day Wes couldn't avoid meeting his little woods walker. He had since learned her name was Julia and she was a "fiber artist." "What the hell is a fiber artist?" he had asked Perry Enders, his informant.

"You know. She does things with wool," leaving him with a vague image out of his grade school history book of a woman carding and spinning fleece.

And then he saw an exhibit of her work at the Liston Christmas Fair: felted mittens and berets tarted up with embroidery, some loose-woven throws with knotted fringes, and something that looked like a rug but was meant to hang on a wall, with interlocking animals woven into it. "A tapestry," he was told. The price tag was $1200, which guaranteed that he wasn't going to buy it. He went back a couple of times just to look at it, to study the stylized animals that seemed to be dancing in tandem around the edges. They were a puzzling procession: what looked like an oversized mouse was linked to a cat, in turn hanging onto a dog that seemed to be chasing a pig. At the front of the little parade, a child. The pattern repeated all the way around. He marvelled at the intricate design, the way the colors shaded into one another. He could see she really was an artist.

The morning of December 10 when her car overtook him on the Grimes Peak Road he wasn't sure how to act, so he nodded and lifted one hand in terse acknowledgment. By the time she came back from town, though, the backhoe was planted across the road and she had to stop. It was obvious to both of them that a brief chat was in order. She initiated it.

"Well, I see you got your deer after all."

"Yup."

"Is it good?"

"Don't know. I sent it over to the Chesley Home."

"What's that?"

"State home for folks that can't live on their own anymore."

"So what are you eating?"

"Oh, lots of things. I got some brook trout still in the freezer from last spring." But then the backhoe finished maneuvering. She bumped the Nova out of neutral and into drive and was gone.

"Hope she isn't planning to drive that hunk of junk all winter," he said to no one in particular.

She was gone over Christmas and most of January. He knew this in the way that small-town news travels. Jimbo Flood, Liston's one plumber, had been called to come out and drain the pipes. He would go back and restart the system on the 20th. He'd had to build a helluva roaring fire just to warm the place up before he dared prime the pump.

Wes didn't have any official reason to run out the Grimes Peak Road but toward the end of January he told himself it might be good to see how the poles were setting up now that there was two feet of snow on the ground. He had heard the sound of wheels futilely spinning, wearing away rubber, before he even got to where the road bends and begins to climb. Her Nova was wedged sideways on a slick patch. There was a sand barrel a little further on; he had a shovel in the truck so it didn't take long to free her.

"You'd best get some grain bags full of sand or even a couple of concrete blocks to carry in the trunk of this thing. Road's gonna get lots trickier than this."

"Thanks. Hey, I wanted to say I'm sorry about . . . that day up there." She gestured behind herself in the direction of the ledges. "This isn't an apology or anything, I still don't believe in hunting, but I'm sorry I spoiled your day."

"S'okay. Now it's none of my business but if you're thinking about staying all winter you oughta get rid of that Nova and pick yourself out something more suitable. Something with a stick shift and four-wheel drive. Automatics are no damned good on these hills."

"I might stay." She turned a smile on him so vulnerable and radiant that he felt heat rush to his face. She held out her hand. "Julia Mather. Soon to be Julia Hesselstrom again."

"Wesley Kingsley. Never been anything else." He smiled back. They shook gloved hands and exhaled little ghost puffs.

"I might stay," she repeated. "I have a little money. My kids are grown and gone. One's in law school, the other's a painter, she's in California." He was frankly stunned. "You don't look old enough to have grown kids."

She made a little face that said she had heard that before. "You?"

"Oh, I'm just a fixture. Born and raised here, work for the telephone company. Had a wife once, long time ago."

They didn't exactly run out of things to say. It was as if, Wes thought afterward, they had both arrived at a crossroad, a four-way stop, and neither was certain who should go first. He thought she could have invited him back for a cup of coffee or to see her work. He thought she thought he might refuse or he might make a pass at her or godknows. He thought he should have mentioned the tapestry, he could have asked her to explain it. He found he couldn't imagine her life, he didn't have enough to go on.

Ten days later his beeper went off just as he was sitting down to his supper. He stashed his plate on top of the fridge where the dogs couldn't get it, shut the cats into the back hall, jammed his feet into his boots, and took off, licensed dome light twirling, for the fire station.

"Fire at the old Chester place," Perry told him.

"How bad?"

"Can't tell. Pumper's already out and so's the ladder truck."

"It'll be a bitch if we have to pump in this weather." He wondered who had turned in the alarm. She must be out there; nobody else would have seen a fire till the place burned down to the ground.

"You better believe. Guess we'll go in your truck," Perry said. "Mine's skippen again."

"Points?"

"Prob'ly."

By the time they got there they were superfluous.

"Chimney fire!" Perry spat his quid out the truck window, half in disgust, half in relief.

Ray Jenkins and Charlie Santos had hauled the steaming woodstove out of the cottage. It sat on the satiny snow crust like a surprised black bear.

Inside, the stovepipe dangled from the chimney flue, its elbow bent at an improbable angle. Windows had been opened to dissipate the smoke. It was almost as cold in as out of doors. Julia Mather stood in the middle of a group of volunteers. She looked pale and a little scared;

80

they always did, after the crisis was over. He hoped she wasn't going to faint.

Apparently she had let the stove go out during the warm afternoon, then attempted to start a fire when she got back from her errands. Cold stoves are stubborn starters. When the fire didn't catch promptly she added several wads of newspaper imperfectly crumpled. These ignited all at once, lodged in the pipe cutting off air flow, and a severe downdraft sucked the rest of the papers into a fiery mass. Clouds of smoke billowed back into the room, a familiar scenario. At that point she panicked and dialed 3434.

" . . . dizzy," he heard her say.

"Get a blanket, somebody," he said, shouldering his way into the group. "Charlie, see if you can heat up some water, she needs some hot tea or something."

It was an electric stove. While they waited for the teakettle to hiss, Wes opened several cupboards in search of a tea bag.

"What's this stuff?" He dangled a square packet with foreign symbols on it.

"Miso," she said. She was now sitting at the table wrapped in a rose-colored comforter and she was still shaking.

"Whaddya do with it?"

"Drink it. It's like soup."

"Smells like a goddam Chinese restaurant. You got some coffee somewhere?"

"No."

"Tea?"

"Any whiskey?" Ray asked.

"Whiskey's the worst thing in the world for shock," Wes told him.

"There's some camomile tea over there, on the left." She gestured above the stove.

"Jesus, not that sissy stuff," Ray muttered to Perry.

"I'm sorry," she said. "I don't keep any stimulants around."

Wes didn't like the looks of her lips. They were still a pinched lavender. Little spasms of shivers were coursing through her body, making her teeth chatter. There was something appealing about her, even desirable. He wondered about the stimulants remark. Was she a former alcoholic? He stirred the miso and handed her the mug.

Within an hour the squad had cleaned creosote out of her stovepipe and chimney flue. Wes himself clambered up on the roof and shone

81

his company flashlight down to check for any obstructions. Charlie and Ray carried the stove back in, with rather more grunts than were required. They reattached the pipe, levelled the stove, relaid a fire and got a good blaze going. They instructed her in the care and feeding of woodstoves in general, airtight cast-iron ones in particular.

"You guys go ahead," Wes said. "I'm gonna stay a while and put up a good pile of kindling so we don't have to come back out here again."

They shuffled around a bit as they were leaving. Perry gave Wes a broad wink. "Don't wear out that little hatchet."

Since there was nothing else, he fixed Julia a second cup of miso; himself, camomile. "Where's your milk? You run out?"

"I don't use milk. I'm a vegan."

"What's that?"

"Someone who only eats plants."

"You mean like a vegetarian? They eat milk and eggs and things."

"Ovo-lacto vegetarians do. Vegans don't."

"Judas Priest. No wonder you're such a slip of a thing. Whaddya live on?"

"Fruits, vegetables, nuts, whole grains. Lots of soybean products."

"You mean like tofu?"

"Tofu is one item. There's also soy cheese, even soy ice cream."

He grimaced.

"Want some peanut butter cookies to go with the tea?"

"Criminy, you mean you eat cookies?"

"Well, I don't have two heads, Wesley. I was stupid about the stove, I don't eat meat or dairy products, but I do have a life."

"Yea-zoo, I didn't mean you didn't, I just . . . "

"Well, you act like you think I live in a cocoon somewhere. I've been around, I've been arrested five times, I've gone to jail."

"Arrested? What for?"

"Criminal trespass. Theft. Destruction of government property. Disorderly conduct. Resisting an officer." She ticked them off on her fingers.

"Come on, Julia, don't bullshit me. Theft of what?"

"Theft of cats, for one. We broke into a lab at Preston University and stole six cats they'd been injecting with various paralyzing agents, cats that were going to be 'harvested'—that's the euphemism they use for killing them."

"Oh, that's it. Animal rights, I remember reading something about it in the paper. Oh yeah, it fits."

"You think I'm crazy."

"I think you're crazy but I respect it, you know? I gotta respect you for living what you believe. You steal anything else?"

"Mink. Primates. Dogs, most of them family pets that were picked up on the streets and sold to biomedical labs."

"Jesus H Christ." Wes was amazed. She looked like a perfectly ordinary person, definitely not the warrior type.

"You have any pets?"

"Dogs. Five of them right now. Summer people drop them off in my driveway when they're sick a them. Some go to the pound, some I keep. I try to keep the puppies, give them a good start."

She winced.

"See, people don't have respect for animals, they treat them like a Nintendo game or something. See, if you needed to take out a license to have a dog or a cat, there wouldn't be so much . . . abandonment."

"Five dogs. I never would have guessed it."

"Couple a cats too." He said it modestly, aware he had just won a hundred brownie points.

"Be careful. Next thing you know, you'll be joining our group."

"What's it called?"

"AA. *Animals All*. Our slogan is: A rat is a cat is a dog is a pig is a boy."

"I get it. Is that what you put in the border around your tapestry?"

She looked pleased. "You saw that?"

"Saw the whole exhibit. You're the first artist I ever knew close up."

"Thank you for telling me."

He closed his hand over hers, felt her stubby, tough fingers. She did not pull back.

He stopped by the next day with a pickup truckload of split hardwood from his own pile.

"You shouldn't have done that."

"You've only got a cord, cord and a half out there. It can get a whole lot colder than this here. You better believe."

"I've got backup electric heat. I don't like to use it much, it's so expensive."

"Well, this'll hold you for a bit." He hesitated. "You gonna ask me in?"

"Certainly."

He ended up staying for lunch, which was surprisingly normal. Vegetable soup, homemade bread, apples and cookies.

"I don't s'pose you'd come over for supper one night? Meet my dogs?"

"I'd love to," she said, never missing a beat. She bestowed that smile on him and this time he felt the flush begin in his groin.

"Another thing. You can call me Wes."

"My friends call me Jules. My fellow thieves call me J.J."

"You're lucky to have two names. I'm just plain Wes to friend and foe."

It snowed steadily Thursday, the day she was to come over. He didn't trust the Nova so he went to fetch her himself. Driving back, he tried to explain about the snow, how it lifted everyone's spirits, how it was good for the pastures—"poor man's fertilizer, they call it"—good for insulating the ground, wells, houses. Good for horses' and cows' hooves, for the skiers, for replenishing the reservoirs.

"Why, that's practically a prayer, Wes," she said, embarrassing him.

He knew she was an animal nut but he wasn't prepared for the reception his dogs gave her. It was downright eerie the way they howled and fussed and rolled over on their backs to have their bellies scratched.

He had given the meal much thought, not wanting to contravene her code. He fixed a pasta sauce laced with plenty of garlic and mushrooms and he put a dish of Parmesan cheese on the table, which he sprinkled liberally over his portion. She passed it by. He'd bought an apple pie from Ella's, an authentic local bakery. He topped his with vanilla ice cream. She had peppermint tea while he doused his coffee with cream. The dogs lolled under the table. Not one growled or snapped at another. The cats sat on top of the refrigerator, the Maine coon cat with the torn ear kept his yellow eyes fixed on Julia while his bushy tail hung down, forming a plume.

"So you don't drink coffee or tea or beer or wine?"

"I'm a recovering alcoholic."

"That's what I guessed. Well, you came to the right place. So's half this town."

"I went off the deep end a few years back, after the really bad arrest. I couldn't sleep so I started pouring myself nightcaps and then I found I couldn't stop."

"What bad arrest?"

"Oh, this was in Michigan the night we broke into the university."

"You broke in?"

84

"You always try to commit your sabotage at night. We destroyed their files on mink research, they claimed it was thirty years' worth."

"You just ripped up the papers?"

She laughed. "No, better than that. We set them on fire. But three of us were caught and the cops were really brutal."

"You take the cake," Wes said. He couldn't picture her in that environment.

"I don't like to talk about it. They hogtied me, if you know what that is."

He nodded.

"And two of them beat me up on the way to jail, ruptured my spleen."

"Jesus. These were men beating on you?"

"State troopers. Good old boys."

Wes made some commiserating sounds.

"The thing is, they'd been staking out the lab for weeks, waiting for something to happen."

"But what I don't get is, why do you want to put yourself on the line like that? When you know people are gonna jump you for it?"

"Wes, I've cared about these things all my life. I care that people still club baby seals for their fur. That fishermen cut the fins off shark for Chinese restaurants and then toss them back in the ocean to die. I've been there, it's so ugly. Even rats. I'm not fond of rats, but if you've ever seen them trained with electric shocks to run a maze . . . "

"So now you're out of jail and on your own?"

"Well, first I had a sort of breakdown. Too much pressure from all sides. I pretty much got out of the movement . . . "

"The animal rights movement?"

"The activist, confrontational part. Then I joined the other AA—"

"Alcoholics?"

"Right. I went to meetings every week for about a year. And now I just try to stay clean."

She got up then and started clearing the table.

"I'll wash," Wes said. "You can dry if you want."

"Delighted."

The last cup was in her hand when he came up behind her, lifted the hair on her neck and asked, "Would you get mad if I kissed you?"

She turned to face him. "Where is this going?"

"It isn't going anywhere you don't want it to go."

"Wes. It's been four years since I've kissed a man."

"Well, let's not wait any longer then, okay?"

She opened her arms and took him in.

Fitted against him he smelled her hair, unperfumed but faintly minty. Her mouth opened under his as she kissed him back. He ran his hands down her sides and cupped her to him as he grew hard. But the dogs went wild, scrabbling to get between them.

"You see who they prefer," Julia said. "Now I'm an interloper."

"Don't be too sure. I could be the one they want to drive off."

After some order had been restored Wes suggested they retreat upstairs.

"It's cozy up here under the eaves," she said in his monastic bedroom. "Toasty warm."

"Warm air rises," he said, and facing each other they began to undress like two teenagers at a strip poker game. At that moment his beeper went of.

"Shit!" He rebuttoned his shirt.

She pulled her sweater back over her head. "I've gotta go, I can't not go, you know?"

"I know."

Her tone was so level that he couldn't tell how she meant it. Was she disappointed or relieved?

"You stay here, Jules. Maybe it won't take long. We get a lot of emergency calls that don't amount to anything this time of year." He swiped his lips across hers, then leapt down the stairs.

Jimbo Flood's parents' dairy barn had burned down. Out of thirty head of cattle they'd only been able to save sixteen. It was the worst disaster in Liston since the 1962 hurricane. There'd been a rash of electrical fires then as the winds brought down power lines, poles, transformers, or so the oldtimers said. This fire was electrical, too; a defective cooler had shorted out.

Wes could still smell the charred timbers, hear the live cows moaning for the others as they milled around directionless. His ribs were bruised from the jostling he took as he and Charlie raced into the barn hooting and shoving, shooing cow after cow into the open. He didn't feel the kicks so much, it was their sheer weight pressing on him. The cows' lowing in terror like the rising of a terrible wind was a sound he hoped never to hear again.

He and the others struggled to round them up, driving them through stinging sleet into the open pasture where all they could do was huddle like football players. It was pitiful. Even though there was a stand of pines at one end of the pasture, the Floods would probably lose some more before they could arrange to get the survivors trucked to neighboring farms.

It was well after midnight when he returned bruised and bone-weary and caked with soot and mud. She had left the outside light on. The dogs, accustomed to the sound of his truck, whined a little but didn't bark.

He tiptoed upstairs. Jules was asleep in his bed, in his flannel pajamas. He took a long hot shower, rooted around in his bureau for another pair, and slipped in beside her.

She woke long enough to identify him. "Wes?"

"Shh. It's 2 a.m. I'll tell you in the morning." He curled around her and spoon-fashion they slept.

When he woke, her side of the bed was empty but the imprint of her body was still there. He could hear her downstairs talking softly to the dogs. The storm had cleared. A brisk wind now whipped up great froths of snow and swirled them into the trees so that it looked like a fresh snowfall was under way. March had come in like a lion, all right.

"There you are. I made you some coffee."

He took the cup with a little salute, then sat down facing her to tell about the fire.

"God. Those poor people! And the cows, cows are so afraid of fire.'"

"All animals are. Don't know how many'll pull through." He was secretly pleased that her first response was sympathy for the humans.

"You must be beat. And hungry. Maybe we can have some oatmeal?"

"Listen to me, Jules. That's the first time I've spent a whole night with a woman in umpteen years."

"Really? How'd you like it?"

"Don't know. I fell asleep so fast I didn't have a chance to . . . appreciate it. I'd like to try again."

"Before breakfast?"

"Before breakfast."

"You'll be late for work."

"I'll call in sick."

As they started up the stairs together she said, "Where's your beeper?"

"In the truck. I'm not taking any more chances."

Word got out around Liston that Wes was keeping company with the lady who almost burned the Chester place down. Although he suf-

87

fered the ribbing goodnaturedly, he didn't volunteer any information about Julia. What they did or said, where they went or spent the night was their own affair. Mostly she stayed over in the cabin. Five dogs were like having children all over again, she said. Days, he went to work and she to her studio in the caretaker's cottage. Her work was going well. She said she had started a new tapestry, this time with cows in it. The Floods sold off the survivors. They were putting the farm up for sale and moving to Florida.

"With the rest of the snowbirds," Wes said, disapproving. Julia said how sad it was to see good people leaving the land. Although she didn't approve of keeping dairy cows.

"Well, what about raising sheep? What about the ram lambs, you can't use but one or two for breeding. If you don't sell them for meat you've got to castrate them. What about that?"

"I know. But shearing their wool once a year feels different to me from keeping cows, breeding them for calves in order to rob the milk. And those little vealers raised in slatted cages in the dark, not even able to turn around, that has to be the cruelest practice."

"I agree with you there. Round here, though, people raise them on grass, mostly they don't pen them up."

"So it's a short happy life. But what right do we have to do it?"

Silence was Wes's first reflex. He rooted around warily for something to say. "Thing is, I wish you didn't care so much."

"I know. I went overboard once. I'm learning not to obsess."

"How do you do that?"

"I use up some of it in my weaving."

"And the rest?"

"I do this with it." She pounced on him, tickling him in the armpits until, howling *I give up!* he caught her in a bear hug.

With something close to sorrow he saw that he had fallen in love with her. To him she was a small mysterious goddess whose values often struck him as bizarre. He saw he was ready to spend the rest of his life unravelling the mystery. Fitted together like spoons they would drop wordlessly into sleep. One night he would awaken inside her dream and then he would know the world that she knew.

Little by little Wes gathered that there had been a major nervous collapse. Not one big dramatic moment the way it happens on TV and you see the person led away drooping between two starched attendants. Jules's had been a sort of gradual decline. Of not wanting to get up in the morning and then not wanting to eat and on top of that, more vodka downed earlier and earlier until evening had backed up into afternoon. She told him that her marriage had begun to come apart well before her breakdown. Her causes sat down with them at breakfast, crawled into bed with them at night, breathing between them in the kingsize bed.

He understood that she was trying to warn him; "I don't scare easy," he told her.

In mid-April he rototilled a space for her garden and watched as she plotted what to plant where. Because the garden was so close to the cottage he didn't suggest fencing it. He didn't count on the lawless ways of several generations of rabbits and woodchucks that had laid uninterrupted claim to that space. All the lettuce went down in one night and about half the peas were nipped off at ground level.

Shooting was out of the question. Gas bombs in the chuck holes were vetoed, too. His Jules was a vegan without a garden. But the Swiss chard pulled through and, cunningly wrapped in hardware cloth, several broccoli seedlings thrived.

He didn't taunt her with questions about how the vegetables she bought at the grocery store were raised. Those acres and acres of soybean fields must have harbored thousands of rabbit nests. Farmers learn how to be ruthless. Did she make the connection on her own?

Blackflies, that terrible scourge of the north country, came on schedule. It was mid-May.

"They'll go as soon as the mosquitoes get here." Wes bought her an Adirondacks hat to wear out of doors, a skullcap with netting that hung down long enough to be tucked in a shirt.

"God. I never thought I'd pray for mosquitoes." She pulled out a packet of seeds and studied the instructions on the back.

"Jules, it's too early for squash."

"Too early? It's got to be eighty degrees today."

"And tomorrow it could frost. You've got to wait till oak leaves are the size of a mouse's ear."

She looked up at the bare branches. "A mouse's ear? What kind of scientific measurement is that?"

She wouldn't come to his June solstice party. It had nothing to do with meeting his old friends. No, it wasn't the rock music. Or the beer. She was around people who drank all the time and she hadn't succumbed.

"Well, what is it?"

"Nothing. I just don't . . . do parties."

"What about gallery openings?"

"That's business, not pleasure."

"Jules, it would mean a lot to me."

She looked stricken. "I can't do it, Wes. I . . . have to go to New York that week."

Sometimes she came sharply into focus for him, like a painting done with a child's primary colors, the outline inked in with a thick black pen. All summer it was the plight of the dolphins and orca whales. It was the relentless Navy teaching dolphins to defuse bombs in the harbor. Teaching them to pick up objects off the ocean floor. Forcing them to dive deeper and deeper, beyond their range. Teaching them to recognize mock-enemy frogmen underwater. Several dolphins had died of mysterious ailments.

She drove down to Connecticut to observe the protests although she swore she wouldn't take an active part. "Never mind the issue of capturing them, taking them prisoner. Just ask yourself, what right do we have to make animals fight our wars?"

"Even if it saves lives?"

"It's a moral issue, Wes."

"Promise me you won't get mixed up in this?"

It was one of the July dogdays. He had taken the afternoon off. They were lying side by side on a mangy strip of beach at the local lake. Her neat, compact body bound in two strips of cloth lay so close to his gangly freckled one and yet not touching; he could not stand the hunger he felt. "Marry me, Jules."

"You want to marry me to save me? God, Wes, what can I say? I'm not sure we're a good match. I'm not sure we're any match at all."

"We're a perfect match. And if you don't get in the water this minute and start swimming I'm going to fuck you here right in front of the good citizens of Liston."

Over the late summer while the squash prospered and a few beans began to climb the tepee he set up for her, he felt her distancing herself from him. She was inundated with visitors—sunshine patriots, she called them, but he suspected they were her fellow conspirators—and after they left she was frequently too tired to come for supper. Even his vegetarian pizza couldn't tempt her.

At the end of August, a gallery in Soho sold her new tapestry. She called him with the news; she was bringing supper.

"Ta da!" Out of one brown bag she took four zucchini. "Home grown." Out of another, some strange-looking yellow things that she identified as chanterelles.

"You mean they're wild mushrooms? How do you know they're not poisonous?"

"Trust me."

He had to admit it was a wonderful if poisonous stir fry. "Marry me, Jules, just in case. We can die happy."

It was an ardent night. Afterwards, they slept as soundly as exhausted athletes. She tickled him awake before the sun came up and inveigled him into making love again and then she left him to get an early start on the long drive to New York City.

"You're wearing a groove in the throughway," he told her, hugging her close at the door of her car. He who had never seen Manhattan, who had only been to Boston once and chose not to go back again.

"I'll be back in a week. I'll call you."

After six days he ran up the Grimes Peak Road to check on the garden for her, although he was damned if he was going to pull any weeds. Her mailbox at the end of the long driveway was stuffed full to overflowing. He gathered up the newspapers and fliers, rifled through the letters—nothing personal, just various agency pleas for contributions—then left the stack inside her screened porch.

What was he looking for? A loveletter? Some clue as to her whereabouts?

On a hunch he shaded his eyes and peered into the living room/kitchen. It looked just as he remembered it, only much tidier. None of her papers, tools, utensils, not even a wilted floral arrangement; she was forever picking wildflowers and assembling sprawling bouquets of the commonest weeds. To Jules, goldenrod was parlor-worthy.

From this angle he couldn't see into the workroom but he knew how to get inside without picking any locks. Around back he shouldered open the bathroom window Jules had slipped through one night when she forgot and locked her key ring inside.

The studio was bare. Her loom, her spinning wheel, all the paraphernalia for her felting were gone. The wall hangings, the assorted mittens and slippers, belts and berets were gone. He couldn't take it all in. She must have spent days packing up, patiently breaking the loom down in order to crowd it into her car. He knew before he entered the bedroom that it too would be swept clean.

91

There was a note on the bureau with some folded-over bills, weighted down by a key.

"Eventually you'll figure this out, dear dear Wes. I didn't have the courage to tell you face to face. My life in Liston was too lovely and a lot of its loveliness was your fault. Meanwhile, my guilt just grew and grew. I've gone back under cover so it's no use looking for me. Just know I will never forget what we had together.

your J.J.

PS. Here's $30 for Jim Flood. Please ask him to come up and drain the system and leave the key under the 2nd brick on the R out front (that's where Mr. Chester hides it)."

It was a week before he contacted Jimbo. He couldn't face the enormity of her absence. And then, one night, making his solitary supper, moving among and talking to his dogs, he thought of Ray Waterman, the tamed, reduced Iroquois who taught music in the Liston primary school forty years ago. Every fall Ray was persuaded to open the music program with a war dance. Decked out in feathers and beads and poster paint, this grown man stomped across the stage and shook his rattles as accompaniment to a high, nasal keening that sent shivers coursing down young spines. Every boy in the class elected to study drums. The girls got penny whistles and triangles and were known as the rhythm section.

They only got to see Ray Waterman once a year in his Indian regalia. The rest of the time he stood at the blackboard in shirt and tie demonstrating half and whole notes on the treble clef.

Jules, he thought, was like that. What he had seen was the tamed Jules. The true terrorist self, J.J., had never surfaced in his presence. He could only guess at its nature.

The hardest thing for Wes was having to face the hopeful excited millings about of his dogs day after day when he drove into the yard. It was clear they had not forgotten. He wondered how long it would take to dim their expectations. As long as her scent lingered, he guessed.

Early in November he took in a soaked mongrel pup not more than three months old. Perry had found it being swept downriver. He named it Jay and let it share his bed until he could get it socialized with the others.

When hunting season opened on the second Saturday of the month, Wes was ready. He rose early, put on his orange cap and vest, loaded his rifle and sling into the pickup, and drove out the Grimes Peak Road.

The sun was just coming up as he started scaling the ledges that led to his tree stand in the glen. It was a flaming sunrise, unusual for autumn. As he climbed up over the granite outcroppings the sun's rays blurred his vision, bringing tears to his eyes, but he was back in his own skin.

Nominated by Joyce Carol Oates and Robert Phillips

THEORIES OF ILLUSION

by MAUREEN SEATON

from THE MISSOURI REVIEW

The panda has a sixth digit we call
a thumb but really it's a greatly enlarged
"radial sesamoid," a simple component of the wrist.

Also, although the panda is a charter member
of the order Carnivora, she eats absolutely nothing
but bamboo from the mountains of Western China.

As for the orchid, we may think brava!
What an amazingly well-thought-out system
for attracting insects. But it's no more

than a zany arrangement of already existing
flower-parts, a jury-rig of pistil and stamen—
much like my ex-boyfriend Will in his many disguises

in and around America, the chilling fact
that he's absolutely Will but can pass for someone
or something else. For example, while bodybuilding,

Will can be heard grunting in his makeshift gym
until his back looks apish, his calves
like a goat's leaping on high places. He can easily

be mistaken for Chinese, Cherokee, Greek, that
might be him right now looking Latino near Montrose.

He used to say he'd find me one day and I'd never

recognize him until he had me pinned in bed.
He said "the strong survive," like the placentals
who roamed across the Isthmus of Panama

and all but extinguished the marsupials—
and then he'd squeeze me for luck and punctuation.
Once he was sitting in a saloon after escaping

from a hospital on the Hudson, and a cop asked him,
point blank, if he'd seen himself. Like a slippery hero,
a quantum leap of light, energy radiating

at different levels of illusion, an insane
physics: Mad Max meets Inspector Clouseau. Once
the dinosaur was ineluctable as dawn

and all the big ones lumbered and the winged ones
tried to fly, and for a hundred million years they reigned,
fit and fervent as the myth of creation.

Now their descendent sparrow zooms above Swan Lake
like a fairy spirit of the coelurosaurus,
and the orchid continues expensive as silk.

Now the panda faces starvation, and some believe
Will has taken his life in Montana after a day of fishing.
My favorite illusion is the one about the relativity

of time. How the humpback with her big slow heart,
her contrapuntal biorhythm, weaves a song in the deep—
half-hour concert to us, to her a minute waltz.

—after Stephen Jay Gould's
The Panda's Thumb

Nominated by Marilyn Hacker and David Wojahn

LAST THINGS

by DEBRA SPARK

from PLOUGHSHARES

MY SISTER AND I step briskly out of the greengrocer to get away from the men behind us in line who have told us, in great detail, what they'd like to do to us, where they intend to put certain parts of their bodies. The clerk, kindly, rings their purchases up slowly, so Cyndy and I have a chance to hurry across the street, almost bumping into two men who are breaking raw eggs in their hands and leaning over to slip the viscous mess into their mouths.

One of those Manhattan nights, I think.

Earlier today, as Cyndy and I were taxiing away from Grand Central to her apartment in Chelsea, we were thrilled, saying: "New York, It's so great. Look at this dirt! Look at the guy peeing in the alley! I love it!" A joke, sure, but only partially. We'd just spent a claustrophobic weekend with our parents and other two siblings in the Berkshires. The occasion, I guess, was Cyndy's mastectomy last week.

Cyndy's nerves are pretty much gone in the right side of her body, so the operation didn't hurt as much as the lumpectomy she had two years ago, when she was twenty-one. Still, I can't help thinking, Wound, especially now that we're out with the crazies. And also, I'm thinking of my own toes, which are so black and blue with cold (a circulatory problem, I will learn later in the month) that I am having trouble walking. Indeed, at the moment, I feel more damaged than Cyndy appears to. We shuffle by the guys with the eggs, and I put my right arm around Cyndy's back—companionably, I think, because I want to restore the playful order that has reigned most of today, that was operative when we were at New York City Opera, and I was meeting

96

Cyndy's co-workers and admiring the Mr. Potato Head doll she had placed over her desk, presumably to supervise her efforts as rehearsals coordinator. My arm has barely touched Cyndy's black coat (the coat I will someday wear) when she says, vicious as possible, "Don't you *dare* try to protect me."

I am quiet—my throat, for a minute, as pained as my toes—and then I say, my voice strangulated, half the words swallowed, " . . . not trying . . . protect you."

Cyndy is dead, of course. That is why I wear her black coat now. She died of breast cancer at age twenty-six, a fact which I find unbelievable, a fact that is (virtually) statistically impossible. When she was twenty-one, she was in the shower in her dorm room at the University of Pennsylvania. She was washing under her arm when she found the lump. She was not checking for breast cancer. What college girl does monthly exams on her own breasts? Laura, my twin sister, says that I was the first person Cyndy called about the cancer. I don't think this is true, though Laura insists. I'm certain Cyndy called my father, the doctor, and that he told her to fly home to Boston. He demanded her return even though the doctors at Penn's health service pooh-poohed her concern. Finally, after a long conversation, I realize why Laura thinks Cyndy called me first and I tell her: "I think you're thinking about the rape."

"Oh, yeah," Laura says. "That's probably right."

When my father called me in Wisconsin to tell me about Cyndy, I said, "Oh, well, I'm sure she's okay. Lots of women have fibrous breasts."

"No, Debra," my father said, sternly. "That's not what this is about."

"Do you think she'll have to have a biopsy?"

He was quiet.

"A mastectomy?"

"That's the least of my concerns."

I guess I wasn't quite able to hear him right then. I hung up the phone and pulled out my copy of *Our Bodies, Ourselves* to look at that book's photograph of a jubilant naked woman—out in the sun, with one breast gone, the stitches running up her chest like a sideways zipper. I remember wailing, literally wailing, at the image and at the prospect of my sister losing her breast.

I didn't know yet that my father had examined my sister when she came home from college. My father is an endocrinologist, a fertility specialist. He examines women every day in his office, but to feel your adult daughter's breast—breaking *that* taboo, because medical care is shoddy and you *do* love your daughter desperately and *appropriately*—and to know, right away, what it is you are feeling . . . I have to stop myself from imagining it. And I think my father has to disremember it, too, because even though he knew, right then, she had cancer, he tells this story about himself: When the x-ray of Cyndy's chest was up on the lightboard, my father pulled the x-ray off the board and turned it over to look at the name. "Spark, C." He looked back at the picture. Turned the x-ray over again to check the name. "Spark, C." He did the whole thing again. And again.

Later, two weeks before she did die, I remember seeing her x-ray up on a lightboard. Not something I was supposed to see, I know, but Cyndy's treatment all took place at the same hospital my father has worked for twenty-five years. I knew my way about and I knew how to take silent advantage when I needed to. I looked, but from a distance. I was out in the hall, standing over Cyndy in her gurney, as orderlies were about to move her out of the emergency ward and up to a floor. My view was oblique and once I knew there was nothing happy to see there, I said, Don't look. Though later, all I would do was say, Look, Debra. Look, this is a person dying. Look, this is Cyndy going away.

My mother was always the most pessimistic of all of us, and I used to hate her for it. "She'll be okay," I'd say. And, "We can't read the future." My mother said we were lucky we *couldn't* read the future or we'd never get through it. Which is probably true. That night in Manhattan, things seemed tragic but manageable. In the past was the lumpectomy and the radiation. Now, the mastectomy was completed. The chemo was to come. Cyndy had cut her hair short so the loss of it wouldn't be too upsetting. Back in Boston, she'd gone with my mother to buy a wig. Now, she was trying to wear it over her hair. That was the advice she had been given: to start wearing it so it would be like a new haircut and no one would notice. I thought, Who cares who notices? I was for announcing the illness as just another fact, among many, about Cyndy. To keep it secret was to imply that it was either shameful, like a sin, or special, like a surprise gift, and it was neither.

The wig bothered Cyndy. It was itchy and, though we'd tell her otherwise, it had a dowdy look, a look that owed nothing to the haircuts

Cyndy had always had—the funky asymmetrical do she'd sported when she'd gone to London for a year or the long red mane she'd had as a child. One day, while I was still visiting with her in New York, we went out to lunch with some friends of mine who had never met Cyndy. In the middle of lunch, Cyndy, impatient and in the midst of a story (she was a magnificent and voluble talker), pulled off her hair—to my friends' surprise, especially since there was another head of hair under the one she'd pulled off.

After all the preparation for baldness, however, Cyndy's hair didn't fall out. At least, not that year. The first round of chemo was bad, but, again, in the realm of the get-overable. Every three or four weekends, my mother would come into New York and take Cyndy to the hospital and then out to my grandmother's house for a weekend of puking. Cyndy handled it well. The biggest long-term effect was that she wouldn't let anyone say the words "pot roast" when they were around her. And she couldn't stand the smell of toast for years to come.

Some time later, after Cyndy had finished up the chemo, she decided to go to business school, to get a degree in arts administration at UCLA. She loved school. She had never been too happy as an undergraduate, but UCLA was right for her. Her goal had been to make opera, which she adored, accessible to people who ordinarily wouldn't go. She had a special column in the school newspaper called "Kulture, Kulture, Kulture"; she was proud of her ability to drag business students (a surprise! stiff business students!) to the opera. I imagine Cyndy as the life of the party in those days. Cyndy going to the graduate-student beer bashes; Cyndy leading the talk at the business-school study sessions; Cyndy still earning her nickname "Symphony."

I know she slimmed down in those years, too. She had an intermittent problem with her weight, and it was probably the real clue that Cyndy—handle-everything-Cyndy—sometimes had her unhealthy way of handling things. When I visited Cyndy in Chelsea, after her mastectomy, we were toying with the idea of living together. At the time, I was profoundly (read "clinically") depressed. I had left the man I had been living with for four years and had been unenthusiastically debating what I should do next. Cyndy was moving up to Inwood, and we had found a small apartment that would accommodate the two of us should I decide to move with her. I remember that one of her real enthusiasms about the two of us living together had to do with food. She was convinced that I'd have her eating large green salads for dinner, that my own good habits would rub off on her, and she would no longer find herself in the middle of secret, ruinously upsetting food binges.

Cyndy had been a chubby kid, but never really fat, even when she weighed a lot. When she was older, her figure was sensual if robust. Still her weight was an occasional issue: my father telling her, at dinner, not to be a *chazar*, my mother spinning her own anxiety about weight onto Cyndy. At Cyndy's college graduation, Cyndy said "No, thank you" to the dessert tray that a waiter was offering our table. We were all too full. My mother said, "Oh, I'm so proud of you," to Cyndy. Cyndy said, "I'll have that chocolate cake," to the waiter. And the rest of the children—Laura, David, and I—hooted with laughter. It was our turn to be proud. After all, the request for cake was her version of "Oh, stop it, Mom."

Still, toward the end of Cyndy's stay in Chelsea, I got my first glimpse of how painful the problem with food could be. Like many women, I had my own issues, and Cyndy and I would often have long talks about what all this meant. Once, she told me about how she used to have a secret way of slipping cookies silently out of the cookie jar and hiding under a dining-room table to eat. This might have struck me as funny—so often our childhood stories charmed me—but I wanted to sob when she told me. I felt stricken but stricken by our— her, my, everybody's—desires. How easily they became desperate or grotesque or hateful, especially to the person who did all that desiring.

Her desires must have been met in L.A., however, because she looked so good. At the end of her first year there, she organized a student show, a big, campy celebration that everyone dressed for. She brought a videotape of the show back to Boston for the rest of us to see. Now, we fast-forward through the tape so we can see the intermission. Someone has filmed her—happy her—backstage exuberantly organizing things. Then we fast-forward again and there is Cyndy in a gorgeous, retro, off-the-shoulder dress. Her hair is long, just above her shoulders. She needs to flip it out of her eyes. She has long dangling earrings. She is glamorous by anyone's account and quite sexy. By this point, she's had reconstructive surgery. The new breast is lumpy and disappointing—not that anyone says this. It's just clear that when my uncle, the surgeon, said, "Sometimes they do such a good job you can't tell the difference," he wasn't one hundred percent correct. Part of the problem is that Cyndy, like all the women in the family, has large breasts. They couldn't reconstruct her breast so it would be as big as

100

the original one, so she had a smaller breast made, and she wore a partial prosthesis. The doctors had asked her if she wanted the other breast reduced—for balance's sake. But she decided no. After all, she didn't want to run the risk of not having feeling in either breast.

In the videotape, when Cyndy starts to sing, the audience is clearly amazed. And they should be: her voice is stunning. She could have had an operatic career if she had wanted it. Months before her death, a singing instructor made it clear to Cyndy that she not only could, but she had to, have a singing career. Her voice was that beautiful.

Now, when I listen to the tape, I watch Cyndy's mannerisms. Each time, I am surprised by the fact that she seems a little nervous about performing. Cyndy nervous? Cyndy is never nervous, as she herself will admit. (Except about men. That's the one exception.) But she gets comfortable as she proceeds, as the audience's approval is clear. She sings, beautifully, the Carol King song "Way Over Yonder." *Way over yonder, that's where I'm bound.*

Even before she died, I knew the irony would always break my heart, once she was gone.

In the summer after Cyndy's first two semesters in L.A., I was living in Lincoln, Nebraska. I was teaching a summer class, and late at night, I'd get tearful calls from Cyndy. Mostly about men, for I was, in many things, Cyndy's confidante. Sometimes, now, I think that I am wrong about this. I *was* Cyndy's confidante, wasn't I? She *was* the person who I was closest to, wasn't she? When we were young, I always thought that Cyndy and I belonged together, and David and Laura belonged together. Laura always had a special way with David. Laura and I were close (the twins, after all), and Cyndy and David (the youngest) were playmates. Still, I felt Cyndy and I were a pair. When they met Cyndy, people used to say, "Oh, so she's your twin?" And I'd shake my head no. "Your older sister?" No, I'd say again. Cyndy loved being mistaken for my older sister. "I really am the smartest one in the family," she'd say, even when she was in her twenties. I'd have to disagree; it was a distinction I thought I deserved if by smart you meant (and Cyndy did) commonsensical.

Our closeness was somewhat competitive. We delighted in being competent—more competent than the one in the family who was spacey, the one who was overemotional. We just had things together, and we understood the world. The one fight I remember us having (I'm sure we had many when we were young, but I can't remember them) is about driving the car. She snapped at me for correcting her driving. She hated it when I played older sister.

When Cyndy first started making her tearful phone calls to me, I was proud. I took a secret pleasure in the fact that she confided in me, that she came to me first. I'd even felt a slight pleasure—mixed with my horror—when she called to tell me, and, at first, only me, that she'd been raped. It was during her first year at college. I was in my senior year at Yale. It was a date rape, I suppose, although that term doesn't fit exactly. The man was someone she met in a bar—a sailor, good God—and Cyndy got drunk and later, after some flirting, he didn't understand that no meant no. I honestly don't think he knew he raped her. I think for a while Cyndy was bewildered, too. Her previous sexual encounters had not amounted to much, and, later in college, her experiences remained disappointing.

Given her history, Cyndy's tears on the phone made sense to me. I thought she was finally addressing the issue that had always so frightened her. She spoke, with uncharacteristic frustration, of the way her women friends were always talking about *their* relationships, and she didn't have any relationships, and how upset it made her. With the encouragement of the family, Cyndy started talking to a therapist. I was all for this, I would tell Cyndy, as I sat late at night in my small rental in Nebraska. After all, I had been helped, enormously, by a psychiatrist. My parents agreed with my assessment, I think, although Cyndy spent less of her time on the phone with them talking about men and more time talking about her headaches, her terrible headaches, that stopped her from getting any work done.

So, it's clear where this goes, no? We hope it's not, we hope it's not—as with each test or checkup we have hoped—but it is. Cyndy has cancer in her brain. When they do the initial radiation on her brain, and later when they do an experimental treatment that *does* shrink the tumor, it becomes clear that all that crying had a physiological base. Her tumor shrunk, her headaches go away. She stops crying or talking about men.

But, of course, she does cry, though only once, when she learns about the brain tumor. When I find out, I am standing in my kitchen and kneading bread. I get the call, and then I phone MIT to tell a friend of Laura's not to let her go to lunch. I want to come get her and take her to the hospital. I feel like a rock when I do all this, like a cold rock. I throw the dough in the trash and hear the *thump-swish* of it hitting the plastic bag. Then, I go and get Laura, who screams—as in bad movies, screams—and I drive to the hospital. Laura, instantly feeling everything, spins out of control with grief. She's sharp with nurses who seem to be blocking her way to Cyndy. She won't allow what my father says when he says it. She just tells him, No, no, you're wrong. She turns to me and says, Why aren't you acting like anything? And I think, Because I am so very competent.

In the fall, Cyndy comes and lives with me in my big apartment in North Cambridge. This is clearly better than staying with my parents in their suburban home. She is immensely disappointed about having to take time off from UCLA. But it is only time off, we reassure her. She will get back there. And she does. After a year with me, she goes back for a semester. But she is too sick and has to come back to live with me for good. She lives with me for two years. This is the part that I'm glad I didn't get to see when I was in my Wisconsin apartment and worrying about the possibility of my sister having a mastectomy. I think now, A mastectomy! A lousy mastectomy! Who cares? I remember once, not long after I'd moved to Cambridge and before Cyndy moved in with me, I was in bed with a temporary lover. He was an old college friend, a doctor, in town to do some work for the year. Cyndy and I had been talking, earlier that day, over the phone, about men. I was encouraging her to approach a young man she was interested in, in L.A. She'd said, "But, it's so complicated. Like at what point do I say, 'Hey, buddy. One of these isn't real.'" I knew she'd be gesturing, even though we were on the phone, to her chest, pointing to first one, then the other. ("I can always tell," she'd said, "when someone knows and they're trying to figure out which one it is.") That night, in bed, I'd said to my friend, "Well, if you loved someone, it wouldn't make a difference . . . say, before you were involved . . . if you found out they had a mastectomy, would it?" He looked at me. "Yeah," he said. "I don't mean to be horrible, but of course it would."

"But," I said, as if he'd change his mind because I needed him to, "I said it wouldn't. That's what I said."

Cyndy and I had fun in the apartment where we lived. My boyfriend, Jim, would come by in the evenings, and they would talk music or we'd go out for dinner. Nights when Jim was working, we'd get George, a musician friend from around the corner, to come over. Cyndy took classes at Boston University. She worked for the Boston

Opera Theatre. She got involved with a project concerning musicians in Prague. Related to that, Vaclav Havel's press secretary and her son came to live with us for a while. And during all this, cancer would pop up in one place or another—her knees, the back of her tongue. Still, it always honestly seemed to me that we could make her better. Healthy denial, I suppose. Certainly, Cyndy had a lot of it. She was always willing to be cheered up, to imagine her future.

Some things stand out, but I can't (I won't) put them in order. Like: the number of times I would be in bed, making love with Jim, and hear Cyndy hacking away in the next room. That would be the cancer in her lungs.

Or the way she would call out to me each morning that Jim wasn't there: "Derba, Derba, Derba," she'd say, in a high-pitched silly voice. And I'd call back, "Der-ba Bird," because that was what she was, chirping out the family nickname for me. Then, I'd go crawl into her bed and rub her back. There was cancer in the spine by then, and she could never get comfortable. Sometimes, she'd wail at her pillows. She couldn't get them in the right position.

Or the way, one night, when I was making dinner, she said, "Oh, God," and I said, "What is it?" and she snapped, angry as could be, "You *know* what it is!"

There was an odd stretch when I felt her oncologist was trying to convince her that her symptoms were psychosomatic. Like when she couldn't get enough energy to move, and we'd spend days inside, only making an occasional trek to the back porch. Perhaps, he seemed to be suggesting, she was only depressed?

The few times Cyndy did snap at me, I felt like I would dissolve. My mother said, "Well, I guess you're getting a sense, before your time, of what's it's like to have an adolescent." In truth, my mother got the brunt of it. When Cyndy was in the most pain, she would leave the apartment for a stay with my parents. When she was well enough, she would come back to stay with me. Wherever she was, though—my house, my parents' house—we were all there, all the time.

And even when she was doing relatively well, there were lots of visits back and forth. One day, in the beginning of her stay with me, Cyndy and I were driving out to our parents' house for dinner. We were talking about death, and Cyndy said, "Oh, well, you know, sometimes I think about death. And I try to force myself to imagine what it would be like but then I'm like . . . whoa . . . you know, I just can't do it."

104

"Yes," I said, for I knew exactly what she meant. "I'm like that, too."

Now I'm even more "like that." For if a parent's job is to protect his or her child, a sister's is to identify with her sibling. Which means, of course, that the whole family gets, in the case of a terminal illness, to fail in what they most want to do for one another. So I push my imagination to death, make myself think "no consciousness." I have, regretfully, no belief in heaven, an afterlife, reincarnation. I believe in nothingness. I try not to let myself pull back, try not to say, "Whoa, that's too much." But my brain—its gift to me—is that it won't let me do what I want.

I think, in this regard, of the time ten-year-old Cyndy came home from school in a snit. She'd learned about black holes in her science class. She'd stomped up to her room and flopped on her bed. As she went, she ordered the family never to talk to her about black holes. I thought she was joking. So, I opened the door to her bedroom, stuck my head in—cartoon-fashion, the accordion player poking his head through the stage curtain to get a peek at the crowd—and I said, rapidly, "Black hole, black hole, black hole." Cyndy, already lying on her bed, threw herself against the mattress so that she bounced on it like a just-captured fish hitting land. She started to sob. "I'm sorry," I said. "I was kidding. I thought *you* were kidding." But why would she have been? What's more terrible than everything going out?

Once, during one of her final stays in the hospital, Cyndy said to my mother, "I'm going to be good now," as if that would make her healthy, as if a planet could blame itself for being in the wrong part of the universe.

"Oh, honey," my mother had said. "You *are* good. You are so *good*."

One trip out to my parents that stands in my mind: Cyndy had the shingles, an enormously painful viral infection that runs along the nerve path on one side of the body. Just getting her down the staircase into my car was horrible. Cyndy was sobbing and sobbing, and ordinarily she didn't cry. I put her in the passenger's seat and cursed myself for having the kind of life that made me buy such an inexpensive and uncomfortable car. The requirement of bending was too much, and Cyndy wept and wept. I drove as fast as I could and neither of us talked. I thought, I'll just get her home and it will be all right. My father, the doctor, would know what to do. My mother would be, as she could be, the most comforting person in the world. When we got there, I said, "It's okay, it's going to be okay," as Cyndy walked, with tiny paces, from the car to the front steps. My parents were at the front door and it was night. My mother brought a kitchen chair to the front hall so as soon as Cyndy got up the stairs, she could sit down. I stood behind her, and my parents stood at the top of the six stairs that lead to our front door. My mother (blue turtleneck and jeans); my father (stooped). Both of them had their hands out and were reaching for Cyndy but they couldn't get her up the stairs. She had to do that herself. And I thought, looking at them in the light, and Cyndy forcing herself up through the night—*Oh, my God. All this love, all this love can't do a thing*.

But that wasn't completely true. The love did do something. It just didn't save her.

Laura, my twin sister, gave Cyndy foot rubs and Cyndy loved them. Laura would give foot rubs, literally, for hours. I gave back rubs but I never liked giving them, would wait for Cyndy to say I could stop. When Cyndy told Laura she could stop if she wanted to, Laura would ask for permission to keep going—as if Cyndy were doing her a favor by putting her feet in the vicinity of Laura's hands. One day, Cyndy was lying on her bed in our apartment and Laura was on a chair at the end of the bed and she was rubbing Cyndy's feet. I was "spooning" Cyndy and occasionally rubbing up and down her spine where the cancer was. We were talking about masturbation. "I can't believe you guys," Laura was saying, telling us again about how amazing it was that, of the three of us, she had discovered masturbation first. We were giggling. The conversation wasn't unfamiliar. We'd had it before, but we could always find something new to tell each other.

"What was that bathtub thing you were talking about," Cyndy said.

Years earlier, I'd instructed both of my sisters about the virtues of masturbating in the bathtub. Something I'd learned from my freshman-year roommate at college. "Got to try it," I said now.

"Exactly how do you do it again?" asked Cyndy.

"Lie in the tub. Scoot your butt under the waterspout and put your legs up on the wall and let the water run into you. Guaranteed orgasm."

"De-bra," Cyndy said, hitting me, as if I'd gone too far in this being-open-with-sisters conversation.

"Sor-ry," I said. "Still, you've got to try it, but wait till this thing gets better." I pointed at her head. There was a new problem these days, something that caused Cyndy to get, on occasions, dizzy. She had some new medicine, so I talked as if the problem would be solved in a matter of weeks. (Aside from the dizziness, Cyndy had occasional aphasia.

106

One night when I was on the phone, Cyndy screamed from her bedroom. I ran in. She'd forgotten a word, couldn't pronounce it, and felt her head go weirdly blank. The word, she realized, five minutes later, was cancer.)

We decided to leave the topic of sex behind for something else. But not before I insisted, once again, that Cyndy try this bathtub thing. I was rubbing her back and Laura was still rubbing her feet, and I was thinking, as I stroked her skin, Yes, an orgasm. Let this body give her some pleasure.

You *do* get inappropriately intimate with a body when the body is ill. Sometimes there's something nice about it. Cyndy used to sit on the toilet in our bathroom and I'd take a soapy washcloth and wash her bald head. I'd say, "Stamp out dry scalpy skin." This struck us, for some reason, as terribly funny. We'd soak our feet in the bathtub and talk about our favorite Gogol stories. We'd walk arm-in-arm. Say: "This is what we'll be like when we are old ladies."

When Cyndy's symptoms were at their worst, my own body struck me, especially my legs, which stretched—it seemed amazing—from my torso to the ground. The miracle of walking. I still feel it. The air behind my legs is creepily light as I move. Who would have ever suspected that you can feel grief behind your kneecaps?

One very bad night: Cyndy was upset about everything, but especially men, relationships, never having had a boyfriend. According to her, I didn't, *couldn't* understand because I had had a boyfriend. This was a point of connection between Cyndy and a few of her intimates, an absence they could discuss and from which I was excluded. It didn't matter that I felt, for the sadness of my own relationships, included. I had had sex. Many times even—enough to have had a sexually transmitted disease which I (paranoid, irrational) thought I could pass on to Cyndy through ordinary contact. It didn't matter that I was cured of the problem. Her immune system was down. Anything I did might hurt her. My own desires might kill her.

This one night, Cyndy was crying, so I went into her room to put my arm around her, and she said, "Don't. Don't you touch me." Fierce, again. Vicious. I retreated to my bedroom. Cried softly, but still felt I had to do something. I stepped back to her bedroom, and she started to scream, waving me away, but saying, "It's just that I realize that nobody but my family or a doctor has touched me in the past five years."

107

It'll change, it'll change, it'll change. That was always my mantra for these relationship conversations. But it didn't. She died before it could change.

After that terrible night when Cyndy had the shingles and had to struggle out of our apartment to the car, she spent six weeks at my parents' house. Those were miserable times. She couldn't move from her bed. We'd all climb onto the double bed, a ship in the ocean of her room, and play word games or watch TV or be quiet because a lot of the time she couldn't stand for anything to be going on. As she started to feel a bit better, she worked on the course that she was going to teach in January of 1992. It was going to be called, "Opera—What's All the Screaming About?" and it was going to be for high school girls, for kids who, presumably, could care less about opera. We rented opera videos and watched them with her. Then, she decided she was ready to come back to our apartment to work on her course syllabus. I cleaned the kitchen while she worked. At one point, she started to faint, but she grabbed the doorjamb, and I came in and caught her, wrapped my arms around her waist—big now, she was bloated with steroids—and set her down on the ground. She was okay, so she started to work at her computer, and I made us some cocoa. She handed me her syllabus to proofread. She sipped, while I read it, and she said, in a sort of campy voice, "Mmmm . . . this is love-ly." I laughed, still reading. She made a funny gurgling noise. I thought it was a joke but when I looked up from the syllabus, Cyndy was slipping out of her chair. I ran the few feet to her. She was crumpled on the ground. I rolled her onto her back and saw blood. There was water on the floor—her urine. "Are you okay? Are you okay?" I screamed. Her wig had rolled off her head and she looked like a gigantic toppled mannequin. She was gasping, breathing oddly. A seizure, I knew. I am, after all, a doctor's daughter. When the convulsive breathing stopped, she said, "What happened? What just happened?" She was as purely frightened as I'd ever seen her.

"Close your eyes," I said. "You just fainted. Close your eyes." I didn't want her to see her own blood. I thought that would scare her. I ran to the bathroom to get a towel and wipe her up. I tried to see where the blood was coming from.

"It's okay, you bit your tongue."

I felt—I have to say this, only because it's so horrible—a slight pleasure. It was the old thing; I would be competent, take care of this trouble. I was good in an emergency. But, there was also part of me—

108

small, I promise myself now, very small—that thought, with some relief, It's over.

The ambulance came. We rode over to the hospital. My parents were there before us. When they rolled Cyndy away, I cried to my mother, "Oh, Mommy. I thought she was dying. I thought she was dying."

Inside, Cyndy was saying the same to my father, "I thought I was dying. I thought I was going to die."

And about two weeks later she did. But not before her body put her through enormous suffering. Not before she had a little more fun with her family. So, last things. The last thing she ever produced was a picture from a coloring book. She had asked for the book and some crayons, and we all earnestly filled in Mickey Mouse's ears and then signed our names and ages. Debra, twenty-nine. Laura, twenty-nine. David, twenty-four. Mommy, fifty-three. Daddy, fifty-five. Cyndy signed hers, "The Queen." (A joke from our two years together. When she was queen, Boston drivers were not going to be allowed to be obnoxious.) Under "age," Cyndy wrote, "None of your damn business." Last meal: gray fish from the kosher kitchen, but she didn't eat it. Last thing she *did* eat: Jell-O. I know, I spooned it into her mouth. Last thing I said to her: I told her that the man she was interested in was in love with her, that I knew because of what he'd said when I called to tell him she was in the hospital. (I was making this up, but who cares?) Last thing Cyndy ever said to me: "Oh, good. Well, tell him we'll get together when I get out of here." Last thing she ever said: I didn't hear this because I wasn't in the room, but she woke up, delusional and panicked and worried because she was going on a long trip and she hadn't packed her suitcase.

As my fiction-writer friends always say, You can't make this stuff up. No one would believe you if you tried.

And I have to agree: real life is just too heavy-handed.

Very last thing: her body still desiring life, she takes every third breath, though her fingers are dusky, though her kidneys have already shut down. We give the funeral director the pretty purple dress she bought for special occasions. We put her in the ground.

Our desires, I sometimes think now, as I'm walking down the street.

Today, outside a bakery, I stop myself and say, "Yes, Debra? What about them?" And I realize I don't know. "What? What?" I stand for a while feeling disgusted with the world—those horrible leering men in the greengrocer's; that stupid sailor in the bar; foolish me, making love with my sister dying in the next room. *Our desires, our desires, our desires.* I know what the refrain is; I just don't know what to do about it. It's a reproach for me, an always unfulfilled wish for my family, and a sad song—it's a dirge—for Cyndy. Still, since I am here, stuck among the living, I have to remind myself that the song owes nothing to the beautiful ones that Cyndy sang. So I go into the bakery and get a shortbread cookie, dipped in chocolate. It is so delicious I start to cry.

Nominated by Michael Bendzela, Rosellen Brown, Eileen Pollack, Ron Tanner, Ploughshares

MY FRIEND

by DAVID ST. JOHN

from AMERICAN POETRY REVIEW

My friend, a man I love as wholly,
    As deeply as the brother neither of us
        Ever had, my friend, who once
Greeted me at the door of his carriage house—
        Having not seen each other in seven years—
    Saying only, as he turned to place
The needle into the grooves of Mahler's unfinished 10th,
     "Listen to this! It's just like the *Four Quartets*!"
        His head, tilted slightly back
As we listened in silence, his black scarf looped loosely
    Around his neck, not an affectation, simply
Because of the cold in the carriage house he'd redone
        With everything but heat,
    The wind slicing off the East River, the mansion
In front of us lit up brilliantly that night
        By chandelier and firelight—my friend,
    Whom I love as deeply as any friend, called
This morning to report the sleet blanketing the East,
        To ask about the color of the sunlight
Sweeping the beaches of California; I tell him, "A lot
        Like the green of ice at night,
     Or the orange of the hair of that girl who once
Lived downstairs from you, in Cleveland. . . . "
        My friend, who said nothing for a moment,
    My friend, who had always lived the pure, whole
Solitude of Rilke, though he fell in love

As often and as desperately as Rilke,
Began to talk about his recent engagement, now
Past, though still not quite a memory, simply a subject
Yet too mystifying to be ignored,
To a debutante, half-British, that is, an American deb
With an overlay of aristocratic parquet—
Albeit with an Italian given name—a stunning woman
He had loved desperately, silently,
The way Rilke loved
The sky at evening as the cloud-laced sunset
Dusted the high ragged peaks of Switzerland . . .
Yet, after a pause, he began
Again to talk, about some new acquaintances, two
Young ladies, both painters (of course),
Who seemed to enjoy his company as a pair; that is,
The two of them, both of the young
Ladies, preferred him as a garnish
To their own extravagances—for example,
They'd welcomed him into their bath one
Evening when he came to visit, only to find them lathering
Each other tenderly. And though quite
Clearly desiring the company of each other to his alone,
They were tolerant, he said, even welcoming,
As the one reached up her hand
And invited him into the froth of the square black tub.
And now this had, he reported, been
Going on for several weeks this way, perhaps longer,
He couldn't be clear about those kinds
Of details, though about other, more
Intriguing things, his memory was exact. The very night before,
He recalled, as the two young women painted
His naked torso slowly into a tuxedo of pastel
Watercolors, they'd both wisely proposed the following:
A joint—triadic—marriage for one month
As they traveled, all three, through Italy and France,
A journey to visit all of the Holy Places
Of Art, as well as
The grandparents of the one, Delphine—about whom Constance,
The younger, had heard so many stories—at their home
In the hills overlooking the beaches of Nice.

My friend, a quiet man, a man who remains as
Precise, in his reckonings, as a jewel cutter, a man whose
        Charm could seduce the Medusa, was,
He confessed, totally at a loss, bewildered, delighted,
        Terrified, exhausted—mainly, he said, exhausted
                From the constellations of couplings
        He'd been exercising, recognizing in the process
He was, as they say, as he said, really not quite so young
                As he'd once been, though certainly still
                As eager for invention
As any artist who takes his life work, well, seriously . . .
        And as we talked about old times, old friends, our
Old lives being somehow perpetually rearranged, at last
                He stopped me, saying, "Christ, you know—
        I can't *believe* how much the world has changed. . . . "

Nominated by Ralph Angel, Henry Carlile, Gillian Conoley, Patricia Henley, Walter Pavlich,
Diann Blakely Shoaf, Michael Walters

SUPER NIGHT

fiction by CHARLES BAXTER

from TRIQUARTERLY

Eᴀʀʟɪᴇʀ ɪɴ ᴛʜᴇ evening, while searching on the bathroom floor for her reading glasses, Irene Gladfelter had noticed a spidery damp spot on the wall under the sink. She would have to take care of it herself; her husband was out, having a beer a few blocks away in the neighborhood bar, The Shipwreck.

On her hands and knees, she'd worried at the wall—Walt could patch it up later—with a screwdriver and a chisel, making a small neat hole. Then she had remembered that the maintenance man should be performing such work, this wasn't her property, and the leak was really none of her business.

But she had found the pipe, rotted away with rust at one of its connection points. The water was dripping down onto a heap of razor blades, a small secretive pyramidal scrap yard. Snaggling the flashlight's beam inward, she saw the piles of . . . *edges*, not all of them lying flat. A few stood propped against each other like sentries. This mound of blue blades had been inserted one by one through the old medicine cabinet's razor slot by Walt and by the unit's previous renters down through the millennia of shaving. The blades had rusted into a soft metallic brown. She unsettled herself by just looking at them. You thought something as simple as a morning shave wouldn't leave a trace, but then it did.

She hated the look of the dull blue metal. It made her shy.

She made her way back to the bedroom. She found her reading glasses on the bedside table, inside a green box of tissues. Inanimate things liked to hide. She had noticed this again and again. She undressed, turned on the TV, and got under the covers, spreading her catalogs around her in friendly disarray.

Thursday was her husband's night out. At around eleven-thirty he returned home from The Shipwreck pleased with himself, ripe with cigarette smoke and beer. Knowing his habits, she always left a single breath mint out for him on the kitchen counter, and the fluorescent light on the stove burning, so he could see his way in.

With the cat snoring at her feet, she sat propped up in bed reading her catalogs and watching the movie on TV with the sound muted. Drawer organizers, peg-and-dowel wood wine racks: a physical pleasure that began at her spine and spread upward toward her forehead like a sunflower filled her whenever she gazed at objects she did not need or want. They were her suitors, and she brushed them away.

She liked these occasional evenings alone, these little shallow pools of rest and emptiness. Here was a swivel bookstand, there a typewriter table. The sunflower bloomed again. She glanced at the TV set. When she was in bed, by herself, she had a queenly indifference to the details of the stories. She didn't have to explain the plots to Walter, her usual task whenever they watched television together. Tonight she checked the screen now and then to see, first, a roadster bursting off a cliff into a slow arc of explosive death, and then a teenager putting a black shoe slowly and sensuously on a woman's foot. Apparently this movie was some sort of violent update of *Cinderella*. Now a man dressed like an unsuccessful investment broker was inching his way down a back alley. The walls of the alley were coated with sinister drippings.

She bathed in the movies more satisfactorily when they didn't make any sense. Tomorrow, at work, during her break, she could reconstruct what the sense was, but she usually didn't bother.

When she looked up from her furniture catalog, hearing Walt unlock the front door and trudge toward the bedroom, she knew the night had gone badly, just from the labored slush of his walk. When he stood in the doorway, his gray hair poking through his oil-stained cap, she forgot to ask him if if he'd taken his breath mint. He had a peevish expression. First he examined the television, then the bedroom window, as if he didn't know what to look at. "Walter," she said. "Now what is it?"

A garage mechanic, now in late middle age having trouble with his knees and his back, he could no longer stand straight. His upper body

115

seemed to perch out at an angle from his waist, like a permanently bent metal beam. And he had pockmarks on his face from an attack of shingles. His spiky hair was his last spirited feature.

"The guy upstairs," he said. "Burt Mink. It beats anything. The guy upstairs is a damn criminal."

She didn't ask Walter any questions. Burt Mink? The upholsterer? *Him?* The more awful the story, the better. But it could always wait. It would have to. With Walt, a person exercised patience. When you rushed Walt, he lost his thoughts' thread, and he became a meaningless old guy who could not make himself understood. He came from a family of reluctant speakers: even his mother had never been able to manage more than about twenty words a minute. His father and his two uncles had been laconic farmers in western Michigan, where every word spoken was begrudged, like a mortgage payment. Irene watched as he shambled off irritably into the bathroom.

She understood the slow procession of his moods and knew how to time them. And she was used to his fumes, the oil fumes at least. With their two sons grown and out of the house, the mechanic's smell made her think of her two boys when they'd been younger, teenagers dismantling cars in the garage, surly and sweatily handsome grease monkeys. That was when they'd all been living in the house on Mackenzie Street, before the boys had become men and had left, and she and Walter had moved to this apartment building north of Detroit to save money for their retirement. They hadn't saved any money. Selling that house had been a terrible idea. Once they sold it, she recognized that she had poured her feelings into every floorboard, every ceiling corner.

She heard Walt brushing his teeth and spitting. When he came out of the bathroom he still had his street clothes on. "There's a mess on the floor in there," he said. "Hole in the wall."

"I made it," she said. "I noticed a dampness."

He shrugged the information off with a somewhat alarming indifference. "I don't feel like getting into bed," he told her. "I don't feel like sleeping. I don't feel like any of that."

"You have to sleep. You'll have to go to work tomorrow."

He walked over to the wall facing the bed and adjusted a tilted photograph of their younger son in uniform. "I can go to work," he said. "I've done it before. I can work without sleep. I can't sleep thinking about Burt Mink."

"What about Burt Mink?"

He turned, not answering, and went into the living room. She heard him sit down in the reclining chair. It always sighed when people sat down in it. She heard him shuffling a pack of cards.

She fell asleep to the sound of the cards.

At four A.M. she put on her bathrobe. In the living room, playing cards were scattered on the floor like snow. To get to her chair she had to step on the jack of diamonds, the two of spades and the six of hearts. Walter was sitting there like a sentry, his hands on his knees, eyes wide open.

"So," she said, almost cheerfully, "what did Burt Mink say? What'd he do?" She was a lapsed Jehovah's Witness. She expected things to turn out badly. It used to excite her—how things always turned out badly—but not now, not anymore.

"You shouldn't hear," Walter said.

"I shouldn't?"

"Pigeon, you shouldn't hear a story like this," he said. He was trying to sound offhand but wasn't succeeding: his voice growled.

"Tell me anyway," she said.

The guy upstairs, the one down the hall, Burt Mink, said he had killed a child and was maybe going to do it again.

He had been completely drunk when he had said this. His mouth'd been open and his words were slurred, and his whole face was a mess, going every which way. He sounded like a man asleep but still talking, one of those still-functioning zombies. His head hung down and his nose got itself to within two inches of the bar.

They'd been talking about fishing, then cars. The guy'd already been drinking too much, and his voice got like a radio that was losing a station. The son of a bitch had been muttering about traffic, then about school buses, like he was interested in school buses. Nobody is interested in school buses. But this son of a bitch was. School buses, for chrissake. With little kids on them.

Somehow this creep admitted he had lured an eight-year-old boy into his car and then done things to him and buried him out at the edge of the county near an apple orchard. The kid had been wearing a yellow shirt. He was buried near an apple tree, what was left of him.

It hadn't taken very long.

He didn't say if he had learned the kid's name. The kid looked like an angel. He actually said that.

117

Nobody knows who I am, he said. No one ever sees inside any-one else.

Dead drunk but not sorry, this guy, like he'd been discussing the price of nails at the hardware store. Walter got up and left him there on his barstool at eleven twenty. They'd found themselves at The Ship-wreck before, but this was the first time he'd ever heard anything ter-rible coming out of him.

He worked upholstering furniture, after all. You'd never guess this other thing about him.

The living room froze for half a minute, then came to life again. Irene could feel her breath coming back.

"But that's a movie," she said when Walter was finished. "They ran that movie on TV last month. Remember? Maybe you were asleep. This boy in a yellow shirt was abducted, and the man buried the body in a grove of apple trees. It was the movie-of-the-week. The villain said that no one knew who he really was. Everyone went around saying, 'Yellow shirt, yellow shirt.' I didn't like that movie," she said, almost as an afterthought. "Dina Merrill was in it. She played a psychologist. Wore a pretty pink scarf. You just heard a plot summary."

"What?"

"It's a movie, Walt," she repeated. "He's telling you about a thing they broadcast last week. You didn't see it. But I did. He's confused."

"No. He told me he did it. He didn't say about movies. He said he killed an angel. That was our exact conversation."

Walt stood up and walked to the window, where he stood gazing out in a speculative posture, though bent as always. "Somebody's got to right the balance."

"Don't you do it," she said. "Drop that thought. Burt Mink just thinks he was a character in a TV show, that's all. He's telling you about the movie. That's his business, what he thinks when he's drunk, I guess. Nobody got hurt. I'd watch him, maybe, but a plot summary, that's what he was telling you. My God, Walt, people do worse than that, telling you about movies they think they were in."

She stood up to walk to her room and felt on her back that Walt was staying put, aimlessly thinking.

From the bedroom, she heard Walt say, "I believed him. That's the bad part."

At seven-thirty she put some bread out on the ledge for the birds and dropped a peanut or two on the front sidewalk for the chipmunk.

A fine fall day, the air so crisp that you could see the Renaissance Center in Detroit if you looked straight south from Mrs. Gladfelter's bus stop. One of her boys worked in Detroit, and she worried about him sometimes, worried that he'd become part of the daily feast, but he was a big strong kid, a peaceful furry bear, knew his work and didn't go looking for trouble.

She wished she had brought along her new point-and-shoot camera. She had a particular sugar maple in mind for a picture that she planned to send to Ed Oskins's weather show on Channel Four. They showed a weather picture every day, usually a landscape, and she thought she had a good chance with this tree right here in Ferndale, growing on the boulevard across from the collision shop. This time of year, the sugar maple looked like a picture more than it looked like a tree. Bright burning red leaves rose from its branches, stopping traffic. It glorified that city block.

You couldn't imagine violent death happening on a day like this. It had to wait patiently for gloom and shadow, a few hours after dinnertime. Just like the movies, it had to have darkness, or it didn't happen.

The bus arrived, hesitated in a jovial roar of diesel exhaust, and Mrs. Gladfelter hoisted herself up.

Although the bus was not especially crowded, she sat down next to a pleasantly dressed woman in a light tan overcoat. Her straight brown hair was braided down one side. Her eyes were alert, more the exception than the rule on these buses. Mrs. Gladfelter liked to sit with other women if she could: less chance of funny business that way.

In the public tone she used with strangers, she said, "They've taken the flowers out." She pointed to a circular area in the median, the marigold spot. "Have you noticed how they put them in to form an F? The marigolds? An F for Ferndale?"

The woman in the tan overcoat turned to Mrs. Gladfelter. She said that she *had* noticed that, yes. They spoke for two more minutes before they turned back to their own thoughts. Mrs. Gladfelter exhaled. Normal people were sometimes hard to find on the bus. Frequently all you saw were people in various stages of medication. But today: no lost souls on either side of the aisle.

Considering the times, she felt pleased to have her job, checking out food; it was steady, and the manager was a kind man, and though the ceiling lights were too bright, like a toothache, and she had to be on

119

her feet all day, the job had its compensations, especially now that management had installed laser scanners. She could talk to customers, briefly, if they initiated it, and sometimes she could chat with Shirley, her best friend among the other checkout girls.

The regularity soothed her. Food, processing, payment, bagging. The work's rhythms occupied just enough of her mind so that she didn't have to think about anything she didn't want to think about. She kept track of the prices. She wrote down the numbers of the check-cashing cards on the checks. She had no responsibility for judgment calls. It was like being an elevator operator.

At two in the afternoon, she saw Burt Mink in her checkout line, two carts back. Looking hung over, one eye seemingly glazed and the other with a drooping lid, he was pushing a cart loaded with no-brand frozen dinners, and pre-cut vegetables for salads from the salad bar. He wore a flannel shirt with a hardly noticeable pale white stain. His wet stringy hair was combed over the bald spot at the top of his head, and he had a narrow rodentlike face with protruding teeth, but when he saw Mrs. Gladfelter, he smiled and waved, and the effect was so startling, his face abruptly transformed like that, a superficially ugly pleasantness, that she felt herself go dizzy for a moment before she waved back and continued bagging the groceries of a very young and very pregnant woman who had paid for her chocolates and eggs and ice cream with cash.

Well, after all, she thought, he's been here before. I've checked him through before, and we're neighbors. There's that.

"Here you are," she said to the pregnant woman, handing her her change. "Take care of yourself, honey. You must be due any day now."

"A week," the woman said, tottering out, and Burt Mink advanced in the line. She checked through the woman ahead of him while he scanned the headlines of *Weekly World News*. Coffee cups had been found orbiting in space. The surface of Mars had been photographed; Graceland, complete with swimming pool, had turned up in the pictures. Earthlings were being teleported to other locales in the galaxy. This was common knowledge.

"Mr. Mink," she said, smiling. "Good afternoon."

He unloaded his cart with all the frozen dinners in front, and he said grimly, "Yeah, but I had too much last night. I got to watch that." He smelled unclean.

"Yes," she said, checking his items through. The frozen dinners chilled her fingers. She thought of him eating the food, putting it into his mouth.

120

"I like to come here," he said. "A familiar face, you know."

"Well, we're neighbors, of course."

"Yeah," he said unpleasantly. "You're downstairs. But I see more of your husband than I do of you."

"Hmm," she said. "Bars aren't for me. He tells me about it."

Burt Mink nodded. "Not much to see anyway. Not much to do but drink."

She nodded. "I'm better off at home. He tells me what people say." Burt Mink did not react, not a twitch or a glimmer, as he wrote his check. He had dandruff on his ears and another stain on his frayed gray pants. Even for an upholsterer, he was unpresentable. She couldn't imagine a woman who would have him. "Time alone, you know. Good for all of us. I'll have to see your check-cashing card."

He extracted his wallet from his trousers and with his scarred fingers began to flip through it. Next to the check-cashing card, in its plastic divider, was a photograph of a child, a boy, a school photograph, rather worn by now, an amazingly unattractive boy with an overbite and a narrow ratlike face, unmistakably Burt Mink himself. Did adults carry their own photos, as children, around with them? This adult did, anyway.

She felt a curious queasy sensation, seeing the rat-faced boy in the photo. She didn't recognize this sensation and wouldn't be able to say what it was. She wrote down his number on the back of the check. After saying goodbye and hoisting two bags of groceries, he disappeared out of the store like all the other customers.

A harmless and ugly man, she decided, who worked upholstering furniture and who, after hours, imagined himself as a dangerous character in the movies. The movies were getting into everything now. They could spread over everyone, like the flu.

After taking the bus home, she carried her new camera to the corner of the sugar maple and the collision shop. She struggled to frame the tree in the viewfinder properly so that the wisps of vapor trails were visible against the very dark blue of the background, and after several tries Mrs. Gladfelter believed that she had managed it.

She had a simple dinner planned, beef stew, already in the refrigerator. She strolled over to the city park, two blocks west of their apartment.

Perched on the last building before the park entrance, a billboard asked HOW TROPICAL CAN YOU BE? The billboard showed tuxedoed men and sequined women dancing on the deck of a cruise ship. Underneath the picture was an 800 number from a travel agency. The men and women appeared, to Mrs. Gladfelter, to be imaginary. They possessed impossible honey-colored skin. Somebody had spray-painted the word FIRB over one of the women's faces.

Carrying her camera, Mrs. Gladfelter strolled into the park.

A man wearing a Hawaiian shirt and army camouflage trousers and flip-flops sat on the first bench, dozing, but still giving off an air of violence and moonshine. He clutched in his right hand a copy of the *Ferndale Shopper's Guide.* She walked past him quietly, wearing her smile-armor.

Kids were kissing on the next bench. They looked about fifteen years old, the two of them, and optimistic, the way people did when they were stuck on each other, their tongues in each other's mouths. Making her way to a little rise in the park's center, she placed the camera on a bench for steadiness, pointed it toward the west gate and pressed the super night button, a feature that held the aperture open for two seconds. Then she put the camera in her pocket and headed toward home.

Just before she passed the man in flip-flops it occurred to her that if you were flying over this park at just the right altitude, the whole assembly, including the trees and the bearded man and the lovers and herself, might look like something—a face, or a letter, or a symbol like the F arranged in the marigolds in the middle of Woodward Avenue. But it might look like something else, something terrible and perplexing. She put that thought away and scuttled toward her building.

A few days later, when she picked up the developed film, she was delighted to see that the photograph of the sugar maple was good enough to frame. The super night shot, however, was terribly blurred: streaks of light crossed the sky in it, like meteors, and the west gate of the park had the appearance of fiery brown gelatin.

She put the photograph out on the dining-room table near the place setting for Walt's fork and knife. For the last several days, he had been quieter than usual, losing the thread of conversation, frowning into corners. She thought the photograph might cheer him up, now that autumn was here, the gray skies and soul gloom of winter.

That night, a Wednesday, he trundled himself in from work, and showered as he usually did, and had his beer and watched the local news, saying very little. She tried not to provoke him. When dinner was served, he sat down and began eating. Then he saw her photograph.

"What's this?" he asked. "This is your picture? You took this?"

She smiled proudly. "I'm sending it in to the weather show."

"It's nice," he said. "Real good. They should appreciate it."

He ate everything. He sopped up the gravy with a piece of white bread, and when he was finished, he placed his fork carefully in the middle of the plate and said, "I'm not going to the Shipwreck tomorrow. I believe I'll stay home."

"O.K. with me," she said, although it wasn't. She would miss her catalogs and the expressive solitary quiet. "But I'll bet Burt Mink'll expect you."

"Don't think so. He's had a thing happen to him."

"What thing?"

"Accident. Car accident." Walt rubbed his jaw with his fist. "He's banged up. Could have died."

"What?" she asked. "Where? How'd you find this out?"

"I heard," he said, not explaining. He shrugged for her benefit. "Then I called the hospital. He's in there all right. But they said it wasn't critical or anything of that nature. Just a few bones broken. He wasn't wearing a seat belt. That part didn't surprise me."

"A few bones broken!" She showed her teeth. "Like saying a little fire claimed your house. Walter, what happened exactly?"

"Something went out in his car, brakes I guess. He hit a lamppole, but not one of the breakaway kind." He examined his fork carefully. "I heard he was speeding."

"Oh, Walter," she said. From the street a car honked. The chipmunk on the kitchen ledge scrabbled back and forth. "Walter, it was just a story! He never did anything."

"What? What are you saying?"

"You know what I'm saying. What did you do to his car?"

"Let's wash these dishes," he said. "Let's make some coffee and we'll clean up here."

She would not move. "I know you," she said. "I know your mind, and don't say I don't. Now answer me, Walter. What did you do, Walter?"

He sat up, as straight as he could with his bent back. He said, "I'm a mechanic. You can't ask me such a thing as that. Besides, it's technical."

"You could have killed him," she cried out, "and him with his only sin being ugliness!"

"No." He stood, but he still would not look at her. "No. He was drunk and he admitted his crime, and he got away with it. I couldn't stand that. I wouldn't tolerate it when I imagined him doing harm like that to our boys when they were youngsters, and I drew a line."

"What line? He's a crazy man," she said. "Just another damn crazy person like you and I see every day on the job. Ferndale's full of them, and Detroit's worse. He saw a story on TV. All he did was repeat it! And who are you to judge, and go and do such a thing to him and his car?"

"The only judge he has," Walter said to her, gazing into her face at last. She raised her hand to cover up the wrinkles. "Hell, I'll do it again. He shouldn't have talked that way. It was so ugly, it kept me awake. Imagine saying those things. I went and thought about it. It stayed with me, Irene. Stayed and stayed. Replacing brake pads, changing oil, there's in my head that boy in the yellow shirt. What kind of story is that, and him wanting to be in it, as the star?"

"You kept it going, Walter. It could've ended with him."

Picking up his plate and taking it into the kitchen, Walter said, "Wasn't meant to kill him, exactly, what I did. Paralyze him, maybe. That was all. Put him out of that hobby of his." He rinsed the plates in the sink. "I'm not a vigilante. One night while you were asleep, I fiddled with his Chevy. I'm a good mechanic. I know what to do. Anyway," he said, smiling now, "I wasn't sleeping, thanks to him, and now I am."

"*It was just a story!*" she said, lifting her hands involuntarily. "Like that's just a photograph!" She pointed toward the sugar maple.

"Some stories you shouldn't tell," Walter said, "if you're in them. From where I sat, he had guilt all over him. True or not, I wouldn't abide it."

Suddenly Irene said, "Why do you people do these things to each other? Why do you?"

"What people are you talking about, Irene?"

"You" she said. "You guys. You gibber and jabber and then you just go after each other, fists and guns out, all because of the tales you tell, to make yourselves so big."

"No, we don't," he said. "Where did you ever hear it before?"

He walked past her, apparently at ease with himself for now, and headed toward the reclining chair, to finish the sports page. The chair sighed when he sat in it.

"I shouldn't have said anything," he muttered. "I should have kept you in the dark. It would've been better all around, that way."

That night she stood at the window in her bathrobe and slippers, sipping tap water from a glass with a scoop of vanilla ice cream in it, for her nerves. She was thinking of Burt Mink in the hospital, and of how, years ago, she herself had left the Jehovah's Witnesses, "defellowshipped," as they called it, after she had met Walter.

She had encountered Walter in all his salty early handsomeness when she and her father had been going door-to-door with copies of *The Watchtower* and *Awake!* Walter had been up on a ladder, cleaning gutters, and somehow found out her name before she'd reached the end of the block. He called her that night.

He talked her out of Armageddon. He replaced the wild beast 666 in her imagination with four-barrel carburetors and timing lights. Before Walter had come into her life, she could gaze at the bedroom ceiling and see Armageddon happening right up there, all the panic and terror. The truth had been explained. God was hungry for vengeance, thirsty for it. The clouds on Irene's ceiling boiled blood. She felt herself uplifted and groomed in all this bedlam.

Then Walter took her for rides in his reconditioned Olds convertible. He showed her how to clean fish and how to swing a baseball bat. He said he loved her and repeated it so often she had to believe him.

After three months of Walter, Armageddon lost interest for her. Could an angel turn into a demon, out of jealousy? No. Did angels kill other angels? Probably not. *Someone had made it all up.*

And after her boys were born, she just didn't care to imagine the death of anything. All that prized calamity was just another story.

Men often puzzled her. A world war wasn't big enough for them. No, they had to have a universe war, and give it a fancy name that most adults couldn't even spell. This end-of-the-world story they could recount until they were blue in the face, going onto strangers' front porches, all dressed up for the sake of the bloodshed to come.

A strange appetite, like something in the *Weekly World News*, and she had once shared it. You certainly had to believe a lot of things to get through a lifetime.

She stood at the window and sipped her tap water and ice cream.

The soul calms down in middle age, she thought, but it does take some doing, getting it there.

125

"Pigeon, honey," Walter called from the bedroom. His voice faded and swelled as if someone were manipulating a volume control. "Where are you?"

"Here," she said. "I'll be back in a minute."

She was thinking that she'd call the hospital tomorrow and find out how Burt Mink was, maybe even talk to him. Just because he had a smile that made babies wail and cry didn't mean you couldn't ask after him. As she was toying with these courtesies, she saw a taxi pull up to the curb in front of the building, and there he was, the subject of her thinking, getting to his feet behind the opened car door, as if her mind had given birth to him—Burt Mink—coming out, wrapped in a raincoat and up on crutches. He looked like a bat in splints.

The cabbie carried his overnight bag to the door, and Burt Mink hobbled his way forward. He glanced up, gave Irene a smile that would freeze dogs and cats to stone, and then was gone, upstairs. After he'd disappeared from view, she waved at him.

Two days later around sunset she put a cooked chicken on a tray and walked upstairs. She knocked at Burt Mink's door, and for the longest duration she heard the sound of crutches being gathered and slippers whispering along the carpeting. After the door opened, and she saw the full distemper of his face, she wanted, rather desperately, to run away. Instead she said, "Hi. I brought you this." She handed the tray toward him.

"Can't take it," he grumbled. "I got my crutches."

"Well, maybe I can take it inside."

"Guess so," he said. When he exhaled, he sounded as if he were quietly gargling. "Thank you." The words came out dutifully. "I'm much appreciative. You can put that in the kitchen there."

The apartment smelled of burnt lamb shank and curdled milk. The kitchen had few cleared areas: a careless convalescent man's eating space, marked by food spillage and catastrophe. She laughed to let the tensions loose. Then she peered into the living room. "Anywhere here?"

"Anywhere," he said. "I gotta sit down. My bones is all broken."

She tiptoed nervously into the living room. Burt Mink sat in a chair in front of a TV set tuned to a news station. The maladjusted color made the announcers appear to be greenish-purple. She heard the bubbling of a tropical aquarium and turned to look at it. The aquarium rested on an aluminum stand near a large ashtray filled with chewing-gum wrappers. At the bottom of the tank, a small metal deep-sea diver produced air bubbles that rose to the surface. The diver's arms were thrust out as if in self-defense. Only two or three fish swam back and forth in the water, their eyes perpetually staring, astonished and frightened. They made panic-striken veerings around the stones and seaweed.

"Sit down if you want," he said. "The news is on."

"Everybody's mixed-up," she told him. "The color needs adjusting."

"Not for me," he said. He pointed at his eyes. "Color-blind. Rare form, the blues and the golds." Just then the screen flashed on her weather photo, the sugar maple she had taken such care to photograph. On the screen, the autumn leaves were a lush purple.

"I wanted to say something." Irene held herself against the living-room wall. "I wanted to say how sorry I am. How sorry I was and am about all of this. I'm sorry about your accident. I'm just so sorry. I'm sorry. I can't stop saying it."

"Well, thank you." He examined her with the fixed gaze of someone who may be making some sort of plan, or is considering an idea he has no intention of articulating publicly. With repellent politeness, Burt Mink said, "Go over there and look at those fish. You might like them. I got some neon tetras in there that're still alive."

She walked closer to the fishtank and was pretending to be interested in them when she heard Burt Mink say, "Jesus has a plan for me."

"He has a plan for all of us," she said, on the other side of the tank. Through the water, fish darting in front of it, Burt Mink's face had a viscous, shimmering irregularity.

"That's not what I meant," Burt Mink said. "He told me I should despair."

"That can't be right," Mrs. Gladfelter said, as the air in the room suddenly took on the smell of aquarium water.

"You arguing with Jesus?" Burt Mink asked. "That'd be something."

Mrs. Gladfelter noticed some dusty plastic flowers in a chipped vase on top of the TV set. Next to the vase was a bright red apple made out of glass. "I have to go now," she said. "I hope you're feeling better soon, Mr. Mink."

He shrugged from his chair. "I'm in Hell," he said. "*That's* a certainty. I could make you a map. But thank you for the chicken. I'm much appreciative."

"Oh," she said, reaching out to pat him on the shoulder. Even as she did it, she saw how pointless gestures of kindness were in this room—

127

how they went nowhere, and stopped right where they happened. Then a thought occurred to her. "You're color-blind? You've never seen a yellow shirt, have you? You've only heard about them. They're just news to you."

He didn't even bother to shrug. He gazed at her for moment with a face so emptied of expression that it seemed like one of those contemporary sculptures she'd seen in museums, so blandly abstract that it didn't stand for anything. He seemed completely absorbed in the TV set again, studying it, as if for a test.

Walking out, her skin puckering from an icy, airy chill that might have originated in the room or might have been in her own mind, Mrs. Gladfelter turned around for a quick last glance. The room looked like a cell inside someone's head, not her own, but someone else's, someone who had never thought of a pleasantry but who sat at the bottom of the ocean, feeling the crushing pressure of the water. An ocean god had thought up this room and this man. That was an odd idea, the sort of idea she had never had before, and it wasn't her own thought, she realized, but Burt Mink's.

She closed the door behind her, imagining the pile of razor blades behind her bathroom wall, maybe behind Burt Mink's, her own good intentions piled up, rusting, somewhere behind a wall, and she had to stop in the hallway for a moment to get her breath.

But in her mind's eye the boy in the yellow shirt appeared before her. His brown hair uncombed, child-debris all over him, a real kid stinking of sweat and mud, maybe a real brat, nobody's close friend. Who would trust him? What d'you want, lady? he asked her. Some respect, she said. O.K., he muttered, O.K., Mrs. Gladfelter, not so sarcastic now, sorry. What're you doin' here?

Just run now, she said, past that apple tree, do it, someone's after you, and she pointed, and the boy took off, arms and legs pumping, scabby knees and all, past the grove until he was a small vanishing point near the horizon, alive this time, free of murder, and she inhaled fully, taking the stairs one by one, thinking: he's gone now, I saved him.

Nominated by Richard Burgin, Alice Fulton, Robert Phillips, Eileen Pollack

THE ERA OF THE VARI-VUE

by GARY FINCKE

from OXFORD MAGAZINE

The spring I was failing the blackboard test
And the exam of the curveball, I thought
Everybody saw with the soft focus
Of myopia, squinted and hunched close
To find the edges of print and faces.

A question of distance, tilt of the head:
In the first, fad years of the Vari-Vue
My father brought home plastic-ribbed pictures
Of Plymouth Landing and Christ on the Cross.
I wig-wagged those Pilgrims ashore, the eyes
Of Jesus up to heaven, and for weeks,
Bobbing my head, signed a reduced, slightly
Blurred Declaration of Independence.

Dog-at-the-hydrant. Cow-over-the-moon.
Finally, I wore glasses. By the time
I mastered contact lenses, I could shift
Nixon's eyes in White House windows. I could
Surface my children's skulls and nod my wife
To bones, flicking her forward, fast or slow,
Like Mutoscope women you could undress,
Once, for a nickel.

        Now, for quarters, men
Can lock up in booths to watch looped films, choose
Sound-suffused channels on the porn network,
Sighed syllables of acquiescence flung
Like dots on this page I'm holding tonight,
In the gallery of unimportance,
Trusting they will leap up as holograms.

I'm staring at a near-wash of purple,
Coaxing "truncated spheres" or "peeled fruit" off
Paper. I'm deciphering instructions,
Learning the principles of SIRD, 3-D
Without glasses. I pull the page haze-close,
One simple step to "deep-sight," the trompe l'oeil
Of computers if we transfix ourselves.
You enter the page, the inventor claims,
And I imagine the third dimension
Of pornography, toxins surfacing
In lakes, futures embossed by tainted blood.
I call each of my chattering, clear-lensed
Children to these pictures, say "hold this close
And stare," prodding them to levitate balls
And fruit, say "pear" and "globe" as if these were
Rorschach blots for the willingness to see.

Nominated by Colette Inez

MY FATHER'S CHINESE WIVES

fiction by SANDRA TSING LOH

from QUARTERLY WEST

MY FATHER DOESN'T want to alarm us. But then again, it would not be fair to hide anything either. The fact is, at 70, he is going to try and get married again. This time to a Chinese wife. He thinks this would be more suitable than to someone American, given his advanced age.

He has written his family in Shanghai, and is awaiting response. He is hoping to be married within six months.

* * *

Let us unpeel this news one layer at a time.

Question: At this point, is my father even what one would consider marriageable?

At age 70, my father—a retired Chinese aerospace engineer—is starting to look more and more like somebody's gardener. His feet shuffle along the patio in their broken sandals. He stoops to pull out one or two stray weeds, coughing phlegmatically. He wears a hideous old V-neck tennis sweater. Later, he sits in a rattan chair and eats leathery green vegetables in brown sauce, his old eyes slitted wearily.

He is the sort of person one would refer to as "Old Dragon Whiskers." And not just because it is a picturesque Oriental way of speaking.

131

"I am old now," he started saying, about 10 years after my mother had died of cancer. "I'm just your crazy old Chinese father." He would rock backwards in his chair and sigh. "I am an old, old man . . . "

At times he almost seems to be over-acting this lizardy old part. He milks it. After all, he still does the same vigorous exercise regime—45 minutes of pull-ups, something that looks like the twist and much bellowing—he did 10 years ago. This always performed on the most public beaches possible, in his favorite Speedo—one he found in a dumpster.

"Crazy old Chinese father" is, in truth, a code word, a rationalization for the fact that my father has always had a problem . . . spending money. Why buy a briefcase to carry to work, when an empty Frosted Flakes Cereal box will do? Papers slip down neatly inside, and pens can be clipped conveniently on either side.

Why buy Bounty Paper Towels when, at work, he can just walk down the hall to the washroom, open the dispenser, and lift out a stack? They're free—he can bring home as many as we want!

If you've worn the same sweater for so many years that the elbows wear out, turn it around! Get another decade out of it! Which is why to this day, my father wears only crew neck, not V-neck sweaters . . .

Why drive the car to work when you can take the so-convenient RTD bus? More time to read interesting scientific papers . . . and here they are, in my empty Frosted Flakes Box!

"Terrific!" is my older sister Kaitlin's response when I phone her with the news. Bear in mind that Kaitlin has not seen my father since the mid-'80s, preferring to nurse her bad memories of him independently, via a therapist. She allows herself a laugh, laying aside her customary dull hostility for a moment of more jocular hostility. "So who does he think would want to marry *him*?"

"Someone Chinese," I answer.

"Oh good!" she exclaims. "That narrows down the field . . . to what? Half a billion? Nah, as always, he's doing this to punish us.

"Think about it," Kaitlin continues with her usual chilling logic. "He marries a German woman the first time around. It's a disaster. You and I represent that. Because he's passive aggressive and he's cheap. But no, to him, it's that rebellious Aryan strain that's the problem.

"You take an Asian immigrant just off the boat, on the other hand. This is a person who has just fled a Communist government and a horrible life working in a bicycle factory for 10 cents a month and no public sanitation and repeated floggings every hour on the hour. After that, living with our father might seem like just another bizarre interlude. It could happen."

Kaitlin scores some compelling points, but nonetheless . . .

I'm bothered for a different reason . . .

* * *

Perhaps it is because in describing the potential new wife, he has used only that one adjective: *Chinese*. He has not said: "I'm looking for a smart wife," or even "a fat wife," he has picked "Chinese." It is meant to stand for so much.

Asian. Asian women. Asian *ladies*.

I think back to a college writing workshop I once attended. (No credit and perhaps that was appropriate.) It was long before my current "administrative assistant" job at Swanson Films. (Makers of the 10-minute instructional video "Laughterobics! Featuring Meredith Baxter Birney," among other fine titles.)

Anyway, the workshop contained 13 hysterical women—and one Fred. Fred was a wealthy Caucasian sixtysomething urologist; he was always serene and beautifully dressed and insistent upon holding the door open for me "because you're such a lovely lady." I always wore jeans and a USC sweatshirt, sometimes even sweatpants, so at first I did not know what he meant.

We women, on the other hand, were a wildly mixed group—writing anything from wintery Ann Beattie-esque snippets to sci-fi romance/porn novels ("She would be King Zenothar's concubine, whether she liked it or not"). We attacked each other's writing accordingly. People were bursting into tears every week, then making up by emotionally sharing stories about mutual eating disorders.

But there was one moment when all 13 women were of like minds. It was that moment when Fred would enter the classroom, laden with xeroxes, blushing shyly as a new bride. We would all look at each other as if to say, "Oh my God, Fred has brought in work *again*."

As though springing from a murky bottomless well, each week new chapters would appear from this semi-epistolary novel Fred was penning about an elderly doctor named Fred who goes on sabbatical for a year to Japan and there finds love with a 23 year-old Japanese medical student named Aku who smells of cherry blossoms.

There were many awkward scenes in which Fred and Aku were exploring each other's bodies as they lay—as far as I could gather—upon

133

the bare floor, only a *tatami* mat for comfort. (Fred would always italicize the Japanese words, as if to separate and somehow protect them from other, lesser words.) But it was all beautifully pure and unlike the urban squalor we find in America—the rock music, the drugs, the uncouth teenagers.

Anyway, I recall the one line that I have never since been able to blot from my mind. I cannot think of it without a bit of a shiver. Nor the way he read it, in that hoarse tremulous voice . . .

"I put my hand in hers, and her little fingers opened like the petals of a moist flower."

*　*　*

It is a month later and, as in a dream, I sit at the worn formica family dining table with my father, photos and letters spread before us.

Since my father has written to Shanghai, the mail has come pouring in. I have to face the fact that my father is, well, hot. "You see?" he says. "Seven women have written! Ha!" He beams, his gold molar glinting. He is drinking steaming green tea from a beaker, which he handles with a Beauty and the Beast potholder.

Remarkably, my father doesn't make the least effort to mask his delight, no matter how inappropriate. He is old now. *He can do whatever the hell he wants*, is how I now understand it. With a sigh, I turn to the photos. In spite of myself, I am wowed!

Tzau Pa, Ling Ling, Sui Pai, Chong Zhou . . . "28, administrative assistant," "47, owner of a seamstress business," "39, freelance beautician." The words jump off the pages, both in English and Chinese translations. These women are dynamos, achievers, with black curly hair, in turtlenecks, jauntily riding bicycles, seated squarely on cannons before military museums, standing proudly with three grown daughters.

One thing unites them: they're all ready to leap off the mainland at the drop of a hat.

And don't think their careers and hobbies are going to keep them from being terrific wives. Quite the opposite. Several already have excellent experience, including one who's been married twice already. The seamstress has sent him two shorts and several pairs of socks; there is much talk of seven-course meals and ironing and terrific expertise in gardening.

Super-achievement is a major theme that applies to all. And the biggest star of all is my father. He clears his throat and gleefully reads from a letter by one Liu Tzun:

> Dr. Chow, your family has told me of your great scientific genius and of your many awards. I respect academic scholarship very highly, and would be honored to meet you on your next visit.

"You see?" my father chuckles. "They have a lot of respect for me in China. When I go there, they treat me like President Bush! Free meals, free drinks . . . I don't pay for anything!"

* * *

"He had his chance. He got married once, for 25 years. He was a terrible husband and a worse father."

Kaitlin is weighing in. All jokes are off. Her fury blazes away, further aggravated by the fact that she is going through a divorce and hates her $50,000 a year job. Her monthly Nordstrom bills are astronomical. MCI is positively crackling.

"He's a single man," I say. "Mum's been gone for 12 years now—"

"And now he gets a second try—just like that?" Kaitlin exclaims. "Clean slate? Start right over? Buy a wife? It makes me sick. He is totally unqualified to sustain a marriage. A family structure of any kind collapses around him. Do you even remember one happy Christmas?"

Twinkling lights and tinsel suddenly swirl before me and looking deeper, through green foliage, I see my mother looking beautiful and crisp in lipstick and pearls, her wavy auburn hair done . . . except for the fact that she is hysterical, and my father, his face a mask of disgust so extreme it is almost parodic, is holding his overpriced new V-necked tennis sweater from Saks out in front of him like it is a dead animal—

"I try to block it out," is what I say.

"Well I was six years older than you so I can't." Kaitlin's pain is raw. "Why does he deserve to be happy . . . now? He made Mama miserable in her lifetime—he was so cheap! I think she was almost glad to go as soon as she did! A $70 dress, leaving the heater on over night, too much spent on a nice steak dinner—he could never let anything

135

go! He could never just let it go! He just could . . . not . . . let . . . things . . . go!"

* * *

Meanwhile . . .

On its own gentle time clock, unsullied by the raging doubts of his two daughters . . .

My father's project bursts into flower.

And 47-year-old Liu—the writer of the magic letter—is the lucky winner! Within three months, she is flown to Los Angeles. She and my father are married a week later.

I do not get to meet her right away, but my father fills me in on the stats. And I have to confess, I'm a little surprised at how modern she is, how urban. Liu is a divorcee with, well, with ambitions in the entertainment business. Although she speaks no English, she seems to be an expert on American culture. The fact that Los Angeles is near Hollywood has not escaped her. This is made clear to me one Sunday evening, three weeks later, via telephone.

"I know you have friends in the entertainment business," my father declares. He has never fully grasped the fact that I am a typist and that Swanson Films' clients include such Oscar contenders as Kraft Foods and Motorola.

"Aside from having knitted me a new sweater and playing the piano," my father continues, "you should know that Liu is an excellent singer—" Turning away from the phone, he and his new wife exchange a series of staccato reports in Mandarin, which mean nothing to me.

"I'm sure that Liu is quite accomplished," I reply, "it's just that—"

"Oh . . . she's terr-ific!" my father exclaims, shocked that I may be calling Liu's musical talent into question. "You want to hear her sing? Here, here, I will put her on the phone right now . . . "

Creeping into my father's voice is a tremulous note that is sickeningly familiar. How many times had I heard it during my childhood as I was being pushed towards the piano, kicking and screaming? How many times—

But that was 20 years ago. I gulp terror back down. I live in my own apartment now, full of director's chairs, potted fici and Matisse posters. I will be fine. My father has moved on to a totally new pushee . . .

Who picks up the phone, sighs—then bursts out triumphantly:

136

"Nee-ee hoo-oo mau, tieh-hen see bau-hau jioo . . . !"

* * *

I have left you and taken the Toyota, Dr. Chow—so there!

Five weeks later, Liu just packs up her suitcase, makes some sand-wiches, and takes off in the family Toyota. She leaves her note on the same formica table at which she'd first won his heart.

My father is in shock. Then again, he is philosophical.

"Liu—she had a lot of problems. She said she had no one to talk to. There were no other Chinese people in Tarzana. She wanted me to give her gifts. She was bored. You know I don't like to go out at night. But I tell her, 'Go! See your friends in Chinatown.' But Liu does not want to take the bus. She wants to drive! But you know me, your cheap father. I don't want to pay her insurance. That Liu—she was a very bad driver—"

"Ha!" is Kaitlin's only comment.

* * *

Summer turns to fall in Southern California, causing the palm trees to sway a bit. The divorce is soon final, Liu's settlement including $10,000, the microwave and the Toyota.

Never one to dwell, my father has picked a new bride: Zhou Ping, 37, home-maker from Qang-Zhou province. I groan.

"But no . . . Zhou Ping is very good," my father insists. He has had several phone conversations with her. "And she comes very highly rec-ommended, not, I have to say, like Liu. Liu was bad, that one. Zhou Ping is sensible and hard-working. She has had a tough life. Boy! She worked in a coal mine in Manchuria until she was 25. The winters there were very, very bitter! She had to make her own shoes and cloth-ing. Then she worked on a farming collective, where she raised cattle and grew many different kinds of crops—by herself!"

"I'm sure she's going to fit in really well in Los Angeles," I say.

* * *

Zhou Ping is indeed a different sort. The news, to my astonishment, comes from Kaitlin. "I received . . . " her voice trails off, the very

137

words seeming to elude her. "A *birthday card*. From Papa . . . and *Zhou Ping*."

My sister continues in a kind of trance of matter-of-factness, as if describing some curious archaeological artifact. "Let's see, on the front is a picture with flowers on it. It's from Hallmark. Inside is gold lettering, cursive, that says, 'Happy Birthday!' At the bottom, in red pen, it says . . . 'Love, Zhou Ping and *your* Dad.'"

"Your 'Dad'?"

"I think Zhou Ping put him up to this. The envelope is not addressed in his hand-writing. Nonetheless . . . " Kaitlin thinks it over, concurs with herself. "Yes. Yes. I believe this is the first birthday card I've ever received from him in my life. The first. It's totally bizarre."

A week later, Kaitlin receives birthday gifts in the mail: a sweater hand-knit by Zhou Ping, and a box of "mooncakes." She is flipping out. "Oh no," she worries, "Now I really have to call and thank her. I mean, the poor woman probably has no friends in America. Who knows what he's having her do? We may be her only link to society!"

* * *

Kaitlin finally does call, managing to catch Zhou Ping when my father is on the beach doing his exercises (which he always does at 11 and at 3). Although Zhou Ping's English is very broken, she somehow convinces Kaitlin to fly down for a visit.

It will be Kaitlin's first trip home since our mother's passing. And my first meeting of either of my step-mothers.

* * *

I pull up the familiar driveway in my Geo. Neither Kaitlin nor I say anything. We peer out the windows.

The yard doesn't look too bad. There are new sprinklers, and a kind of irrigation system made by a network of ingenuously placed rain gutters. Soil has been turned, and thoughtfully. Cypresses have been trimmed. Enormous bundles of weeds flank the driveway, as if for some momentous occasion.

We ring the doorbell. Neither of us has had keys to the house in years.

The door opens. A short, somewhat plump Chinese woman, in round glasses and a perfect bowl haircut, beams at us. She is wearing a bright yellow "I hate housework!" apron that my mother was once given as a gag gift—and I think never wore.

"Kat-lin! Jen-na!" she exclaims in what seems like authentic joy, embracing us. She is laughing and almost crying with emotion.

In spite of myself, giggles begin to well up from inside me as if from a spring. I can't help it: I feel warm and euphoric. Authentic joy is contagious. Who cares who this woman is: no one has been this happy to see me in ages.

"Wel-come home," Zhou Ping says, with careful emphasis. She turns to Kaitlin, a shadow falling over her face. "I am glad you finally come home to see your Daddy," she says in a low, sorrowful voice. She looks over her shoulder. "He old now."

Then, as if exhausted by that effort, Zhou Ping collapses into giggles. I sneak a glance over at Kaitlin, whose expression seems to be straining somewhere between joy and nausea. Pleasantries lunge out of my mouth: "It's nice to finally meet you!" "How do you like America?" "I've heard so much about your cooking!"

My father materializes behind a potted plant. He is wearing a new sweater and oddly formal dress pants. His gaze hovers somewhere near the floor.

"Hul-lo," he declares, attempting a smile. "Long time no see!" he exclaims, not making eye contact, but in Kaitlin's general direction.

"Yes!" Kaitlin exclaims back, defiant, a kind of winged Amazon in perfect beige Anne Klein II leisurewear. "It certainly is!"

My father stands stiffly.

Kaitlin blazes.

"It's good to see you!" he finally concludes, as though this were something he learned in English class.

Feeling, perhaps, that we should all leave well enough alone, the Chow family, such as we are, moves on through the house. It is ablaze with color—the sort of eye-popping combinations one associates with Thai restaurants and Hindu shrines. There are big purple couches, peach rugs, a shiny brass trellis and creeping charlies everywhere.

All this redecorating came at no great expense, though. "See this rug?" my father says proudly, while Zhou Ping giggles. "She found it in a dumpster. They were going to throw it away!" "Throw it away!" she exclaims. "See? It very nice."

Over their heads, Kaitlin silently mouths one word to me: "Help."

Beyond, the formica dining room table is set. Oddly. There are little rice bowls, chopsticks, and a sheet of plain white paper at each place setting. It is good to know some definite event has been planned. Kaitlin, my father and I are so unaccustomed to being in a room together that any kind of definite agenda—aka: "We'll eat dinner, and then we'll leave"—is comforting.

My father goes off to put some music on his new CD player. "That bad Liu made me buy it!" he explains. "But it's nice." Zhou Ping bustles into the kitchen. "Dinner ready—in five minute!" she declares.

Kaitlin waits a beat, then pulls me aside into the bathroom and slams the door.

"This is so weird!" she hisses.

We have not stood together in this bathroom for some 15 years. It seems different. I notice that the wallpaper is faded, the towels are new—but no, it's something else. On one wall is my mother's framed reproduction of the brown Da Vinci etching called "Praying Hands" which she had always kept in her sewing room. Right next to it, in shocking juxtaposition, is a green, red, blue and yellow "Bank of Canton" calendar from which a zaftig Asian female chortles.

"I can't go through with this!" Kaitlin continues in stage whisper. "It's too weird! There are so many memories here, and not good ones!"

And like debris from a hurricane, the words tumble out:

"I go by the kitchen and all I can see is me standing before the oven clock at age five with tears in my eyes. He is yelling: 'What time is it? The little hand is most of the way to four and the big hand is on the eight! It was 3:18 twenty-two minutes ago—so what time is it now? What's eighteen plus twenty-two? Come on—you can do it in your head! Come on! Come on!'

"I go by the dining room and I see him hurling my Nancy Drew books across the floor. They slam against the wall and I huddle against Mum, screaming. 'Why do you waste your time on this when your algebra homework isn't finished? You . . . good for nothing! You're nothing, nothing—you'll never amount to anything!'

"I go by the bedroom—"

"Please—" I have this sickening feeling like I'm going to cry, that I'm just going to lose it. I want to just sit down in the middle of the floor and roll myself into a ball. But I can't. Kaitlin's rage is like something uncontainable, a dreadful natural force, and I am the gatekeeper. I feel if I open the door, it will rush out and destroy the house and everyone in it. "Please," is what I end up whispering. "Please. Let's just eat. We'll be done in a hour. Then we can go home. I promise. You won't have to do this again for another 10 years—or maybe ever."

* * *

At dinner, endless plates of food twirl their way out of the kitchen, Zhou Ping practically dancing underneath. Spinach, teriyaki-ish chicken, shrimp, some kind of egg thing with peas, dumplings packed with little pillows of pork.

And amazingly, there is no want of conversational material. Photos from Shanghai are being pulled out of envelopes and passed around, of her family, his family . . .

I do recognize three or four Chinese relatives—a cousin, an aunt, a grand-uncle? Their names are impossible for me to remember. We had met them in China during our last trip as a family. I was 15; it was right before our mother started to get sick.

Shanghai is a distant, confused memory for me, of ringing bicycle bells and laundry lines hanging from buildings. What I do remember is how curious my father's family had seemed about Kaitlin and me, his odd American experiment, oohing over our height and touching our auburn hair. There were many smiles but no intelligible conversation, at least to our ears. We probably won't see any of these people again before we die.

Zhou Ping, though, is determined to push through, to forge a bridge between us. She plunges ahead with her bad English, my father almost absent-mindedly correcting her.

Their lives are abuzz with activity. Zhou Ping is taking piano lessons at the community college. My father is learning Italian and French off the Learning Channel—he sets his alarm for four in the morning. "So early!" Zhou Ping hoots. They listen to Karl Haas' "Listening to Good Music" on the classical station at 10. "Mot-sart—he very nice!" They have joined the Bahais, a local quasi-religious group. "I must cook food all the time!" My father suddenly puts his spoon down. He is chewing slowly, a frown growing.

"This meat . . . " he shakes his head, "is very greasy."

He turns to Zhou Ping and the lines at both sides of his mouth deepen. His eyes cloud. He says something to her in Chinese, with a certain sharp cadence that makes my spine stiffen . . .

Zhou Ping's face goes blank for a moment. Her eyes grow big. My stomach turns to ice.

How will she respond? By throwing her napkin down, bursting into tears, running from the room? Will she knock the table over, plates sliding after each other, sauces spilling, crockery breaking? Will we

141

hear the car engine turn over as she drives off into the night, to leave us frightened and panicked?

It is none of these things.

Zhou Ping's head tilts back, her eyes crinkle . . .

And laughter pours out of her, peal after peal after peal. It is a big laugh, an enormous laugh, the laugh of a woman who has birthed calves and hoed crops and seen harsh winters decimate countrysides. Pointing to our father, Zhou Ping turns to us with large glittering eyes and says words which sound incredible to our ears:

"Your Papa—he so funny!"

My jaw drops. No one has ever laughed out loud at this table, ever. We laughed behind closed doors, in our bedrooms, in the bathroom, never before my father. We laughed sometimes with my mother, on those glorious days when he would be off on a trip—

But Kaitlin is not laughing. She is trembling; her face is turning red.

"Why were you always so angry?" Kaitlin cries out in a strangled voice. It is the question that she was waited 30 years to ask. "Why were you so angry?"

There is shocked silence. My father looks weary and embarrassed. He smiles wanly and shrugs his thin shoulders.

"No really," Kaitlin insists. "All those years. With Mama. Why?"

"I don't know," my father murmurs. "People get angry."

And I know, in that moment, that he doesn't have an answer. He literally doesn't. It's as if anger was this chemical which reacted on him for 20 years. Who knows why, but like some kind of spirit, it has left him now. The rage is spent. He is old now. He is old.

* * *

Dusk has fallen, and long shadows fall across the worn parquet floor of the dining room. After a moment of silence, my father asks Zhou Ping to sing a song. The hausfrau from Qang Zhou opens her mouth and with an odd dignity, sings simply and slowly. My father translates.

> From the four corners of the earth
> My lover comes to me
> Playing the lute
> Like the wind over the water

He recites the words without embarrassment, almost without emotion. And why shouldn't he? The song has nothing to do with him personally: it is from some old Chinese fable. It has to do with missing someone, something, that perhaps one can't even define any more.

As Zhou Ping sings, everyone longs for home. But what home? Zhou Ping—for her bitter winters? My father—for the Shanghai he left 40 years ago? Kaitlin and I? We are even sitting in our home, and we long for it.

Nominated by Quarterly West

THE STORM CHASERS

by WILLIAM OLSEN

from THE GETTYSBURG REVIEW

Just short of danger the camcorder stops;
one van keeps plodding forth past the rain-beaten
Yield sign in the headlights, past Andover, Kansas, farm kids
stationary beside stationary pickups
(the engines must still be clicking, hoods still warm),
past even the squad car pulled to the side of the road
and the sheriff holding up his end of astonishment,
watching a string of streetlights pop like flashbulbs
as someone's farmhouse is shriven into tinder.
Behind them the past goes abnormally clear for once,
ahead of them the future is crossed by the sheering force
we who have been twisted into apperception call form. . . .
I used to look for tornadoes over my parents' country-club golf
　　course
and car lights used to glow through stable trees like
long grievous letters to those who are already dead,
those who, on their separate voyages, hear nothing
troublesome as they dispatch from our grief
at practically the speed of changeling light,
the awkward beings we knew as ancestors.
What was there to do but watch the houses
darken to wilderness while the streetlights
came on prematurely,
the greens flags snapping in wind and yet
there was nothing bereft about it, so much space
all the grief in the world can't begin to fill that space.

Then, once, the first blue-black tenuous twist or two
of cloud-stuff, a single careless lock of heaven,
and then the houselights rising and rinsed clean
as if out of amnesia they surfaced, negotiating hope,
far off as a moral out there in the offing of recall—
and the insinuation went back into its cloud.
It turns out I had seen one after all—
the unlikely twisted beginning of a funnel,
a faint ringlet of cloud like the wisps of hair
my mother turned and turned around her index finger.
Worry tracked down the remainder of her freedom.
It was as if there was nothing but haystacks of lightning
for her troubled nights to pile up on the horizon.
In dreams the shape of worry constantly changes: strange
chalice stems, then wriggling ceaseless revisions
roar across dreamed prairies of sleep paralysis.
Awake, the earth with its streets prematurely lit
and scrub oak lifting glowing earfuls of cicadas
had already ended eons ago, the storm
could do its worst yet not erase a thing—

as if the earth were merely ending all over again.
I don't remember anything else of the hugely agitated
except how the final fairway shone like the deck
of an aircraft carrier upon the face of the void.
I used to time-lapse lightning over that golf course,
set the f-stop at a long preternatural minute,
and let emulsion go varicose with chaos theory
til above the horizons loomed a latticework of trouble
that would outshine the sun if we could see all time at once.
Twenty-three, I thought my parents insufferable that summer
because I lived insufferably unemployed with them
and every storm I errored and looked for disaster
until each storm exampled every storm, the first storm
and the first ever to be except for the fact
that long after the clouds have been removed and the last
raindrop has ticked through the ratchet leaves
there'd be another storm to chase, another firefly
to take up its place in its intolerable weakness—
and every dawn across the greens the tarantulas made their shadows

145

and every night the streetlights of the universe
blinked on above me lying down lost
in dazzling explanations of the heart—

remembering already, as if they were ancient,
soon to come in but for one careless instant
patinaed green in unearthly possibility,
two parents freeze-framed by distant lightning,
statuesque on the eighteenth green—
like beings permanent after all—
each bolt echoing the hour our universe,
when it could no longer take eternal confinement,
exploded into everyday heartbreak.

Nominated by Linda Bierds, Reginald Gibbons, Brigit Pegeen Kelly, Lisa Lewis, The
Gettysburg Review

THE END OF THE WORLD

fiction by MICHAEL COLLINS

from THE ANTIOCH REVIEW

THE END OF the world was a school day. There was even homework due. It seemed strange. It was hard to think of homework due on the day the world was set to end. The priests stood before the classes and paged through the math books and the Irish books and picked out problems, the odd ones from one to fifteen. A long passage of Irish was assigned.

The day before the end of the world was like any other school day for Patsy. He was walloped twice, once in geography and then again in history. He was pure thick, a dosser of the highest order. The priests said no boy alive could have that little aptitude for a written language.

There was going to be no letup on educational pursuits on the day before the end of the world. The routine was well established. Catholicism guarded against idlers.

Patsy traveled the cold corridors between classes, obligingly good humored. He gripped the ribs of the heaters with his callused hands, squeezing the hot iron. Patsy's ability to take abuse had a formal status among the other fellows. He let the strap lick its way up his palms and wrists. It didn't hurt him the way it hurt the others. In English class he was caught with the word *Armageddon* written into his notebook where he should have had his homework listed. Tierney demanded, "Where did you get that word?"

Patsy shrugged his shoulders. He held his hands out for punishment, but Tierney punched him in the face. Patsy fell out of his desk. His nose bled. "Where did you get that word?" Tierney roared again. He was a head taller than Patsy and had huge slop-

147

ing shoulders and a strong rugby player's neck. "Where did you get that word?"

Patsy finally admitted he'd seen it in a comic from America about Superman saving the planet. His nose was still bleeding. The bell rang for the next class. Tierney kept Patsy back and then the two of them went down to the toilet and filled up a basin of water.

"Hold your head back, you fool."

Patsy tilted his head back and thought of nothing except how nice it would be when the end of the world came. He presumed there would be no school in heaven, and that all things would be revealed to him. He maintained his solemn ignorance, especially in the presence of a man who could beat him to death. If the world had gone on a little longer, Patsy felt he would have gotten Tierney back. But now was a time for forgiveness. Patsy knew the beating was frustration on Tierney's part. The school had lost early on in the Munster school rugby championships. Tierney was the coach.

"Head off now, Patsy." Tierney shook Patsy's hand and said, "May we meet in heaven, please God."

Patsy took the hand in a genial manner, winked and said, "Maybe they'll have a rugby championship in heaven."

Nobody was really sure how the world was going to end. The Pope was supposed to have an envelope that held the secret of Fatima. It was believed by all the Catholics that when he opened it the world would end.

The Religion teacher was a pious old priest, Father Mackey, who had stories about the famine and what it did to Ireland. He came around every week and spoke about the missions in other countries and always tied things up by relating a story about the famine in Ireland. Father Mackey was in his eighties. On the day before the end of the world, the classes were brought together in the study hall for what everyone thought would be a sermon by Father Mackey.

It began without a prefatory remark. The boys were still chatting when Father Mackey climbed up on the podium, teetering with old age, and said, "Now boys, how will the world end?" He asked it three more times in the same modulated croaking voice. He hadn't the ability to speak loudly. He'd been a heavy smoker of rolled cigarettes in his day. His neck was cut up from numerous operations. The boys had to lean forward in their desks, trying to catch what he was saying. The question finally reached everyone. The place was dead silent. Nobody had actually mentioned the end of the world all day. It was unspeakable. It was good to finally talk about it. There were questions that needed to be asked.

"How will the world end?" Father Mackey said again.

"Maybe an angel will come down," the school swat said resolutely, standing up.

Father Mackey had a stooped spine, and when he smiled it became a perfect arch. "Could somebody draw what it will be like?" Father Mackey gasped for breath.

Father Mackey looked out at the boys. The gray vacuity of the back of the room contrasted with the intensity of the boys before him. A window rumbled behind the boys, letting in a cold rainy breeze.

"Draw me a picture, boys," Father Mackey said. "How will the world end?" he repeated over and over again. "Draw me a picture."

The boys worked away in their copy books. Father Mackey checked the drawings, walking up and down the aisles.

"Go up to the board, Donovan, and draw what you have," Father Mackey said, holding Donovan's limp hand.

Donovan drew a picture of an ark pulling in down at the city docks. People were getting on in twos.

"What's that?" Father Mackey asked, pointing to a small creature that looked like a dog.

"It's a dog, Father. It's me and my dog getting onto the ark down at the docks." Donovan touched the knot of his school tie, suddenly feeling self-conscious. Maybe dogs weren't going to heaven. He assumed a schoolboy position of defense, cowering sideways, holding his hand over his ear.

Father Mackey put his hands together in prayer. "Sweet Jesus, humor at this hour—"

Somebody else had a flying ark driven by Noah through the sky. The boy was asked to draw the picture.

The priests at the doors were shaking their heads in an ambivalent way. Everybody was scared.

The English boy Wilson stood up and said, "My mother says the Germans killed all the Jews in the world. That is why we are going to die." Wilson's father had died in the trenches in France. His mother was Irish.

"Was Jesus a Jew?" Father Mackey asked Wilson.

Wilson said nothing.

"Are we part of the Church of Ireland or the Church of Rome?"

149

The class mumbled back and forth among themselves. This was a trick question that Father Mackey always asked them, but they never could remember which was the right answer.

Wilson ran to the doors crying. The priests let him go.

Father Mackey's spine was still arched. "Let him alone, God love him. He will be with his father soon."

"When Wilson sees his dad, will he— Well, you know, Father, Wilson's dad was blown up. Will all the souls of people look like new?"

"Everybody will be about thirty," Lawlor shouted. "That's what my mother says. The age of Jesus—thirty three—isn't that right, Father Mackey?"

"That seems reasonable," Father Mackey coughed. He had lost control of the boys.

"You mean we'll be thirty as well?" Kingston shouted.

"No, our mothers and fathers and all the grannies and the old fellows, they'll all be thirty. We'll be the way we are, right, Father?"

"That seems reasonable," Father Mackey's small head turned on its thin neck. He needed help.

"Will we have wings?" a fellow asked from the last row.

Patsy said, "When the Pope opens the secret of Fatima, will the world begin to end at that moment?" He had seen something like it in his comics where codes had a message in caps saying: THIS WILL SELF-DESTRUCT IN 5 SECONDS.

Father Mackey sat down on a chair and spread his legs apart, leaning over, drawing breath. He spoke from the seat. "You boys should be praying, not scheming."

"What happens if he doesn't open it, Father?" Patsy pressed on.

The two boys beside Patsy moved out of the desk and shoved in beside some other fellows. Then there was a moment of silence. Father Mackey said to Patsy, "Are we part of the Church of Ireland or the Church of Rome?"

Patsy said, "The Church of Ireland," and twitched his injured nose.

"Come up and reproduce your drawing, Patsy."

Patsy went up and drew a picture of Jesus coming down on the great orb of the sun which was in his copybook. He had seen something like this in the same Marvel comic from America that had the Armageddon. But, in the comic, Superman came down to save the world. Patsy ad-libbed from the original drawing in his copybook and added a big "J" on the chest of Jesus in a diamond and a great mushroom cloud rising above the smiling face.

Father Mackey took Patsy by the arm. "What's this?"

"It's Jesus. Don't you see the J? It's how He saved the world from nuclear war. Armageddon, Father." Patsy looked at the class with a pat, apish stare.

Everyone thought Father Mackey was going to break in half. His body creaked and cracked audibly as he went at Patsy. He was flogged before the class, his hands held out before him. Each wrist in turn took the long tongue of the leather. The nosebleed opened again with the pressure of his face holding back expression. He managed a smile at the end. The boys wouldn't look at him. They turned to the fogged windows. This was the eve of the end of the world. Everybody resented Patsy's antics. It was supposed to be a time of prayer and family.

Father Mackey raised his small leathery hands and roared, "The end of the world has nothing to do with the Supermen or Nuclear War!" He referred to something from the Book of Revelations.

Patsy was beginning to understand something. He swallowed the sweet trickle of blood, but he knew he was winning. He remembered something back at his house about how the world was saying the Church and the Pope had done nothing, even though they knew the Jews were being burned alive. He figured Superman would have been on to that.

The school ended an hour early for everyone to get a start on their homework. The senior boys went to the back of the class and began their homework. Even Patsy worked hard, laboring over a long-division problem. Over half the class had completed their homework before they left the study hall. However, Patsy was one of the unfortunates who would go towards eternity with the nagging specter of long division remaining as one of those earthly conundrums. He braced himself for the patent sideburn pull from a priest who saw him struggling with the dual anxiety of ignorance and diminishing time. "You're pure thick," the priest said, but didn't touch him. Then the bell rang and the boys were let out.

All the boys walked silently down the long drive to the school gates, sometimes stopping, looking back at the great structure of the school in the field, flanked by grazing cows. The priests lived off in one section of the school. The evening was getting dark, the trail of lights from the town off in the distance. The priests had solitary lights on in their small rooms, each one distinct and cold. Patsy stopped and began to laugh. The other fellows around him moved away. He pointed at the priests' quarters. "Jasus, look at that. Just think of them spending their

151

last night praying alone." He had stopped laughing by the time he had said it.

•

"What happened to your nose?" Patsy's mother said when he came into the kitchen.

"I bumped into a door."

His mother had bought a big roast and cooked the family's favorite dish for the eve of the end of the world.

"Well, change your shirt and get ready for mass." Patsy went out of the kitchen and looked in on the small living room. Everything was like Christmas, the best tablecloth spread out on the table, the good cutlery and the china. A big fire going. Patsy's father came in in solemn humor. He nodded at Patsy and noted the damaged nose. "Acting the maggot until the end, no doubt. Do you have any fear of hell?" he said, passing into the kitchen. "Are you ready, Mother?" He took off his shirt and filled the sink. He rubbed a cloth between the rolls of his white belly, washing his face, ears, and neck, and then shaving.

Patsy waited with his sisters in the living room. The lashing rain streamed down the window. If the world was going to end, this seemed to be the weather for it. Patsy looked in the mirror and touched the soft scab forming on his nose. It had turned a dark brownish-black. "You told a lie, Patsy" one of his sisters said. "You'll go to hell for that, you will."

Patsy spat on his palm, parted his hair, and plastered it with saliva. "I wonder if Rita O'Brien will be up above?"

"Cut the messing out," Patsy's father said, coming into the room. He smelt of soap. "Let's get going. Look lively, you fool. Are you ready, girls?"

The girls smiled. Patsy gawked at his father.

The street was black with people going towards the churches. The town accepted the raining, cold vulnerability, the penitent slogging their way to mass, all the houses oozing the black dribble of the faithful. For all the crowd, the street was silent, only the scrape of shoes, or the occasional cough. Patsy's mother had her hair styled, protected by a transparent rain cap.

All the churches were packed. Patsy stood with his parents, bewildered, cold, and hungry. The atmosphere died in a drowsy smoking in-

152

cense. A tremulous singing began in strained discord. Nobody could sing. Teeth chattered. From the ceiling, the faded murals looked down silently. Twenty minutes passed and nothing started.

Patsy thought of the food warming at home. He looked at his father's severe face. His father's eyes turned to him and squinted. "Pray," he said. "This is your last chance at salvation."

A priest came out and announced there would be confession first for the adults. A rumble of thunder rolled through the vault of the church. The dark mahogany doors of the confessionals opened. Patsy was astonished to see that there had been priests in them since they had come in. The confessions were administered rapidly. Patsy waited in his seat.

In the few minutes, the earthly mysteries of sin were revealed, the dark mouths pouring out guilt, drunkards who beat their wives, men who had harbored impure thoughts, and the mystery of the young girl who had been murdered three years earlier revealed by a man with his lips pressed up to the mesh.

Patsy sat in his seat, freezing. The mass was a long, arduous affair. Patsy listened to none of it. He looked around for Rita O'Brien, waiting for the inevitable retraction by the priest.

The priest said nothing about how it would end. "All is in God's hands," he said, breathing through the speaker, sending a storm of breath through the congregation. "Pray to our Blessed Mother in heaven, the intercessor of all our petitions, the patron of our parish." The priest left the altar.

The congregation looked at one another. Patsy felt a grim satisfaction. He had known this would happen. But sure, hadn't the others?

Patsy went with his father to the side altar. The priests looked through the bars of the confessionals, sitting silently, their unblinking eyes like animals watching people light candles, omniscient of all the evil of their parish. The world seemed ready for its end to Patsy. The sickness of revealing everything was followed by downturned-eyed shame for the people, vulnerable and cold. Death was what they needed. They had been coerced into revealing everything about themselves, to move through this sham requiem. They were now praying for the end of the world.

The small side altars crowded with people. The brass boxes were so full of money that people had to leave the pennies on the floor of the altar. Patsy took a small candle off a pale blue saucer and gave it to his mother.

From down in the storage room, the priests brought up all the candles. The congregation scrambled to get candles for petitions, passing around lit candles to light the others. The candles were a constellation of light that trailed up the aisles when the small altars filled.

Patsy lit his own candle and placed it beside the squat red candles of his sisters and his parents. Patsy's father moved his eyes around his family. Touching Patsy's calloused hands, he turned them over. He had never acknowledged what had been done to his son before. Patsy knew his father was ready for death. He had always wanted to die without a sin on his soul. It was the death he had prayed for. "Forgive me," he whispered.

Patsy swallowed and looked away, feeling the pressure on his hands. Even Patsy prayed for the end of the world at that moment.

At home the meal was eaten in silence. The lingering smell of incense in their clothes and the effect of mass had drained them. The rawness reminded Patsy of the nausea of a carnival ride.

The girls pulled the couch over to the fire and curled up. Patsy opened his buckle and unbuttoned the top button of his trousers. He drank the last of the tea and then stretched out before the fire. He looked at the fat of his mother's arms, his father's weak mouth, vacant and dark. They had committed their souls to another life. Sleep had fallen on them.

Patsy set two blocks and a bed of slack on the fire. Behind him, the dishes remained, the remnants of their last meal on earth, the shriveled roast guarded by a ring of potatoes. Outside the houses stood in dark rain, the beginning of a great flood? Patsy looked out into the darkness. How was it going to end? A seagull took sanctuary on the window sill, its eyes shining. Patsy felt like letting it into the house, wanting to fill the room with all of God's creation. Fiddle music drifted on the rain. He hoped death would come in sleep. His lips touched his mother's head, then he placed a hand on his father's shoulder. He tucked the blanket around his sisters. Stretching out before the fire, he knew he would not dream as his eyes closed for one last time. He whispered his last words on earth. "I am sorry for what I was, Jesus."

It was the radio next door that woke Patsy. He turned over, his shoulder blades stiff from sleeping on the floor. He sat up slowly, looking at the legs of his parents. They'd taken their shoes off during the night.

The room was still darkish. Patsy turned his head to his sisters. They were under the same blanket.

The sounds of the day filtered into the room, the hiss of tires on the wet road outside, the clank of the milk bottles being left on the porches.

It would have been good if the world had ended during the night. He hated to disturb his family. In the kitchen, he put the kettle on the boil. When he came back in, they were all awake. Nobody knew what to say. The big meal from the previous night still hung in the air.

His father worked the embers of the fire and got a small red coal and blew on it, fanning it with bits of paper. It took quickly.

Stares lingered. Patsy took the milk from the porch. The street was empty.

"Well," his father said. "Lets move the couch back then." It all seemed like a cruel joke. Were they going to die during the day, separated from one another? Patsy's mother went over to the table and cut slices of meat off the roast, wrapping them into the evening paper. Her long gray hair hung over her face. Patsy stood in front of the mirror, touching his nose, watching his mother's reflection. He went up to the bathroom and washed his face with cold water, then came down again.

The girls stayed in the room with their mother. Patsy opened the front door. A dirty day for the end of the world. God must have hated his own image to let the world run down to this horrible rainy weather. He had destroyed Sodom and Gomorrah in the Bible by fire.

Patsy pulled the collar of his coat up around his neck. His father came out of the room. "Come on." He pulled the front door closed. Patsy could hear the girls crying behind. Patsy stopped. His father shook his head. "Leave them be."

At the end of the street his father stopped. He reached for Patsy's hands and held them. He tried to say something, opening his mouth, but he turned aside and stiffened. He gripped the hands. Patsy looked away. "It's nothing, Dad, please." The hands were blistered, the calluses white from the cold. "Bastards," his father whispered, touching the knuckles deformed from years of the backs of rulers. "No, I should have done something." He showed his own hands, the leathery skin sealing hidden secrets. Patsy turned his head away. He did not want to cry. His father took it as a rejection. He let the hands go. "I knew and I did nothing. That can't be forgiven by even Him!" His father closed his eyes to hide the tears.

At lunch time, nobody wanted to go outside. Sandwiches were left on the windowsill, uneaten, half-drunk bottles of milk in doorways. The fear hung solidly as the day wore on, trying to clear up. The sun came out in patches. Patsy loitered around the toilets, smoking a cigarette with some other fellows. He felt sick thinking of how he had caused such trouble in school and drawn the beatings on himself, and now for his selfishness his own father was going to hell because he felt guilty for not standing up for his son. Patsy knew he should have said something. He shouldn't have left his father standing there like that.

Patsy went out into the yard. The place was dead silent, boys standing in a daze. The air smelt of fire. It came from down in the town. The priests came out and crossed themselves. "It has begun." The sun turned a dark orange off over the town, then the first drift of light smoke descended on the school. Embers floated in the air, pulsing a deep red, carried on the wind. The boys shielded their heads with their coats, and peered off, seeing that even the church steeples were on fire. In a few minutes, the sky billowed in dark smoke. The town was obscured. The hot smoke burned Patsy's eyes. A fallout of ash rained silently down on everyone. "We will go to the chapel to wait for Him," Father Mackey said, shivering and wheezing with the thick smoke.

Patsy went back into the toilet. It was true. The world was ending. He slumped down on the floor, curling up. His people were dead. The smoke seeped in through the doors and windows. Patsy tasted it. His faced touched the cold porcelain urinal. He had robbed his father of a good confession. His father was dead now. Who else had sinned since last night; was his father to endure purgatory alone? Patsy called out to his father as though he was haunting the earth already. There was no response. "I deserved it!" Patsy screamed. "Da, I deserved it! You couldn't have done anything!" He knew what he had to do. He opened his mouth. "You fuckin bastard, God!" His voice trembled, feeling the sin enter his soul. He would be with his father.

A priest came into the toilet and glared at Patsy on the floor. The priest blessed himself and took Patsy by the arm. "What are you saying?" He dragged Patsy away with him.

In the chapel the boys were on their knees. Father Mackey held the host from the tabernacle in his old hands. "He will enter it now in His own flesh and blood."

156

The priest with Patsy went up to the altar. He whispered something to Father Mackey. Two priests held Patsy steady. "Repent!" Father Mackey quivered. Patsy struggled. Two other priests held his arms apart. Father Mackey whispered, "In the name of the Father, I absolve you." He sprinkled holy water on Patsy, holding the tip of the cross on the tabernacle to Patsy's head. Patsy tore his arm free and slapped the tabernacle with the back of his hand. The cross cut his hand. Father Mackey collapsed and the tabernacle fell on the cold marble. "Fuck the lot of you! Let you all burn in hell!"

The congregation of boys went insane at the horror of Jesus coming down the road hearing this roaring blasphemy. Hands dragged at him, tripping him by the ankles, pulling him down into the mire of bodies, the twisted faces of desperation, boys without mothers and fathers, screaming boys waiting for Jesus to come and save them, and here was a boy who didn't care and wanted them all to die and live in hell. The entire school fell on him, grabbing his face and holding him, clasping hands over his mouth to keep him quiet, to stop the devil in him from damning them. Patsy lay deep beneath the pile.

Amidst the flames and smoke in the town, the wailing started, "Where are our sons?" a woman cried. The girls from the convent had come home dazed and confused. The men had left the factories. But where were the boys?

The people moved off towards the school. They called out their sons' names.

The school was deserted. There was vomit and blood on the floors, copybooks were flung around the place. The classrooms were empty, chalky numbers and sentences still on the blackboards, school-bags beside the desks. They saw the ark pulling in down at the docks in the study hall. Someone mentioned the last plague that had visited the House of David, the slaughter of the first-born sons. It was here again, the people left without their sons.

"We must pray!" a priest said solemnly. People were holding one another, mothers and fathers calling the names of their sons. They moved towards the chapel.

In the chapel the boys and priests hid behind the altar. The place was in darkness except for a few candles.

The men stopped outside the locked door. "Go on," someone whispered.

"It is locked," a man answered.

"Locked?" the people murmured among themselves. They sensed the presence of something within.

The men pushed the outer door, forcing the bookcase to crash against the marble floor. Then one person and then everybody began to wail the names of their boys in a great roar.

The priests and the boys huddled by the altar. "We believe in One God, the Father Almighty—" the priest cried out. The boys began saying the words.

The people heard them and shouted louder, pushing one another forward, kicking and pulling at everything. The inner door gave way.

In the study hall, the names of all the boys were read off a list by Father Mackey. The people were shaking, holding their sons. The absurdity of the day was beyond them. But the people did not dare curse or complain. It was still the day that the world was to end.

Patsy's and Gerald Taylor's names were called out over and over again. Everybody else had been accounted for. Patsy's and Taylor's fathers went down with three men to the chapel. They carried candles since the lights had been smashed inside the chapel.

The men found a body under the benches. The head was unrecognizable, it had been trampled so badly. The men turned away and blessed themselves. They looked through the rest of the shambles. They found Taylor sitting in a confessional. "Are you an angel?" Taylor wept as his father took him in his arms.

Patsy's father sat down beside the broken body. It was dark.

The men stood to the side, looking at one another. "Come on," Malloy whispered tentatively, putting his hand on Patsy's father. They brought the light on the body, moving it from the bloody face down to the huge hands clasped together. The small imprint of a cross was embedded on one of the hands. Patsy's father collapsed.

The day passed into the night and into the next day. The secret of Fatima was never revealed. It was said that the Pope fainted when he read it. He kept the secret to himself.

Patsy's funeral was held three days later, at a makeshift church down at the parish community hall. His was the only death associated with the end of the world. They did a lovely job with him. The hands were never separated. A bishop came to verify the mark of the cross on the left hand. It was pronounced a miracle. The red imprint on the hand looked as though it had been touched up. It was a perfect cross. People pressed pieces of clothing against the sign to get holy relics. They came from all over the place.

A cast was taken of the hands. The priest gave a sermon disputing the rumor that it was the thousands of candles in the churches that had set them on fire. He said, "It was a sign, a miracle. We have been given another chance. We must rebuild the temples of the Lord. We must clasp our hands like Patsy, with the faith of one who was taken to heaven, who gave us the very symbol of faith." He looked at the mahogany coffin. "We lived amidst a saint." The congregation bowed their heads. They were a holy people. The priest looked up with tears in his roving eyes, his hands clasped together like Patsy's. His mouth opened, "From now on there will be two collections at mass, until we have a sign that our work is done."

Nominated by The Antioch Review

SOLO, NEW ORLEANS

by DIANN BLAKELY SHOAF

from THE ANTIOCH REVIEW

Crossing Lake Pontchartrain, vertiginous, hands gripping the wheel,
    the bridge beneath me
swaying—I could have sworn it—as a dented maroon Ford passed,
    radio blaring,
back seat crammed with children, the Madonna stuck on its dashboard
    clutching a horseshoe
of roses. Homelife closing in, I'd scrimped for this day away,
    not expecting haze,
heat already swathing the filthy narrow streets, their beer joints

    and souvenir shops
selling beads, half-price masks after Mardi Gras, not expecting
    the fat hotel clerk's
"Don't go past Dauphin, don't go out alone at night" when I asked
    directions. Wary
at 10:00 a.m., I skittered down Bourbon, darting from strippers
    in a round-the-clock
bar, tassels swinging, siliconed and sweat-beaded breasts, again
    when I saw a man

on his knees at the corner of St. Ann begging for mercy,
    the same cry I heard
at noon mass in St. Louis Cathedral, where a woman dusk-skinned
    as Jeanne Duval sobbed
the response, her accent thick and seductive, like the coffee
    I sipped with salad,

my take-out lunch. I backed into a tiny bookstore, spotted
    a moldy volume
of Baudelaire, his willing confusions of love and disgust,

    that mistress' nipples
like rubies, syphilis blooming inside her. Hooves clopped nearby;
    a guide recited
the history of the Ursuline convent next door to couples
    lapsed in his buggy,
those stucco walls, murmur of *nones*—still I'd prayed already, purged
    to bone in shelter
and safety, and now zydeco percussed, delta blues wafted
    around the statues

in Jackson Square; a young mother balancing a cherub-cheeked,
    drooling baby dealt
Tarot cards, told a story of my life so true I tipped her
    ten dollars, replaced
my wallet with fingers that trembled, walked smack into two men
    swapping envelopes,
their knife-like stares no match for the Lady of Situations,
    her stern-eyed blessing
from a card that explained a past, while confirming the future

    was mine. "When I leave
this town . . . ," but not yet, though the cathedral bell struck its hour;
    I reversed my heels'
stiletto to sprawl on grass, sniff azaleas, watch mimes, painters,
    a shot for a film.
Humid skies haloed the city; a man asked me directions
    as if I'd lived there
always. "When I leave this town," "Cocaine, lady?," "Want a good time,
    sweet little sister?"—

if I answered, perhaps I'd remember these swells and surges
    back home, allow them
to transform a life I couldn't bid farewell. And how can we
    belong anywhere
except by peeling shrimp, drinking beer at bars then divining
    the way back to cheap

hotels, blurred copies of Baudelaire? Pigeons' stupid cooing
    finally woke me;
I rushed to make check-out time, filling two cracked glasses to rinse

    my parched mouth, throwing
matches, a sweaty nightgown in my duffle. Nearing the bridge,
    which looked more solid,
somehow, than before, I pulled over, seeing a procession
    encircling raised white
tombs, next stopping to jewel one with flowers, joined a woman
    who opened her throat
in long vowels to echo and celebrate loss in that city
    of flesh and the dead.

Nominated by William Matthews, David St. John, David Wojahn

SEX

by IRMA WALLEM

from ZYZZYVA

It was Sunday afternoon, the loveliest time of the week, and I had just come out of the reading room when Melvin asked me if I wanted a ride to my room. I decided I would rather go out into the yard for some fresh air, which was O.K. with Melvin. He is a blond man with a slight build, but he was strong enough to hold open the heavy outer door and push my wheelchair through at the same time.

We went along the walks and I admired the flowers with absolutely no idea of what was about to happen, when suddenly he said, "I'm going to put it right on the line. What I'm interested in is sex. I haven't had any since a year before my wife died, seven years ago, and that makes eight years."

Nothing in my past had quite prepared me for Melvin's problem. The men in my life had done a lot of stuff before they asked me. Or they hadn't asked. "Where do you plan to do this?" I managed to reply.

"My roommate is gone for the day," he told me. "We can go to my room."

We went in the big door and past the nurses' station. No one was around to stop us from doing what we were apparently planning to do. We headed straight for Aisle C, Room Six. He opened the door and we went in. On Melvin's side of the room there was a bed, an overstuffed chair and a big oak dresser. Since there was nothing pretty anywhere, not even so much as a plastic rose stuck in a coffee mug, I could tell it was the sort of room no woman had anything to do with.

"Do you want to sit in the chair?" he asked.

163

I explained that the chair was too low for me. I had to stay in my wheelchair. We sat facing each other. "What if a nurse comes to check on you?" I asked.

"They always knock." He seemed to have an answer for everything.

"Where have you been the last eight years?" I asked.

"I've been living with my daughter, helping her husband on their farm."

"So you didn't know many women down there? There are lots of women here, how did you happen to choose me?"

"I don't know," he said. "I just thought you'd been around the block."

"It isn't that I don't want to help you," I told him. "It's my arthritis. It takes me five minutes to lay flat in bed."

Then he truly surprised me. He stood up and leaned over my wheelchair and gave me a kiss on the lips.

"That's the way to start," I told him. "Next time you find somebody, you don't ask. You have to do a lot of stuff first, but asking isn't one of them."

"Maybe I should take you to your room," he said, looking like he'd been swatted with a newspaper. We went out the door and nobody noticed.

Before Samuel first moved in, a woman at our table acted a little doubtful when she heard that he was coming. "He's quite a ladykiller," she told us, "and he has only one hand."

I wrote a letter to my daughter, Marsha, and told her we were about to get a ladykiller in our midst. It was a pleasant thing to anticipate. Soon after, I saw a new man at the snack bar with a stub where his left hand should have been. I said, "Hello, Samuel." He looked surprised and pleased.

Next day I said, "Hello, Samuel," again, and then I asked him about his life since supper wasn't ready yet. "It'll take a while," he said. It did.

Because Samuel turned out to be hard of hearing, a two-sided conversation wasn't easy, but I soon learned that if you asked him almost any question he'd get going so fast that it wasn't easy to stop him and not too necessary to ask any more questions. I soon wished I was younger, with enough time to write his story in a novel.

Samuel's grandparents had moved to the Ukraine at the invitation of the queen, to have free land and teach the peasants how to farm, Mennonites, he told me, practically have topsoil in their blood. Then the Communists took over. They had entered Samuel's home one night, told everyone to leave, and killed the oldest son to show they weren't kidding around. Samuel's family left with all nine children, taking only what they could carry. Samuel said they "lived like dogs" for two years, until they got to Turkey, where the Mennonites were building a school. The church people contacted other Mennonites in Pennsylvania who sent $750 for boat tickets. When they got to America they found a foreclosed farm ready and waiting for them, with a pantry full of food. The Mennonites had even butchered a hog. Everything was perfect, except that two of Samuel's little sisters had died on the way.

When Samuel was 20, his father decided he needed a wife. He knew of a family of Mennonites in Canada who had four marriageable daughters. He got in touch and sort of ordered up one of them. Then Samuel went to Canada and returned with his bride. She turned out perfect in every way. They bought a farm. She saved her egg money, and he grew tobacco, and they paid off their mortgage in three years. He told me there was a write-up in the paper that had a headline reading, "Russian Farmer Shows Americans How to Farm." Nobody burned down their house, so I guess nobody got riled.

Working in the fields the day after their first baby was born, Samuel got his hand caught in the cultivator. The doctor happened to be visiting at the time, so he cut off the smashed hand and sewed up the stub. The hardest part for Samuel was that it spoiled his wife's joy in the new baby.

It all sounded romantic and wonderful, but it isn't always enjoyable to listen to men brag on their dead wives, especially if the wives were just too perfect and the men are still attractive.

One day my roommate at the time, Mamie, and I were given the job of making a big thank-you card for the free pizza served us at an outdoor lunch. I painted flowers in the corner and printed a big THANK YOU across the top. Mamie's job was to take the card around to all the residents to sign. When she came back after taking a look into every room, she told me, "Samuel has the most beautiful furniture of any room and his place is as neat as a pin."

The next time Samuel started to push me home from the snack bar, I asked if I could see his room. He hesitated a minute and then turned and headed back to C wing and pushed me inside his room, leaving the door ajar in a sort of disappointing way. There was a huge wall cabinet with mirror and shelves filled with china and figurines. It covered

165

half the wall space. "These all belonged to my wife," he said. "She liked beautiful things."

I exclaimed over the carved bed and dresser and he said, "My wife liked beautiful furniture."

He then showed me a picture of his wife and himself standing together, looking calm and happy. She had long hair, brown, parted in the middle and drawn back from a face that was neither beautiful nor homely. She was wearing a long-sleeved, blue polka-dotted dress, very plain. So this was the woman, I thought to myself, who was perfect in every way and who would come to his bed naked, Samuel told me, and slide in beside him. She had been his beloved for 59 years and he still had love left over. Gently he touched the head of a beautiful, brown-eyed German doll with a brown velvet dress. He said it was on his wife's pillow the night she died, five years before.

Feeling it was time for a change of subject, I asked him how he had happened to become a carpenter and then a contractor who had built 104 houses, all with one hand.

"My wife wanted a house," he said, and I thought to myself, "Oh dear, of course." He went to where some men were putting up a house and he stood around until they offered him a job. Then he built a house on his own and somebody liked it so well that he sold it and built his wife another house. He did that six times, until she said finally that she'd had enough of moving and wasn't going to pack everything up ever again. So Samuel built her a house with windows that looked out over the valley and there she stayed until she died.

My favorite Samuel story is the one he told about making babies. He said, "She wanted a little girl so I worked and worked and got her one. Then she wanted a boy, so I worked and got one of those for her, too. Then she wanted another boy and so I worked until she had one. Then I told her, 'You don't have to make babies when you make love.' I was afraid we wouldn't be able to send them all to college."

Samuel didn't like the food when he first came because, he told me, they didn't cook like his wife had. Nobody could quilt the way she had, either, or can preserves. Nobody could do anything half as well as she could.

I decided it was time for me to return to my own room, with its yellow painted dresser and worn-out easy chair and nothing at all perfect in any way. Samuel bent down and gave me a good smacking kiss, the kind that makes you forget about a man's perfect wife and her Best-of-

Show piccalilli relish. "If you were a little bit younger, I'd ask you to marry me," he said.

The next time my roommate was at the doctor's office and he felt free to kiss me again, he said, "I'd ask you to marry me, but I guess I'm getting a little old. I'm afraid I couldn't handle you." What he said was true, except it still would've been nice to have been married to him for maybe a week or two, until we ran out of anything new to talk about. There was still a lot of life left in his kisses. He might constantly talk about his wife's virtues, but he still seemed to have a little love left for all the other women he knew—and they knew it.

I asked him, "Do you watch television?"

He said he owned one but never watched it.

"Then who taught you how to kiss like that?"

He took my question seriously. "Nobody taught me. This is all me."

Since I had written to my daughter that Samuel was coming, and that he was known as a ladykiller, I wrote her another letter explaining that, though I had been warned, I was his first victim.

One of Samuel's best moves is the face hug. He gave one to 94-year old Viola, and she said, "I guess I'm not as old as I thought I was." I told my daughter how he gave shoulder squeezes, a new thrill with his stub where his hand had been, and how different pressures with his strong good hand seem to mean different things. When someone else got hold of the handles of my wheelchair, there wasn't the same electricity.

My daughter wrote back and asked, "Aren't there other women there as beautiful and sexy as you are, so the boys won't have to fight over you?" I said of course there were, but they weren't in wheelchairs. Not long after that, Marsha called to wish me a happy birthday and I told her, "It's happened—a new woman and she's younger and more beautiful. I don't know about sexy," I told her, "but she's very thin and is in a wheelchair." She also had been moved to our table, I told Marsha, and that she was a once-blonde person who thinks she is on vacation. Plus, she got Samuel to play Bingo, which I never could.

"You just stay in there fighting," Marsha said. "There's probably some flaw in her character."

When I wrote my next letter to Marsha, I told her how right she had been. There was no need to worry about Hilda. She had definitely not "been around the block." She had been in Chicago and San Francisco all of her life, was well educated and had been a legal secretary. She didn't tell us anything about any man in her past, she only talked about

167

her sister. She had never had a cherry coke at the corner drugstore, because she had gone to a private boarding school. She had never been bitten by a chigger or a wood tick. She had no respect for the black-eyed peas, which we know kept starvation away in Depression days, and she never heard of salt pork or huckleberry pie. She had never tasted fresh-butchered pork chops fried fast to keep the flavor. She would never think of listening to replays of the Lawrence Welk Show.

Now Jim, who was born in Oklahoma like I was, decided that we had to educate her since she'd missed out on most of the good things in life. This was an uphill battle. When Ray and I crumbled our biscuits into the white gravy, Hilda said it was gruesome. Though she is thin and has a citified sort of style, there was no standing in line to give her a push because she is a hard woman to please. Still, it was heartbreaking to hear her make plans for a future of travel and study. Samuel came over to our table, not too long after we'd heard they were "a couple," and gave her some arm squeezes, but they didn't seem to thrill her, which made up my mind right then that she was no competition. However, by then Jim was looking better and better to me and those arm squeezes had lost a little of their electricity.

Then Samuel left in order to make sure his daughter didn't run through all his money, and soon after Ted went, too, which made me sorry because he was a good conversation-starter. Plus he had the only mustache in the room. He had been to every place in the United States and told us at our table about every single one of them. Everybody else kept quiet and ate because they couldn't match his experiences. He only stayed a month, but during that time he took it as his duty to push my wheelchair whenever he could because, he said, his wife had been in a wheelchair for 15 years and he was used to them.

His place to my left was quickly taken by Frank, whose arthritis had bent him until he was hunchbacked. He was enduring great suffering, but he insisted on coming to the table and taking part in our conversation, which always is the liveliest in the dining room. We all talked about our lives and Frank said he'd been married 63 years to the same woman and had nine children. He had married when he was 18 and never had another woman.

I was the only person who answered him. "I've been married twice," I said. Then I felt a need to give him a small shock. "Twice, legal," I added.

That was the night he pushed me to my room, even though he had to use one of those four-cornered walkers. He could see, and so could

168

I, that Samuel—who was by now disappointed in Hilda's lack of romance—was heading our way from his table on the other side of the room, and that Jim also seemed inclined to give me a push, too.

Frank whispered to me, "You carry my cane and I'll push you." He grabbed the handles of my wheelchair, and I grasped his cane. The women at the other tables stared at us as we swept by. When we reached my room, Mamie, my roommate, was there ahead of us. She also stared. She had been expecting one of my usual pushers, not this man who was all bent over and panting as if we were an Olympic bob-sled team.

Frank didn't make it to breakfast next morning. I felt to blame because, as it turned out, he was hardly able to walk. At noon the nurses brought him to our table in his wheelchair. He had been in lots of pain, but he managed one of his slow smiles. He could only eat a little bit of food, but he came again that night, still in a wheelchair. He was able to wheel himself out into the reading room after supper, and I followed him on my own steam this time. I parked beside him and tried to find something to say that would make him look more cheerful, but he was deep in gloom. "I'm ready to go home to be with Jesus," he said. "I hope he calls me soon to get me out of this misery."

I reached over and patted his hand. There was so little to say, and it seemed as if I had done enough damage without getting him all fired up again. "I'd like to ask you two things," he said. I expected a mighty serious question from a man about to meet his Maker. "Did a great big man ever get on top of you?"

"No, all the men who got on top of me were small," I answered.

He nodded, letting this sink in. "Which one was the best?"

"The one with the most experience," I told him.

That night he was found dead on the floor when the nurse went in to give him his nine o'clock pills.

Now our table was all filled with women, except for Jim. This kept him busy pouring our coffee and tea, because the coffee containers we have are heavy and their tops often stick and the milk cartons are difficult for us to open. Besides, it's nice having a man do these things and Jim, who is a manly sort of man, enjoys feeling needed.

Nominated by M. D. Elevitch

EIGHTEENTH-CENTURY MEDICAL ILLUSTRATION: THE INFANT IN ITS LITTLE ROOM

by ANN TOWNSEND

from THE NORTH AMERICAN REVIEW

Little sympathy, who kicks beneath my ribs
    for comfort, the clock reads 5:10
        and I am awake. Even held inside,

lightly under water, you hear everything
    and answer back to laughing voices, high music
        and the heartbeat, unceasing:

insistent baby, whose hands press out,
    who wakes me before light,
        the house is quiet except for us.

I don't know the moment I turned
    from one to two, when I began
        to think in plural. But long ago,

before sonograms and the x-ray's touch,
    before the Doppler monitor, one man drew
        what he thought was there, cupped inside

the cradle of the pelvis: another man,
    arms outstretched, a gold ring
        on each tiny finger.

Eyes raised, he looked
    for the place where music calls,
        where he might find a new world unfolding,

all glittering candlelight,
    graceful girls and bobbing flowers.
        Little one, we have this body

to ourselves, its ticks, its murmurs.
    We have a pulse, a subtle pressure.
        It drives us forward now, in time,

a late, insistent rhythm
    that plays as background
        for the waltz you've learned to dance.

Nominated by David Baker, Marilyn Hacker, James Harms, Sherod Santos

THE NEARNESS OF
THE WORLD

fiction by STEVEN HUFF

from AMERICAN SHORT FICTION

THE HEADLIGHTS THAT came down the north hill, running the last mile into Geary Falls, seemed as remote to her as fish in a black stream. Although sometimes she worried about how visible she might be to those drivers through her trailer windows, out in the middle of the wide bottomland field. Once she bought a male mannequin at a garage sale with the notion of propping its head and shoulders in a window to delude travelers who might hope to find a woman alone. Only in late summer and early fall, when the corn on both sides of her lot was high, did she feel she had a modicum of privacy.

But on this warm night in early July, when the muddy corn was only knee-high, she watched every pair of light beams, though she tried not to; she tried to watch television and drink her soda, but always involuntarily she turned again. Then she heard a singing of brakes as a car turned too quickly into the driveway, kicking up stones, its high beams filling her lattice windows. She went out on the roofless porch and stood with her fingertips pressed into the tight pockets of her jeans as he got out of the car with a carrying bag. "Can you manage it all, or you need help?" she asked.

"Would you get this?" he answered.

She stepped out on the driveway and took his bag. And as he handed it over, he dropped his eyes in a characteristic expression of his in which he seemed to be looking down into his beard. At the door she turned and saw he was pulling one of two large boxes from his back seat. He lugged them inside one by one along with another smaller box, and set them on the kitchen table, filling the surface. "I guess I could move the books later," he said. "But I don't really think there's enough room for them here."

"Sure there is," she said, with disappointment in her voice. "We'll make room. You know that."

He lugged the boxes into the tiny second bedroom where her sewing machine had been, which she had moved to her kitchen-living room in anticipation of the equipment Gray was bringing.

"I didn't start dinner because I didn't know when you'd be getting here," she said. "So I figured I'd just order a pizza."

Gray looked up from the floor of the little room where he was squatting next to the largest of the boxes and smiled broadly. "Thanks, Eileen," he said. "But I've eaten. You go ahead."

She didn't go ahead, though. She didn't want to order a whole pizza for herself; not even a small one. There was something too communal about pizza, which was why she never ordered one when she was alone. Instead, she stood in the doorway and watched him work, determinedly setting up his equipment in a new room with unfamiliar electric outlets. The computer came out of its box first, then the monitor, and finally the printer with a nest of wires attached to a surge strip: a maze she believed she could never have figured out even with an instruction book. How odd this all was—she would have expected him to bring a typewriter. Perhaps an old manual Royal like her own would be right. But, a poet with a computer!

"You can put your books in here, too," she said, envisioning the bookcases she had never seen because she had never been to the city house where his apartment had been. "More can go in the living room and more in the bedroom if you want."

He sat back on his buttocks with his thin knees up to his chin, pushing two plugs into the wall outlet and smiling up at her again. He hadn't kissed her when he came in, and perhaps, she thought, he was realizing that now. But there was such haste about him. She wondered, was he even staying the night?

"To tell you the truth, I've got more books than you could fit into this whole trailer," he said.

"Then what'll we do?"

"Dunno, my dear."

He leapt up suddenly with a look on his face that frightened her back into the hallway, but he caught her in a hug. "You got the wine, didn't you?" he asked.

"Yes."

"Bordeaux?"

In fact, she had—a dusty bottle from a low shelf at Quaterman's Spirits in Geary Falls. The price had stunned her, a good half of what she paid for groceries some weeks. But she plunked the money on the counter anyway. How could she do less when her life was about to improve so immeasurably?

"Good," Gray said. "Because we're going to need it after." And he drew her lips up into his, and bumped her into the plywood sliding door of her bedroom—theirs now—knocking it off its thin metal track.

He had forgotten that his car doors were still open and the dome light was on, which during the night, would run his already weak battery down, and she would have to give him a jump start in the morning from her old slant-six Dodge.

*

The cost for poetry classes had come close to being an insurmountable obstacle for Eileen Shepherd. Funded by a Rural Outreach Grant from the state of New York, they still carried a hundred-dollar registration fee. She finally got seventy-five of it by selling her ex-husband's Fender amplifier that she had been using in her bedroom for a nightstand. "Too bad, Shep," she mumbled to his absent spirit as she tucked the money into her jeans, watching a teenage boy lug the amp away from her trailer. The classes were to be held in the Nordhoff Community Center in Kliner, the Loggins County seat, on three mornings in June, part of a series of workshops in the arts.

The advertising poster, which she had found on the wall of the laundromat one night in April, gave her an inkling of depression. She had no clue who the instructor Gray Carter was. But she had decided she wanted to be a poet. She couldn't remember what had instigated her to declare herself—privately and inwardly—for that nebulous profession, but after years of stupefying menial work she had felt instantly lifted in spirit when she had. Sure, she told herself, why the hell not? Didn't she have a wealth of living experience? Hadn't she criss-crossed the floor of hell a hundred ways in her twenty-eight years, working since her last divorce in a crappy outlet store in the middle of a nowhere county; living in a tin trailer with leaky windows in the summer, frozen pipes in the winter, and a toilet that didn't flush when the bottomland became permeated with spring runoff? Hadn't she learned to live with dizzy spells and collections calls and yet still laugh at herself? And what did all that give you—if you survived—but poetry? Her three-ring binder of verse written in bed had swelled to four inches thick. There had to be a nugget of epiphany in some couplet, on one of those pages. If she could see it she could learn to make an art of the accident that made it.

The first morning of the workshop Eileen drove her Dodge out of the driveway under a cloudburst of such force that the mud danced among the new corn shoots. She arrived twenty minutes early, intensely nervous, and sat on a wooden bench inside the building as four elderly women also gathered. One of them had blue hair and eyed Eileen with something like disdain, perhaps for her willowy body and long reddish-brown hair, or for her casual top that exposed three inches of her belly. But none of them spoke to her, and she was afraid to talk to them. Then Mrs. Hartley from the Arts for Loggins County office arrived and unlocked the classroom and plugged in the coffee urn.

The same prudential silence resumed around the table in the room until they heard the outer door of the community center again, and the sound of heavy feet clomping over the wood floor. Through the inner doorway came a bearded, graying man with a wild smile across his gaunt face, disarming the tightness in the room. "I'm Gray Carter," he announced. Later she would remember how thin his arms were in his short-sleeved shirt as he set five folders and a couple of books on the table. His eyes seemed both feral and ascetic, and he often closed them as he spoke as if out of an overwhelming modesty. The folders contained the packets of poems that each of the students had nervously submitted to him through the arts office three weeks before.

"All right," he began, after some preliminaries in which each student introduced herself. "This is a mixed group, I think. By that I mean that we have one or two who have apparently been writing some time, and others who seem—I stress the word 'seem'—to be new at it. Or at least, new to poetry. However, I think we can accommodate everyone, and give each a little of the encouragement we need" —(and he smiled wryly)—"to go forward with this thankless, uncalled-for, and yet absolutely necessary art."

She wondered which category he perceived her to be in. Hell, she had only a year and a half of college behind her. But that first morning reassured her, as Gray read samples from the packets and led the critical discussion. Most of them had never sallied beyond the old themes of Jesus, flowers, and grandmother's rhubarb recipes. Most of them, he would later tell Eileen, grumpily, "wouldn't know a poem if it crawled up her leg." But he worked hard with them and was gracious, though Eileen knew—and she knew the others knew and resented it—that he favored her work, and favored her.

One of the old women seemed a more serious writer, and viewed the attention Gray gave Eileen with sardonic humor. Her name was Helen Weir. She was the only one who was already familiar with his work, making reference to one of his poems that had appeared in the January issue of *American Poetry Review*. Eileen knew that she had to get acquainted with Helen—she needed writing friends—if she hoped to keep up her determination after this teacher was gone.

She'd never felt so good, so energized. For those three days Eileen lived for the classes, felt buoyant when they were over, and couldn't make herself go home to her trailer afterward but instead went to diners and bars, just to stall her return. She tried to engage Helen in conversation after class while Gray made his rapid exit (driving back to Syracuse University), but the woman seemed absorbed and busy. On the second evening Eileen drove to Binghamton to a plaza bookstore that she knew carried poetry and bought a copy of *Breaking Bread: Poems by Gray Carter*. But they were hard poems, full of puzzling references. When class opened the final morning she gave it to him to inscribe for her. It threw him off balance at first.

"Where did you get that?" one of the women asked, startled and apparently jealous.

Gray held it for a moment and then said, "Perhaps I could do it when the class is over. I'd do it better justice then. Would that be all right?"

Instead of ending at noon, the last class ran until one o'clock, when Gray suddenly hoisted a paper bag to the table and ripped it open. It was a two-liter jug of cheap red wine.

"Now, I prefer to end my workshops with a bit of merriment," he said, "so that we may all part ways warm in our blood and warm in our memory."

It caused an unexpected stir. Two of the women snorted at him and left. Helen and a fourth woman stayed for half a Dixie cup of wine before thanking him and excusing themselves. Eileen was astonished to be where she was now, alone in a room with a poet, a real poet, drinking wine. This kind of thing didn't happen to women in Geary Falls, nor in Kliner for that matter. As they talked, boys came into the outer room of the building and hauled the town's baseball equipment outside where a loud game was starting, but they were only shadows. She told him about her two marriages and listened to the stories of his three (the last of which had ended the previous winter) and to all his complaints about his publisher, who had released *Breaking Bread* two years before but wouldn't schedule his next book for another three years. They were deliberately stalling his career, he grumbled, reddening in the face, and he was bitter for having signed such a contract. For Eileen, it seemed a dazzling privilege in her tough life to be let in on such information blurted by one whom she now realized was among the finest poets writing in English—a blurb on the jacket of his book had said so. Jittery, she almost forgot to hand him the book again to sign.

"Oh, it pops up again," he giggled, and flipped it open to the title page. "You know, I'm not good at this. Especially when I like the student, and the student is doing some very good writing, and I want to say something particularly . . . meaningful."

He shut his eyes again, and she said, laughing, "You want me to look the other way while you do it?"

"Yes."

She went into the outer room, leaned on a Ping-Pong table for a minute, and then went to the women's room to brush her hair. When she returned her heart plummeted as she saw him gathering his things, stuffing the bottle in his canvas bag.

When he saw her, he said, "Mrs. . . . uh, Hartley—is that her name?—will be coming and locking up this little room here. So . . . why don't we go to lunch?"

He was lifting her out of what had been an ugly, spiritless seven years. Growing ridiculously enthusiastic about the rolling drumlins and black muckland as they drove, he began to give color back to a landscape that had been lifeless and remote for all the time since the beginning of her first marriage to a body-shop worker with three children from a previous wife. Gray made the world come near to her again, where she could see and feel herself a part of it. None of her husbands or lovers had done that; none of them could have understood the need. None.

He went back after that, back to the environs of Syracuse University where he taught, though he had the summer off and mentioned vague travel plans. She was left wildly restless and began packing to move, somewhere, anywhere. But she unpacked again the first time he phoned her. She was astonished and unsettled to hear his voice betray loneliness, almost a helplessness. He began driving down to spend weekends with her. Far from the most skillful lover she had ever had—his skinny gray body seemed to nearly break in her clutches—he was still the most intriguing, and for a while that made him the most satisfying. Weeknights between visits she worked hard on her poems, and read them aloud to him on Saturday mornings in bed. He didn't mind the cramped little trailer, though the lack of a visual barrier from a mile of bottomland highway unsettled him, and so when they were outside he preferred the back lawn.

Finally he dumbfounded her by suggesting that he move in with her. It would be a long drive to his job at SU when fall came, and the winter drive, she warned him, would be treacherous; but he seemed not to care about those variables. Anyway, he told her, he wanted the quiet country of Loggins County to allow the bedlam from his divorce to settle out of his spirit and begin to write again.

*

He seemed frantic in the morning about his dead battery. She drove the front of her car up to his and joined them with jumper cables, a little surprised that he didn't know how to do it himself. Rain during the night had left a mist on the fields that would be burned off by the sun in a couple of hours. She had to be to work in twenty-five minutes, and she hadn't showered yet, which meant she was going to miss breakfast. That wouldn't matter except that she had skipped supper the night before and her stomach was growling.

"Let the car run awhile and charge your battery up," she told him as she went back inside to shower.

At one o'clock she called home to check in with him, but got her own answering machine. Then, since she hadn't taken time to pack a sandwich, she broke her recent resolution against extravagance and went out to lunch. She was startled when she saw Gray in a back booth, reading a book and eating a large pizza. The man seemed able to eat enormous quantities of anything without gaining weight—it just became wiry energy. He shared the pizza with her, but he seemed annoyed by her interruption.

"I thought you'd be writing," she said.

"Yes, I was," he said irritably. "But it's too hot in the goddamned trailer. It's worse than India."

"Oh," she answered, "Well, we can get a fan. We'll go out and get one tonight."

He nodded and went back to his book.

It was a difficult, tropical afternoon. The store's air-conditioning was broken, and the half-dozen fans that employees had brought in barely moved the leaden air. Eileen sweated profusely until her hair was a mass of strings and she smelled like a homeless woman; so she tied her hair back before she went home. To her great surprise and relief she found him in a jovial mood, almost silly, coming in from the backyard with iced tea. He demanded that she take him immediately across the field to the woods and introduce him to the swimming hole that she had told him about.

So they went, though she was starving, and they had a cool, reviving swim in Kennicutt Creek, naked and satisfied to be together alone. Back at the trailer he surprised her by cooking an exotic Risotto Milanese, cracking a tube of saffron over the pearly Italian rice and serving it with mussels and martinis.

She hardly knew how to eat it. "Where'd you get all this stuff?" she asked.

"It can be had if you drive a little way. We've got to get you out of this hamburger-and-pizza rut that people seem to be in down here."

He had been everywhere: Europe, Africa, Israel, India, Australia, Iceland, Alaska, Mexico, Belize, and Guatemala—drinking, carousing, and occasionally teaching. He had a continuously revealing list of friends and acquaintances—writers, luminaries whom he casually brought up in conversation, most of the same people whose books he pushed on her. And it chilled her to think a time might come when she would answer the phone and one of those titans would be on the line looking for him. But she believed he had no notion, no glimmer of an idea of how he and all his vast influence and experience were altering her life.

"Oh sure, he didn't," Helen would say later, trying not to smile. But she couldn't help it. And opening Eileen's copy of *Breaking Bread,* she read the inscription in a quiet, toneless voice: " 'Best wishes, Gray'." Eileen knew she was thinking that a lover—even just a prospective lover as he had been at that moment—should have written something more. She knew Helen was also thinking that a man like Gray who had never brought his books along, leaving most of them in storage, had never actually moved in.

179

She had learned from his flares of temper not to bother him during the daytime—his writing time—and so she stopped calling home at lunch, even to leave a message on the tape. So she was unsettled one afternoon in August when he walked into the outlet store, purchased a T-shirt, and asked her if she had any plans for the evening—teasingly, as if he had ever noticed her making any particular plans independent of him.

With a little hope as sweat poured down her front, she asked, "Is this a swimming night?"

"Well," he said, "I got a call from my friend Bob Murmer. You know, Robert Murmer the poet?" No, she didn't, but she nodded. "He's at Syracuse in the department with me," Gray explained. "And I suggested we go up and meet him for dinner. Tomorrow's Saturday, right? That means we can come in tonight as late as we want."

She was ebullient, and bought a new top off the rack that she couldn't afford, even though it was a second. And when she drove in the driveway—the corn was neck-high now, giving the trailer the ambience of a jungle home—she found him about to put a quart of oil into his car, into the radiator. She stopped him just in time.

It was the mildest chiding she gave him: "My God, Gray! Don't they have cars on your home planet?"

But his eyes blackened with anger and he stalked into the trailer. She was left with the full oil can and the hood up. She poured it into the oil intake and then slammed the hood down so hard that she wondered if she had jammed it. She was hot and sticky, she needed a damned beer, and he was threatening to blow a night out she wanted like a fortune in gold futures. So she went inside and tugged his new T-shirt from behind and apologized, inducing him to talk again, to kiss her, and finally to laugh. How like Mick the body-shop man, and Shep the county road foreman (her second husband) he was. Sometimes the only difference was that Mick and Shep had never heard of most of the dishes he liked to cook, and probably would turn their noses up at them anyway, if not also at the chef. Other times the difference was so profound that he made her feel like she'd been living half born before he came along and raved to four elderly witches about the power of her best lines of poetry; as though he had raised her heart up above their heads in his two cupped hands.

180

But this night was not to be like she expected. They met Professor Murmer at his home in a shady section of Syracuse, where she shook hands with the little nasal-voiced man who seemed to look right past her. Introducing her, Gray said, "She's got some of the strongest work I've ever seen in a young poet, and all she's got is half a community college education, Bob. It just goes to show you." Murmer seemed to think that was very funny. And for a moment she hated them both.

They went to a crowded restaurant near the campus where, rather than talking about poetry and poets and reminiscing about other writers as she was desperate to hear them do, they talked about their computers. Their computers! She was uncomfortable with Murmer's squinting questions whenever Gray left the table. He seemed amused by what she did for a living, clerking in an outlet store, and wondered aloud what she could have done to "lure" his old friend to the "wilderness." She woke up on a couch in an unfamiliar room in the wee hours of the morning, near a gurgling fish tank with no Gray in sight anywhere. She was drunk; there had been nothing else for her to do but drink.

*

The fall semester began. Gray was driving to Syracuse three mornings each week and returning late. At home, his edginess seemed peculiar, had an odor to it. She was unable to write now when they were both home—Tuesday and Thursday nights and weekends—and she hadn't shown him a new poem for more than five weeks. When he'd read her last one, he was impatient with what he said was her overuse of simile. "A sumac is a goddamn sumac," he snapped. "It has its own identity. It has nothing whatever to do with your heart and ovaries."

She led him out in the field one warm evening to the rows of sweet corn near the woods and showed him how to distinguish the edible ears from the vast acres of feed corn by their tassels. "He won't mind if you pick some?" he asked, referring to the farmer who owned the fields.

"Nah," she laughed. "I slept with him twice. That ought to be enough for a lifetime of corn, don't you think?" Eileen was referring to a brief relationship between her two marriages that Gray already knew about.

But somehow he didn't like it. " You eat the corn then," he grumbled and began to walk away.

181

But she was in no mood to run after him now. "I got another idea," she told him. "Let's have a corn roast on Saturday night? Invite your friends from the college? What do you say?"

She hadn't expected him to agree, but he did, and she was excited. They picked six dozen ears on Saturday morning. She showed him how to soak them in a tub of water, dig a pit, and get a slow fire going that would build up a fortune in coals by evening. One car arrived at six-thirty, half an hour after they had told guests to come, navigating in the long, stony driveway towered on both sides by the high corn. It was Murmer with a heavy, painted woman in a sack dress who wore a be-jeweled engagement ring. No one else came.

With the acres of corn at peak growth, the trailer and its backyard were like a secret place. Murmer was in a jollier, friendlier mood, even complimenting Eileen on the corn. And the woman—an SU instructor named Sandy—though she acted abrasive at first, turned out to be a pleasant woman who seemed to like her redneck hostess. They ate enormous quantities of corn, as though they had to make up for the crowds who didn't show, while ears that no one could eat smoldered on the coals and filled the air with a distinct smell of harvest burn. The two women wandered off together in the dark field to the creek. Eileen brought a mosquito torch along and plunged its stem into the ground next to a fallen tree that they sat on together near the water.

Sandy sucked on a beer. "So, how the hell did you get together with Gray?" she asked abruptly.

"He was my teacher for three days."

"Oh God! He was always doing that."

"Doing what?" Eileen asked irritably. She had met few academics in her life, and she was soured on these three already, and suddenly ready to push this one into the creek.

"Falling in love with a student," Sandy pronounced. Then she looked at Eileen in the moonlight and said, "Oh, don't be pissed. He loves you, or he wouldn't have been here this long. I won't guarantee he'll hang around forever. But he must be happy to be here."

The heavy woman was out of breath from the short walk. She drew on her cigarette—she had smoked constantly since she arrived—mingling her smoke with the hissing vapor from the mosquito torch.

"I won't shit you," she continued. "I'm in a position to know when he's in love. He divorced me last year." Then she laughed.

Eileen grabbed her chubby arm with both of her hands, not as though she were about to hurt her, but as though she needed suddenly to hang on.

"Christ, you're young yet," Sandy told her, seeming not to feel Eileen's clutch. "You can deal with it. I'm getting ready to retire in two more years, if I live that long. I need a fucking rest."

Eileen could hear the wild laughing of Gray and Murmer far away in the yard, like wild horses. It seemed everything was a joke to those two. And why shouldn't it be, she thought, to men who had never been trapped in a valley, in a mill store? Who had yodeled over the hilltops and cityscapes of the world? Who knew how to hook up a computer, but not to put oil in an engine? Who could prepare escargot, but couldn't cook corn? Who could give you triple entendre, but could not say, simply, "Excuse me"? Sure, they were as right as anyone could be—life was a leg-pull, a comedy of stimulations. Sandy coughed and spat, throwing her cigarette out into the swimming hole.

*

Helen bought slippers. Eileen surmised by the way she barely looked at them that she didn't need them, that she only wanted to visit. They went to lunch together and, as it happened, were given the same back booth of the pizza parlor where she had discovered Gray sitting ten weeks before. Helen was widowed—that didn't surprise Eileen. And had written books of poetry—three of them, in fact—which did surprise her. The second of the three, *The Furies,* had gained some attention in the 1950s, which quickly faded in the 1960s after the ill-received *The Earth Turns with the Searcher.*

She told Eileen that she came to Loggins County with her husband from Boston after he suffered a nervous breakdown, and her writing career was shelved. They had also lived in London, Brussels, and Berlin while he worked for the U.S. State Department, though she never really knew what he did for them. They bought a small, fallow farm where they raised nothing but roses and rhubarb. Gardening was almost the first thing she had truly shared with her husband other than sex and dinner. Roses and rhubarb became an obsession of reclaiming love missed.

Now Eileen understood the poem about a woman searching through old scrapbooks for her grandmother's rhubarb recipes, which had sounded so banal in the workshop. "You should have said more in that poem," she blurted, though she thought it would have been better not to mention it. "We would have understood it then." She was afraid of offending yet another accomplished poet.

But Helen nodded in agreement. "That was a problem for a long time. When he was still alive I couldn't finish that poem—he would have been so wounded. The same is true of a lot of my other poems. Now maybe I can finish them. I needed the impetus to get started again, and that's why I joined the workshop."

They met several times on Gray's moody Saturdays. Helen had now become the one Eileen brought her poems to, a writing friend. One Saturday, when she rushed home about six o'clock to start dinner, the corn was almost completely harvested, the acres around the trailer denuded. Far away she could see Craig, her old flame, a nub on the tractor seat. Gray's car wasn't there, and when she went in she noticed an eerie difference—things were misplaced or weren't there. She rushed to the little room and saw that the computer and all the related equipage were gone.

Some wine was left in the cupboard, a little Vouvray, which she had learned to like from Gray, and a red that she couldn't pronounce. And two pieces of pizza in the refrigerator that she'd brought home from a party at work, which she sprinkled capers over. She ate her simple, funny dinner at the table and watched the tractor from the window stripping the fields all the way to the wooded hills. She was letting the shock—or surprise, really, more than shock—take its effect on her slowly, and almost peacefully.

There was the black muckland in the rutted rows, which next year she had heard would be planted with cabbage. The woods were brown; and there was the stark, gasoline smell of the growling John Deere that sent up clouds of blue smoke. Cars were coming down the hill, beginning to turn on their lights in the falling dark. All was near, real as the food on her plate.

Nominated by Kim Edwards

FILM NOIR: TRAIN TRIP OUT OF METROPOLIS

by LYNN EMANUEL

from ANTIOCH REVIEW

We're headed for empty-headedness,
the featureless amnesias of Idaho, Montana, Nevada,
states rich only in vowel sounds and alliteration.
We're taking the train so we can see into the heart
of the heart of America framed in the windows' cool
oblongs of light. We want cottages, farmhouses
with peaked roofs leashed by wood smoke to the clouds;
we want the golden broth of sunlight ladled over
ponds and meadows. We've never seen a meadow.
Now, we want to wade into one—up to our chins in the grassy
welter—the long reach of our vision grabbing up great
handfuls and armloads of scenery, our eyes at the clouds
white sale, our eyes at the bargain basement give away
of clods and scat and cow pies. We want to feel half
of America to the left of us and half to the right, ourselves
like a spine dividing the book in two, ourselves holding
the whole great story together.

And then, suddenly, the train pulls into the station,
and the scenery begins to creep forward—a friendly but timid tribe.
The ramshackle shapes of Main, the old-fashioned cars dozing
at the ribbon of curb, the mongrel hound loping across a stretch

of unpaved road, the medals of the Lions and Chamber of
    Commerce
pinned on the town's chest, the street lights on their long stems,
the little park, the trolley, the faint bric-a-brac of park stuff:
bum on the bench, boy with the ball come closer and closer.
Then the pleasantly sinister swell of the soundtrack tapers
to a long wail. The noise of a train gathers momentum
and disappears into the distance leaving us stranded here,
and our names are strolling across the landscape in the crisply
voluminous script of the opening credits, as though these were
our signatures on the contract, as though we were the authors of this
    story.

Nominated by William Matthews

VIDEOTAPE

fiction by DON DeLILLO

from ANTAEUS

Iᴛ sʜᴏᴡs ᴀ ᴍᴀɴ driving a car. It is the simplest sort of family video. You see a man at the wheel of a medium Dodge.

It is just a kid aiming her camera through the rear window of the family car at the windshield of the car behind her.

You know about families and their video cameras. You know how kids get involved, how the camera shows them that every subject is potentially charged, a million things they never see with the unaided eye. They investigate the meaning of inert objects and dumb pets and they poke at family privacy. They learn to see things twice.

It is the kid's own privacy that is being protected here. She is twelve years old and her name is being withheld even though she is neither the victim nor the perpetrator of the crime but only the means of recording it.

It shows a man in a sport shirt at the wheel of his car. There is nothing else to see. The car approaches briefly, then falls back.

You know how children with cameras learn to work the exposed moments that define the family cluster. They break every trust, spy out the undefended space, catching Mom coming out of the bathroom in her cumbrous robe and turbaned towel, looking bloodless and plucked. It is not a joke. They will shoot you sitting on the pot if they can manage a suitable vantage.

The tape has the jostled sort of noneventness that marks the family product. Of course the man in this case is not a member of the family but a stranger in a car, a random figure, someone who has happened along in the slow lane.

It shows a man in his forties wearing a pale shirt open at the throat, the image washed by reflections and sunglint, with many jostled moments.

It is not just another video homicide. It is a homicide recorded by a child who thought she was doing something simple and maybe halfway clever, shooting some tape of a man in a car.

He sees the girl and waves briefly, wagging a hand without taking it off the wheel—an underplayed reaction that makes you like him.

It is unrelenting footage that rolls on and on. It has an aimless determination, a persistence that lives outside the subject matter. You are looking into the mind of home video. It is innocent, it is aimless, it is determined, it is real.

He is bald up the middle of his head, a nice guy in his forties whose whole life seems open to the hand-held camera.

But there is also an element of suspense. You keep on looking not because you know something is going to happen—of course you do know something is going to happen and you do look for that reason but you might also keep on looking if you came across this footage for the first time without knowing the outcome. There is a crude power operating here. You keep on looking because things combine to hold you fast—a sense of the random, the amateurish, the accidental, the impending. You don't think of the tape as boring or interesting. It is crude, it is blunt, it is relentless. It is the jostled part of your mind, the film that runs through your brain under all the thoughts you know you're thinking.

The world is lurking in the camera, already framed, waiting for the boy or girl who will come along and take up the device, learn the instrument, shooting old Granddad at breakfast, all stroked out so his nostrils gape, the cereal spoon baby-gripped in his pale fist.

It shows a man alone in a medium Dodge. It seems to go on forever.

There's something about the nature of the tape, the grain of the image, the sputtering black-and-white tones, the starkness—you think this is more real, truer-to-life than anything around you. The things around you have a rehearsed and layered and cosmetic look. The tape is superreal, or maybe underreal is the way you want to put it. It is what lies at the scraped bottom of all the layers you have added. And this is another reason why you keep on looking. The tape has a searing realness.

It shows him giving an abbreviated wave, stiff-palmed, like a signal flag at a siding.

You know how families make up games. This is just another game in which the child invents the rules as she goes along. She likes the idea of videotaping a man in his car. She has probably never done it before and she sees no reason to vary the format or terminate early or pan to another car. This is her game and she is learning it and playing it at the same time. She feels halfway clever and inventive and maybe slightly intrusive as well, a little bit of brazenness that spices any game.

And you keep on looking. You look because this is the nature of the footage, to make a channeled path through time, to give things a shape and a destiny.

Of course if she had panned to another car, the right car at the precise time, she would have caught the gunman as he fired.

The chance quality of the encounter. The victim, the killer, and the child with a camera. Random energies that approach a common point. There's something here that speaks to you directly, saying terrible things about forces beyond your control, lines of intersection that cut through history and logic and every reasonable layer of human expectation.

She wandered into it. The girl got lost and wandered clear-eyed into horror. This is a children's story about straying too far from home. But it isn't the family car that serves as the instrument of the child's curiosity, her inclination to explore. It is the camera that puts her in the tale.

You know about holidays and family celebrations and how somebody shows up with a camcorder and the relatives stand around and barely react because they're numbingly accustomed to the process of being taped and decked and shown on the VCR with the coffee and cake.

He is hit soon after. If you've seen the tape many times you know from the handwave exactly when he will be hit. It is something, naturally, that you wait for. You say to your wife, if you're at home and she is there, Now here is where he gets it. You say, Janet, hurry up, this is where it happens.

Now here is where he gets it. You see him jolted, sort of wire-shocked—then he seizes up and falls toward the door or maybe leans or slides into the door is the proper way to put it. It is awful and unremarkable at the same time. The car stays in the slow lane. It approaches briefly, then falls back.

You don't usually call your wife over to the TV set. She has her programs, you have yours. But there's a certain urgency here. You want her to see how it looks. The tape has been running forever and now the thing is finally going to happen and you want her to be here when he's shot.

Here it comes, all right. He is shot, head-shot, and the camera reacts, the child reacts—there is a jolting movement but she keeps on taping, there is a sympathetic response, a nerve response, her heart is beating faster but she keeps the camera trained on the subject as he slides into the door and even as you see him die you're thinking of the girl. At some level the girl has to be present here, watching what you're watching, unprepared—the girl is seeing this cold and you have to marvel at the fact that she keeps the tape rolling.

It shows something awful and unaccompanied. You want your wife to see it because it is real this time, not fancy movie violence—the realness beneath the layers of cosmetic perception. Hurry up, Janet, here it comes. He dies so fast. There is no accompaniment of any kind. It is very stripped. You want to tell her it is realer than real but then she will ask what that means.

The way the camera reacts to the gunshot—a startled reaction that brings pity and terror into the frame, the girl's own shock, the girl's identification with the victim.

You don't see the blood, which is probably trickling behind his ear and down the back of his neck. The way his head is twisted away from the door, the twist of the head gives you only a partial profile and it's the wrong side, it's not the side where he was hit.

And maybe you're being a little aggressive here, practically forcing your wife to watch. Why? What are you telling her? Are you making a little statement? Like I'm going to ruin your day out of ordinary spite. Or a big statement? Like this is the risk of existing. Either way you're rubbing her face in this tape and you don't know why.

It shows the car drifting toward the guardrail and then there's a jostling sense of two other lanes and part of another car, a split-second blur, and the tape ends here, either because the girl stopped shooting or because some central authority, the police or the district attorney or the TV station, decided there was nothing else you had to see.

This is either the tenth or eleventh homicide committed by the Texas Highway Killer. The number is uncertain because the police believe that one of the shootings may have been a copycat crime.

And there is something about videotape, isn't there, and this particular kind of serial crime? This is a crime designed for random taping and immediate playing. You sit there and wonder if this kind of crime became more possible when the means of taping and playing an event—playing it immediately after the taping—became part of the culture. The principal doesn't necessarily commit the sequence of crimes in order to see them taped and played. He commits the crimes as if they were a form of taped-and-played event. The crimes are inseparable from the idea of taping and playing. You sit there thinking that this is a crime that has found its medium, or vice versa—cheap mass production, the sequence of repeated images and victims, stark and glary and more or less unremarkable.

It shows very little in the end. It is a famous murder because it is on tape and because the murderer has done it many times and because the crime was recorded by a child. So the child is involved, the Video Kid as she is sometimes called because they have to call her something. The tape is famous and so is she. She is famous in the modern manner of people whose names are strategically withheld. They are famous without names or faces, spirits living apart from their bodies, the victims and witnesses, the underage criminals, out there somewhere at the edges of perception.

Seeing someone at the moment he dies, dying unexpectedly. This is reason alone to stay fixed to the screen. It is instructional, watching a man shot dead as he drives along on a sunny day. It demonstrates an elemental truth, that every breath you take has two possible endings. And that's another thing. There's a joke locked away here, a note of cruel slapstick that you are completely willing to appreciate. Maybe the victim's a chump, a dope, classically unlucky. He had it coming, in a way, like an innocent fool in a silent movie.

You don't want Janet to give you any crap about it's on all the time, they show it a thousand times a day. They show it because it exists, because they have to show it, because this is why they're out there. The horror freezes your soul but this doesn't mean that you want them to stop.

Nominated by David Wojahn

SEIZURE

by LINDA BIERDS

from FIELD

When his eyes took the half-sheened stillness of fish roe,
he tightened his helmet, cinched its inner cap of
canvas straps until the dome above wobbled, swayed
with a life of its own. We were not to touch him,
he said, but wait on the sidewalk until his soul returned.
His hat had a decal that captured light
or hissed out a glow when the light diminished. We were
not to touch him, but watch the ballet of his arcing arm
as he opened the fish, the chum and ponderous king,
flushing the hearts, the acorns of spleen. We were young
together, fourteen or fifteen, and still he returned
to the fish houses, his sharp hands working the knives,
disappearing in flaps of cream-tipped flesh that
closed like a shawl. He showed us the opaque archings
of ribs, brought into our schoolroom the weightless gills,
book-pressed and dried, the spine he had saved that
snapped apart into tiny goblets. We saw him one night
fallen by the river—saw the light from his helmet,
that is, lurching in the long grasses, slicing its
terrible path like a moth grown fat and luminous:
if what flashed there could be seen as a body,
could be stopped in the human hand.

Nominated by Andrew Hudgins, David Wojahn

BAD

by FREDERICK BUSCH

from PLOUGHSHARES

In THE PRACTICE of my trade, as writer and teacher, I lie by omission, I sometimes think, as much as I tell the truth. I note, for an eager, untalented first-year student, that her story is *interesting,* that it *shows terrific energy,* that *there's some marvelous insight here* into waking up hungover on Saturday morning after a debauched night at ATO. At summer writers' conferences, I am not about to tell a seventy-year-old woman that her personal diaries, recorded since World War II and bound in leather, need to be buried or burned before she can think to write what consumes her, the story of her life. In book reviews, it is unusual when you or I say, outright, that a book by one of our colleagues is ordinarily lousy.

Mercy is all to the good, and maybe it's another name for being afraid—often for obvious, sometimes honorable, reasons—of telling what seems to be the truth. But sometimes I find myself, as I read a set of essays for school, or put down a stranger's galleys after not many pages, wanting to stand, and flap my featherless wings, and howl that, goddammit, this is outright bad. I've been thinking about what constitutes badness, and reflecting on the pleasures of announcing its presence in the room.

Bad, I recall, was once good. In novels and poems—and especially at poetry readings—of the fifties and early sixties, to call a musician or writer bad was to say he was excellent beyond words. Because jazz was the music of the revolution, and because the best musicians were black or admirably, like Gerry Mulligan, blackened in their art, the sense of life as protest, the sighing song about being Beat, was punctuated by what used to be called negritude. When one was good at being in a state of protest, at being, through one's art, not only accomplished (conventionally good) but also avant-garde and crazy with this life and showing it, one was bad (*un*conventionally good). Norman Mailer wanted the badness of *The White Negro* but wasn't, he might in his sixties admit of himself in the sixties, good enough.

If you're bad, nowadays, you no longer swing: you dance to rap, you fight the power by wearing angry T-shirts and by doing what, if you're white, you think black people do. If you're black and smart, like Stanley Crouch or Ernest J. Gaines or Toni Morrison or David Bradley, you've been watching the white folk strive to be bad while you've labored to make your work as good as you can.

Bad, in other words, is protest-and-Perrier unless the badness takes place in the real arenas of race—the streets or the voting booth or sometimes the page. People who call themselves or others bad, in that old-fashioned sense, are no longer good enough to get away with it.

Of course, conventional bad remains to us. Richard Nixon did well by doing bad. He was bad, he is bad, he died bad, and we will miss him because his badness helped to define what many of us think is, in public life, good. Vietnam was bad. The invasion of Grenada was bad. The failure of nerve by the West in Bosnia was bad. Desert Storm was done well for bad reasons; to the hundred thousand non-Westerners who died in it, badness abounded. Our confrontation of Haiti began and will end badly. Hollywood's renditions of teachers and writers, no matter how many times they are attempted, are bad. Journeyman baseball players who earn a million dollars a year to hit .243 and play average infield represent something bad. Pop Warner football, with its emphasis on winning at every conceivable cost, before rapaciously howling parents, is bad. Spectators at Little League games tend to the bad. Television commercials for beer are bad. Songs on jukeboxes that take as their subject sundown, long nights, or truck rides are bad. Women who feel constrained to dress for business by looking like men and carrying cordovan attaché cases have been subjected to what's bad. MTV is bad. Press secretaries are bad. Plastic bottles for whiskey are bad. So is most beaujolais nouveau and the fashion for giving it as a gift. So is the airplane announcement about *smoking materials.* So is the seating space on the plane. The old *New Yorker* was bad. The Anglophile new *New Yorker* is bad. People who talk about the old or new *New Yorker* are bad. So are writers who comment on them. Men's vertically moussed haircuts are bad. The cheap shots in *Spy* are bad, especially any referring to me.

Bad is what you call an applicant for a job at a university who describes her method of teaching the writing of fiction "an empowerment of the gender-oppressed and racial minorities." She adds, promptly, that she has also found her method to work in "bringing out silenced white males." Which leaves us with no one to do the *oppression,* she forgot to say. She will be hired, I've no doubt, and will go on, canons firing, to become a star in some department. She will teach her students that they're victims. She will teach them how to prove it.

Also bad are literature professors who think that contemporary writing is, at its best, the cream in the departmental coffee. They tolerate writers although it is their secret, they think, that Geoffrey Chaucer, were he to make application for work, would not be hired because he is a dead white European male and because his degree isn't good enough, and because he doesn't do theory. These people do not understand that literary art is not only the cream in their coffee, but the hillside on which the coffee is planted, the earth in which it is grown, the sweat on the skin of the men and women who pick the beans, the water in which the ground beans steep, the mouth that, savoring it, speaks by expelling words in shapes of breath it scents.

It is bad that black writers do being black, Chicano writers do being Hispanic, lesbians do being homosexual, and feminists do being feminist—instead of each doing art, or professing English, or writing about the nature of the world that has the temerity to exist outside them. It is bad for their souls and our minds that careerism so drives their critical faculties and their prose. A young artist or professor knows that you achieve success now by writing, painting, composing, or critiquing by way of your genes and the color of your skin. Authors once strove to get good by being more than the total of their birth weight multiplied by their genetic code. It's bad that they now claim credibility (and royalty checks) on the basis of the accident of their birth.

In a burst of badness, Peter Brooks, in a review in the *Times Literary Supplement,* yawns that "We have known for some time that fictional characters are linguistic constructs, that the impression of mimesis of real persons that they may give is a mirage, and that to ask how many children Lady Macbeth had is the wrong way to interrogate literature." Professor Brooks bends backward into the professorial critical wars to recall the feud between A. C. Bradley and L. C.

Knights, whose *How Many Children Had Lady Macbeth?* is evoked by his question. Brooks reminds us that Shakespeare's characters aren't, you know, real; they're, you know, language; when you speculate about the biology of a linguistic construct, you're believing in the language instead of prodding at it, disproving it. You aren't cool.

I am of the body heat school, the school uncool. I think that to ask ourselves—so long as we don't require a specific number in reply—how many children Lady Macbeth might have had is to believe in her as a person-on-the-page, a figure-on-the-stage, and is to ask questions in *a* right way. Has she not sexed her husband past all inner and social restraint—meager as they might have been—and into dark, maddened criminality? What was she like in bed, we well might wonder. Was she cold and withholding? All nakedness and surrender? Did she claw at his flesh? Startle him with his own appetites? Do we not imagine about what's not made explicit? Is that not one reason for a writer to withhold instead of delineate? Does the writer not, him- or herself, speculate or intuit or *feel*—there, I've said the F-word—about the secrets of his or her self as well as these metaphors for self, these people, pulled up from the page?

And note: such thinking "is the wrong way to interrogate literature." Literature, then, is not studied or read, it is not considered or enjoyed: it is interrogated. Tie it in a chair beneath hot lights. Pump it full of chemicals. Apply electrodes to its most delicate parts. Beat it, steal its family, *disappear* it. The aggression in the word is noteworthy, and it is bloated with self-delight, with arrogance. We know the right way, that sure locution says. And it is bad, and a symptom of bad education in the graduate schools, and a guarantee of bad education by graduate students turned college professor and high school teacher, and an assurance, for years to come, of literary papers and essays and books that hum with contentment and cover the field—a living blanket of flies on the body of literature.

Mr. Brooks reminds us that "we really haven't found a vocabulary, or a conceptual framework, that takes us much beyond the formative cultural work done by Dickens, Tolstoy, George Eliot and the rest." Don't you love that "the rest"? Thackeray and Emily Brontë, Gaskell and Chekhov: the rest.

Why not think a moment of those Victorians, of those "the rest": Thomas Hardy, for example, clumsy and obsessed and brilliant in spite of a self-professed disdain for his own prose. He writes *Tess of the d'Urbervilles*, in 1891, intending, according to his subtitle, "A

Pure Woman," to assert that purity has less to do with having borne an illegitimate child and having committed adultery and having murdered the child's father and her adulterous partner than his readers might think.

Hardy presupposes Tess. He doesn't only write her: he believes in her. He doesn't see her as "an illusory ideological formation, another product of Western logocentric metaphysics," which is how Brooks defines character. "The concept of character," Brooks goes on, "is the reification of a figure, in which the sign itself ('character' as an engraved mark) is substituted for what it signifies ('character' as the traits constituting selfhood)."

Hardy didn't know that. He wrote about a woman he conceived as flesh and blood in his imagination and whom he tried to make tangible and persuasive on the page. He believed in her enough, the dolt who was "one of the rest," so that in the posthumously published, putative biography of Hardy by his wife, Florence—it was actually his own grindingly discreet autobiography—he twice describes women to whom he was attracted in these terms: one had "quite a 'Tess' mouth and eyes: with these two beauties she can afford to be indifferent about the remainder of her face"; of the other he says, "In appearance she is something like my idea of 'Tess,' though I did not know her when the novel was written." Thomas Hardy is in love—with, I guess, "an illusory ideological formation."

I think, sometimes, that many postmodern critics do not love anything except the control they exercise in alleging the artist's uncontrol. They are well-fed revolutionaries, bourgeoisie in guerilla costumes. Their field is power, and some of it resides in their knowing what they say and your not knowing what they say because they use bird whistles, eyebrow twitches, invisible ink codes, furtive-fingered recognition gestures, and secret handshakes understood mostly by them. I'd like to call that smug codification bad.

But I know as well as you that what's bad is also found in language perpetrated by writers in the name of love and of loving their characters. I am thinking of a first novel I won't name. It's done; the author can't be helped with this one, and there's always hope that someone—editors have been paid, in the past, for such work, and some have even done it—will warn him or her about such writing. In that novel, the birth of a child is exhaustingly awaited and then the child dies. The mother is crushed, but plods on through her life. At the end, at a reception, a handsome restaurant owner asks her to dance. She "folded herself into" his arms, and they "sailed across the room." Those terms are of course bad: they are constructed of received language, and they are not speaking to us; they show that the writer believes he or she *is*, but we know he or she cannot be. For how does the human body fold itself into someone else's embrace without breaking or at least bending very painfully? How does it sail across a room unless someone has pitched it? The character ceases to be particular when expressed in such language; she here becomes an echo of ten thousand writers and ten thousand characters who enjoyed being held by a man while dancing. Each time a writer fails to particularize such a moment, a character dies, and we are left with television: the general idea of, the electronic signal about, a woman who dances. It's the jokester's convention, and the master of ceremonies calls out "Number Eleven," and everyone knows to laugh.

Suddenly this character knows—but only because the author has decided that the book is going to end here—that "she had survived, it was all that mattered, to survive and endure and let go." She knows that "the future belonged to her." The handsome man dips her and she laughs. "Looking at the ceiling, she thought she heard soft applause, the sound of baby hands clapping."

Those are the last words of the novel. They are bad. They are failed feeling—the failure of a writer to find the right words about emotion: sentimentality, that is to say, and the careless use of language as a rhetorical weapon—to, in this case, bludgeon the reader into acceding to the novelist's postulations about emotional life. We know that we long to speak to the dead and to be consoled by them. And good writers have made this common knowledge uncommon. Here, the author has made this impulse embarrassing and the protagonist infantile. By asking the reader to be infantile, too, the author invites the sort of antagonism we reserve for baby talk between lovers we're not. Bad.

Also bad: *The Bridges of Madison County*, a *New York Times* best seller for, it seems, most of my adult life. This paragon of dead prose is about a Marlboro Man photographer and the woman whom he makes beautiful with his great art. It was at first reviewed almost nowhere. Word of mouth made it sell so many copies, its author installed an 800 telephone number on which his enchanted readers could leave messages about their powerful response. In turn, book-chat people have begun to write as if they take the book seriously. The earning of money unfailingly has this effect.

The woman made beautiful says, "If you took me in your arms and carried me to your truck and forced me to go with you, I wouldn't murmur a complaint. You could do the same thing just by talking to me. But I don't think you will. You're too sensitive, too aware of my feelings, for that. . . . My life . . . lacks romance, eroticism, dancing in the kitchen to candlelight, and the wonderful feel of a man who knows how to love a woman. . . ."

The next morning, as cowboys who know how to satisfy a woman always do after satisfying her, he leaves. "Her mind was gone, empty, turning. 'Don't leave, Robert Kincaid,' she could hear herself crying out from somewhere inside."

Why is this bad? The entire phenomenon is bad—the work itself, and its enormous popularity, which tells us that we, as a reading populace, are in love with what's bad. What we love, apparently, is talk that doesn't sound like people, but that does sound like speeches made by a person-on-the-page written by someone who doesn't listen to the rest of the world or know how to make plausible an imitation of the world. If you agree with me, you are asking for homage to the world in what you read, not homage to theory about "'character' as an engraved mark."

If you agree with me, you know that the dialogue I quoted from the novel is a summary of points—he's sensitive, she's needful, and he is a dervish in her cold bed—and not the statement of a soul with whom your soul, you feel, needs communion. Indeed, then, you probably believe in something like souls and something like communion which is available, without brain death, to readers.

If you agree with me, you marvel (to say the least) at a woman whose mind is not only "gone," but is in its absence still present enough to record that it is "empty" and that, while vanished and hollow, it is "turning." While turning stomachs are appropriate, perhaps, a turning mind suggests something like those whirling plastic barrels from which women in tights pluck lottery winners on cable TV. Note further, please, that while her mind is both gone *and* enough on the scene to record its empty *tour jeté*, it can assist her to "hear herself crying out from somewhere inside." You can only cry "out" from someplace that's in, of course; so logic is not what the statement's about, but emotion. She hears herself with a mind that's not there, yet, turning, cries out when she does not, in fact, cry out. It's a silent cry, then, and yet the author feels the need to tell us that it's "from somewhere inside." From where else?

This is the language of television, of bodice rippers, of the Harlequin Romance. It is incapable and irresponsible writing, unmediated by thought or the gift of artifice, or by the author's belief in a character sufficient to move him. It's what the majority of readers seem to want. That's bad.

What's good, then? Am I not defending the old-fashioned and ignoring the hard-edged new? Well, the hard-edged new is old, I'm saying. No one has yet written a more profoundly moving, vast, and encompassing novel in America than Melville did in his *Moby-Dick* of 1851. Surely, it is the template by which we judge both our jokes about and our attempts to write—or, as readers, to find—The Great American Novel. William Gaddis's *The Recognitions*, Ralph Ellison's *Invisible Man*, Thomas Pynchon's *Gravity's Rainbow*, Eudora Welty's *Losing Battles*, Maureen Howard's *Natural History*: these come to mind as candidates; each is vast, encyclopedic, steeped in American history and in the lives of characters about whose fate we care. Only in the Pynchon are the characters flat, two-dimensional—commentary, in effect, on the difficulty of dealing in contemporary terms with emotion. The others, including the Melville, deal with *feeling* as well as intellection. Remember that *Moby-Dick* begins with an 1851 rendition of the blues ("Whenever I find myself growing grim about the mouth; whenever it is a damp, drizzly November in my soul; whenever I find myself involuntarily pausing before coffin warehouses, and bringing up the rear of every funeral I meet").

Contemporary fiction of the unemotional sort plays off the emotions it seems to forswear; the narrator—these are usually first-person novels—manifests the pain he or she then insists he or she doesn't care about and that the prose, it's insisted, doesn't reflect. And then the author factors the pain into his or her passages, so that you feel them on the author's behalf. At its clumsiest, we have the author turning you into a parent or lover and you're feeling just terrible on his or her behalf. At its best, we have *L'Etranger* with a chaser. "Mother died," Meursault announces, and then he boasts that he can't recall when. We respond by supplying the emotion our protagonist claims not to feel. Our participation in that transaction consists of this: we have endured a parent's death, or we fear it, or fear our own, and fear for the strength of our love, or fear to be *un*loved. We are loyal to those tawdry elements of life, that is to say, which a professional postmodernist pretends to believe one can afford to put, as they like to term it, under erasure. But they are human, and we are, too, and the fiction we read

200

for our souls' sake—and not for the sake of advancing our career—is what responds to our humanness. Find out which detective stories about passion and trespass your neighborhood theorist reads during the campus vacation.

If you don't agree with me, give up: you will. You will remember the death of a parent, the loss of a friend, the terror or illness of a child you tried to protect. It is those moments—they are lived at body temperature, there is nothing cool about them—that define a life. In the art about which you're serious, you seek, willy-nilly, examinations of, metaphors about, the heat of your existence. Even if your blood has run cold, you don't want anybody else being cool about such times. They are your times, and you were on the face of this earth and in trouble or love, and while you are perfectly willing to be attractively disenchanted and invulnerable in public when you need to, you know that the warmth of flesh, the muddiness of earth, the terror of madness and death, the hugeness of institutions, and the brevity of your life and the lives of those you need are what your seriousness involves. Such moments help you to define your morality. You seek them and it in the art you make or surrender to.

What resorts to trend and gossip, to evasion and gloss, to the cutely second-rate, or what drops its bucket all the little inches down into the mud and gravel of jargon and career, is the opposite of what your soul requires, and it's bad. And maybe what is worst is the noise of some tired writer who, preaching and confessing, flaps his unfeathered wings in your face. Doesn't he know better?

Nominated by Stanley Lindberg, Robert Phillips

THE BARBARIANS ARE COMING

by MARILYN CHIN

from THE PHOENIX GONE, THE TERRACE EMPTY (MILKWEED EDITIONS)

War chariots thunder, horses neigh, *the barbarians are coming.*
What are we waiting for, young nubile women pointing at the wall,
   the barbarians are coming.
They have heard about a weakened link in the wall. *So, the*
   barbarians have ears among us.
So deceive yourself with illusions: you are only one woman, holding
   one broken brick in the wall.
So deceive yourself with illusions: as if you matter, that brick and
   that wall.
The barbarians are coming: they have red beards or beardless with a
   top knot.
The barbarians are coming: they are your fathers, brothers, teachers,
   lovers; and they are clearly an other.
The barbarians are coming:
            If you call me a horse, I must be a horse
            If you call me a bison, I am equally guilty.

When a thing is true and is correctly described, one doubles the
   blame by not admitting it: so, Chuangtzu, himself, was a barbarian
   king!

Horse, horse, bison, bison, *the barbarians are coming*—
and how they love to come.
The smells of the great frontier exult in them.

after Cavafy

Nominated by Michael Dennis Browne, Henri Cole, Jane Cooper, Rita Dove

THE SWING OF THINGS

fiction by JENNIFER C CORNELL

from PITT MAGAZINE and *DEPARTURES* (University of Pittsburgh Press)

YOU GO ANSWER IT, my father said when the doorbell rang. I was up to my elbows in lemon bubbles, a butcher's apron around my waist, but he took the pot and scrubber off me and held a clean towel while I dried my hands. Go on, luv, he said. I'll finish these.

Brian and Jack were my honorary uncles, and though I'd just seen them the previous evening they still hugged me close when I opened the door, the scent of cologne fresh on their collars, their cheeks newly shaven and smooth against mine. My father came from the kitchen and stood behind us with folded arms.

Is he ready? Brian asked me, before he saw him. I ordered a taxi.

I'm not going, my father said.

You are, Jack said.

Now look, said Brian, we've been through this already. He unbuttoned his coat with determination and aimed his voice at the other room. You don't mind, do you, Mr. Scully?

Of course he doesn't, Jack said. He went over to where the old man sat in his chair by the fire and crouched down in front of him, eye-to-eye. Alright, grandad? he said. What's the forecast?

There's too many chickens, the old man said.

So there are, Jack said, straightening up, I've always said so. See— what d'I tell you? Sharp as a tack.

For God's sake, said my father. Can't you see I can't go?

Listen, comrade, Jack said, it's not immigration; it's one night on the town. We'll have you back here within twenty-four hours.

I don't know, said my father. What about the child?

She's a good big girl, aren't you, luv? How old are you now? Seventeen? Twenty-one?

She's nine, my father said. Too young to be left in the house on her own.

But she's not on her own, Brian said, she's with her granda. You'll look after her, won't you, Mr. Scully?

We've got to get'm out, the old man answered, but my father shook his head.

He doesn't know what he's saying. That's not about this.

He knows more than you do, Brian told him. They looked at each other in silence for a moment. C'mon, now, Brian said finally. You'll be in by midnight, earlier if you want. And you don't have to do a damn thing you don't want to, alright? Just get out of the house for once, that's all, have a few pints and watch the match.

My father sighed. Who d'you say's playing?

Liverpool, Jack said. And this time they'll win.

For the next twenty minutes they stood beside him in the downstairs toilet watching his razor move in the mirror, lifting their chins with the same squint and pout as he scraped the blade carefully across his throat. Then they followed him up to the back bedroom to help him match a clean shirt and tie, where they shook out his suit and condemned its condition, spit-polished his shoes and vetoed his socks until my father gave up and let them choose a pair. I heard them arguing about financial matters—who'd pay for the pints and the grub if they got any, how much to save for the cab fare home—until my father came in for his jacket and cap and the spare set of keys, kissed the old man on the top of his head and said, Alright, luv, I suppose we're away.

A man was closing our front gate behind him when we stepped outside looking up, testing the odds in the blush of clouds above us of another summer evening ending in rain.

Hiya, the man said, and shook hands with Brian because he was the closest. Gus Holden. Is one of you a John Scully? I was told I could find him at this address.

Is that right? said Jack.

What for? Brian said.

Your name's not Holden, my father said. You're a McCulla. Pascal McCulla, from the Ligoniel Road.

Not any more, the man said. I've been Gus Holden for ten years now.

Your father owned a sweetie shop when I was a boy, my father continued. Remember, Brian? Across from the post office, near Leroy Street. How's he doing, your dad? Does he still have that shop?

No, no, it burned down years ago. He and my ma live in England now.

McCulla's a good name, Brian said. Why'd you change it?

Part of the job, the man said. You do what they tell you or you don't get paid.

Listen, Pascal, my father said, John Scully's my father but he's not very well; I don't like to disturb him. Can I help you at all?

The thing is, the man said, it's your da won the prize. I don't think it's transferable.

Jack shook his head like a man clearing water. He's done what did you say?

He won a prize, the man repeated uncertainly. He was in a competition. He won a day out with me.

And who are you?

I do stunts, the man answered. He seemed embarrassed. For the cinema, mostly. Sometimes just for show.

What kind of stunts?

Lots of things. Get set on fire, jump off of buildings. The usual stuff.

That's not true, Brian said. You do that thing with the catapult, don't you? Off an eighty-foot bridge with a plane going by. You catch hold of it. I saw it on TV.

Yes, that's right, the man said. But I do the other stuff, too.

You should see that one, Brian said generally. That's really something.

It's a bit late for a day out, isn't it? my father said. It's almost seven now.

Aye, I know, the man said. But youse aren't on the phone, and I have a cousin in Velsheda Park I haven't seen for a while, so I reckoned I'd stop by here first and make plans for tomorrow or whatever day suits.

Jesus, Jack said. How about that.

A competition, my father repeated. What kind of competition? What did he have to do to win?

Oh, I don't know, said the stuntman. Just be a fan, I suppose.

No offense, Jack said, but that's just not possible. You sure you have the right address?

It says John Scully here, right enough, Brian answered, examining the letter the stuntman had taken from inside his coat. And it's your street and number. He refolded the letter and returned it, shrugged and shook his head. Looks like it's him.

Have a look in his room, Jack suggested. He might have the rule sheet or something up there.

No, said my father, he's got to have privacy. This is his house, too, after all.

So what do you want to do? Brian asked quietly.

We were on our way out, see, Jack told the stuntman.

Oh sorry! he said. I can come back tomorrow.

You're here now, Jack said. Hold on—you wouldn't mind staying here for a while, would you? Just for a couple of hours, to keep an eye on things. You'd be doing us a real favour, letting this fella have a night out for a change. He grinned at the stuntman and patted his back. Don't worry; you'll understand everything when you've met the old man.

Now wait a minute, my father protested, that's not on.

What about your cousin? Jack asked, ignoring him. Is she expecting you?

No, not at all. She doesn't know I've arrived.

Well that's it, then! Jack said. We'll be down at The Joxer for a couple of pints. They're showing the match on the big screen. You can see it yourself, if you want to. He's got a TV.

I don't feel good about this, my father said.

Don't be silly, Brian said, it's a great idea. As long as you don't mind, of course.

It's alright, the stuntman said, really. I don't mind.

When they were gone I led him inside. The old man was sitting just as I'd left him, and I went over and collected his plate from the table beside him and removed the napkin from his lap. His fingers shook as I wiped them clean.

What's all this for? said the stuntman, looking round him.

For him, I explained, so he doesn't get lost.

I'd written the first set myself, one for every door in the house. But bright colours confused him so my father made new ones, simple black letters on white, unlined cards—one to say TOILET, another, COAT CLOSET, the three bedrooms upstairs identified by occupant, the back of both exits reading, THIS LEADS OUTSIDE. In our kitchen too everything was labeled. A note on the bread basket reminded the old man where to find butter, another on the kettle told him how to make tea. TURN THIS OFF! said a sign on the cooker. My father had changed it over to electric after he found the old man still looking

207

for matches an hour after he'd switched on the gas. The following week he'd stepped through the gate the postman had left open and struck out for Carnmoney, where he used to live. He'd gotten as far as the city center, had even managed to find the right bus, but the coins in his pocket had made no sense to him, and though he'd lived all his life within a twelve-mile radius he was disoriented completely when the driver pulled away. He'd entered a shop but lost sight of the exit, had drawn the attention of a security guard, then stood in front of the Linen Hall Library counting the same fifty-pence piece over and over until the thought of the sum he believed he was carrying had paralyzed him with dread. A whole afternoon of pedestrian traffic had moved him gradually to the opposite side of Donegall Square, where Brian walked into him on his way home from work. From then on we kept the gate bolted beyond comprehension, and he carried a card on his person printed in large letters with his name and address.

I checked the carriage clock on the mantel, stoked the fire and switched on the pump.

It's time for his bath, I told the stuntman. Do you want to come up?

We followed the same procedure each evening. The first thing was to sit him down on the toilet, get his clothes off and then fill the tub. I'm going to unbutton your shirt now, da, my father would tell him while I got the old man's toothbrush ready and tested the water against my wrist—Lift your feet up now, let's pull off those socks. After the bath there were ointments to use for poor circulation and swollen joints, plus an assortment of tablets and liquids which had to be taken before going to bed.

I took everything off him but his vest and pants, then I opened my mouth so he'd open his and pulled my lips back in the grimace necessary for the brushing of teeth. My father shaved him every morning but by teatime his chin bristled against my palm, the short white stubble on his jowls too sparkling like frost in the bright light of the bathroom.

I don't think they cleaned it, he said as I wiped his lips. It's gone now, anyway. Audrey, luv, did I give you this one? There was something else the last time, you tell him. Did he take that one away with him, too?

Okay, I said, stand up a minute. I fastened a towel around his waist, reached up underneath it and pulled down his briefs. As he stepped into the bathtub I took the towel away and helped him sit down, and when he let go of the handrails I lifted his arm up and pulled off his shirt.

Aren't you going to answer him? the stuntman asked me.

No, I said, he's not talking to me. It's your hair, I explained. Audrey's my mother. She used to wear hers that way, too.

Hers had been thicker than his, however, and even longer, and when she tied it behind her the dark strands moved in lazy unison, like the tail of a horse. Who do I look like? I'd asked her one evening when my father and I were sitting beside her, one on either edge of the bed. We were looking through a shoe box of photos he'd come upon earlier while searching the closets for something to have ready for Mrs. Mercer, who collected donations on behalf of the church. Like your father, she'd answered promptly, but he'd disagreed. He'd lifted the soft rope of hair from her pillow and tousled his own head next to mine. Look at that colour, he'd said, there's your answer. You see that, wee girl? You're a bit of us both.

The stuntman examined the ends of his own hair curiously, as if he'd only just realised how long they'd grown. I gave him the soap to hold so I wouldn't lose it, and the shampoo to pour when the time came for that.

Listen, he said, can he go outside?

I recalled the forecast, the violet horizon, the mild breath of the evening on me as I'd waved Brian and Jack and my father goodbye.

I think so, I said. But not for long.

It's just that he did win this competition, the stuntman continued. He deserves something for it. There's got to be something outside I could do.

I dressed the old man in the clothes my father had already set out for him to wear the next day, a combination of garments he'd been fond of once. To be on the safe side I put a cardigan on him, then I led him downstairs and out into the garden where the stuntman stood, contemplating the house.

He was in his bare feet and he'd taken his shirt off. White gauze bound him from midwaist to abdomen, swift movement seemed difficult, and I don't know why but I thought of my father, whom I'd happened to see once stepping into the bath. The door to the bathroom had been slightly open and I'd caught a thick glimpse of flank and buttock before he sank in, lifted the sponge from the water beside him and squeezed its load slowly over his head; all the strength with which he'd been fooling us drained away from him then. Some time before that I'd observed the woman who lived across from us step into her garden perfectly nude. Her body was a nest of soft folds and deflations, like those of the models who posed for night classes in Life Drawing and Sculp-

209

ture in the art room at school. The first time I saw them disrobe with such confidence and then mount the platform to pass the interminable hours outstretched on cushions or straddling a chair, I'd been with friends—we'd just finished Swimmers, and waiting for someone to come fetch us home we were wandering the corridors, intrigued by all that the building was home to after school hours, independent of us. From then on I watched regularly the Adult Ed students seated at easels, the hesitant strokes of their pencils and chalk, the thoughtful perambulations of the silent instructor and the all the while oblivious expression of whatever naked man or woman was in front of them that week. The old man had recently moved in with us then, my mother had only a few months to live, and I already had doubts about my own body, already imagined I could see proof of its impermanence in my own face and limbs. The woman's husband, returning from work as she stepped from the house, had dropped the plastic box he was carrying which still held his crusts and wrappers from lunch. He'd put his arms around her and held her, and it occurred to me then that this is why we fall in love: because we need another's eyes to convince us we remain things of beauty, because without another's tongue to tell us we assume such words can not be said.

The stuntman touched his bandages gently.

Bad back, he told the old man as if he owed him an apology. It's going to catch up to me one of these days.

How'd you get it? I asked.

I'm not sure, to be honest. The littlest thing can cause an injury. Bobby Dunn knocked an eye out doing a high dive—there was a match on the surface and he hit it coming in. I've been doing a lot lately with airplanes and ladders; that kind of thing can throw your spine out of whack.

He carried a chair out from the kitchen and I had him put it where the old man could see, then he excused himself and returned to his survey, tugging briefly at the drainpipe, gauging the likely strength of the gutters, testing the soundness of the moulding and quoins.

I don't know, he confessed finally. I haven't done anything like this in ages. Everything's so high tech these days. I used to work a lot with animals, too, but I hardly do anything like that now. That's how I got started, actually—training horses in Connemara. The first film I did was with Peter O'Toole.

Sargano wrestled lions, the old man said, Bostock boxed with kangaroos.

The stuntman stared at him. That's right, he said. So they did.

I put money on the barber, the old man went on. I'd've like to've been there. Your uncle, he was living in Lancashire, he wrote me about it, but it wasn't the same.

Not Tom Helme, the stuntman said cautiously, but the old man was plucking at the cuffs of his cardigan and didn't respond. Helme shaved a man in a cage with six lions, the stuntman told me, must be forty, fifty years ago now. It was a dare; the circus was in town and he was a big talker.

So what do you think? I inquired at length. He'd inspected the house now from every direction, and I'd seen him eyeing the distance to the roof of the garage from one of the windows on the second floor. By now dusk had dulled the edges of everything, and although his fingers were as warm as ever still I worried about the old man.

I could make up a rig if I had some boxes, the stuntman offered.

There's a Spar round the corner, I told him. You might find boxes there.

I'd need a lot of them, but, he said, his eyes on our chimney, that drop's thirty foot if it's an inch.

There weren't enough but he took what was there. A cardboard wall rose quickly in front of him, its layers compact and orderly, printed with CORNFLAKES, WHITE CLOUD, and ARIEL AUTOMATIC. He found the old sheets my father had used to cover the furniture when preparing a room for the old man's arrival; the cotton still smelled of turps and was stiff as rubber where the paint had congealed. He threw these over the boxes and bound it all loosely with twine.

Don't try this at home, he said when he'd finished, then climbed easily up the drainpipe onto the short roof of our scullery, turned and sat down.

Not to worry, he said. When I first started out I worked with this fella who used to say there's no such thing as a more dangerous stunt. That was true then, it still is, a little, but there are some stunts now that're more easy than others.

They told him he was finished, never lift'm again, the old man said. In some places they were half an inch deep.

Jesus, the stuntman said. Dick Grace. Now he was one of the greats. Outlived eighteen professional rivals; another four had to quit cuz of injury. He was a mess himself after that accident, right enough—786 square inches, burned so badly his arms ended up webbed to his sides—but he cut the scar tissue with a razor so he could keep on working. It was him used to talk about outwitting gravity. The stuntman laughed softly, then shook his head. Jesus, he was fearless. It just didn't trouble him, the thought he might die.

When I was much smaller my mother told me that should we ever be separated in a shop or department store I was to stand by an exit, and she would come and look for me there. You still remember that? she'd said when I reminded her of it—though I suppose, she'd added, it's not so long ago. She'd been weak, however, and a doctor was coming, so I never did explain the reason I mentioned it—the conclusion I'd come to regarding death. The way I see death, I had wanted to tell her, it's a circular room in which I'm at the centre, and though I fight hard through the people to get to a wall, though I travel along it and feel for a door, the same faces keep passing with the slow regularity of unclaimed luggage, and I end up repeatedly where I began. But no other opportunity ever presented itself, and later I realised what I'd been describing was not death at all, but the waiting room outside it where all the rest of us are.

That's madness, I said.

The stuntman shrugged. We have to go sometime. I suppose he reckoned with the end coming at him it'd do him no harm to meet it half way.

He stood up. I heard the sound of scuttling gravel, a clump of moss dislodged from our shingles fell swiftly past and vanished into a flower bed, then I spotted his head and shoulders, his elbows cocked on either side, and in an instant he'd levered himself over and was coming towards us across the roof of the house.

It's okay, he called down from the edge. The rig's a wee bit smaller than I'd like it, but you can fall fifty feet on dry land without damage if you know what you're doing. He crossed his arms over his breastbone, his fingers clasping the back of his neck. Backwards and sideways, he explained over his shoulder, and spread-eagled on impact. That's the safest way, usually, for this kind of thing.

He described the mathematics of arcs and projectiles, the various forces that determine a fall, but all I understood of what he was saying was the margin of error, something they'd tried to teach us in school. An explosion in town the previous evening had damaged a gas main near the building, and as we were already facing evacuation we'd gone on a field trip to the Ulster Museum to see an exhibit on the concept of chance. The rest of the group moved on without me while I lingered at one of the first displays, an upright contraption of transparent plastic through which a torrent of ball bearings perpetually bounced down from a single opening into a row of compartments below. Though their descent was described by the force of gravity, it was the force of their knocking against the short, even pegs which were there to obstruct them that shunted them into a bell-shaped curve—and I thought as I watched them repeating the pattern how everything in life was this accidental. Despite all the care of the hands that place us, trying to centre us so we fall just right, still our paths remain unpredictable, we're so easily sent veering by a single peg—success, disaster, and recovery all equally uncontrollable, whatever the odds and calculations.

All set below? the stuntman said.

Out of sight around the corner I heard our gate hum.

All set, I answered.

The stuntman nodded and stepped back with long strides, disappearing in sections from the bottom up. Then my father was beside me, our front door key ready between his fingers.

I thought I heard your voice, he said. What are you two doing out here? He touched the old man's forehead with the back of his hand. Are you alright, da? he demanded. Where's Pascal?

Again the gate groaned and shuddered. My father, glancing back to see who was coming, said Ah, no, and shook his head.

Now what did you think? Brian replied before he could say anything.

I told you, my father said. I just wasn't up for it. Why didn't youse stay there, enjoy the match?

Who needs football when there's home entertainment? Jack answered. Just in time, by the look of it. Have a look up there.

It seemed he spun from the edge in slow motion, off by many inches and almost certain to miss the rig, and I thought of the way glass shatters, the regal burst of liquids when they land. The cord around the boxes snapped when he struck them, the sheets leaped up with the sound of someone heavy elbowed out of slumber into turning over in bed, and flattened bits of cardboard shot out from under, scattering leaves and twigs. Grit and plaster pattered softly on the bushes as the pieces stopped revolving and slowly came to rest.

Jack was the first to reach him. He pulled the sheets and cardboard away like a man in a hurry rifling through drawers while my father and Brian followed behind him, stepping gingerly into the path he'd cleared. What I saw first when they finally reached him was the stuntman's chest heaving, the careful way he drew up his knees.

Easy, now, my father said urgently—Hold on! Don't move.

I'm alright, the stuntman said, sitting up. A thin strip of bandage grew taut behind him and he stopped abruptly.

Just wait a minute for god's sake! Brian said, We'll ring for an ambulance. There's a hospital just down the road.

It's okay, the stuntman said, I feel fine. With an effort he stood and brushed the dust from his trousers. Miscellaneous joints clattered irritably as he stretched.

You are one daft bastard, Jack told him with admiration.

C'mon inside, my father said. I don't care what you say—you ought to have someone look you over.

I'm alright! the stuntman insisted. But I could do with a drink.

Good idea, Jack said, we'll go to the local. I'd very much like to buy this man a Bass.

Not me, thanks, said my father, youse three go. I want to get that child to bed. Da? he called, and they all turned with him to look back at us. You okay?

The old man had risen when the stuntman fell. The last time I'd seen him move so quickly I'd been much younger and spending the day with him at his house. A year before that he'd tackled the bare, uneven land that lay behind him and created a pond, and I was keen to see proof of what he'd told me, that from the first bucket of silver he'd spilled into the water had come a whole population of healthy fish.

We'd approached the bank quietly but still the pond's rhythms had been disturbed; it was many minutes before they returned.

There he is, he'd whispered finally, pointing to the source of that retching bellow whose tremor I'd felt in my own throat and chest. He'd eased himself off the log on which we'd been sitting. I saw his arm strike with a heron's speed, and all at once he was crouching beside me, his shirtfront splattered, the frog with its large golden eyes and vulnerable belly afraid but uninjured between his hands.

I put my hand on the old man's shoulder. He said, You're a good girl, Audrey, and placed his hand over mine.

We're alright, I answered. We're okay.

Nominated by Ehud Havazelet

HISTORY BOOKS

by THOMAS LUX

from AMERICAN POETRY REVIEW

That is, their authors, leave out
one thing: the smell. How sour, no, rancid—bad cheese
and sweat—the narrow corridors of Hitler's bunker
during the last days powdered
by plaster shaken down
under bomb after bomb. Or (forward or backward
through time, history books take you) downstream
a mile or two from a river-crossing ambush
a corpse washes ashore
or catches in branches
and bloats in the sun. The carrion eaters
who do not fly
come by their noses: the thick,
ubiquitous, sick, sweet smell.
Most of history, however,
is banal, not bloody: the graphite and wood smell
of a pencil factory, the glue- fertilizer- paper-
(oh redolent!) shoe- hat- (ditto malodar
and poisonous) chemical- salt cod-
munitions- canning- shirtwaist- plastics- box-
tractor- etc. factories—and each one
peopled by people: groins, armpits, feet.
A bakery, during famine; guards, smoking, by the door.
Belowdecks, two years out, dead calm, tropics.
And wind a thousand miles all night combing
the tundra: chilled grasses, polar bear droppings,

glacial exhalations . . . Open
the huge book of the past: *whoosh!:* a staggering cloud
of stinks, musks and perfumes, swollen pheromones, almond
and anise, offal dumps, mass graves exhumed, flower
heaps, sandalwood bonfires, milk vapors
from a baby's mouth, all of us
wading hip-deep through the endless
waftings, one bottomless soup
of smell: primal, atavistic — sniff, sniff, sniff.

Nominated by Stuart Dischell, Stuart Dybek, Sharon Olds

THE MORE I LIKE FLIES

fiction by REGINALD McKNIGHT

from THE KENYON REVIEW

ALL right, man, so I'm busing down tables—we gotta do our own here, and we gotta sweep, mop, wash dishes, and do just about everything else, too—*and* I'm trying to keep flies off my arms and the sweat out my eyes and the seam of these polyester monkey-suit pants from working into the crack of my ass. I ain't even gonna tell you how disgusted I am with all this wreckage these ape-neck cadets have left behind. And we gotta throw all this crap away, too. Three and a half gallons of milk; four, maybe five pounds of scrambled eggs; a whole pig's worth of bacon; enough French toast to feed France, and I'm saying to myself, like, Yeah, like I really need this crap. Up at three-goddamn-thirty in the morning, so I can drive to the Air-god-Force-damn-Academy to spoon-feed and clean up after these little dweebs. . . . Six-thirty-three-the-hell A.M., and I been at this gig for two hours already—already driven up all these hills and black curves to sweat into my eyes and sling food. Love it. But then, like, from nowhere ol' Kelly, my partner, goes, "What's so great about bein' goddamn white?"

Hello! I say to myself. There he goes. Good ol' Kelly. But I keep my mouth shut, naturally. No sense going into it. This is Kelly.

But still, I get to thinking, How about this, ya dope: Try walking down the street at night, minding your own beeswax, and a white couple comes at you from the opposite way? and it's hot outside, so you're ambling, just ambling, and it's not all that late, just blue black with a few stars, like you like it, and you're thinking about, say, nothing really, OK? and you don't even mind the water sprinklers spritzing your right side.

217

And the crickets sound nice, don't they? Then when Ken and Barbie get within half a block of you they cut across the street like you're a hissing viper hell-hound man, bristling with Uzis and hypodermic needles. You can barely keep yourself from hollering, *Oh, come ooonnn, I gotta Korean girlfriend and my best buddy's white, and you people got to simply lay off watching so many goddamn drug-lord movies.*

What's so great about being white is you get to act like everybody else in the world is a scary monster.

Like I say, all this I keep to myself 'cause once this old melonhead's got his mind made up to say something, you can't stop him. He starts from nowhere, gets nowhere, if you ask me. But you can't stop him. He's like a four-foot stack of plates tipped at a forty-five-degree angle. Get 'em that far gone and you can kiss a big hunk of your paycheck good-bye. That's Kelly. Soon's he opens his mouth he's already at forty-five degrees. Too late. Man says what he's gotta say. "You think we'll get our pay today?" I ask him, even though I know it won't make a damn bit of difference what I say. I look at him, see him working them bones in his temples, working 'em. You'd think he was chewing corncobs. But didn't have a damn thing in his mouth but his own words. He says, "You colored guys make it sound like don't nobody else in the world feel pain."

"Hey look, Kelly, I ain't said jack to you, man. Go talk to Mendez; he's the one pissed you off."

"Move," he says, then he sweeps in front of me, then behind.

I say to him, "You know, we'd get done quicker if we sweep at the same time and clear at the same time, and wipe at the—"

"Mendez don't listen." He swipes his hairy hand through the air, stands straight and leans on his broom. "At least you listen. And Mendez gets loud, too. I can't talk to him, 'cause no matter what you say he gets loud. I can't talk to loud people." He tweaks at his nostril hairs, rolls his fingers together, then flicks the invisible speck to the floor.

"Do you wanna get the mop, or me?" I say.

"A guy like that'll never learn shit. You look at him. He's supposed to be our shop steward, setting an example for younger lads like yourself, and what's he been doing?"

"Same as usual, walking around with a pitcher fulla drumsticks and talking smack while he's supposed to be working."

"Fat son of a bitch."

"Yeah, well, I'll mop and you can clean the silverware and plates." I walk into the kitchen and just about drop from the heat. Jesus, how can these cooks take this nonsense? I walk past the ovens and see they're empty. They haven't even started lunch yet, I notice, and I start wondering where Mendez got the chicken legs. I look for George, which is easy, 'cause he's the only cook here who wears a cloth chef's hat. Everybody else wears paper. I find him at the chopping block, skinning garlic. This is pretty much where you can expect to find George, and that's what he'll be doing when you find him. Skinning garlic. He's got a year before he retires, so I guess no one'll say squiddly to him about goofing off.

"Georgie Porgie. How's your old Chef Boyardee lookin' ass?"

"Say Babe, what's to it?"

I don't care much for the way guys around here call each other "Babe." I know they don't mean nothing funny by it, but the only person I call Babe is Hwasook, my girlfriend. But lately I've been kind of joking with my best bud Ray by calling him Babe. He'll walk into our apartment and I'll say, "Hey, Babe," and he'll say, "Hey Babe," and we'll both get a grin out of that. We did it once when Hwasook was over, and you could tell it made her uncomfortable. Even after we explained it was a joke she still didn't get it.

"Say, George, where'd Mendez get the bird legs?"

"Cooler."

"He's grubbing a whole pitcher full of cold chicken legs?"

"Microwaves 'em in Salazar's office."

"You mean Salazar don't care?"

George said he didn't care, so I said, See you, George, and went back to the soap room to get the mop and bucket. I was a little twicked off about finding out that a guy like me'll get written up by Salazar for snatching a handful of shrimp, while Mendez gets away with a pitcher or a plate full of whatever the hell he wants all day long. We're not supposed to eat any leftovers, but most guys do. Even me sometimes. Don't get caught, though, 'cause they *will* nail you, even though it takes an act of Congress to actually fire a civil servant. But Mendez does whatever he wants. Maybe it's because most everybody likes him. Maybe because he's shop steward. But it isn't because, like Kelly says, that Mendez is a "colored Mexican," and in cahoots with Salazar. Mendez'll tell anybody who wants to listen that he's Panamanian. But to me the guy's all Brooklyn. I figure a guy like Kelly, though, thinks anyone with a Latino name is a Mexican.

As far as I can see, Mendez and Salazar despise each other, and it's clear that Salazar's terrified of Mendez. Mendez knows it and loves to rub Salazar's face in it. Calls him Sally, throws his arms over the little dude's shoulders, musses his glossy pompadour. Salazar smiles back with tight white lips, and never says much. I mean all you gotta do is compare one to the other and you can see why. Salazar can't be taller than five-foot-four, and if he weighs much over one-twenty, on any given day, it's 'cause he's carrying his grocery money in quarters. And he's got about as much personality as he's got body weight and height. Big ol' meaty Mendez could have the dude fried up crispy, carry him around in a pitcher, and munch him in maybe four quick bites. Mendez is all personality. The big, quick-stepping, fast-talking lug is everywhere at once, in sight and sound. Cahoots my butt. Mendez owns the place, and you gotta admire him sort of. But still this chicken-in O'-pitcher crap twicks me off, and I tell Kelly about it when I get back to our section. All Kelly says is, "Proves my point." And before I can stop myself I ask him what he means, and he says, "When you finish mopping, we'll take a break."

So, after I'm done, I sit down for break and Kelly comes from the kitchen with the usual yogurt, the usual orange, and the usual sausages. He bathes the sausages with Frank's Louisiana Hot Sauce, and as per usual asks me why I'm not eating, and as usual I tell him I don't eat breakfast. Then I say, "You know, if we don't get our checks today, I'm gonna tell Salazar to pay my rent."

"It's just like I'm saying, Scott, what's so goddamn great about bein' white?"

Plates, I tell you. Plates, stacked four feet high, heading straight down like a gunshot victim, and there's nothing I can do.

"I mean look," he says, "You don't get your check. I don't get my check. How's my color make it any better for me?" He clicks his flat hazel eyes twice, runs his freckly hand over his crewcut, sliding his paper hat a couple notches to the left.

"Couldn't tell you," I say. "All I know is that Civil Service pay is supposed to be guaranteed on time."

"And do I get a tax break 'cause I'm white?"

"Nine extra days is just too damn long to wait, if you ask me. Hey, how come it's taking so long anyway?"

"Scotty. You know why I retired early from the Corps?"

I give up on getting him to swing my way, so I say, "You got shot. You told me."

"Know why I got shot?" He pushes his paper hat back off his brow, then dumps salt and more hot sauce on his sausages. I tell him no I don't know why he got shot. "You know who shot me?" he asks.

"You weren't shot in Vietnam?"

Kelly stabs a sausage with his fork, pops it into his mouth, and chews it so hard I can hear his teeth knock together. I wave a fly off my ear. After a minute Kelly says, "There was this kid in my company, well, not really a kid like some of the boots in my company. This lad had seven years in. Did a couple tours in Vietnam, too, but was only a private first class."

"So why'd he shoot you?"

"Did I say he shot me?"

"Well, get to the—"

"No, I didn't, so let me—"

"All right! All right!"

"You never listen."

"Kelly, just ten minutes ago you said . . . OK, Kelly, you're right. I don't listen."

"They called him Barney for some damn reason, but at the inquest and the court martial they called him by his real name, but I don't remember it. Never forget what he looked like, though. This fella had one a'them bull necks, built like a little oak stump. Heavy beard. Black eyes. Had eyelashes that looked, you know, like a woman's. No, I won't be forgetting that mug for a long time. The guy was Indian, but I don't know the tribe or nothing. But that's what made him wild. Mean, lazy, and smart, too, I'm telling you.

"You know, I'd walk into the squad bay sometimes, for some reason or another, and I'm telling you, it'd be like ten, eleven hundred in the morning and there'd this kid be, in his boots, trousers, and undershirt, just snoozing like a papoose. Course I'd wake him up and he'd tell me some kinda bullpuckie like he'd just give blood or was suffering heat stroke, or didn't nobody bother to wake him up at reveille, or like that, and I'd go, 'Well, where's your med-pass?' or 'Why come you're in uniform?' or something and he'd get pissed off, get his ass up, put on the rest of his uniform, and get his Indian ass to work."

Kelly sniffs and holds his coffee cup under his nose, just staring off into space. I look at his nose hairs and his bushy knuckles and his arms, which are fuzzy as a dog's leg, and I say to myself, Well, looks like some white people got it better in winter, but I sure wouldn't wanna be you in all this heat. Kelly sniffs again and sips his coffee. "Goddamn *right* I did," he says, as if I've just said, Gosh, Kelly, really?

"But nobody else would," Kelly says. "Company commander didn't say shit. Hell, his own platoon sergeant didn't say shit. I did. Good ol'

221

Gunny Sergeant William P. Kelly did. I never understood this, Scott, I never did. Some guys seemed to respect this Barney guy 'cause of all the chest cartoons he'd picked up in combat. Man, you shoulda seen that boy in dress uniform. Had a chest fulla combat ribbons, more'n me. Enlistment stripes on his sleeve, too, of course, but just one god-damn strip on the upper sleeve. One." Kelly's pointing a finger in my face like I can't count. "That told me everything I needed to know. It was like he was saying to everyone, 'Lookit me, I done my time, so lea-me alone and lemme collect my paycheck.' Nobody but me seemed to care. Kid wasn't even in my platoon. I was motor pool; he was comm, but you think any one a'them shitbirds in the comm platoon'd say something to 'im.

"Well, one day I caught him in the rack, and it was something like thirteen hundred hours in the afternoon or what have you, and so I nudge him with my foot and he sits up like a dead body'll do if it lays around a few days. Well he says, 'What time is it, gunny?'

" 'It's time somebody wrote you up,' I say, 'if you don't have an ex-cuse for being in that rack, PFC.' And get this: He jumps out his rack, throws his blouse and cover on, telling me he's got an excuse, but that he's gotta go get it. Well, that little son of a bitch walked out and never did come back. I wasted twenty minutes waiting for his dumb ass to come back, but he never did. Well, I was mad enough to piss fire, but I let it go. Wasn't in the mood that day, I guess."

Kelly pops the last sausage into his mouth and has some more cof-fee. Those little skull bones are working like he's got at least a dictio-nary or two worth of words in his mouth. He stares down at his plate, and chews. I sit back and wait. This obviously ain't his point. The plates ain't hit the floor yet. I swipe at a fly, and it vanishes somewhere past Kelly's ear. "So what's this got to do with why white folks got it so bad?" I say.

"You know, breakfast is your most important meal of the day, Scott. You oughta take advantage. Only thirty cents a meal, lad." I just hiss and shake my head. Then my heart pops when I'm jolted by someone's meathook slapping down solid on my shoulder. I hear, "What you boys think this is?" When I turn I'm staring right into little Salazar's mus-tache, even though I'm sitting and he's standing. " . . . a retirement home?" he says.

"Break ain't over yet," says Kelly. Salazar ignores him and looks at me. "I need someone to hit your section one more time with the mop,

Mr. Winters. Sergeant Klutsky spilled some coffee between table five and table six."

"Someone. You mean me."

"Everybody else is eating," says Salazar, and he looks a little stunned that I'm irate. I'm not usually irate, but Kelly's kinda rubbing on my last nerve.

"Hey," says Kelly, "we getting paid or not?"

"Paychecks are in my safe," says Salazar, then he scoots away on those size six patent leather shoes of his. Damn things squeak and glimmer like a couple mechanical toys. Kelly's looking at 'em too, them shoes. Looks at 'em like he hates 'em. "Why's he always come to me for crap like that?" I say. "He never says jack to the other new guys."

Kelly says he does it 'cause I let him. I guess that's true, but I *am* new here and can't afford to act like I own the place, like I'm Mendez. I've got a month and a half of probation left. But even if I was a full Civil Service employee I don't think I'd play the jigaboo some of 'em expect me to. That's the kind of thing you just can't explain to an old bonebrain like Kelly. It means something different when a black guy skates at work from when a white guy does. It might not be so, but you always feel white people are watching you, waiting for you to screw up, pissed off a little if you don't. And they can't really make up their minds about us. I mean, they call you lazy, but every so often you overhear white dudes in the locker room say, "Yeah, Babe, busted my ass today, worked like a nigger, I'm telling ya." But, I can't make up my mind either, 'cause what I can't figure is whether I look more like a "jigaboo" if I try to slide by with hardly any work, or if I kowtow to de boss man and bust ass. Can't win as long as someone else calls your game, I guess. And, like, would it be OK working during break time if a white guy had asked me to? What if Mendez was the boss? Would I feel like a Tom then? Skip it, I tell myself. All I wanna do is keep my job. I get up, stretch. "Well," I say, "by the time I get back from the soap room, break'll be over anyhow."

"Fuck Salazar."

"Not my type."

"Sit down."

"Well, what damn difference is it gonna make two minutes from now? The point is *I'll* be the one who has to do it anyway. You ain't gonna do it. Mendez, Piper, Ski, Morales, those guys ain't gonna do it. So . . . " And I just stand there with my knuckles on my belt, trying to look tough, but my trouser seams are wedged up my butt; and in my paper hat, short-sleeve white shirt, and red monkey jacket, and knowing that I'm on my way to the soap room so I can clean up a mess that I know no one else will, I don't feel so tough. Kelly gets the message anyway. He sits there, staring at me with his flat hazel-blue eyes jiggling side to side like they always do when he's twicked. It always makes me sort of nervous. I can't understand how a guy's eyes could do that. Must be some kind of palsy. Then he squints and says, "You noticed how hot it is? It ain't even lunchtime yet, and it's just plain damn hot in here."

We're setting up the lunch dishes. In less than an hour we'll be shoveling chow at the junior flyboys and girls. That's what I really hate about this job. That, and cleaning up after 'em, which pretty much means I hate the whole job. I'm not saying I've got anything against these cadets, not personally. They're smart and polite and everything, but I hate the way the upperclassmen harass the doolies. I hate it when the kids have to stand up at attention right in the middle of a meal and spout the chain of command, or the parts of the M-16 rifle. I hate when a bunch of 'em are made to stand up and shout football cheers or wing cheers or flight cheers or squadron cheers. I hate when you're just getting the ravioli or whatnot to your hundredth flyboy when the first ten are asking for more milk and juice, and after you give 'em the milk and the juice, ten people here want more green beans and twenty there want more corn and bread, and there's cheers and chants, and heat and steam and flies and Air Force blue and pink heads everydamnwhere you look, and you're pulling your hot cart all overthedamnplace and it's big, the size of a V. W. bus, when you're tired, but then the flybabes split all neat and orderly like, leaving you all this cleaning up to do. All the waste. All the waste. It really gets to me: feed a Boy Scout Jamboree with the leftover burgers. Fatten every poor baby on the south side of Colorado Springs with the leftover milk. Ship the green beans, the rice, the macaroni to the shelters all over town and you ain't gotta feel guilty for at least half a week. Abscond with the spuds—fried, baked, au gratin, hashed and browned, boiled, ranched—and open up your own damned potato restaurant at zero percent food cost. But whatta we do with it? We toss it. It's criminal. I mentioned this fact to Kelly once and he told me, "Volume buying. Don't cost 'em nothing. And don't give me that trash about starving people and all that, 'cause the gover'ment pays for it, and pays your

224

rent, food, clothes, and gas, too, and they can do what they please with us *and* the food."

But I can't think about all that now, 'cause I got to hustle buns and get the stuff laid out. Yesterday. 'Cause lunch is just about ready, and I know Kelly ain't gonna be much help today since he's steady yabbering my ear off about this Barney guy. "Well," he says, "I had duty that very night, anyway, which means I had reveille the next morning, and you could bet your sweet ass that little shitbird was getting outta that rack at oh-five-thirty sharp. I knew how to get jarheads up, I tell ya. I'd rap my nightstick on their bedposts, wink the lights, kick over shit cans, and if that didn't work, I'd grab an ankle and pull the guy out. And see, with this Barney kid, I'd not only wake him, see, but I'd make sure he stayed up by giving him a lawful order to help me get other Marines up."

I say to Kelly, "Say, you want me to get the pitchers laid out or you want to?" Kelly wipes his brow with the inside of his wrist and says, "But when I grabbed his ankle the boy went three kinds of ballistic. Scott, I tell you that not only did this boy take a swing at me, but he pushed over five or six wall lockers and racks. Goddamn things went over like dominoes. . . . You better polish them spoons; they look like hell—and then, see, and then he starts screaming, 'motherfucker! motherfucker! I got something for your ass!' And next thing you know he starts punching out windows."

"With his fist?"

"Hell, yeah, with his fist. He punches out four before I even know what the hell he's doing. Rattled me pretty bad. That's one of the reasons I retired from the Corps when I did. Crazy hopheads like that, well, you never knew *what* they were gonna do.

"Well, so this big colored fella, name of Lance Corporal Whitaker, just pushes by me and says, 'Dust,' which I thought was some kind of colored cuss word for white man, but I found out later he meant what they call angel dust, PCP, know what that is?"

He misses my sarcasm when I say, "Tarzan no know. What angel dust?" 'cause he says back, "It's a goddamn drug is what it is. A goddamn drug." He pauses to let this sink in, then says, "So this Lance Corporal Whitaker just walks over to Barney when he's on his seventh or eight window, cutting himself and shedding his blood like he's got an extra couple quarts in his wall locker and don't care, see, and this Whitaker guy just touches Barney on the shoulder and says something like, 'Morning, Barn,' and Barney just stops. Stops dead. I mean he

225

don't move, and neither does anybody else. Everybody's just staring at this kid's bloody hand and arm, and all the blood here and there, in drops and smears. But then this Whitaker fella, just as calm as you please, grabs a towel off Barney's rack, wraps up Barney's arm and walks him to the infirmary. Hey, Scott, we got some bent forks here. Scrounge some good ones, will ya, lad?"

The dining hall is wall to wall blue, and Kelly shuts up for a while. But I know he's at sixty degrees 'cause those bones are struggling under his skin like a bag fulla kittens. Things are going smooth, and my mind's not even on my work. I'm thinking about taking a long shower, getting into some non-polyester clothes, and calling up Hwasook to make plans for the weekend. Since we're getting paid today, the weekend's looking good. We'll go to Deckers, maybe, and she'll take her suntan lotion, a nice bikini, and a book, and I'll take my fishing stuff and wine and crackers, cheese, fruit, and so forth. Maybe I'll bring a good sci-fi pulp, myself. If the sun cooperates, we'll be fine. As long as we don't run into a bunch of gawking rednecks. Hwasook doesn't understand, but that's why I don't care much for going to the mountains, big, blue-green quiet and beautiful as they are, 'cause of all the RV, truck, and motorcycle necks who stare at her like she's some kinda slut and stare at me like they know she wouldn't be as close as a parsec to me if not for my twelve-inch unit and my briefcase fulla heroin.

Hwasook argues that a neck's neck is just as red in town as it is in those hills, and she's got a point, but I have my doubts. Something funny happens to some people when they start huffing pinewood air, drinking beer in the hot sun, eating ash-flavored food. They start feeling like pioneers, muleskinners, cowboys, desperadoes. To them Hwasook and me start looking like runaway slaves or bloodthirsty savages. They start up with the yee-haaaaws, and revving their engines, yelling hey nigger out their windows as they drive by. She doesn't get it, though, and neither does Kelly. I'm getting pretty twicked off thinking of all this stuff and can't wait till things slow down and he can get to his point, which I plan to shoot down with all this stuff I've been thinking about.

Finally, things do slow down, but before I can talk to ol' Kelly, I spot Mendez coming our way with a hamburger in his fat mitts. "Hey, Mendez," I say.

"Hey, Babe."

"Is it true we're getting paid today?"

Mendez shrugs. "Ask Salazar."

"Fuck Salazar," says Kelly.

"Too skinny," I say, and at the same time Mendez says, "Nobody's talking to you, Kelly."

Kelly's eyes start to jiggle. "You can kiss my ass, Mendez."

Mendez swells up bigger than the usual huge, and looks at Kelly. "Wouldn't kiss that wrinkly thing with your *own* lips, old man. Don't start with me again." Then he turns back to me. "Look here, bruh, Salazar needs someone to help Peggy clean up a mess on the east section."

"He don't have to—"

"It's OK, Kelly, I got it."

And I do get it, leaving Mendez and Kelly to argue with each other over the rattle and clatter of ninety waiters in monkey suits cleaning up after 4,500 cadets; throwing away, probably a quarter ton of food; telling jokes, lies, stories. I hear Mendez say "racist" at least a half dozen times. I hear Kelly use the phrase "silver platter." I roll my eyes and keep walking.

My only problem working with Peggy is that I'm pretty sure she's got a crush on me. I'm not being conceited, or anything, 'cause I'm no stud and Peggy's no fox. She's tall, skinny, forty-five-ish with platinum hair, veiny hands, and sky-blue, ice-blue eyes. She always calls me gorgeous, which I find hard to respond to in a likewise way. She ain't ugly, but I don't like giving her ideas. Right now I'm trying to be polite to her but keep my eyes on the grape juice I'm swabbing up. The flies are having a party. There's a zillion more in her section than there are in Kelly's and mine. "Who's your partner today, Peg?" I ask.

She locks her unbelievably blue eyes on me and smiles at me the same way Mendez smiles at ribs. "Freddy Washington, but I'll trade him for you, gorgeous." I ignore that and ask her where Freddy is. "Salazar's got him in the office, chewing him out for coming in at four-fifty this morning. I'm sure Salazar's having a tougher time than Freddy in there."

I chuckle and say something like Yeah, or, I'll bet, but I notice my hands are trembling, and I feel almost sick to my stomach. I'll admit that Peggy usually makes me nervous, but there's something more right now, something I can't get the finger on till two things happen. One: a fly lands on my hand, and I flick it away so hard I drop my mop. Then two: Peggy bends to pick it up for me, and as I bend over she looks me right square down deep in the eyes. Then I remember.

"So where is Freddy?" I say. Peggy smiles, no doubt thinking she's got me in one of those magic moments where a guy finally notices how beautiful a woman is. "Someone's been working too hard," she says. I shake my head dramatic like, and say, "I mean, what time did Freddy come in, you say?" I notice her neck is all mottled up red, and I say to myself, Oh Lord, and I look up at her face, and she winks and says, "About five, gorgeous." I wish I could tell her it's not her half-moon beauty, but it does have to do with her, and these flies, and Kelly, and her color and mine, and especially her eyes, the most beautiful thing about her. And now that I really look at her it's got to do with her thin, chapped lips, her hawk nose, her long neck. She reminds me of this girl I thought was my friend for about a semester back in high school. Her name was Dianna Dillman, and she was my lab partner in tenth-grade biology. I never had, like, a crush on Dianna or anything, but I liked her a lot. She was extremely funny, and used to write little notes to me while Mr. Buller was yammering about pond scum, or mitosis, or some such crap. I figure because of Dianna I got Cs instead of Bs in that class, but for almost a whole semester it was worth it. If her little notes didn't crack me up, she'd go for what Buller used to call the "lowbrow" stuff like pretending to get high from breathing the Bunsen-burner gas, or just filling her cheeks with air and staring at me for five minutes. Guess you just had to be there. But one day all that stuff just stopped. Dianna acted like I was absent. Bad day, I told myself, and let it go. So pretty much near the end of my bio class, Mr. Buller asked me to stay after. I nudged Dianna with my elbow and whispered to her, "Wonder what this is all about. Nobel Prize, you think?" Dianna didn't say jack. She stared straight ahead and blushed red as her own lipstick.

Turns out the day before, Dianna'd had her wallet lifted from her purse, and since she noticed it missing after bio class, and since I sat right smack next to her at our little black table, she figured I'd snagged it. I didn't take her wallet, and I was glad Buller believed me, but he told me that Dianna didn't want to be my lab partner anymore. I didn't see her the rest of the day, so I never got the chance to argue my case. And the next day I found a note that she'd slipped into the vents of my locker. I knew it was her, 'cause it was in the same microscopic hand-writing of all those funny little notes she'd slip me in class. It went, and I quote, "Only two things in this world that I despise / One of them's niggers/The other one's flies/Only one thing to say about each of these guys/The more I see niggers/The more I like flies." That was it. Not even a "Love, Dianna" stuck on the end.

228

So this is one more thing to tell Kelly. One thing that's great about being white: The rest of my sophomore year I never could figure out the words to hurt Dianna as much as she'd hurt me. Fact is, I still don't think I could. Six, seven years now, and I still don't think I could.

When I got back, Kelly's so hot I'm surprised his little paper hat hasn't burst into flames. "What is it you people want?" he says.

Dominion over nature, time, and the bodies and minds of the white race, I think to myself, but I say, "What'd he say?" and he waves his hairy hands in little circles like he's lost his balance while standing on a log. "Man, that guy burns my ass," he growls. I don't say nothing. I just start collecting silverware and fighting flies, scraping plates, wiping sweat from my forehead, pulling the seam from the crack of my behind. Hell with these jerks, I say to myself. Hell with spooks, ofays, spicks, gooks, flies, cadets, paychecks, heat, color, kinks, straight, curls, black, brown, freckles, white. I hate this stuff, I say to myself. I hate all this stuff.

"So," says Kelly, and I'm about two seconds from sticking a fork in his neck. I don't care. I just don't care, but the best thing I can do is let him finish his crap and then blow him away with all this stuff inside me, all this crap I been thinking.

"So," he says, "I figure the guy's crazy, and I don't say nothing to him or even look at him when him and Whitaker leave the room. If the United States Marines Corps wants to give welfare to a goddamn lazy hophead that's OK. I'm a short-timer and I don't care. I was in long enough to retire, even though I'd always wanted to do a full twenty-five years. But I just forgot about him. Washed my hands, so to speak. Just went about my business, you see. Least everybody was awake. That was that. I figured I just wouldn't deal with the kid no more.

"But one morning the first sergeant ast a bunch of Marines to redo the squadbay. Seems it was a pretty bad mess. You know it gets like that sometimes. The lads get in a hurry to get to morning chow and miss a spot or two with the swabs and brooms—Will you look at this. Sloppy sons a bitches. Look at this. Some idiot spilled a whole container a milk all over a tray of succotash."

"So fucken what, Kelly, it's not like we're gonna put it in a Tupperware container and stick it in the refrig—"

"So I don't know why I went up there, but for some reason I had to go see somebody in the company office. I don't know, but in order to get to the HQ, you gotta go through the squadbay, see? So I'm going up the stairwell, and I hear all this yelling and cussing, so I run up the rest of the way, and Barney's got some little boot private pinned up against the wall. Got his forearm jammed into the kid's windpipe and four other Marines are trying to pull Barney back, but like I told you, Barney's one stout little fella and they're having a pretty tough time getting him to let the kid loose.

"Well, shit, what was I supposed to do? I help grab Barney's leg. Then his arms, and finally we get him off the kid. This kid's name was Hernandez, Mexican fella, and big old Whitaker was there, and then there was this Samoan fella, Tapua, and another Mexican fella, a guy from Comm Platoon I didn't know, and this white fella name of Grice, a radio tech, I think he was. Looked like the goddamn United Nations, I was thinking. Sure wasn't like the Corps I joined. Not that I got anything against you people being in the service. Just never got used to it."

"Roll me the beverage cart, Kelly," I say, and then I tell him to go ahead. My palms are sweaty, hands trembling. Kelly walks the cart to me and says, "Well, I don't know why we did this. Maybe it was the way Barney relaxed so sudden, the way he just stared out the window like we wasn't even there. Made everybody else relax, too. We all just let him go. And I whispered to Grice to go get the police, and was just getting ready to walk Barney over to the office. I said, 'All right, leatherneck, let's go.' But he just stood there, staring out the window. Then in this real quiet voice he goes, 'I got something for your ass. I got something for all of you.'

"He was at his locker so fast nobody could do nothing. Besides, who the hell knew he'd come back with a pistol? But there he was, waving a silver-plated snub nose thirty-eight in all our faces. Next thing you know, Hernandez is on his knees, begging for his life. Whitaker's looking sick and pissed off. He sits down on a rack and just starts cussing kinda quiet like, saying how hard he's tried to be a good Marine and how every time he turns around it's some new bullshit. And the Samoan's waving his hands and backing up to the wall, speaking Samoan like he ain't never hearda the United States. The other Mexican kid's just standing there looking white, sweaty and scared. And then there's me. After looking at all these scared, young boys I closed my eyes and lowered my head, see, and it's like I got two brains. One brain's going, Now what the fuck am I supposed to say to this hophead to get him to put the stinking gun down. The other brain's going, I don't give a rolling fuck what he does. I've had it. I've had it. Don't even care anymore—You better get that mop and broom. I'll get these carts."

"We got time, just finish!"

"Well, he shot me."

"I thought you said he *didn't*."

"No, that's not what I said. I just told you I didn't say that. I swear, Scott, you just don't listen. Hell yeah he shot me. Right in the thigh, splintered my femur bone like it was rotten bamboo. But the way Hernandez started screaming you'da thought that Indian bastard'd shot him. But I was the onliest one he shot, and even though Whitaker was on top'a Barney before he could get off another round, I knew he was only gonna pump 'em off into me if he'd had the chance."

"So you think he shot you 'cause you're white."

Salazar walks by before Kelly answers and he tells us he'll be passing out the checks at the end of the shift. Kelly glares at Salazar. At his squeaky shiny shoes, really. Like he hates 'em. "Man," says Kelly, "I got no respect for that little prick."

"So you think he shot you 'cause you're white, right?"

He looks at me a real long time, like I'm stupid. I'm not stupid.

"A guy who wears patent leather shoes is too lazy to shine," he says.

"Kelly."

"Huh?"

"Is that your point? What's your point?"

He raises one batwing eyebrow. *I* know what he means. *I* get his point. "That's another reason I retired from the Corps. Lot a lazy goddamn boot officers'd wear patent leather 'cause they were just too damn lazy to put a good spit shine on their shoes. Why, do you know that some a them bastards were getting away with wearing patent leather combat boots? Where's the tradition? Where's the pride? Hopheads, shitbirds, AWOLers, rock-n-goddamn-roll, hippie-jive talk a guy can't understand, wash-n-wear uniforms, no-discipline-having, dope-smoking punks, and people, all these people who don't like me . . . for no damn good reason. You think I'd wanna be part a that after twenty-one years of life the way it's supposed to be? No sir, I don't think so. No thank you. . . . Look here, I'll swab this time. You sweep, and then let's get outta here. We're getting our pay, Scotty boy."

That's exactly what I did. I swept. I tried to get him to talk more, but he'd just scoot his words around me. I just wanted to talk to him. Talk. But he wouldn't even look me in the eye. It was like sweeping up a four-foot stack of broken dishes. Big pieces with razor-sharp edges, little pieces with needle points, tinier pieces, like little daggers, pieces fine as moon dust that you'll never get up. After I finished sweeping, I grabbed my check, went to the locker room, and doffed the monkey

231

suit, slipped into my jeans, sneakers, and T-shirt, and broke camp. But all the way home I still felt like I was sweeping broken china, from under tables, under chairs, from corners and cracks, and across wide-polished floors, military clean and quiet as the mountains.

Nominated by The Kenyon Review

THE ANACONDA

by DENNIS SAMPSON

from THE AMERICAN VOICE

The man with the anaconda around his neck
seems proud, letting it coil and slide

across his outstretched arm and cupping
the throat as gently as a sparrow.

He has arrived
to flaunt his fearless love at noon

to traffic on the highway,
wrapped up this tough-minded muscle that shares

his days in a cage of glass demanding all,
flickering its tongue, the habitual

tic of a thief alone in the night,
thick and glistening, threading its length

gently up around his shoulders now
and weaving the delicate wedge-head in the air.

The anaconda does not seem to care
that it will be carried out to be admired

on Greensboro Avenue with its master
smirking at those who linger along the highway,

as if he alone possessed
the courage to confront this gliding dream

embracing everything. The anaconda feels
but begins to hunger for something other

than what it feels, flashing
between the master's spreading feet,

projecting its sexual head
like a wild idea, looking behind and around,

like a hand thrown up by a child,
nude, with nothing human on its mind.

And when the master grows tired
of presenting this labyrinth of flesh to the crowd,

folding and unfolding above the ground,
too feverish to receive his several kisses

offered to demonstrate his love,
he unwinds the willing creature with difficulty,

pouring it into the cage beside his bed
with patience won from doing things right,

as if the anaconda were the embodiment of knowledge,
consciousness wedded to consciousness

in a moment of clarity, hidden in stillness:
vainglorious, passionate, precise.

Nominated by Philip Levine, Sandra McPherson

THE UNDESIRABLE TABLE

fiction by JOYCE CAROL OATES

from RARITAN

WITH MUMBLED apologies, the maître d' seated us at an undesirable table in our favorite restaurant Le Coq d'Or. The men in our party protested. But there was nothing to be done. It was a Saturday night in the holiday season, the more desirable tables had been booked weeks in advance. Our reservation had been made practically at the last minute, what could we expect? Even though we were—are—frequent patrons of Le Coq d'Or, and had imagined ourselves on special terms with the management.

As we took our seats, reluctantly, at the undesirable table, in a front bay window of the dining room, one of our party remarked, bemused, yet serious, that perhaps the maître d' had expected a twenty dollar bill to be slipped surreptitiously to him. Was *that* it?

Seated at the undesirable table, in a front bay window of the dining room of Le Coq d'Or, we discussed this possibility in lowered, incensed voices. We are highly verbal people and much of dispute in our lives is resolved, if not satisfied, by speech. The more cynical among our party believed that yes, this might be so; though, in the past, and we'd dined in this restaurant innumerable times, the maître d' had not behaved like an extortionist. The more optimistic among our party believed that, no, that wasn't it, at all; surely not; our reservation had been made late, just the day before, the holiday season was frenzied this year, it *was* a Saturday night. And so why not enjoy ourselves? As we'd come out to do?

Even if it was something of a disappointment, and a rude surprise in a way, to be seated at an undesirable table in Le Coq d'Or.

And so, seated at the undesirable table, in a front bay window of the dining room of Le Coq d'Or, with an unwanted view of the street outside, we gave our drink orders to the waiter; we smiled gamely, and took up our hefty Le Coq d'Or menus (parchment-bound, gilt-printed, gold-tasseled, with elegantly scripted French, and English translations below) and perused the familiar categories of appetizers, first courses, entrées, desserts, wines. We chattered to one another discussing the dishes we might order, recalling previous meals at Le Coq d'Or, previous evenings in one another's company that had been both intellectually stimulating and emotionally rewarding, evenings that had had *meaning* of a kind, precious to consider. For food consumed in the presence of dear friends is not mere food but sustenance; a sustenance of the soul. A formal meal, with excellent wines, in a restaurant of the quality of Le Coq d'Or, in the right company, is a celebration. Yes?

So it was, we smiled gamely. We chattered happily. We were not to be cheated of our evening's pleasure—for most of us, a well-deserved reward for the rigors of the previous week—by the accident of being seated at an undesirable table. We gave our orders to the waiter, who was all courtesy and attentiveness. We handed back our hefty menus. When our drinks arrived, we lifted them to drink with pleasure and relief. We were almost successfully ignoring two facts: that the undesirable table in the bay window of the dining room was even more undesirable than the most pessimistic of us had anticipated; and that those of us unfortunate enough to be seated facing the bay window were particularly afflicted. Yet such was our courtesy with one another, even after years of friendship, and so awkward was the situation, that no one, not even those facing the bay window and the street, chose to speak of it. For to *name* a problem is *to invest it with too much significance.*

We, who are so highly verbal, whose lives, it might be said, are ingeniously amassed cities of words, understand the danger as few others do. Ah, yes!

There followed then, with much animation, a discussion of wines—in which several of our company, male, participated with great gusto and expertise, while others listened with varying degrees of attentiveness and indulgence. Which wines, of the many wines of Le Coq d'Or's excellent list, were to be ordered?—considering that the party was to dine variously on seafood, fish, poultry, and meat. Our conversations about wine are always lengthy and passionate, and touched with a heartfelt urgency, even pedantry; yet there is an undercurrent of bemused self-consciousness, too—for the wine connoisseurs are well aware of the absurdity of their almost mystical fanaticism even as they unapologetically indulge in it. After all, if there is a simple, direct, unalloyed ecstasy to be taken by the mouth, savored by the tongue like a liquid communion wafer, how can it be denied to those with the means to purchase it?—and by whom?

So, the usual spirited talk of wine among our party. And some argument. Where there is passion there *is* argument? Not that the wine connoisseurs dominated completely, despite their loud voices. Conversation became more general, there were parenthetical asides, the usual warm queries of health? recent trips? family? work? gossip of mutual acquaintances, colleagues? If there was a distracting scene outside the window, on the street (which was in fact an avenue, broad, windy, littered, eerily lit by street lamps whose light seemed to withhold, not give, illumination) or even on the sidewalk a few yards away from those of our company with our backs stolidly to the window *we knew nothing of it: saw nothing.*

At last, our appetizers were brought to us. And the first of the wines. Their ceremonial uncorking, the tasting—exquisite!

Red caviar, and arugula salads. Giant shrimp delicately marinated. Pâté maison. Escargots. Coquilles St. Jacques. Consommé à la Barigoule. Steak tartare. And of course the thick crusty brown bread that is a specialty of Le Coq d'Or. As we talked now of politics. Foreign, national, state, local. We talked of religion—is there any *demonstrable difference* between the actions of "believers" and "non-believers"? We asked after our friends' children in the hope and expectation that they would ask after ours.

(One of our party, her gaze drawn repeatedly to something outside the window, which, facing it as she was, at this undesirable table in the dining room of Le Coq d'Or, seemed to possess a morbid attraction for her, suddenly laid her fork down. Shut her eyes. As conversation swirled around her. But she said nothing, and nothing was said to her, and after a pause of some seconds she opened her eyes and, gazing now resolutely at her plate, picked up her fork and resumed eating.)

(Another of our party weakened. Laid his fork down too, pressed the back of his hand against his forehead. Again, conversation continued. Our eyes were firmly fixed on one another. And after a minute or

237

so he, too, revived, with steely resolution lifting his wine glass to his mouth and draining it in a single swallow.)

Boeuf Stroganoff. Pompano à la Meunière. Bouillabaisse. Sweetbreads à la York. Chateaubriand. Blanquette of veal, coq au vin, sole Lyonnaise, and an elegantly grilled terrapin with black mushrooms. And jullienne vegetables, lightly sautéed in olive oil. Another generous basket of crusty brown bread. And another bottle of wine, this time a Bordeaux.

One of our party, a woman with widened moist eyes, said, Oh!—what are they doing—? staring out the window in an attitude of disbelieving horror. But adding quickly, a hot blush mottling her face, No really—*don't look.*

No one of us having looked, nor even heard. In any case.

(Yes, certainly it crossed the minds of those gentlemen of our party with their backs to the offending scene to offer to exchange seats with the women facing it. Yet we hesitated. And finally, as if by mutual consent, said nothing. For to *name* a problem, in particular an upsetting and demoralizing problem over which none of us has any control, is *to invest it with too much significance.*)

How popular Le Coq d'Or is!—a region, an atmosphere, an exquisite state of the soul rather than merely a *restaurant.* In such surroundings, amid the glitter of flashing cutlery, expensive glassware, and crystal chandeliers, animal gluttony is so tamed as to appear a kind of asceticism.

At Le Coq d'Or, a perfectly orchestrated meal—which, we were determined, ours would be, even at an undesirable table—is rarely a matter of less than two hours.

Casting our eyes resolutely *not* in the direction of the window, the avenue, the luckless creatures outside. But, rather, with some envy at parties seated at desirable tables. Impossible not to feel resentment, bitterness, rancor. Even as we smiled, smiled. Even as the maître d' hovered guiltily near, inquiring after the quality of our food and drink and service, which we assured him, with impeccable politeness, and a measure of coolness, was excellent as always. Yet: *Why are these other patrons favored with desirable tables, while we, equally deserving, possibly more deserving, are not?*

Perennial questions of philosophy. The mystery of good, evil. God, Devil. More wine?—a final bottle uncorked. Through the plate glass bay window an occasional unwelcome, unheard stridency of sound. Keening wails, or sirens? No, mere vibrations. All sound *is* is vibrations, devoid of meaning. Coffee, liqueurs. Desserts so delicious they must be shared: Sorbet à la Bruxelles, profiteroles au chocolate, meringue glacé, zabaglione frappé, strawberries flambé. And those luscious Swiss mints. It was observed that the rose-tinted wax candles in the center of the table had burned low, their flames had begun to flicker. A romance of candlelight. The circular table, draped in a fine oyster-white linen cloth—the rose-patterned cushioned chairs—were floating in a pool of darkness. Staring intensely at one another, friends, dear friends, the fever of our love for one another, our desperate faith in one another, transfixed by one another's faces. For there lies *meaning*. Yes?

You expected me to weaken. To surrender to an instinctive narrative momentum. In which the *not-named* is suddenly, and therefore irrevocably, *named*. Following the conventions of narration, I might have proceeded then to Events B, C, D, the horror of disclosure increasing in rhythm with the courses of our elaborate meal. By the climax—the emptying of the very last bottle of wine, the paying of the check, our rising to leave—a revelation would have occurred. *We would never be the same again after our experience at the undesirable table.* You expected that.

But that was not my way, because it did not happen that way. There was no *naming*, thus no *narrative*.

The check was paid, we rose to leave. One of us, fumbling for her handbag, dropped it and it fell onto a chair and from the chair to the floor spilling some of its contents with a startled little cry.

We walked through the dining room of Le Coq d'Or without a backward glance at the undesirable table.

(Let the maître d', who wished us happy holidays with a forced smile, worry that we'll never return to his damned restaurant. Let him worry he's insulted us, and we'll spread the word to others. Our revenge!)

Fortunately, there is a high-rise parking structure directly accessible from Le Coq d'Or so that patrons are spared walking along the windswept, littered avenue, and the possible danger of this walk. We'd parked our cars there, on Level A, and in the cooler air felt a sudden giddy sense of release, like children freed from confinement. We were talking loudly, we were laughing. We shook hands warmly saying goodnight, we hugged one another, we kissed. Old friends, dear friends. Now the ordeal of the undesirable table was behind us it was possible to forget it. In fact, we were rapidly forgetting it. We would retain instead the far more meaningful memory of another superb shared meal at Le Coq d'Or, another memorable evening in one another's company. Of course we'll be back—many times.

For Le Coq d'Or is, quite simply, the finest restaurant available to us. It might be said we have no choice.

Nominated by Robert Phillips

STILLBORN

by MARIBETH FISCHER

from THE IOWA REVIEW

"Nothing hurts as bad as they say it does," she told me later. "And clear, pure memory doesn't hurt at all. What hurts is forgetting."
Josephine Humphreys, Rich in Love

A FEW SUNDAYS AGO my mother phoned as I was eating dinner in front of the TV, her voice startling me because it wasn't her usual time to call. The minute I picked up the receiver, she said, "I don't want to talk, but I just had to phone you, Beth."

"What's wrong?"

"Nothing, nothing at all," she told me. "It's just that I found another book—" She paused. "It's about a mother who leaves."

She didn't need to say anything else. I scribbled the title and the author's name on the back of a mail-order catalogue and hung up after promising to buy the book as soon as I finished with classes the following afternoon. "It's hardback," she cautioned just before I got off the phone. "I'll send you the money if you need it."

After hanging up, I sat still for a moment, listening numbly to the voices on the TV and remembering that summer five years before when my mother first left our family to be with a man who was nothing more to me than a name and a photograph from her 1959 high school yearbook. I was twenty-two at the time, newly married and living in Iowa. It was a summer of drought, of endless bone-white skies and acres of dying cornfields. I could hardly imagine then, as the sun brutalized the landscape, that grief wasn't simply something to get through, like a bad season or a dry spell.

I stared down at the new title in my hand. Ever since my mother left, I've been reading novels and short stories about women who leave their families. I know, of course, that the books won't give me the answers, but that's not what I want anymore. I am simply trying to find in fiction what I can not find in real life—understanding.

When I read Richard Ford's short story "Great Falls," my mother had only been gone for three months. It was September and I still believed that she'd be home in time for Christmas. The story was told from the perspective of an eleven-year-old boy named Joe, who made me think of my younger brother Mark, only a year older. Home in New Jersey, Mark would have started school already and I tried to picture him in the mornings, waking up, realizing—as I did every day—she's gone and, worse, *she left*.

"And my mother herself—why would she do what she did?" Joe asks at the end of the story. I have never known the answer to these questions, have never asked anyone their answers. Though possibly it—the answer—is simple: it is just low-life, some coldness in us all, some helplessness that causes us to misunderstand life when it is pure and plain, makes our existence seem like the border between two nothings, and makes us no more or less than animals who meet on the road—watchful, unforgiving, without patience or desire."

I read that quote ten, fifteen times, the words "low-life" and "coldness" echoing in my head long after I'd put the book away. How I hated what those words suggested; how I still do: that ultimately our most painful decisions are borne *not* of grief or fear, love or regret or joy but, instead, of a terrible selfishness which lies beneath the surface of our lives like a cancer. I hated the implication that it was that simple, that arbitrary, that just as anyone could be struck with illness—so could any of us be struck by this "coldness," this numbing inability to distinguish right from wrong.

There were other books. In one, the mother who left had dark permed hair and long blood-red fingernails. She drank too much whiskey and talked too loudly about the men—and the women—she had loved. In another, the mother was sick, abusing her daughter sexually. And in the novel my mother phoned to tell me about a few Sundays ago—*Father Melancholy's Daughter* by Gail Godwin—the mother who left her family dies before she has a chance to come home, before her daughter can understand.

Last week I read the novel *Rich in Love* by Josephine Humphreys. In this story, the mother leaves so abruptly that when her daughter comes home from school the door of her mother's car is hanging open and her macramé purse, along with a bag of groceries, is still sitting on the front seat, where a container of butter pecan ice cream has melted. Two hundred pages later, the mother returns, her leaving "like a television serial that had gotten so complicated the plot could only be resolved by calling itself a dream, backing up and starting all over again."

I realized, then, that for most people, most women, what my mother did five years ago truly is unimaginable. And yet I, her oldest daughter, not only have to imagine it, I have to understand it.

Recently I listened to a friend of mine an artist, talk about how she wants to go to an artist's colony to work on some paintings. But she can't bear to leave her children—in ten years she has never been away from them for more than a few days. As she talks of leaving, something happens in her face, to her eyes. Although the children—a boy, ten, a girl, six—are not here with us in this restaurant, they are present in the tightening of my friend's jaw, in the way she nervously grips the stem of her wine glass. She is suddenly so anxious that her husband reaches to cover her hand with his own. Susan has heard my mother's story; she hasn't judged it, and wouldn't judge it, yet I know that she cannot imagine ever doing what my mother has done. I also know, however, that until the day she left, my mother herself could not have imagined it either.

I wish I could explain to Susan how it happened so quickly. *Nobody* thinks she can do it. Maybe that's why, of all the books I've read, the only insight that rings true for me is the detail about the ice cream melting all over the front seat of the car. I know it really does happen this way, as you are carrying groceries into the house or ironing your son's favorite soccer shirt or standing in front of your closet wondering what to wear. I know the unimaginable becomes imaginable in a moment just that ordinary.

Until the day my mother walked out, I naively thought that it was only a certain kind of woman who would do such a thing; a woman who shouldn't have had children or never really wanted them in the first place; a woman whose daughters spoke of her with contempt and shame. And if she was a good woman and she just happened to have made a mistake, well then, she'd come back, wouldn't she? Just like Meryl Streep in *Kramer vs. Kramer.* She'd come back full of regrets and promises never to leave her son again.

Two weeks before my mother left and flew to Montana with Nick, her former high school sweetheart, my husband and I came home

243

from Iowa to visit. It was then, my first morning back, that my mother confessed to me her longing to leave. Dan, my stepfather, had left for work over an hour before; my younger brother was at school; my husband was asleep in my childhood bed. My mother and I were sitting in the kitchen, picking at a plate of hot blueberry muffins. Rain clattered against the bay windows, which were steamed from the heat of the oven.

"I think I'm in love with someone else," my mother said quietly, staring down at her hands. She spoke the words so quickly that I couldn't understand them at first. They sounded like pig Latin; *mai nai ovelay ithway omeonesay*. I remember feeling frustrated, wanting to shout at her. What are you talking about? Even now I'm not sure if she repeated what she'd said or if the words themselves unscrambled. All I know is that I heard them as an echo, blurred and distorted, as if she'd shouted them across a distance. *I'm in love with someone else.*

Outside everything looked very shiny and very green: Bottle-green, Apple-green, Sea-green. Olive-green—as if my sister and I were still kids and had just gone down a row of Crayolas and scribbled long streaks of that color over and over across the window. Nick, my mother called him, this man she apparently loved. *Nick*. The name was familiar and I recognized the way she said it, the same way that I could identify songs I hadn't heard in years. Vaguely, I remembered kneeling on the living room floor with my mother when I was still young enough not to be in school. It was raining then too, a slow-silent drizzle like lines of static across an old black and white movie. Twenty-eight years old, already divorced from my father, she was showing me her scrapbook and high school yearbook, pointing to a photograph of a thin, dark-eyed boy I didn't recognize. I wondered if this was when I first heard my mother say Nick's name. "This is the boy I dated before I married your father," she might have confessed. Five or six years old, I would have looked at her in amazement, shocked to think of her dating or going to parties, incredulous to realize that once my mother had been young—as young as the high school girls who lived across the street from us.

Whenever I asked my mother why she and my father had divorced, a divorce they had always described as "amicable," she would turn away and answer quietly, "Your dad and I are good friends now, Beth. That's all that matters." Or, "Our marriage was pretty painful," she would say, "I really don't want to talk about it." The minute I heard about Nick, though, I questioned that "painful marriage." I wondered

244

if he was the real reason I couldn't remember my father ever living with us.

Sitting in my mother's kitchen two weeks before she left with Nick, I heard her say that she had practically been engaged to him when she was twenty and that her parents had convinced her to break it off. "They never gave him a chance," she said. She sounded distant as she spoke of it, a cadence of sorrow in her voice that I'd never heard before. I thought of how, when my older brother and I were kids, we used to tie rubber bands around empty shoe boxes and pluck them as if they were guitars. But we could never control their deformed, squeaking twang; we could never make real music. My mother's voice had that same wire-tweaked quiver. I wanted to lay a steady palm against the shuddering cords of her throat.

"I don't mean to make this sound like a soap opera," she said. "It wasn't. It was just the fifties. But we wanted different things then, Beth. I wanted a nice house and good clothes for myself and my children—I don't think there's anything wrong with that either—and my mother kept telling me that I'd never have that with Nick, that Nick would never amount to anything, that if I married him it would be the biggest mistake of my life." She shook her head, brushing the memory away like a strand of hair fallen in front of her eyes. "When I look back, I don't understand it," she whispered. "I was twenty years old then. Why didn't I stand up to my parents?" She spoke so softly that I could barely hear her: "I was afraid." Her face was lacquered with tears; I felt as if I was staring at her through a window. Without looking at me, she continued: "So, I ended it. I sent Nick a Christmas card and told him I'd decided to marry your dad. I wanted to write a letter, I wanted to explain, but didn't know how, I didn't know what to say. . . ." She shrugged and tried to smile, as if to show me that she understood how ridiculous this all was, but her face crumpled and she began to cry. Outside the rain had stopped. The sky, a flat yellow-brown, was the color of water stains on old love letters. "What I did to Nick was the cruelest thing I have ever done to another person," my mother said. "And I've never gotten over it."

It was then that she told me that Nick had phoned her one afternoon a few weeks before. It was the first time she had heard from him in over twenty-eight years. He was at his sister's, he said. Her name had come up, and he got to wondering how her life had turned out.

"What did you tell him?" I didn't look at her when I asked, afraid of the truth I might see in her eyes.

245

Gently, she touched my arm. "I told him I was happy," she said. "And I meant it. I was."

"Then what—"

But she held up her hand to stop me. "Nick told me he had business in Philadelphia, and he wanted to know if I could meet him for lunch—" She glanced at me hesitantly. "I told Dan about it, Maribeth. I honestly didn't think it would be a big deal and certainly I had nothing to hide." She started crying again. "It's not what you might be thinking. The entire lunch Nick and I talked about our kids and afterwards we didn't even hug goodbye. I figured I'd never see him again."

"So *what* happened?"

"I don't know. Dan brought me home and then went back to the office for a few hours and I—" She drew in her breath, seemed to hold it in her throat for a moment and then blew the words out like smoke. "I phoned Nick, Maribeth. I told him I'd never stopped loving him."

"You did?" I asked incredulously. "You?"

She left abruptly on a Monday morning. For the first time in her life she rode in a taxi alone, then boarded an airplane without her husband or children. She went to Milwaukee, the city where she and Nick had grown up, where they had met and fallen in love. The following morning they flew to Montana, a place my mother had never been. Later, try as I might, I couldn't picture her in such barren, open surroundings, in "a landscape dominated only by sky" and "punctuated," as she would eventually write, "not by sounds but by stillness." Earlier that spring, however, Nick, a roofing consultant, had been contracted to fix the leaking stone walls of a small church near the town of Hardin, Montana. Stone by stone his crew would take the building apart that summer and then slowly rebuild it. My mother would spend her afternoons in a tiny café, drinking iced tea and trying to concentrate enough to read. Most days, she would tell me, she couldn't get through more than a page.

In Iowa the drought continued. For weeks at a time it seemed this was all anyone talked about. In the afternoons the local pancake house where I waitressed was filled with farmers drinking cup after cup of coffee. There was nothing to do except pray for rain, and hope. Often, driving west along Route 30 towards the next town, I would see women standing on their porches, staring out at the flat expanse of yellow-blue sky, waiting. In July there was talk of bussing in a tribe of Sioux Indians from South Dakota to perform a rain dance.

I too spent the summer waiting, first for letters, then for the sound of her voice over the phone. At night I would sit for hours, watching as the sun set and the Iowa sky darkened, tightening like skin around a wound. I tried to picture her in Montana, tried to imagine her sitting at a dinner table with him, laughing softly as she took a sip of wine. I wondered what he looked like and what about him was special enough that my mother would abandon her life to be with him. Each time I thought of him, though, all I could see was the vague image of that dark-eyed boy from the yearbook; and all I could hear was the echo of my mother's voice: "I never stopped loving him."

By the autumn my mother and Nick had returned to Milwaukee and were living in a small two-bedroom apartment just off the interstate. Alone, with no friends, no one she could talk to in the long afternoons when Nick was at work, my mother often phoned me. She told me of the different recipes she was trying; she described the books she was reading—Jane Smiley's *The Age of Grief;* Mona Simpson's *Anywhere but Here;* she tried to laugh at herself for feeling such exhilaration the day she passed the Wisconsin driver's test. "I did it," she said, her voice ebullient. "Can you believe it, Beth?"

Quietly, I congratulated her. I knew it didn't matter that my mother had been driving all her life. It was as if she were seventeen, as if she had gotten her license for the first time.

When she phoned me on September fourteenth, however, I knew the minute I heard her voice that everything had changed. "It's me," she whispered when I picked up the phone. She sounded scared.

"Are you all right?" I said.

"I don't know. I was okay when I woke up. I was going to do some reading and I'd taken some spaghetti sauce out of the freezer for dinner—" She began to weep. "All of a sudden the pain just started washing over me, Beth, and I couldn't stop it. I realized it was Dan's birthday yesterday and our anniversary tomorrow and I didn't understand what I was doing here anymore. *Why* am I taking spaghetti sauce out of this freezer, *why* am I not home in my own kitchen?" She was sobbing now. "And that's not all."

She was waiting for me to remember and, of course, I did: on this day fourteen years ago she had given birth to a stillborn, a seven-pound boy named and baptized Daniel Joseph. In all the years since it had happened, she had spoken of it to me only once before.

247

"There's been so much loss," she said. "And it's too much, Beth. It's just too much."

I remember feeling frightened for her. There was such unrestrained sorrow in her voice that I thought of water, black ocean water on a moonless night—and how afraid I was to enter it, to wade deeper than my calves.

Outside it was a bright autumn day. A breeze riffled the papers spread out on my coffee table. I heard a bus pull away from the stop outside my apartment. I thought of the other September fourteenth, of the day the baby had been born.

It had been a rainy Friday. My sister, brother and I had come home from school to an empty house and a neighbor waving at us from under a dark umbrella across the street. "Over here, kids!" she called. 'Your parents aren't home." The three of us raced across the street, kicking up arcs of rain behind us. My older brother won as always, beating my sister and me to the neighbor's porch. "She's having the baby, isn't she?" His delighted squeal seemed to skip over the puddles like a stone flung sideways across the surface of a pond. My sister and I were also shouting by now: "Is she having the baby?"

The neighbor offered a tenuous smile. "I think I'll let Dan tell you all about that when he gets here," she said.

A few hours later, my stepfather picked us up and took us home. "Your mother had a boy," he told us as he tried to get us to come sit with him on the couch. But we were jumping and screaming in celebration. My brother was yelling to the tune of "Old McDonald"— "B-B-B-O-Y, B-B-B-O-Y, B-B-B-O-Y, Yes I have a Bro-ther!"—until finally my stepfather blurted it out—that the baby was dead.

On the phone now, fourteen years later, I asked, "Is it the baby, Mom? Is that why you're so upset?" I was upset myself. "Should I call Dan?"

"There's really no point," she whispered. "I've hurt him too much already."

"It's not irreparable," I said. "You can still go home."

For a moment she didn't say anything. I felt how the echo of that word—*home*—hung between us, static in the line so that it seemed we were losing our connection.

"I can't," she said finally. She sounded surprised, as if this wasn't what she had planned on saying. Again she repeated it, testing the words the way I had once tested a snowflake on the tip of my tongue.

"I can't." Her voice was choked with something I couldn't name—panic or resignation perhaps, or maybe simple grief. After she hung up, I remember standing for what seemed a long time with the phone against my ear, coiling the cord around and around my fingers as if, somehow, I could reel my mother closer.

She is driving home from the food store one morning in late September. It is early, only a little past seven, but she has been unable to sleep lately and decided she would get the shopping out of the way. It is cold out. When she came out of the apartment this morning she noticed the windshields of the cars were covered with a layer of frost as thin as parchment paper. Already she wears a winter coat and, as she is setting the grocery bags into the back seat of her car, she sees her breath dissipate into the cold morning sky. In New Jersey it would still be warm, she thinks, she would be having coffee on the side porch, twelve-year-old Mark would be getting dressed for school in the clothes she bought him last spring.

She is almost at the turn-off to her apartment complex when she sees the children waiting at the bus stop, sees the group of women, their mothers, standing in a huddle around them, trying to shield the children from the wind blowing off Lake Michigan. Suddenly she feels ill. She thinks of Mark, of how each morning, after he was dressed and his bookbag was packed, he'd come to her room and wake her by laying a warm washcloth on her face, the same way Dan had woken him. She thinks of his face in the window of the school bus, remembers that he was so scared on his first day of kindergarten that he threw up. She is afraid she herself will be sick and pulls the car onto the shoulder of the road. Later she will call me. She will tell me this story.

Still, she will fly home to see Mark twice that autumn and, twice, despite the obvious pain she is feeling, she will return to Milwaukee.

I picture her that autumn in the various gift shops near her apartment, where she spends afternoons hoping to find in some pre-printed Hallmark card words which might somehow neutralize her family's anger. Too dressed up in the clothes she has no other place to wear, she lingers at the racks of specialty cards: "To A Special Daughter"; "To A Wonderful Son"; "Have I told you I love you lately?"; "How much do I miss you, let me count the days." I wonder if she notices the blue and white posters one aisle over advertising Yom Kippur cards. Does she know this means "Day of Atonement"? Does she know that all she has to do to be forgiven is come home?

My mother and Nick returned to Montana for Thanksgiving, hoping, I imagined, to find again the brief happiness my mother must have felt there earlier that summer. I was convinced, however, that waking to the silence of a hotel, eating Thanksgiving dinner in a restaurant—being without her children on a holiday—would only remind her of all that she had lost. Consequently, I allowed myself to hope: as I stood alone in my own kitchen on Thanksgiving morning, making stuffing the way she had taught me and baking the traditional pies she had always made, I promised that soon she would come home. She had to, I thought. How could we get through the holidays without her? And how could she get through them without us?

I pictured her in Montana, lying alone in the queen-sized bed of the Western Inn where they were staying, waiting for Nick to return from the dining room with the pot of coffee and the freshly baked brioche which the concierge set out each morning. I could see her growing impatient and hungry, wondering what was taking so long, could see her wrapping herself in the thin chenille bedspread and walking to the high latticed windows, which reminded her more of Europe, she wrote, than of the "Wild West."

In Iowa, as I set out the china and silver we'd received as wedding gifts, as I served turkey to the friends my husband and I had invited to dinner, as I wrapped leftovers for them to take home, as later that night I sat in the dark eating piece after piece of French silk pie, I pictured my mother standing at this window, her head against the glass, the sunlight falling over her like a white slip. Perhaps this is when she would feel the heaviness in her body, the stillness. Perhaps this is when she would realize that the new life she had wanted so much with Nick had quietly died inside of her. I could see her crying now, could see her moving slowly across the room towards the phone. . . .

I replayed this scene in my mind until it became spliced into all our other home movies: my older brother and I as toddlers fighting over a tricycle; my younger sister's first birthday party; the endless reels of my mother and stepfather's trip to Arizona the month before Nick phoned—minutes and minutes of blurred purple and red canyon walls like the insides of the huge heart we had walked through as kids at the Franklin Institute in downtown Philadelphia. And then I pictured my mother standing at the window in that hotel room, her pain so focused it became its own landscape.

250

The Thanksgiving weekend passed, however, and nothing happened. When I talked to my mother a week later, she admitted that the holiday had been horrible. But it no longer mattered, because whatever "horrible" meant, my mother hadn't called us; she hadn't come home.

"Was her life that bad?" I sobbed to my husband. "Was it so awful that she'd rather be in pain than come back to us?"

When I recall those weeks between Thanksgiving and Christmas, weeks which a poet once referred to as "the unimaginable present," I remember only the confusion and disbelief: she wasn't coming home. Maybe this was why I watched the documentary about stillborns that was on TV that November. I was willing to look anywhere for a clue—some hint—which would help me to understand: *Why?*

I learned that in Australian hospitals, unlike many in the US, doctors allow a woman who has had a stillborn to hold her baby after delivery. A nurse will take pictures of the child, sometimes let the mother dress the baby in something special to be buried in. Psychologists say that the greatest regret of the mothers of stillborns is that they never held their child, never got a chance to say goodbye. Their sons or daughters were simply whisked out of sight as if they had never existed.

I hadn't expected the show to upset me. But as I clicked the TV off and watched the screen fade from green to grey to black, I felt as if something was blackening inside of me too. I couldn't stop thinking about the dark-haired woman on TV who had given birth to three stillborns. For each she had a photo album filled with pictures of her dead child and of herself as she underwent labor. As she was being interviewed, she had almost frantically flipped through the pages of these albums, ordering the cameraman to focus in on the pictures. At one point she had stopped him, pointing to a favorite photograph and trying to explain why she liked it. She tried not to cry when she spoke, but her voice cracked and she had to turn away. I had been horrified.

Later, however, I realized that this horror was unjustified. Those photographs were all she had, the only proof of the life she had borne, a life which *had* existed, despite what everyone told her. And it struck me that perhaps what was truly horrible was *not* that a woman would save a photo album full of pictures of her dead child, but that she wouldn't; that instead, afraid of being called crazy or morbid, she would do what everyone said she should—she would forget.

251

I remembered the afternoon before my mother's stillborn was delivered. By then he hadn't kicked in almost two days. Already she must have known that he was dead. My sister and I had no idea that anything was wrong, however, and so we spent the afternoon coloring pictures for the baby's room.

My mother lay flat in the four-poster double bed, a heating pad rolled like a washcloth beneath her breasts. Each time we finished a drawing we brought it to show her. As we stood hesitantly near her bed, she would smile, momentarily looking away from my stepfather who sat at the desk near the window, absently rolling a pencil over the wood in harsh, jerking movements. "Thanks, guys," she'd say, holding the picture in front of her face and studying it before she set it carefully on the night stand with all the others. There must have been twenty or thirty of them. My sister and I would have colored all night, I think, if it hadn't been for my stepfather.

Entering the room once again with another drawing, my sister behind me, I saw my mother softly punching her clenched fist against her distended stomach. She froze when she saw us peering in the doorway, our pictures held in front of us like invitations for admittance. She cupped her hand slowly, protectively, to her stomach then. In that split second before my stepfather turned away from us, I thought I noticed tears on his face. But he snapped his dark eyes away from me before I could be sure. All I could see was his back, a grey shape outlined by a too-bright September sun, which seemed to lie to us about the season.

"It's okay," my mother said, staring not at us but at my stepfather. And then turning her strange quivering smile on my sister and me, she gestured with both arms. "Come here. Let me see what you colored this time," and we scrambled into the room, hopping knees first onto the bed. I remembered her softness, the damp sweaty smell of her thin velour robe, and then the surprisingly sharp grip of my stepfather's fingers clamped tight around my wrist as he jerked me from my mother.

"That's enough," he said. He tried to hold his voice rigid with control but it came out shaky and painfully frazzled.

My mother said, "It's okay, Dan, really."

In their odd watery stares, I saw an entire conversation that I didn't understand.

My stepfather shook his head and then more gently pulled my sister and me from the bed. "No, it's not okay." Then, "God damn it, Laura, you don't need to do this right now."

She started to cry. "Yes, I do, this is exactly what I need."

"How can it be?" he snapped. "You're not all right."

"I will be if you'd just let it alone," she said, her voice growing louder.

But my stepfather pulled us away. "I'm sorry, girls. I don't mean to make you feel bad, but your mom needs to rest for a while."

My sister and I went back to our room. We began to clean up and, without talking, arrange the crayons into systematic rows of colors. Midnight-blue, navy, ultramarine, cornflower, skyblue. Darkest to lightest. And then another color.

Fourteen years later, the November after my mother had left, it wasn't so easy to find a means of ordering the world. As I paced about my apartment in Iowa, pictures of the Australian woman in my mind, I sensed for the first time that my mother probably wouldn't come home—not because of Nick, not because of the baby who had died, but because somehow, in all the years of forgetting, some part of my mother had died. How dramatic this sounded and yet as I got up from the couch I couldn't help but recall a conversation I'd had with my mother earlier that autumn. She had been seeing a psychologist in an effort to understand how a woman like herself, a woman who had always prided herself on being a good mother, a good wife, could so suddenly leave. The psychologist, she told me, had written under diagnosis "prolonged grief." My mother had laughed at this. "What do you mean?" she had asked. "What do you think I'm grieving for? I was happy."

"So happy that you left," he reminded her quietly.

Absently, I flicked on the stereo. Anne Murray, one of my mother's favorites, was singing "Daydream Believer": "Cheer up, sleepy Jean/ Oh, what can it mean. . . ." Through all those conversations when I had asked her to come home, when she had whispered, "I can't, Beth. Please try to understand," she must have known, as I did now, that if she returned we would pretend once again. We would pretend that her leaving had been a whim; we would pretend that she was happy. We would forget—just as we had after the baby died.

She had talked to my sister and me about the stillborn only once, years after the fact. I don't know how the conversation came up or why we were discussing it. I simply remembered her describing how her friends pretended nothing had happened, how they acted as if the baby hadn't been real.

"He would have been so sick," they had told her.

"It's better this way. . . ."

"At least you didn't bring him home and start loving him. . . ."

She told us, too, that when my stepfather reached out to hold the baby in the delivery room, the nurse had stepped back and abruptly pulled him away. "It's better if you don't," the nurse apologized. "There's really no point."

"Dan said he had black hair," my mother had told us. "That's all I know." She had turned to stare outside the window, something she did often when she was upset, as if looking at another landscape was all it took to distance herself from the one she was in.

After a moment, she said, "Nobody understood that the baby was already real to me, that he had a personality even in the womb. At the end of the pregnancy, he used to wake up every night at four in the morning—right on the nose. I'd go into the room Dan had fixed up and sit in the rocking chair and sing to him and rub my belly until he settled down." She had laughed quizzically, the way people do at jokes they don't understand. "I mean, I knew even before he was born that he wasn't going to let me sleep through the night the way you guys did—" She had shaken her head in wonderment. "To think that I hadn't already started loving him," she'd said.

I put a pot of water on for tea and went to sit at the table, waiting for it to boil. When I began to cry, my sounds seemingly enormous and out of place in the quiet and darkness, I thought it was for the Australian woman with three dead children, but then it occurred to me that I was crying for my mother, for all that I had never understood. I realized too that I was crying for my own loss. Because all through childhood and adolescence, when I thought I was getting to know my mother, and later, after I was married, when the two of us would sit at the kitchen table for hours, talking and drinking tea—all that time, she had been so distant to me, as unknown to me, as that dark-haired woman on the other side of the world, that woman who, unlike my mother, had understood what it means to grieve.

It's not the stillborn baby I think of so much anymore when September fourteenth interrupts my life like a cold, leaving me achy and tired. It's my mother's wobbly but bright smile as she fixed our lunches before school the morning before the baby was born, knowing that he hadn't kicked or moved for more than two days. It is her making sure we each had a quarter to buy a soft pretzel at recess; it's her going to the hospital without the diaper bag packed full of pastel-colored baby

254

clothes. It is my mother carrying a dead baby inside of her and never letting go of that pink crescent of a smile, which, when I think of it now, seems almost separate from her face. As if that smile had nothing to do with my mother at all.

Nominated by The Iowa Review

A HISTORY OF PAISLEY

by AGHA SHAHID ALI

from THE PARIS REVIEW

*Their footsteps formed the paisley when Parvati, angry after a quarrel, ran away
from Shiva. He eventually caught up with her. To commemorate their reunion, he
carved the Jhelum river, as it moves through the Vale of Kashmir, in the shape of
the paisley.*

You who will find the dark fossils of paisleys
one afternoon on the peaks of Zabarvan—
Trader from an ancient market of the future,
alibi of chronology, that vain
collaborator of time—won't know that these

are her footprints from the day the world began
when land rushed, from the ocean, toward Kashmir.
And above the rising Himalayas? The air
chainstitched itself till the sky hung its bluest
tapestry. But already—as she ran

away—refugee from her Lord—the ruins
of the sea froze, in glaciers, cast in amber.
And there, in the valley below, the river
beguiled its banks into petrified longing:
(O see, it is still the day the world begins:

and the city rises, holding its remains,
its wooden beams already their own fire's prophets.)
And you, now touching sky, deaf to her anklets
still echoing in the valley, deaf to men
fleeing from soldiers into dead-end lanes

(Look! Their feet bleed; they leave footprints on the street
which will give up its fabric, at dusk, a carpet)—
you have found—you'll think—the first teardrop, gem
that was enticed for a Mughal diadem
into design. For you, blind to all defeat

up there in pure sunlight, your gauze of cloud thrown
off your shoulders over the Vale, do not hear
bullets drowning out the bells of her anklets.
This is her relic, but for you the first tear,
drop that you hold as you descend past flowstone,

past dried springs, on the first day of the world.
The street is rolled up, ready for southern ports.
Your ships wait there. What other cargo is yours?
What cables have you sent to tomorrow's bazaars?
What does that past await: the future unfurled

like flags? news from the last day of the world?
You descend quickly, to a garden-café:
At a table by a bed of tzigane
roses, three men are discussing, between
sips of tea, undiscovered routes on emerald

Seas, ships with almonds, with shawls bound for Egypt.
It is dusk. The gauze is torn. A weaver kneels,
gathers falling threads. Soon he will stitch the air.
But what has made you turn? Do you hear her bells?
O alibi of chronology, in what script

in your ledger will this narrative be lost?
In that café, where they discuss the promise
of the world, her cry returns from its abyss

where it hides, by the river. They don't hear it.
The city burns; the dusk has darkened to rust

by the roses. They don't see it. O Trader,
what news will you bring to your ancient market?
I saw her. A city was razed. In its debris
her bells echoed. I turned. They didn't see me
turn to see her—on the peaks—in rapid flight forever.

for Anuradha Dingwaney

Nominated by David Romtvedt

KINGDOM OF THE SUN

fiction by ALICE SCHELL

from STORY

M Y FATHER CAME home, cured of his enchantment with the dusty little towns where he'd lost himself barnstorming, sometimes playing as many as three games a day with one inchmeal team after another. Always hoping to make it with one of the big ones, the Crawfords, the Grays. Never making it at all except for a game in Pittsburgh once, where he'd managed to sit close to the bench, a spectator only, coming home with autographed snapshots of Satchel Paige and Josh Gibson and a clouded half smile. This time he was back for good, he said.

There was no steady work in those years, not in New Sharon or any place else, but he pieced together odd jobs, filthy work more suited to a younger man, someone whose armor of pride was less brittle. He cleaned toilets at the fairgrounds, hauled junk for Ottendorfer Salvage, unpacked maggot-riddled hides at the tannery. My grandmother, wordless and grateful, fixed his lunch bucket as before with baloney sandwiches and thermoses of hot tea, sometimes a chunk of gingerbread. As if nothing had changed, as if he'd never left. I was the one who sat close-mouthed and sullen when he reappeared out of nowhere, who teetered dangerously on the edge of my chair.

Did he break his promises to Dory and Grammum, or just me? He was always leaving, saying he would stay but leaving even as he said it. My earliest picture of him, a winter picture, too far back to see clearly except for the colors: as he was going out the door, a quick flash of scarlet, the back of his hunting jacket pinned with a bright square of heavy flannel. He came home that day with a gunshot wound, an accident, he told us, runnels of blood streaking his face.

When he was taken away to see Dr. Holt, he promised to come right back. I stood waiting at the window where I could see all the way to the end of the street. My mother, still alive then but coughing up blood, already sleepwalking toward the last week of her life, whispered to me from her chair: *Elizabeth. Littlebits.* She tried to coax me to sit on what was left of her thighs, to take comfort in the bony cradle of her arms. But I refused to come away from the window, fighting to stay awake, at last being put to bed to the sound of her dry gasps for air, the certainty that both she and my father would disappear for good.

He did come home after the hunting accident, but he left the summer after my mother died to travel with a baseball team on the other side of Harrisburg. I was to begin elementary school that fall and he'd promised to wait for me when the first day of school was over; he said he'd take me with him to batting practice; we'd go to the picture show with Dory and Gram on Saturday afternoon. He was gone, of course, weeks before I entered school.

I tried to pretend it was a game like hide-and-seek; he had not disappeared like my mother, he'd hidden himself somewhere. I looked for him among the bushes and weeds in the yard; at the post office when I went with Gram to pick up the money he sent in thin dirty envelopes; in the colored cemetery where they'd sunk into the earth a blunt little stone with my mother's name on it. I ran up the alley, across Lafayette Street to the ball field behind the school, searching for him. Grammum came after me, telling me I should be ashamed of myself, a big girl like me, six years old, crying for her daddy.

I learned to sheer away from myself, to separate from my body and its incessant threats to blow apart: the vomiting spells, night terrors, dizziness, sieges of holding my breath. I often woke Dory up with my nightmares, my stomach aches, punching at her until she stumbled out of the bed we shared and groped her way to Gram's bed across the room—"Grammum, Lizabeth's sick, wake up, Grammum!"—all the while my heart dithering under my ribs, alert for her voice—*go back to sleep, Elizabeth.* But she never failed to appear at my bedside; if I asked, never failed to stay with me until morning, the three of us squeezed together tight, the way I liked best, with Gram and Dory on the outside, me safely in the middle.

When my father came home at last, limping up on the porch as if he'd just gone to the store for a poke of Silver Cup, I stood on the other side of the screen door, my mouth walled shut, while Dory leapt into his arms with happy shrieks of *Daddy,* and Gram stood smiling at him, her last living son, her hands lightly touching the banister for support. When Dory snatched at his yellow baseball cap, knocking it to the floor, he lifted one hand quickly to smooth his hair, still dense and woolly but stippled with flecks of gray.

He set my sister down and reached for the screen door, peering through the mesh with that two-sided look of his—bashful, even reserved, but agitated too, like water with unseen creatures abruptly disturbed by light. "And how's Littlebits? How's my girl?" I fled through the kitchen into the backyard, glancing quickly behind to see if he'd followed me. He had not.

That evening when we sat down to supper I saw a change in the grudging light that usually filtered in through the kitchen window. A tense glittering brightness touched the room as he told us the stories I'd waited for with such longing, such resentment: The places he'd been without us, the teams where he'd picked up jobs, playing every position from shortstop to second base to left field. Once, even the catcher's spot for a team called the Hill Hawks, a team too poor to own a catcher's mask or uniforms, he said, but who sported bright yellow caps with a brown hawk design on the front.

He told us about Brockridge where a shallow creek lay on the far side of the outfield, about the balls that wound up in the creek and the right fielder with water in his shoes, sopping wet up past his ankles. About the coon games he'd refused to play up there: clowning, Tomming; foot shuffling and boot licking just to fill up the maw of the white crowd, making them forget what it was that made them hungry.

He said he was batting close to four hundred. He'd hit twenty-three home runs, five of them grand slams. He told us about the stolen bases, the double plays, about being gouged by cleats more times than he could count.

Sitting next to my father, I felt his heat, his sun-charged dreaming. I wanted to ease myself onto his lap but I kept my head down, pushing chicken potpie around on my plate. After supper I waited for him to fold me against his chest, say he'd never go away again. But he only tugged mischievously on my plaits as he got up from the table. He said, "Seems like the onliest time I play real good is when I'm out there on the road."

My father started going to the ball field behind the school every chance he got. He would stay out there alone, batting balls into the wire mesh behind home plate. From the window of Miss Zieger's classroom I could see him, wearing his yellow cap. He would throw the ball just high enough to ready himself for the swing, sometimes missing, sometimes cracking it into the mesh. He would run to retrieve the ball, loping forward with his fast awkward gait. Every once in a while he would bend over and massage both legs as if he had cramps, kneading and stroking the slightly shorter leg he'd been born with. I imagined him looking over toward the school, waving his cap at me.

When we met after school, Dory stopped to watch him from the Lafayette side of the field. She called out, "Daddy!" but he didn't hear her. I jerked her arm and told her to shush. She screwed up her face. "Ow, that hurts!"

She hopped neatly off the curb, where she planted one foot on the sidewalk, the other in the gutter. "Why're you always mad at Daddy?"

I answered with a careless swing of my chin, tilting it up and away from her. "Who says I'm mad at him?"

"You're not mad at him?" Her voice was hesitant, hopeful.

"No, I'm *not*. Now come on, Dory, quit fooling around. You said you'd walk me home and you're not gonna break your promise."

She scuffed her feet and slowed down, but she kept walking; as always, afraid to displease me. Dory—my shadow, Gram called her because I insisted that she go everywhere I went—was a year younger, but most people took her to be the older one; she was sturdy, taller by at least two inches, with an almost adult air of self-confidence and a knockabout kind of fearlessness. Next to her I looked frail, someone who had yet to grow into her own face. I was left back in first grade because I'd missed so much school; all I had to show for that year was a paperweight I'd fashioned from a chunk of rock painted with bold swirls of color. I'd made it for my father. Dory joined me the following year when I repeated first grade, sitting directly behind me. My sicknesses scared her. If anyone bothered me with so much as a word or look, Dory would be there bristling, ready for a fight. "You leave my sister alone!"

My father went back to playing shortstop for the Corinthians, his old position. Grammum took us to his first game at home in over a year. I told her I didn't want to go, I had a stomach ache, but she cajoled me: "Elizabeth, that ache will fly away on its own wings soon's you get yourself out of this house." She propelled me through the front door with brisk pats on the backside. "Do you know, honey, sometimes you cut off your nose to spite your face?"

Dory hung on to Gram's fingers all the way to the ball field. I straggled behind them, rehearsing under my breath how I would say *I told you* when we found that he was gone again. But he was there, showing his autographed pictures to the rest of the team, spinning tales about night games he'd seen, with lights that were hauled around on flatbed trucks. I gave him a sidewise glance as I trailed Gram and Dory to the bleachers. Using her worn-out bandanna, Grammum dusted off her favorite seat just behind the first-base line. She placed herself between Dory and me, but I moved behind her to the next level, where she couldn't see me chewing my lip. I settled on the edge of my seat, braced my toes against the warped board in front of me, and stared at my shoes.

Grammum turned to me. "How long are you fixing to carry that long face, child? Your daddy's home now. You should rejoice!"

He was standing at the water bucket, finishing off a drink from the gourd that was tied to the handle. Amos Fortune, the manager, looked him over and laughed. "Well, ole man! Ain't you about forty by now? Ain't it time for you to quit them sorry-assed dreams?"

The other players laughed along with Amos. My father let the gourd slip into the bucket and picked up two bats, swinging them together, smiling good-naturedly at the razzing. "Aw, you-uns don't know nothing! You ain't seen no ball like I seen. By George, I can tell you this much. I was batting just about four hundred all last season."

They groaned, rolled their eyes, laughing and shaking their heads. "Aw, tell us another one!"

Early Keyes, the second baseman, put in: "How 'bout batting four hundred for us?"

Amos, with a quick glance at Grammum, said, "OK, boys, get yourselves ready to play ball."

The Corinthians, a haunted ball club forever cramped by their fear of jinxes, were mired in another losing streak. During the first couple of innings, the spectators tried to talk it up as usual: *OK, OK, let's move it, move it, move it, look alive!* But they gradually lost patience. Before long, there were little firecrackers of discontent among the crowd: *Aw, come on. Aw, shit, wake up, you boys.*

I kept my eyes down, covertly watching Grammum's back. Every time I caught the small shift in her posture, a barely visible quiver in her narrow shoulders, I knew my father was at bat, shaking out his muscles, shrugging and hunching himself into his stance as meticulously as a man trying on a custom-made coat. He had already popped

263

out twice. The one time he got on base he was thrown out in a run-down between first and second.

Now Early Keyes was razzing him again. "Hey, here's the man that hits four hundred! Mr. Four Hundred, Mr. Four Hundred! Show us what you got!"

I looked at my father as he crowded the plate. He had just drawn three balls, but his stance was coiled tight, like someone staring into the face of a full count. The crowd grew quiet. Instead of taking the walk on the next pitch as everyone expected, he stepped into it sharp as an exclamation point. A lightning *thwack* splintered the silence as he connected with the ball, a bare, wooden clapper of a sound that jolted people from their seats. All along the bleachers startled faces turned up to the sun, eyes searching the sky. The sound of clattering shoes echoed on the boards as people scrambled to their feet.

Gram, rising halfway from her seat, then standing straight up with the rest of the crowd, turned to me and cried softly, "Look up, child! Look up!"

Something was prying me loose, catapulting me up, forcing my gaze to the sky, where the ball, swallowed by sunlight, soared over the center field fence. As I watched my father circle the bases in his strange, hurt-footed way I was suddenly on my feet, my small voice mingled with the others in one long jubilant roar.

Dory and Grammum hugged me, laughing, their eyes shining, and Grammum said, "You see, Elizabeth, you see!"

My father won the game for the Corinthians that day, but the victory was a lone shooting star, for him, for the team. They lost a string of games after that. One Sunday, when just about everyone on the street had made the trip to Blue Gap only to see the Corinthians shut out by eight runs, Amos called the team together before they boarded the bus for home. He was afire with rage, disbelief. The Corinthians had flubbed balls and racked up enough errors, according to Amos, to fill half the almanac. And the times they'd swung at air! He nearly danced with the pain of it. My father, who'd been pulled from the game after five innings of strikeouts, stood outside the loose circle of players listening to Amos's tirade and looked down at the ground where he'd tossed his glove, digging at the earth with his cleats.

I waited until the bus was nearly loaded before I said it. He was staring over my head, but I forced him to notice me, grabbing his glove and hiding it behind my back. I struggled to look up, squinting against the sun. "You're not gonna leave again, are you?"

264

His baseball cap shadowed his eyes. He said, "Leave? Course not, Littlebits." I stood looking up at him. He forced a smile. "Now gimme my glove."

My father kept his word. He stayed at home for the next eight years, finally able to get steady work when the Lester Ordnance Depot opened the year the war started, and played with the Corinthians on weekends. Night games had begun to put in an appearance here and there, but most of the ball fields around New Sharon were not equipped with lights, so he was home nearly every evening. Dory ceaselessly pivoted around him, chattering, giggling, asking questions, never shy about interrupting whatever he was doing, even able to make him laugh.

During those years I saw how greedily he studied the sun, the sweep of color striations above us, the massed cloud shapes. Not anyone I recognized. A sky watcher, chasing distance and light.

"Did I tell you about that game up in Brockridge, the time I hit that there ball right into the crick? Bases loaded, by George. And what about them other games? All over this damned state, and Maryland and West Virginia too, yes sir. If I'da kept on like that, by George, I would've hit over four hundred. . . ."

He often sat at the window, adrift in memory, watching yesterday's skies. When he sank into one of those reveries, bewitched and out of reach, I was silent. He talked on about the games as Dory and Gram repeatedly asked the same questions; the more they asked, the more he worked and reworked his stories like fine pieces of stitchery. I did not ask him anything. But even as I tried to remain outside that bright nimbus of memory, I was lured into its radiance. I came to know every game he played, every town he traveled. I said, "Tell me about the time in Brockridge. . . .Tell me about the time in Mount Eden. . . .Tell me. . . ."

• • •

By the time we entered high school, Dory had lost interest in my father's stories. She lost interest in the Corinthians too, unless it was an away game where she thought she could meet new boys. She was leaving me, by the smallest increments drifting away. She said she couldn't walk home from school with me on Tuesdays because she'd joined the Press Club; then she was on the committee to plan a trip to the battlefield at Gettysburg. She made the honor roll every term and frequently stayed after school for one special project or another. She joined the chorus. I taunted her about how they'd let colored students into their precious chorus but just try to get a part in one of their dumb operettas.

She said, "Lizabeth, I'm not just going to fold up and sit in the house all the time. What do you want me to do?"

Grammum intervened. "Elizabeth, you've got to stop this, all this grabbing. . . .Dorothy has a life of her own, you know." She added: "Don't you want to get out of the house yourself? You're so smart, honey, don't you want to do things at school like your sister?" But I was barely passing most of my courses. The only subject I liked was English, where I wrote rambling essays, everything I could remember beginning with my father's blood-streaked face, the blood in my mother's handkerchiefs; I composed a jumble of verse, squandering page after page in my notebook.

By the time Dory's schedule filled up so much that she no longer had time to walk home with me even one day a week, I told her, "You lie, Dory, you don't keep your promises, you're just the way he is."

I heard a new sharpness in her voice. "He's home, Lizabeth. What's the matter with you? Do you want to hold a grudge forever?"

The years settled in my father's bones like squatters. There were stiff agonizing times when he would slump badly, times of shut doors and long naps. Times when he'd spend whole evenings looking over the photographs he cut out of the *Pittsburgh Courier:* the ball players, the big stadiums, especially the ones in New York he vowed he would see some day. His slump would start off with a steep drop in hitting, then his fielding would plunge, with one error after another and a fearful loss of power in his throwing arm. Finally, his legs, already a source of betrayal, would fail him, the muscles, ligaments, tendons undone, his base-running not just the usual hobbling accommodation but a series of jerks and stumbles. Amos, playing his younger men, kept him on the bench.

It was during one of his worst slumps that I wrote the poem for him. He wasn't batting two hundred then, not even close, and hadn't been for a long time. The poem, celebrating the dazzle of his barnstorming games, his sunlit home run for the Corinthians, was published in the School Corner section of the *New Sharon Bugle.* My father never tired of hearing me recite that poem. He clipped it out of the *Bugle* and

266

mounted it on a piece of wood, shellacked its surface, and hung it on the wall in the parlor. He kept another clipping in his wallet and showed it to everyone. He could not read, so he would unfold the clipping with great care and ask who would like to read it out loud. He bought a half dozen copies of the *Bugle* and displayed them fanwise on the sideboard.

His slump worsened. Gram told him he should start to take it easy, maybe not play so much ball; she made gossamer-light jokes about his getting on in years. He shook his head, "Aw, there's plenty of other fellas out there . . . I seen them, in their forties, fifties. I seen plenty of them." He watched the sky, as if for a sign.

My father's shorter leg had always bothered him, sometimes causing a dull ache in his left hip, but that had never stopped him from playing ball. Now the pain was keeping him up at night. Sometimes I heard his uneven footfall as he made his way downstairs to wait out the night on the front porch. He took to packing ice around his hip in the evenings. Long after the season was over he continued his solo batting practice, regardless of the pain, regardless of the weather, even when there was snow. I followed him to the field one day, holding my breath as he ran hitching and stumbling after the ball, then massaging his leg, settling into his stance again, swinging at the wind. It was almost dark when he finally quit, muttering, "Them bats they make nowadays ain't worth a red cent."

One warm April morning during my sophomore year in high school, he left home again. Gram said he'd found a couple of fellows out of Philadelphia putting together an all-star team. They wanted to try their luck with the Mexican League, maybe Puerto Rico or Cuba. She talked too fast, too low, her back curved against me as she bent over the washboard.

I stood there hating her, hating the smell of brown soap, the hot damp misery of the kitchen. I wanted to tear the words from my throat and fling them at her: Him, an all-star? Batting one seventy-five, if that, an all-star? *An all-star?* But she had gone out of the door to hang sheets on the line, and I was left holding fast to the sink.

I said to Dory, "I'm going to find him. I'm going to make him come home, he can't just up and leave any old time he wants." I tried to talk her into helping me but she shook her head, training her eyes on me like lamps. "Lizabeth, you're crazy."

I tracked him down that summer. My father wasn't on any all-star team. He'd been barnstorming with the Beacons, then jumped back

267

to the Hill Hawks. They were due for a game on Saturday with the white team in Brockridge. A four-hour bus trip. Grammum didn't try to stop me. I kept telling her, every chance I got, that I was sixteen, old enough to take a bus ride by myself. She let out a wisp of a sigh. "If you're old enough to take a bus ride by yourself, Elizabeth, then it's high time you stopped acting like a child."

I winced at the way she delivered her reprimand, quiet, all pained forbearance. I'd rather she slapped me. But Gram had never lifted her hand against anyone; she'd never even raised her voice, and she didn't raise it now. "I will talk with you, Elizabeth, when you get back," she said.

The bus did not go directly to Brockridge; it went as far as Altboro, a much bigger town a couple of miles to the north. I got off there and walked. These were hard little towns, mostly white, on the edge of coal country, Brockridge itself an anemic huddle of two-story houses with slanting porches and air that weighed heavy and gray under a too-distant sun.

The game had started by the time I made it to the ball field, a scruffy space behind what looked like a defunct factory. I saw by the crude wooden squares on the scoreboard that it was only the second inning. There was no score. The bleachers were small, probably seating less than three hundred people. I took in the drabness of the place, the weedy outfield, the corrugated tin roof sheltering a small portion of bleachers. All this time I had imagined my father playing before tier upon tier of enormous crowds in real stadiums with immaculate diamonds, banners flying. The sad squalor of this ball field made me uneasy, as if I'd pushed open a forbidden door.

Some of the spectators had come with folding chairs, three-legged stools, crates. The faces of the people who stood a short distance from me were a pale blur, except for a man who narrowed his eyes and looked at me as if he expected some kind of trouble. A couple of the others glanced at me and looked away. They'd left a dry little moat of space around me, but I still felt hemmed in. The Brockridge team moved slowly onto the field. Someone called to the pitcher in a loose friendly baritone, "Let's git them coons today."

My shoulders tensed. Not because I was afraid of that kind of talk, I'd heard it before. My real fear was that my father would go hitless, the bat a fifty-pound weight in his hands; that his legs would trick him into a long stumbling fall.

I waited, looking for him when the Hawks took the field. Where was he? Maybe he wasn't barnstorming with them after all; maybe he *had* gone to Mexico, an unimaginable distance. I began to sweat under the hazy sun. The game was still scoreless in the sixth inning when the Hawks snapped to life with a string of base hits, a solid line drive that turned into a double. They were up by three runs, then another three.

I felt the shift, the change in the air; restless movement among the spectators, a low rumble of voices arguing, something pulling loose. Someone threw a pop bottle that went skittering along the third-base line and into foul territory. The man with the narrow eyes looked at me again. The blur of whiteness around me sharpened into a frieze of faces, chiseled and grooved with frustration; yet soft, too, with anticipation, a blank soft yielding to the thing that had been tied up inside them.

There were still no outs when, for no reason that I could see, the Hawks sent in a pinch hitter. A black ragpicker of a man, painted with a minstrel-red mouth, who sidled up to the plate with an exaggerated limp. His mismatched uniform was a joke, a clown's outfit. Apple green trousers, like baggy pajama bottoms. Shirt with a garish black-and-white checkerboard pattern, at least three sizes too big. On the back of the shirt a huge zero in red paint superimposed on the checkered design.

He reeled in a slew-footed circle, swaying like a drunk. He did a little Stepin Fetchit footwork, repeating it several times, until the mutters in the crowd turned to cackles. He twirled his bat like a baton, dropped it, twirled it again, dropped it, pretended to lose his balance. He rolled his eyes, bending over to grin at the crowd, his head upside down, staring at them through the triangle formed by his legs. He adopted a wobbly stance, holding the bat high above his head. The crowd cackled, hooted, gleamed at one another: now that's more like it.

My father.

When he smacked a sharp grounder through the infield, almost clipping the pitcher, he made it to first, gimping and high-stepping all the way, then doffed his cap with an obsequious flourish, fanning his face, his feet, his buttocks. He rolled his eyes and flashed his teeth on and off, a macabre semaphore that sent the crowd into screams of laughter. He was fitting his cap back on his head when his eyes swept past those of us who stood behind the first-base line. He saw me.

269

He fastened on me, so stricken the air between us seemed infected. He stepped forward, heedless of being tagged out when his foot left the base, crisscrossing his hands like windshield wipers, an odd frenzied signal: *No. Stop. Don't. Please.*

A small terrible sound was rising behind my teeth. I wanted to spit but my mouth was full of dust, a sheet of pain spread from my chest out to the margins of my skin. He was still trying to get my attention but I looked right through him. I pushed blindly past the spectators and walked, then ran, toward the road that would take me back to Altboro.

At home in the parlor that evening, I pulled the poem on its plaque from the wall and took it with my father's copies of the *Bugle* to the kitchen, where Grammum and Dory were finishing supper. Earlier, in preparation for heating her irons, Gram had laid the stove with fresh kindling drizzled with kerosene. There I crammed my father's old copies of the *Bugle,* the plaque on top of them. Both Gram and Dory leapt up from the table when they saw what I meant to do. Grammum's voice reached me before she did with a stern *don't you do that, girl,* as she tried to grasp my arm, but I had already dropped the match. I did not step away from the heat as the flame etched a tiny path along the edge of the newspaper and devoured its way to the center. Gram moved fast, pushing me aside, upending a teakettle of water on the fire, jerking her hand away from the rising cloud of steam as she slammed the stove lid back in place.

She touched my elbow. "Sit down here, Elizabeth."

I took the chair she thrust beneath me, turning my head to the wall. She moved back to the table, as if to cool the distance between us, and sat down. "Now look at me."

I turned my head stiffly and looked at her. Dory, eyes wide, stood behind the chair with her fingers on Gram's shoulders. My tongue felt thick, gritty. "If you could've seen him. . . ."

Gram gave me a mild look, a warning. "I don't know what all happened up there in Brockridge and I don't want to know."

"But you should have *seen* him. . . .Gram, you would have been so ashamed."

Dory's voice, fluttering. "What . . . what did you see? What did he do? What?"

Grammum reached up behind her to place a quiet hand on Dory's cheek. "Never mind, child. Don't fret yourself so."

When she turned back to me she shook her head, talking to herself, I thought, as much as to me. "There are times. . . ."

I stared at her, heartsick. What was she talking about, there are times? What times? I hardly had the energy to speak. "He's a fake."

"Elizabeth, you do not know what you're talking about."

"A liar."

Grammum rose from her chair. "Not another word."

"A fake, a liar!"

She supported herself on Dory's arm. "Do not speak ill of your father, Elizabeth."

Turning end over end in a flash flood of words, that's what my body remembers: "A fake, a coon, a dumb coon, a liar, liar, liar!" At the edge of the torrent, Dory shrinking against the wall; the sound of my father's broken step, his shadow in the doorway; Gram advancing on me like a monolith in a dream, a granite statue mysteriously in motion.

The light in her eyes was not steady, it flickered, enlarged by sorrow, the flame of her loyalty trembling in gale-force winds. I tried to push away from her, sliding my chair backward along the linoleum, but she was already there, leaning over me, close enough for a kiss. She did not raise her voice, in fact she almost whispered, "Didn't I tell you not to speak ill of your father?" And she struck me in the face with her fist.

The blow was fierce enough to snap my head sideways but the pain floated free, distant, not my pain. I gazed up at her, stunned by the heartbreak I saw in her eyes. *Oh, Gram.* She had known about the game in Brockridge all along.

A time of ragged edges. I expected something to happen, some act of completion, but Grammum had closed the door on Brockridge, she expected us to go on as before, and we did. Nothing happened, except that my father became a fugitive. The depot no longer had a place for him, so he went back to doing odd jobs, including two nights a week as janitor at the high school. After dark I sometimes stood outside one of the narrow windows of the gymnasium, watching as he limped around that expanse of glossy floor with his cart full of buckets, bottles, brushes, mops. When we had classes in the gym I studied the varnish, searching for spots he'd missed.

He never returned to the Corinthians lineup or attended the games, although I saw him once in a while watching them from the edge of the ball field or from the other side of Lafayette Street. His hip was visibly worse now, it had begun to deteriorate into a crippling rheumatism. He looked worn, planed and sanded down like wood, stripped, peeled away. His hair had turned completely white.

271

Sometimes I wondered how, in our small house, we managed to avoid one another, yet each of us found our own way: my father working at night, usually sleeping during the day; Dory filling herself up with school, looking away from me when I talked to her; Grammum, sitting in the rocker near the window the way my mother used to sit, quiet, turned inward.

I found a place to anchor my rage, touch the roots of my grief. I retreated with one of my notebooks to the cemetery, where I sat on the ground near my mother's stone, writing the same word over and over in microscopic letters: *liar.* By the time I'd filled half the book, the pages were nearly indecipherable, dense with scratched-out words and interlinear notes. When I switched to ink, dark splotches leaked through to the opposite side of the paper, sometimes staining the next couple of sheets as well.

One afternoon, hunched over my notebook like someone trussed up in a straightjacket, I stopped writing and traced the numerals on my mother's stone with my finger: 1900–1935. When I was a child, Grammum had tried to convince me that my mother had not really disappeared, she would be with me always, she'd simply *gone to her resting place.* I never believed her. Still, I put my lips to the stone and whispered, "Mama?"

I didn't hear my father as he made his way up the gravel path and stood a few feet away from me, leaning off-center, favoring his bad hip. I jumped up and moved away from him. We had not spoken to each other for weeks. He looked at the notebook hanging open in my hand, his throat working. "Hey there!" When I didn't answer, he coughed lightly and looked up at the sky, then back at the notebook in my hand. "You writing something about me in that there book?"

I heard a defensive tremor in my voice. "Why should I write about *you?*"

"I don't know. Maybe, I thought. . . ." His words trailed away.

As we stood in silence, watching the western light, a surge of malice welled up in me and I thrust the notebook at him. "Read it for yourself!"

He bit his lip and accepted the book, holding it away from him in both hands, peering at the muddled pages as if he might find a key to their meaning simply by staring hard, perhaps searching for his name. He shook his head and handed the book back to me.

"It's about what I done that one time, it's about me, ain't it?" I caught the tiny phrase: *that one time.* Was he trying to offer an excuse?

He repeated the question. "It's about me, ain't it?"

I held myself rigid, crumbling only a little when I saw how fiercely he struggled to stand upright to correct his posture against the tug of pain in his hip. He waited for my answer. Still I remained silent. His lips parted slightly as if he was about to speak, but he swallowed whatever it was he wanted to say. Instead, he lifted his hand in a half wave, a small dignified salute, and limped away.

I sank to a sitting position next to my mother's stone. I opened the notebook, for a long time studying the pages crammed with my peevish script, tiny and sharp as tacks—a long list of grievances, a crabbed documentation of my father's every transgression from the time I was old enough to remember. Pitiless variations on the same sin: leaving me.

There was no sudden epiphany, no shaft of insight, only slow unfolding knowledge, the gradual opening of a swollen fist. I seemed to be walking out of a thicket, blinking in the light. I closed the notebook, wanting to call after him but he was gone: "No, it's not about you, not at all. It was never about you. It's about . . . me."

I found him in the backyard, where Gram had set up a rickety old chaise for him. His legs were covered with a thin counterpane that had fallen to one side, the bottoms of his trousers were bunched up, exposing the twig-like shins, pocked with dark scars from the cleats that had gouged him years ago. I pulled the cover back over his legs.

He was dozing, his head nodding toward his chest, wearing his old cap turned backward like a catcher. His breath shuddered out in ragged little sighs; his feet twitched under the covers as if he were running the bases in a dream. Next to the chaise I found an upturned apple crate. His wallet lay there beside a glass of tea with ice chips thinned to a glimmering translucence. The edge of a newspaper clipping, held down by a yellow-and-green-painted rock, stirred lightly in the breeze. My first-grade paperweight.

I picked up the clipping. Someone had printed in smudged pencil along the top margin: "*New Sharon Bugle,* September 10, 1944." There was my poem, intact, the paper shredded to a fine lace where it had been folded and unfolded so many times. The breeze played with the paper as I read the poem, long ago buried in memory. The first part was an intricate chronicle about my father's barnstorming days, a stanza for each town. Mount Eden, Brockridge, Schillersburg, Blue Gap, Lester. The second and longer part of the poem described the game he'd won for the Corinthians.

273

I had sketched the picture with fine, detailed strokes, starting with a panoramic image of the sky, blue as glass rinsed clean of any cloud; the Corinthians lined up starch-stiff in front of the bench. The spectators buzzing and hustling bets; Grammum, Dory, and I in our accustomed place behind the first-base line. The game described inning by inning, an epic battle with heroic antagonists. My father's deliverance of the team with the home run. It was a schoolchild's fable. The ball, struck by the lightning of the hero's bat, goes spinning into a mythic field, vanishing somewhere in the Kingdom of the Sun.

I knelt on the grass next to my father, adjusting his cap, turning the brim to the front. I saw that his eyes were open, but I could not tell whether he saw me, recognized me. He finally said, "Hey, Littlebits." He lay very still, his breath coming more easily. He closed his eyes, he was falling asleep.

I picked up the newspaper clipping again and re-read the poem. My father used to say he was partial to the last lines, the one stanza, I realized now, that I still knew by heart but had forgotten I ever wrote: where the ball leaps into the sun, for a jeweled instant pulling him along in its trajectory; where he is riding the stream of blue air yet miraculously touching the bases; hardly limping at all as his cleats come down with a soft *choof* on home plate, and we are there waiting, shining for him, all mirrors.

Nominated by Kim Edwards, David Madden, Susan Moon, Story

SUNG FROM A HOSPICE

by CYRUS CASSELLS

from PROVINCETOWN ARTS

Still craving a robust
Tenderness and justice,
I will go on living
With all I have seen:
Young men scourged
And lusterless;
Against my blind cheek—
Blessed be the frangible
And dying,
The irreplaceable dead—
In my crestfallen arms,
With breath,
Then without it,
With flesh,
Then freed of it—

And the indurate man I heard
Condemn the stricken,
While my cousin was dying,
If he had walked these wards,
Armorless, open
To the imperiled,
Surely he would have gleaned
To sit in judgment
Is to sit in hell—

Lesions, elegies,
Disconnected phones—

Rain, nimble rain,
Be anodyne,
Anoint me
When I say outright:
In the plague time, my heart
Was tested,
My living soul
Struck like a tower bell,
Once, twice,
Four times in a single season.

Nominated by Jane Miller, Provincetown Arts

THE INSTINCT FOR BLISS

fiction by MELISSA PRITCHARD

from THE PARIS REVIEW

F RANCES WAYTHORN, her face ghastly as a mime's from a souring paste of yogurt, scrubs walls and wainscotting, praying for bleach, polish, order, something, to check her daughter's latest slide from innocence. Pockets the Bic lighter, so Athena can't smoke. Weasles under the bed, dredging out a feculent nest of candy wrappers, cigarette butts, lewd notes, blood-soiled underwear, so Athena won't get fat or have sex or die. Frances's motions are selfless and efficient, her behavior a worship extending into grief. She refuses to acknowledge the poster of Jim Morrison. If she follows her own heart, stripping his deviant's baby face off the wall over her daughter's bed, who knows what might happen. Mothers like Frances are no longer immune from the retaliation of their daughters. Her face beginning to itch under the dried yogurt, Frances swivels a plush bunny into the center of the eyelet-edged pillow. Her child's room is pulled back, once again, into an immaculate relief of white, except for the poster, unexpungeable as a stain.

Athena, legally halved, is batted lightly between her parents. On alternate weeks she is not at her father's, she resides with Frances, her white room declining into a dank, fetid emporium of sloth. Those Sunday afternoons when Athena arrives, a canny refugee, on her mother's doorstep, a soiled, lumpy pillowcase of belongings over one shoulder, declaring she is an atheist who has drunk the blood of stray cats, Frances's labor, much like that of Sisyphus, begins anew, no hope for reprieve, only the diligent untanglement of familiar, defiant knots.

Frances is, in fact, uncrumpling and reading, rereading Athena's smutty notes before packing for her drive to a Navajo wool workshop when the doorbell rings. Hollering, "Wait," then "Sorry," unlocking the door, her face dripping water and patchy, as if with plaster, she sees he has a lovely, surprisingly tender face, this Officer Ruiz, telling her Athena is at the police station with another girl, arrested for shoplifting. He has been busy, attempting to notify the girls' parents. (Guiltily, Frances remembers three distinct times the phone rang as she scavenged under Athena's bed.)

"Where in God's name is her father? She's staying with him this week."

"Ma'am, from what your daughter claims, Mr. Waythorn is in Albuquerque until tomorrow."

He then informs Frances she can come get Athena, or agree to her being held overnight in juvenile detention.

"Of course I'll get her, though I am about to leave for Arizona. What about the other girl?" Frances asks, not really caring, angry that once again, and predictably, Athena's father has left her in the dark, told her nothing of his plans, neglected his daughter, and spoiled her own small hope for independence.

"Her parents have requested she be held overnight."

"In the Taos jail? Good lord. At their age I was in a convent. Reciting Shakespeare. Doing as I was told. Though Athena's father was a delinquent, a truant, he's boasted that often enough."

Frances's tone is bitter, as if she had known him even then, as if she had been harmed, even then, by her husband's errant boyhood.

•

So far, Frances decides, this driving across the hammered-flat desert is largely a matter of virulent silence.

Athena catches at a shifting avalanche of cassettes falling from her lap.

"May I play the Red Hot Chili Peppers? Their lyrics are banned." With Frances, almost any 'Mother may I?' worked.

"Banned?" Frances attends carefully, thinks she identifies the phrase *donkey juice* shouted over and over.

"I can't clearly make them out, honey. The words."

Pleased, Athena spritzes her face and arms with water from the plastic spray bottle she's brought, fogging herself like some fragile, costly plant.

278

"Want some?"

Tepid mist hits Frances, wetting her face. She has a pale rash from the yogurt.

Right now she would rather feed than punish Athena, pad her with double cheeseburgers, damp fries, chocolate shakes. If she's fat, no boy will want to have sex with her. If she's fat, she might not steal. Possibly no one but her mother will want her. She casts a look at Athena, the combat boots, unpolished and heavy looking as bricks, shredded jeans, black tank top, the front of her hair in two taffeta-like maroon flaps, the back of her head a shaved greenish stubble. The starlike design inked onto her upper arm, Frances is afraid to ask if it is a satanic emblem or simply the declaration of an atheist. What if Athena belongs to a cult, a gang? Frances remembers the heavyset woman in a purple tunic on Oprah Winfrey, sobbing, saying you never, ever, know what your children do once they leave the house, you think you do, but you don't. Her son had been machine gunned outside the front door. Actually, it is Frances whose stomach is bloating, whose thighs have widened.

"Ma-maah." Athena says it like a doll. "Where are you heisting me?"

"To a workshop on dyeing wool. I signed up for it at an arts fair last month, a freak impulse because I've never woven or dyed a thing in my life. But Athena, at my age, let me tell you, inventing a new life is no zip-i-dee-doo-dah flick of the wrist."

"May I drive?"

"No."

"Pleeze, Ma-mah? Dad lets me drive his truck sometimes."

"Absolutely not. You're supposed to be in jail. And your father's decisions, as you well know, are never mine. Look how he's abandoned you."

"He lets me do what I want, that's different. It is grotesque out here, Ma-maaah."

"Really? I think it has its own beauty. Deserts are spiritual places. Points of transcendence."

This observation rebounds, stilted. And why is Athena talking to her like a rubber doll?

"A couple of things we're to remember when we get there. Can you lower that a bit?"

Athena blunts, reluctantly, her music.

"When you're introduced, you're not to look any of the Navajos directly in the eye."

"Why not?"

"They consider it overly intimate."

"Cool."

Frances glances over. She never knows what will be cool or why.

"A simple enough thing for you."

"What?"

"You never look me in the eye, Athena. Not anymore."

"Not." She pins her mother with a look startlingly lethal.

"Is that genuine? That's frightening."

Athena shrugs. "What was the other thing? You said there were two."

"Fish. You can't eat fish around them. Navajos believe fish are embryonic, unformed humans, something like that. I can't remember. It's in here." Frances pats the guide book on Navajo culture she has brought, largely unread.

"Fish sticks make me puke anyways."

"Anyway."

"Any-waaaays . . ."

With the toe of her boot, Athena turns up the banned, incoherent lyrics.

•

What finally wakes her, after the others are up, is a sullen drone of flies along the heat-warped window ledge. In a white plastic bucket, blacking the surface of their drinking water, is a cobbled rug of drowned flies. A single fly still walks, if walking, she wonders, is how to describe it, along the battered lip of a tin cup. Frances rolls her sleeping bag next to Athena's, against one of the eight cinderblock walls of the hogan. She hasn't the least idea how to function in a Native American environment, but neatness is never an error. Manners are the same the world over, to quote her mother, and politeness, not sex, the true mortar of civilization. Frances's resolve, now that she is divorced against her will, is to "follow her bliss," a phrase she'd recently heard at a Wild Women of the West seminar, where one of the most astonishing things she had participated in was humping the earth to release pent-up male energy. This is why she has driven all the way out here, to a Navajo reservation. On instinct for bliss. She hasn't the least experience with dyeing wool or weaving anything. She can't even sew. What attracted her was being told this would be a place where, temporarily, no men were allowed.

Scraping open the wood door, Frances sees her red car parked under the mercury yard light, haughtily disassociated from the three trucks, two of which have I ♥ SHEEP stickers on their bumpers while her car has a blue sticker, stuck there by Athena, an upside down cow on it saying MEAT IS DEAD. Athena had left the window on her side down, and with the car so close to the hogan, Frances sees a ratty tailed, saffron rooster patrolling the front seat, back and forth, back and forth, its flat eye proprietary, arrogant.

"Hey Ma-mah, coffee."

Athena holds out a green, chipped mug, wearing yesterday's clothes, her mouth smeared a pinkish mahogany, a beauty dot pencilled above the bow of her top lip. Over Athena's bare shoulder, if she squinches up her eyes, Frances can make out a half circle of Navajo women bent over an animal of some sort, trussed and quivering on its back.

"Ma-mah, poke on your glasses. You need to see this. They're going to kill a sheep."

Before leaving the hogan, neatly dressed in ironed jeans and a white-fringed, turquoise sweat shirt, Frances, her eyeglasses on, hesitates before a Navajo loom, its cotton warp a pale and tranquil lyre rising up from the muted, traditional design. Cocoons of wrapped yarn hang neatly along the rug's perfect edge, where the weaver stopped. Reluctant to go outside and face any sort of butchery, Frances traces the design's black fretwork with one slowed finger, out to its edge.

•

She drinks her coffee, sitting on the ground beside a small cedar fire that burns with tallowy, weak effect in the morning sunlight. The grandmother squats behind the animal's throat, in a wide, pink-fanning skirt, red argyle socks and tennis shoes, her skirt the same medicinal pink as the outhouse, angled downhill as if it might tumble any time, exposing whoever sits, unfortunate, inside. Athena stands near the workshop instructor, a young Navajo woman named Valencia, who brushes a cedar branch, in blessing, over the animal. The grandmother, a white kerchief splashed with red roses concealing most of her face, pulls hard on its head, twists it, breaking the neck, then saws her long knife like a resined bow so blood sprays then spills with a green rushing of spring into a low white bowl, and the animal's bowels loose a sheen of knobbled dung onto the flat, colorless ground.

The fleece is split into a kind of jacket, its creamy lining veined with rich coral. The carcass still cinched within its parchment membrane, legs splayed four airy directions, suggests to Frances, except for the knob of breast, an upside-down table, fit to work on. The head, facing Frances, is set down in the fire. One eye swells, a black, glazed plum, the other sears and spits shut, then both eyes close, though unevenly, so it cannot look back upon its old form. The tongue doubles, prizing open the charring jaw. The yellow wool blackens, crisps, stinks. Now the spirit of the animal is released from all boundary, is everywhere.

This placid slaughter consoles Frances. A useful dismemberment, ritualized and strangely clean. The carcass squarely hung by hind feet from a cedar pole near the outdoor kitchen, the parchment membrane flensed back, the pursey insides unlocked, emptied out. The wine-brown brooch of liver, for Frances goes to touch it, like warm sea glass. The taupe gray skeins of intestine are pulled and stretched, the Navajo women pour hot water through the lengthened guts from an old tin coffeepot, squeezing and dribbling out the dung-colored stuff. A ripe jeweling of ruby and pewter, pearled matter, a supple kingdom falling over the plain hard canvas of dirt, the dull, droughted, trouble-seeming earth spotted with blood like vital specklings of rain. The stomach with its sallow chenille lining, the drying gloss of lungs, liver, kidneys, draped over a narrow pole. And rising under the callus of blood in the milky flat-faced dish, like a mineral pool, strings of bubbles, a languorous spitting of bubbles, as if something deep under its weight still breathed.

Frances studies these women, the practical details of their butchering, their reverent pulling apart of a life and making it into other, smaller, useful things.

•

Two emergency-room nurses from Lubbock are the only other participants in this workshop, and Frances has made no effort to talk to either one of them. A Married Rule, that pretense of sociability. The nurses, both skinny, both earnest and, for some reason, wan looking, stick close to the Navajo women, speak in enthusiastic twangings. Frances prays she doesn't resemble them, though she has signed up and paid for this experience, is conscious of being that evil necessity, a tourist with money to purchase a 3-D postcard, "Navajo women at

282

work on the reservation." She wants to tell these Indian women she understands, but what is it she understands, and does she?

"Maa, Maaah. . . ."

Bleating, Athena shuffles outside the tilting outhouse, her nose pinched, her voice nasal.

"You realize there are no males here. None. Except the sheep, and we've just killed him."

"Oh, there are men." Frances's voice is muffled, weary. "Always and eternally there are men." She steps out of the terrible smelling pink box. "My intent, Athena, was to go someplace where, for once, there weren't any. And where the Navajo men who usually live here have gone, I can't imagine. I'm sure it's rude to ask."

They walk back down the slope, Frances whacking at her dusty pants. White pants. What had she been thinking?

"I need some smokes. I have to go into town."

"Town. For heaven's sake, Athena, look where we are."

"Well, a trading post then. Plus I gotta wash my hair, it's getting completely gross. There's a bathroom in their house, I went in and found it, but no water. You turn the faucets and air spits out. There's not even water in the toilet."

"There's a bad drought. I heard Valencia say it's got something to do with the strip-mining, with the slurry water the mines use. All month they've been hauling water from town."

"These people should move to where there's more trees, more water. God." Athena narrows her eyes over the arid, hopeless, scrabbly landscape, blowing mournful smoke from her last cigarette. "Look. That dumb chicken's still on your front seat."

Athena runs, arms flapping, cigarette dangling, to swat the rooster out of the car. The Navajo women stop what they're doing to look, and Frances cannot interpret their faces. She jogs to catch up. She had looked forward to this trip by herself. She had hoped to learn something, or at least stop thinking about what exhausts and obsesses her. Now, looking into Athena's bright, provocative face, Frances sees how precisely, like a scissorcut, it matched her own at that age.

"Athena. you have to behave yourself. When you're the guest of another culture, you blend in, you ask intelligent questions."

"I am. I'm going to ask where the nearest store is and where the men are stashed."

"Athena."

"What."

"Please."

"What."

"You could be in prison right now. I could have left you there until your father decided to come and get you."

"Yada yada yada."

"What were you stealing?"

"Undies."

"Underwear? I just bought you plenty of . . . "

"Sexy underwear, Ma. You've never bought me that."

"May I ask you a simple question? What makes you so sure you are Jim Morrison's wife reincarnated?"

"You're the one who told me about reincarnation."

"Yes, but you can't just make up who you wish you had been. Oh, wouldn't I love to think I was once Thomas Jefferson or Sarah Bernhardt or even Luther Burbank."

"Thomas Jefferson?"

"I've always wanted to be Thomas Jefferson. Do you know who I was in love with at your age?"

"Dad?"

Frances pauses dramatically. "Carl Sandburg."

"Who's that?"

"He's dead now, but he was a famous poet. I wrote Carl Sandburg several passionate letters. He was in his seventies."

"Cool. Mom in love with an old dude."

"I never mailed them. I knew he had a wife and a goat farm in North Carolina, and probably he was happy."

"What about Dad? Oh, never mind. You'll just say something nasty. You're in that stage now."

"Stage?"

"Of divorce. Denial, rage, stuff like that."

"Where'd you pick up that idea?"

"Dad. He has books on divorce. Just like you."

"The same books?"

"Yup. Exactly. You guys are exactly alike."

Right, Frances thinks. Except he's chosen someone else. He's betrayed me.

•

Doing as she is asked, Athena drags the charred head from the fire by one gristled ear, sets it on a wood block, scrapes off filings of ash with a stick so the head can be wrapped and baked. And when she is certain her mother sees, for isn't her mother always watching, spying, jealous, easy to fool, a cinch to scare, to give her something really to be scared about, Athena swoops one finger across the bowl of dulling blood and drives it deep into her own mouth. Not long after that, Frances will stand in the parrot-yellow kitchen, stuffing gray, salted mutton into her mouth until the women, laughing, caution her to stop, until they stop laughing and take the plate away, saying this will make her sick. Mutton hunger is what they will say she has.

·

After lunch, they ride in the nurses' truck to the base of a sort of mountain. Everybody gets a plastic grocery sack. They are to follow the grandmother, collect twigs, leaves, roots and mosses, plants Valencia names for them, mullein, lichen, sumac, mountain mahogany, chamisa.

Athena lags behind with the most tired looking nurse, while Frances tracks the grandmother, what she can of her, two red argyled ankles flashing up a rigorous incline. Frances slows from the midday heat, the altitude, the enervating whiteness of the sun. In every direction, sealike troughs of land push up clumps of piñon and cedar, like rich, bronze-green kelp. A hawk skates the air above her in fluid, mahogany curls.

Frances nearly trips over the grandmother, crouched by a blunt formation of black rock, on her knees with a table knife, chipping chrome yellow powder from the rock and dusting it off her hands into a plastic bag.

Valencia looks up kindly. "We use this to get our black, mixing it with piñon pitch and cedar ash. It's pretty hard to find, but grandmother is amazing, she goes right to where it is."

The taller nurse stands like a sentinel, a lank poplar, behind Frances.

"That stuff looks like uranium. Exactly."

Frances takes her turn scraping, grazing her knuckles, the uranium idea has unnerved her.

"You could hike up here once a year, get a gigantic load of this stuff to last you."

Frances thinks no one has heard, though the nurse's voice is tactless enough. The grandmother is resting in the compressed, thick shade of a piñon tree, while Valencia, wiping sweat from her forehead, answers, a perceptible teacher's edge to her voice.

"We take only what is needed each time. And Grandmother has taught us to leave an offering, a gift, before separating anything from where it is found."

"Halllooooo!" Athena, her arms making rapid pinwheeling motions, appears to be urging them up to the next highest ledge. Frances is busy, spit-washing a smudge of uranium off her turquoise shirt.

When the three white women attain the highest ledge, they hold their plastic bags of roots and twigs, panting, confounded by what they see. Inches deep across the ground lay thousands of pottery shards. The women, winded, hot faced, are told they are standing on a trash dump, where Anasazi Indians, centuries ago, had thrown their broken pots and garbage.

The Navajo women sit and rest, observe the three white women stooping and bobbing, pecking about for bits of clay, their arms blooming with what they cannot seem to gather up fast enough. At first, the women call back and forth excitedly, then lapse into an almost funereal quiet, the weight of anthropology, the burden of choosing among priceless relics falling almost gloomily upon them. Like children, their greed eventually tires them, and they become aware of the Navajo women, quietly watching. They stop, arms and pockets and bags loaded down, their small congress embarrassed, bits of pottery dropping off them like leaves.

"Perhaps just two or three," says one nurse.

"Those that mean the most," suggests the other.

As Frances sets down her cumbersome pile, Athena, who had wandered off, returns. Between her hands, rests a large, perfect potshard, a black lightning streak down its reddish curved flank. Exclaiming over its size and near perfect condition, Frances begins to thank Athena, grateful for the largeness of gesture, the love implied.

"It's for Dad," Athena says softly. "I wanted to bring him something."

"Oh." Frances drops to her knees, shuffling through her little clay bits, as if to choose.

"Did you leave an offering?"

"Yuppers. My last cigarette, one I copped from the nurse."

On the ride back, they stop beside a faded sprawl of prickly pear to pick its mushy, red fruits for pink dye. The driving nurse, feeling unwell, decides to drive to the trading post for stomach medicine. Both nurses drop the women back at the hogan except for Athena, who's begged a ride.

•

Frances labors alongside her instructor, hefting enamelware kettles and a halved oil drum filled with hauled water, onto different fires. She sorts through gathered plant materials, carries bags and baskets of handspun wool skeins out from the hogan, admires Valencia's long, black hair, twisted in a shining bundle at the nape of her neck, noting its resemblance to the skeins of wool, to the little bundles of yarn dangling from the edge of the rug inside the hogan. She wonders how Valencia would raise a daughter, how do the women raise teenagers out here, how, in her own case, could things get much worse.

Swirling the stained waters with an ashy stick, made sleepy by the steam of plants, bitter or sweet smelling, or dense as soured earth, Frances begins to hope Athena might not return until much, much later.

At once she hears the truck, observes it dipping and rising over the rutted gullies, with Athena, cross-legged in the bed of the truck, in a somber corona of dust, brandishing a cigarette. As her daughter trips unsteadily past her, blowing smoke out both nostrils, her maroon hair tangled and shreddy looking, Frances studies the shaven back of her head so disturbingly infantlike, watches her wobble around a cast iron pot of chamisa dye, right herself, then pitch behind one side of the hogan and begin, audibly, to vomit.

One of the nurses comes up to Frances.

"I found this in the truck bed."

Frances stares at the half-empty bottle.

The bottle lodged under her arm, Frances uses a peeled stick to raise out of the water one of the skeins of yarn. It hangs from the end of the willow stick, a twist, an eight, of deep, ardent gold.

•

Worse than finding Athena on the ground, is seeing the rooster, pecking with cold disregard, at her daughter's vomit. Frances is about to kick the rooster, when suddenly, admitting nature's genius, she leaves it to clean the mess Athena has once again made of things.

"G'way." Athena's tattooed arm takes a sodden, backwards sweep at the air. "G'way, stupid."

Her profile, smooshed into the ground, is a mask of vomit and dirt.

"All right, I will go away. I will go get something to wash your filthy face with. You disappoint me, Athena."

Athena's visible eye stays blearily fixed on the rooster.

Inside the dim, stifling hogan, Frances finds the one available cloth, her pink western bandanna. The only water she knows of is in the white plastic bucket. Biting her bottom lip, plunging her arm deep to wet the bandanna, she has to shake off a burred sleeve of flies. She stands quiet before the loom, an object of great dignity, a pursuit, elusive to Frances, of stillness and purpose. Hadn't she tried to make their marriage like that, into fine cloth, an enduring design?

Balling up the tepid pink bandanna, wringing it hard, she squats behind Athena, turning her head and wiping her soiled face. As she scrubs under her daughter's chin, a muddy backwash of rage hits.

"There." She throws down the stained rag. "You find something to do with that. I'm taking our things to the car. We're going home, not that either of us has much of a home anymore."

As she finishes stuffing the trunk with their few things, Frances hears the nurse, the one who had shown her the half-empty whiskey bottle, behind her.

"Mrs. Waythorn, your daughter took off running that way. If you take the car, you'll catch up to her. It won't be dark for another fifteen minutes."

The woman's voice is so nursely, so merciful, so professionally equipped for trauma, Frances wants to collapse against her ordinary sweatshirt, her calm and practical shoulder. She wants to say, Oh you take care of this, somebody else manage this, I only want to rest.

•

Even in the drought-smeared violet light, Frances easily makes out the skinny speck of her daughter shambling along the gravel and dirt road. In the middle of nowhere. Going nowhere.

As her car creeps closer, Frances, seeing Athena's set, miserable profile, does a most unexpected thing. She pumps hard on the accelerator and shoots past her daughter, steering with great angry lurches and radical swerves, up over the crest of a small hill and down.

She stops, exhilarated, considering what she has done. Abandoned her daughter. Gone beyond her. Swooped by. Yes.

Her arch has a dark wetted gash across it. Athena's pot shard, the gift for her father, has rolled off the seat and smashed into pieces

288

around her foot. Frances rests her forehead on the steering wheel. After a long while, she becomes aware of darkness. My God. She switches on the light overhead, lifts up to see the top third of her face in the little mirror. Smeared with dirt, tears, old mascara. Her pants, too, ruined. Her shirt, poisoned with uranium.

Wildly, she feels for the ignition, in a panic, shoves into reverse, backs up the car, coasts down the little hill she's concealed herself behind.

Frances gets out of the car, sees blurrily, a mile or so away, the mercury yard light she had aimed for the night before. Hears, as if it isn't hers anymore, the sound of weeping.

The car light switched on, Frances is on her knees, searching under the seats, trying to gather back pieces of the clay pot. On the day she had been scrubbing down her child's room, on the day of her daughter's arrest, she had found, while on her belly under Athena's bed, a green cardboard shoebox. Inside the shoebox were the souvenirs Frances had kept hidden from everyone. The dry, yellowish triangle of Athena's umbilical cord, a wavy, black shank of her ex-husband's hair, the auburn braid of her mother's hair, cut six months before she'd died, and like twin, eerie rattles, two tiny boxes of Frances's own ivoried baby teeth. Athena, searching through her mother's secret things, had taken, out of instinct or curiosity, all she needed.

"Ma-mah? What is it? What are you doing?"

"My foot's cut."

"Poorest Mommy. You can't drive, bleeding and crying like that. Shh, shh, okay, shh. I'll help you. Shh."

Stripping off, wrapping the black tank top around her mother's foot, Athena, not bothering to ask, gets her old wish to drive. And as the reservation night covers, uncovers her white, scarcely touched breasts, as her mother guards, unyielding, the broken potshards, bits of hair and dried cord, Athena will piece together a stubborn, defiantly remembered, child's way home.

Nominated by Roger Weingarten

DANTE'S *INFERNO,* CANTO XXXIV (THE FINAL CANTO)

ROBERT PINSKY

from AGNI

"And now, *Vexilla regis prodeunt*
    Inferni—therefore, look," my master said
    As we continued on the long descent,

"And see if you can make him out, ahead."
    As though, in the exhalation of heavy mist
    Or while night darkened our hemisphere, one spied

A mill—blades turning in the wind, half-lost
    Off in the distance—some structure of that kind
    I seemed to make out now. But at a gust

Of wind, there being no other shelter at hand,
    I drew behind my leader's back again.
    By now (and putting it in verse I find

Fear in myself still) I had journeyed down
    To where the shades were covered wholly by ice,
    Showing like straw in glass—some lying prone,

And some erect, some with the head toward us,
    And others with the bottoms of the feet;
    Another like a bow, bent feet to face.

When we had traveled forward to the spot
    From which it pleased my master to have me see
    The creature whose beauty once had been so great,

He made me stop, and moved from in front of me.
    "Look: here is Dis," he said, "and here is the place
    Where you must arm yourself with the quality

Of fortitude." How chilled and faint I was
    On hearing that, you must not ask me, reader—
    I do not write it; words would not suffice:

I neither died, nor kept alive—consider
    With your own wits what I, alike denuded
    Of death and life, became as I heard my leader.

The emperor of the realm of grief protruded
    From mid-breast up above the surrounding ice.
    A giant's height, and mine, would have provided

Closer comparison than would the size
    Of his arm and a giant. Envision the whole
    That is proportionate to parts like these.

If he was truly once as beautiful
    As he is ugly now, and raised his brows
    Against his Maker—then all sorrow may well

Come out of him. How great a marvel it was
    For me to see three faces on his head:
    In front there was a red one; joined to this,

Each over the midpoint of a shoulder, he had
    Two others—all three joining at the crown.
    That on the right appeared to be a shade

Of whitish yellow; the third had such a mien
       As those who come from where the Nile descends.
       Two wings spread forth from under each face's chin,

Strong, and befitting such a bird, immense—
       I have never seen at sea so broad a sail—
       Unfeathered, batlike, and issuing three winds

That went forth as he beat them, to freeze the whole
       Realm of Cocytus that surrounded him.
       He wept with all six eyes, and the tears fell

Over his three chins mingled with bloody foam.
       The teeth of each mouth held a sinner, kept
       As by a flax-rake: thus he held three of them

In agony. For the one the front mouth gripped,
       The teeth were as nothing to the claws, which sliced
       And tore the skin until his back was stripped.

"That soul," my master said, "who suffers most,
       Is Judas Iscariot; head locked inside,
       He flails his legs. Of the other two, who twist

With their heads down, the black mouth holds the shade
       Of Brutus: writhing, but not a word will he scream;
       Cassius is the sinewy one on the other side.

But night is rising again, and it is time
       That we depart, for we have seen the whole."
       As he requested, I put my arms around him,

And waiting until the wings were opened full
       He took advantage of the time and place
       And grasped the shaggy flank, and gripping still,

From tuft to tuft descended through the mass
       Of matted hair and crusts of ice. And then,
       When we had reached the pivot of the thighs,

Just where the haunch is at its thickest, with strain
    And effort my master brought around his head
    To where he'd had his legs: and from there on

He grappled the hair as someone climbing would—
    So I supposed we were heading back to Hell.
    "Cling tight, for it is stairs like these," he sighed

Like one who is exhausted, "which we must scale
    To part from so much evil." Then he came up
    Through a split stone, and placed me on its sill,

And climbed up toward me with his cautious step.
    I raised my eyes, expecting I would see
    Lucifer as I left him—and saw his shape

Inverted, with his legs held upward. May they
    Who are too dull to see what point I had passed
    Judge whether it perplexed me. "Come—the way

Is long, the road remaining to be crossed
    Is hard: rise to your feet," the master said,
    "The sun is at mid-tierce." We had come to rest

In nothing like a palace hall; instead
    A kind of natural dungeon enveloped us,
    With barely any light, the floor ill-made.

"Before I free myself from the abyss,
    My master," I said when I was on my feet,
    "Speak, and dispel my error: where is the ice?

And how can he be fixed head-down like that?
    And in so short a time, how can it be
    Possible for the sun to make its transit

From evening to morning?" He answered me,
    "You imagine you are still on the other side,
    Across the center of the earth, where I

Grappled the hair on the evil serpent's hide
  Who pierces the world. And all through my descent,
  You were on that side; when I turned my head

And legs about, you passed the central point
  To which is drawn, from every side, all weight.
  Now you are on the opposite continent

Beneath the opposite hemisphere to that
  Which canopies the great dry land therein:
  Under the zenith of that one is the site

Whereon the Man was slain who without sin
  Was born and lived; your feet this minute press
  Upon a little sphere whose rounded skin

Forms the Judecca's other, outward face.
  Here it is morning when it is evening there;
  The one whose hair was like a ladder for us

Is still positioned as he was before.
  On this side he fell down from Heaven; the earth,
  Which till then stood out here, impelled by fear

Veiled itself in the sea and issued forth
  In our own hemisphere. And possibly,
  What now appears on this side fled its berth

And rushing upwards left a cavity:
  This hollow where we stand." There is below,
  As far from Beelzebub as one can be

Within his tomb, a place one cannot know
  By sight, but by the sound a little runnel
  Makes as it wends the hollow rock its flow

Has worn, descending through its winding channel:
  To get back up to the shining world from there
  My guide and I went into that hidden tunnel;

And following its path, we took no care
    To rest, but climbed: he first, then I—so far,
    Through a round aperture I saw appear

Some of the beautiful things that Heaven bears,
Where we came forth, and once more saw the stars.—

Nominated by Gail Mazur, Lloyd Schwartz, David Wojahn

ELIZABETH BISHOP

by FRANK BIDART

from THREEPENNY REVIEW

ELIZABETH never saw her mother in the hospital because her family didn't want her to, and by the time she was old enough, Elizabeth was afraid to. Elizabeth told me that each time she went to Vassar, the train passed the hospital her mother was in—she shuddered when she said this. It was a source of pain, but she didn't simply say (as if the question were simple), "Oh, I should have gone to see her." How does one visit a parent not seen since the age of five, in a mental hospital, when you have been taught to think of her as dead? Then, suddenly, when Elizabeth reached the age when she might have been able to come to an independent judgment about the matter, her mother *was* dead.

*

Robert Sever wanted to marry her and finally she didn't want to marry him. She broke it off. It was at this point that Seaver killed himself, and before he did, he mailed her a postcard on which he had written, "Elizabeth, Go to hell." It arrived after his death.

*

The person Elizabeth was really in love with in those early years was Margaret Miller. They never had a physical relationship. Elizabeth felt that Margaret was not homosexual. She had been in love with Margaret since they were roommates at Vassar. Once she told me that, after years of being obsessed with Margaret, when she woke up one morning, the knot in her chest always present when she thought of Margaret simply was gone. After years suddenly she was over it. (She told me this trying to assure me that an obsession *I* had about someone would end.)

Elizabeth never talked about being in love with Louise Crane. She gave the impression that they had some sort of an affair. When Elizabeth had been drinking a lot, or was sobering up, the relationship with Margaret Miller haunted her, and certainly the relationship with Lota haunted her. The relationship with Louise Crane didn't.

*

Elizabeth had been sick in Brazil and Lota had nursed her. One morning, Elizabeth was in bed and Lota came into her room and asked her to stay with her in Brazil. Elizabeth said yes. She was surprised she had said yes. She liked Lota, but she was not in love with her. Over the next few years she really fell in love with Lota.

*

Lowell once said to me that Elizabeth changed tremendously with Lota, at least in political terms, and that after about five years, Elizabeth became, from the point of view of someone from the States, conservative. Lota was Brazilian aristocracy; it was an oligarchy. Elizabeth clearly had accepted that. The poems she wrote in Brazil, and her poems earlier, seem to me often radical in perception and feeling; but, Lowell said, Elizabeth would defend their friend the Governor, that sort of thing. She began to sound like Lota. Lowell didn't find this particularly attractive: it wasn't the bohemian Elizabeth Bishop that he had known in the Forties in New York. The only poem, I think, that reflects this is "Manuelzinho," with its whiff of *noblesse oblige.* The speaker of the poem isn't Elizabeth, but Lota; perhaps the title character is perceived too comfortably as helpless and funny. (This is very different from, for example, "The Riverman.") Her last poem about Brazil (and the last poem she finished) is one with enormous, unameliorated social consciousness, "Pink Dog," which is lethal about a society that informally solves the problem of its beggars, its outcasts and crippled, by throwing them into the river.

*

Elizabeth said that the main reason people in Brazil were angry with her was that she took Suzanne back so soon after Lota's death. She and Suzanne went to the country club, and people cut her. Elizabeth was tremendously upset and bitter about this. People knew Elizabeth had had a relationship with Suzanne before Lota died. Elizabeth felt that in their minds this contributed to Lota's death. Elizabeth said that people there felt that she had murdered Lota.

*

I met Elizabeth in 1970, when she came to Harvard to replace Lowell. He wrote me a letter saying that I should call on her; and wrote her saying that he had asked me to. Obviously I couldn't have had a better introduction. Elizabeth was staying in Kirkland House then, a month or six weeks after she arrived. We met at her room, and then went out for lunch—we just immediately got on. With me she was extremely easy, and very warm, very funny. I was quite worried about going to meet her; just because I was Lowell's friend, and shared his opinion of her work (she was his favorite poet among his contemporaries), didn't mean we'd hit it off. I do think the fact that I was close to him mattered a lot. In a way, she wanted to get back into much better touch with him. Elizabeth trusted me because she knew Lowell trusted me.

That first day she was extremely generous about Lowell, grateful to him. She was diffident about her work and reputation. She felt that because she had been out of the country so long she was unfashionable, half-forgotten. (Years later, visiting my apartment, she plucked *The Modern Poet*, a volume of essays edited by Ian Hamilton, off my shelves. There were essays on Lowell, Plath, Berryman, Jarrell—nothing on her. She scanned the table of contents, then putting the book back said, with woe in her voice: "It's like being buried alive.") She was very affectionate about Lowell, and said that when she first met him he was unkempt, but handsome as a movie star. (With delight she told a story I had never heard before: around 1946 a movie producer actually tried to get Lowell to go to Hollywood for a screen test.) Many times she had gotten something—a grant or a prize, or her present Harvard job—because he worked to get it for her; sometimes she had only learned years later that he had anything to do with it.

Somehow it came up that in an interview he had said that she was one of the four greatest women poets who ever lived. The praise was spoiled because women were placed in a separate category, cordoned off: far better just to be considered a poet, however low the ranking.

In later years, as others have written, considerable tension developed in Bishop's feelings about Lowell. Some of the ground of this anger seemed clear at the time: when he planned to come back to America in 1973, his return (despite his offer not to return if it did) seemed to threaten her job, which she needed. (Brazil—where she became so unhappy she couldn't stay for more than a few months at a time—was by now a kind of black hole for her; and she needed the money.) People who never read poetry knew who Lowell was and what confessional poetry was; though Lowell himself was ironic about "confessionalism" and the flood of bad poems about parents, often full of Lowellisms, filling the magazines, hegemony breeds loathing. Bishop herself had greeted *Life Studies* with a great tribute, printed on the hardcover jacket; now, in the early Seventies at Harvard, in the heyday of his fame, she felt suffocated. (Such reasons ignore the residue, the traces of promises, failures, blindnesses, angers left after a friendship of twenty-five years: "heavy as frost, and deep almost as life.") The loyalty, what was obviously love between them was never quite broken; but in the final years it existed in a crucible.

*

A few weeks after first meeting Elizabeth—after we had seen each other several times—when I called one day she said that she had been sick, but I could come by. At the door, she was in her robe, without makeup, straightforward but full of self-reproaches about the fact that several days earlier she had begun drinking and at last stopped only when she was so sick she couldn't continue. Alice Methfessel, the secretary at Kirkland House, now was bringing her food and trying to get her well. Elizabeth was shaky: more or less sober, but ravaged, with a terrible cough (she was asthmatic). She was ashamed, but didn't want to be alone. So we talked. She talked about the painful things in her past that tormented her, events that she never discussed when she wasn't drinking or struggling in the aftermath of drinking.

Perhaps at this point I should bring up something that *I* am tormented by: almost nothing I've said about Elizabeth's life would she want said. That's why, after her death, I decided I didn't want to be the source of anything that appeared in print about her drinking, sexual life, etc. But the intensity of interest in her work, and the nature of

299

contemporary biography, made revelations that she would have found intolerable in her lifetime inevitable. I just didn't want to be their source. What I *could* do was treat these subjects in as un-flamboyant, adequate a way as I was capable, once they had already become part of the record. At this point, Elizabeth would gain nothing from my silence. That's the peace I've made with myself on the issue.

I think it would be stupid of anyone to attempt to locate a single "reason" for her drinking (as if it had a single cause), to condescend to her by "explaining" what she couldn't explain or devise a strategy to escape. So what I am about to say is not an explanation of why she drank: it's the experience I had. There was in Elizabeth the "lady" who liked to talk about food, travel, things you've seen, what happened to you, friends—and, to a lesser degree, books. To be in her presence was constantly to feel her originality, freshness of perception, vulnerability. The "lady" wasn't boring or self-important; Lowell said that she was more fun to be with than anyone. But enormous ranges of her feeling she seemingly couldn't bear to express—even, I think, with her closest friends—unless she was drinking: subjects like Lota, especially Lota's death; her own sexual life; those she had been in love with; betrayals; guilt; her mother; drinking itself. When she drank it seemed that she had ripped down the self-possessed facade of her life, the poise that intelligence and luck and accomplishment had given her. She descended into an inferno of still-alive, wholly unreconciled feeling, the wholly present past.

At times Elizabeth could simply drink socially; at times one drink made her drunk; at times she drank for days and only stopped when her body collapsed, often ending in hospitalization. Without fail she was furious with herself for having inflicted this on herself and those who cared for her, especially Alice. She was terrified Alice would leave her because of it. The thing she couldn't stop doing threatened to kill the relationship that she felt she couldn't live without.

*

Elizabeth considered herself a feminist, and had since she was young; she viewed SOME developments in the contemporary feminist movement with skepticism (particularly the development of women-only collections or anthologies), but she was passionately feminist, and could be bitter about how the world had treated her because she was a woman. Late in her life, in a mood of anger, self-doubt, and bitterness, she told me that she felt she would have written much more had she been a man. She brought up how little she had written in contrast to Lowell (his *Selected Poems* had just come out, and in particular once again she was overwhelmed by "Waking Early Sunday Morning"). I can't quote her words exactly, but she felt that certain kinds of directness and ambition—because of gender—had been denied her, had been impossible.

The skepticism she felt about the gay rights movement was based on her sense that straight society would never truly accept homosexuality, that sooner or later it would punish writers for "coming out." She was worried that the candor of what I had written would at some point be used against me professionally, and in warning me said that she "believed in closets, closets, and more closets." One must remember that for the vast majority of her life, in both social and literary terms, *not* to be in the closet was to be ghettoized; people might know or suspect that one was gay, but to talk about it openly in straight society was generally considered out-of-control or stupid. (Bishop thought famously polemical works like *The Well of Loneliness* weak, simplistic, an embarrassment.) Out of her distrust of the straight world she didn't want people to know she was gay. She certainly didn't want people to talk about it. The irony, of course, is that everyone at least in the literary world *did* know, and didn't care; but she could never believe that this was the case.

*

The period when she thought she would lose Alice certainly was the most terrible period in Elizabeth's life during the years I knew her. And I think her way of working her way out of it was writing "One Art." It did look "like disaster." And the poem is also the desperate attempt to tell herself that it isn't disaster. "One Art" was seventy to eighty percent finished when I saw it. My memory is that there were two or three stanzas that weren't finished. There was a draft with a list of rhyme words, and I think I suggested a rhyme out of that. It was already a villanelle; the present ending was basically as it is. We talked about the punctuation of "Write it," whether to italicize the "Write," how to do that. Elizabeth was very open about the occasion that drives it.

I think Elizabeth was magnificently inconsistent. On the one hand, she could talk a blue streak about how people shouldn't be writing all those confessional poems, and yet when she had to do it, she did it, and without apology. At a certain level, the aesthetic position was quite irrelevant to Elizabeth. I also think she was able to cut off certain parts of her mind in order to make the poem. For example, someone once said something to her about how "Crusoe in England" is a kind of autobiographical metaphor for Brazil and Lota. She was horrified by the suggestion. And obviously the poem is. I certainly never said to her, "Elizabeth, 'One Art' is a confessional poem," but on the other hand, she was entirely straightforward about how it was directly related to what was happening in her own life. I don't think she wanted to confront the way that contradicted her stance. One evening at her apartment, Elizabeth had just shown Octavio Paz the poem, and he was amazed at both how wonderful and candid it was; that evening he said to me in astonishment: Why, it's a confessional poem.

*

Elizabeth once told me on the phone from Florida that, that day, she had wanted to throw herself under a car. She would see cars go by, and she had a tremendous impulse to do it. Without Alice life seemed intolerable. Of course I can't know how much of this was theater to convince Alice to come back. But I was scared to death.

*

I don't remember that there was any sort of big declaration one way or the other. It was clear at some point that Alice decided to give up the man she intended to marry. Suddenly they were together, going on a trip or something together, and there was just no more talk about him. After that Elizabeth was a little unhappy at how extremely candid she had been during this period. For months she had called up a number of people late at night, drinking too much, in despair talking for hours. When things abruptly were resolved, it was as if there had been no crisis.

*

Elizabeth wished she had written more. Before publication she worried that *Geography III* was too short. As I said earlier, she once said to me she felt that if she had been a man she would have written much more. Of course I was dismayed: one of the great things about her work is that she *didn't* write too much, that there is such concentration, perfection, about so much of it. But in certain moods—particularly when she was drinking—she could be savage about her work, and no assertion that she was a great writer (and she is, without question, a great writer: and she had many friends who knew that) seemed to reconcile her to what she had done.

Elizabeth wanted to write and talked a lot about having begun a long elegy for Lota. She was very worried about the way it would or wouldn't be candid. In the background of all this, I suppose, was a certain inevitable competitiveness with Lowell, the fact that he was so prolific. She felt very ambivalent about the fact he wrote so much; but she also envied it. The elegy for Lota (so far as I know, never written), mired in so many contradictory aesthetic and personal emotions for Elizabeth, brought these issues to a head.

In the years I knew her—the last nine years of her life—she didn't (so far as I know) write every day, or in any kind of regular pattern. When she went to North Haven she took manuscripts with her and might come back at the end of the summer without much being written, if anything. When an idea for a poem possessed her, she carried it as far as she could, and then might let the fragments lie waiting to be finished for immense lengths of time. She was, at the same time, an infinitely careful craftsman (I don't think she'd object to the traditional word), and believed in at least the possibility of something like inspiration. Once, when I told her how great the end of "At the Fishhouses" is, she said that when she was writing it she hardly knew what she was writing, knew the words were right, and (at this she raised her arms as high straight above her head as she could) felt ten feet tall.

*

Elizabeth never showed me drafts of poems at as early a stage, or in as much detail, as Lowell did. A new poem was mostly finished by the time I saw it. The first uncompleted poem I saw was "Poem." Elizabeth was already living on Brattle Street, so it was her second year in Cambridge. Two or three spots still were giving her trouble, and she had variants handwritten in the margins. I still see her standing over her kitchen table, puzzling over what became "A specklike bird is flying to the left./ Or is it a flyspeck looking like a bird?" The other rough passage, written and rewritten over the next few weeks, was the great passage about "art 'copying from life' and life itself," in the last stanza. The problem here, of course, is how to use such abstract, even academic language and not have it swallow up, flatten, banalize the poem; it's characteristic of her that she felt both the necessity of it, of reaching this level of generality, and had to find some way to put a "skin" on such language, ground it in the skepticism and specificities of her own speaking voice. (She struggled in the same way with the "literary interpretations" passage in "Santarem.")

There are two instances in which I think I was useful to Elizabeth. After she had sent "The End of March" to *The New Yorker*, she was unhappy with the last stanza and rewrote it again and again. She dictated a set of final changes to me over the phone; clearly it was improved. I retyped the stanza so I'd have a clean copy with the changes. (By now it was too late to incorporate them in *The New Yorker*.) *Geography III* was set by Farrar, Straus, and Giroux from magazine copies of the poems. When page proofs arrived (I don't think there was a separate set of galleys) the poem had the magazine ending; I was upset. By now the poem was just old enough that Elizabeth had forgotten that she hadn't been able to let it go without revising it; and now she couldn't find the revision. So the single typed copy I made was the source of the version in the book.

In some sense, for Elizabeth, getting a poem right was almost a Platonic act; once she was satisfied, the details over which she had struggled so much ceased to have some of their reality. (There is an important stanza break missing in "Over 2,000 Illustrations and a Complete Concordance" in her first *Complete Poems,* which she didn't notice for years; David Kalstone caught it.) She also had a confident, decisive, original sense of details: she told me once that she had to fight with *The New Yorker* for years before they would let her use a dash at the beginning of a line.

Finishing "The Moose" was a crisis: she had promised a new poem for the annual Phi Beta Kappa ceremony during Harvard's graduation week. About a week before it was to be read to hundreds of people, "The Moose"—long, intricate, begun at least fifteen years earlier— still wasn't completed. She had never promised a poem by a deadline before. It was the only new poem she had. Her insecurity about academia, fed by the fact that she hadn't begun to teach till late in life, became terror. (I've heard that Frost, before delivering his Phi Beta Kappa poem, was in a similar panic.) Elizabeth, Alice and I had made plans to go to Bermuda for a weekend; both insisted we must go. Elizabeth took the poem with her.

On the plane, as she showed me the lines for the first time, it became clear that the poem already—except for a handful of connectives, a handful of phrases—was there. In *Return of the Jedi* there's a wonderful image of a planet that isn't finished. There's the sphere, but there are all these gaps and holes in the sphere as it hangs in the air. Elizabeth's stanzas were like that. She would have the first line. She would have the last line. She'd have maybe two lines near the end and maybe even several phrases in the middle, but not quite enough to make the rhymes and the lines come together. What she needed was an audience to lead through the narrative line of the poem: in deciphering her handwritten corrections for me, having again to move from the beginning of the poem through to the end, having to talk out what the stanzas filled with gaps needed to accomplish within the narrative frame, she filled the gaps. Later many phrases again were changed; but when the plane reached Bermuda, she had a continuous draft of the whole.

*

Elizabeth said that she never read *The Group*, but from what people said to her she was convinced that she was the model for Lakey. She knew that Mary McCarthy insisted she wasn't, but she thought she was. She was bitter about this, very angry. The first time I met Elizabeth, in Kirkland House, she said that she had made a million dollars for Mary McCarthy in *The Group*. She had known McCarthy very well and had helped McCarthy through various crises. There's a chapter of the book which was originally a short story, about Dotty being fitted for a pessary; Elizabeth had indeed gone on a similar first trip to the doctor with McCarthy.

Because of the figure of the countess in *The Group*, she was very sorry that she had ever let McCarthy meet Lota. In the last summer of Lowell's life, when Elizabeth and Alice were staying at North Haven, the Lowells were at Castine, and McCarthy lived in Castine. McCarthy wanted to come over with the Lowells for a day trip, and Elizabeth wouldn't let her come. Elizabeth said that she didn't want Mary to meet Alice, because she felt it would end up as another episode in a novel. She certainly didn't forgive McCarthy.

305

*   *   *

Trying to rewrite interview material on Elizabeth Bishop, I thought I saw in fragments of reminiscence the possibility of something faithful to mystery like fiction, but accurate to memory.

*

In 1937, Louise Crane, Margaret Miller and Elizabeth were in an automobile accident in France, Louise Crane driving. The car turned over and Margaret Miller's right arm was severed below the elbow. Margaret was rushed to a hospital; Louise stayed with her. Elizabeth stayed behind at the scene. She found the arm. She sat next to it and covered it with her dress. She waited for the police, or at least more help, to arrive. She told me she had always wanted to write a poem spoken by the arm, but couldn't.

Nominated by Marvin Bell, David Wojahn

LOSS

by CARL DENNIS

from POETRY

Just because your cousins perjured themselves
On the stand to steal the house you inherited
And have settled in, and are filling the rooms
With furniture your aunt would have hated,
Doesn't mean they're getting away with it.

Just because their lights will now burn late
In the house you love, and the sound of their dancing
Will be heard in the street, their drums and trumpets
At birthday parties, graduations, and weddings,
Doesn't mean they're not paying the penalty,
Living lesser lives than they might have lived,
Possessing lesser amounts of comeliness.

And if they're not aware of the loss,
Couldn't that show how shrunken their spirits are,
How you wouldn't want to be them as they fall asleep
At the end of a day they regard as perfect?

Of course it's hard not to wish them ill,
A pain that even their thicker souls can feel.
But that won't widen your cramped apartment.
That won't give you the spacious, airy life you admire
With windows opening out on the horizon.

Pity them if you can't forget them.
And if that's too hard for now, pity the house.

Think how it's losing out on the care
You'd have bestowed on it, on the loyalty
You'd have shown to its style and character,
Not to your fancy, a distinction too fine
For the new owners to handle.

Be like those angels said to enjoy the earth
As a summer retreat before man entered the picture,
Staggering under his sack of boundary stones.
They didn't mutter curses as they fastened their wings
And rose in widening farewell circles.
They grieved for the garden growing smaller below them,
Soon to exist only as a story
That every day grows harder to believe.

Nominated by Robert Pinsky, Ken Rosen

CLOSING OUT THE VISIT

fiction by JOHN BARTH

from THE IOWA REVIEW

GOOD VISIT, WE AGREE—fine visit, actually, weatherwise and otherwise, everything considered—but as with all visits agreeable and disagreeable its course has run. Time now to get our things together, draw down our stock of consumables, tidy up our borrowed lodgings, savor one last time the pleasure of the place, say good-bye to acquaintances we've made, and move along.

"The *light*," you want to know: "Have we ever seen such light?"

We have not, we agree—none better, anyhow, especially in these dew-bedazzled early mornings and the tawny late afternoons, when sidelit trees and beachfront virtually incandesce, and the view from our rented balcony qualifies for a travel poster. That light is a photon orgy; that light fires the prospect before us as if from inside out. Mediterranean, that light is, in its blue-white brilliance, Caribbean in its raw tenderness, yet paradoxically desert-crisp, so sharp-focusing the whole surround that we blink against our will. That light thrills—and puts us poignantly in mind of others who in time past have savored the likes of it and are no more: the late John Cheever, say, in whose stories light is almost a character, or the nineteenth-century Luminist painters, or for that matter the sun-drunk Euripides of *Alcestis:* "O shining clear day, and white clouds wheeling in the clear of heaven!"

"Such light."

Major-league light. This over breakfast bagels and coffee on the balcony—the end of these Wunderbägeln, freckled with sesame- and poppyseed, as good as any we've tasted anywhere, fresh-baked in the little deli that we discovered early on in the village not far inshore from "our" beach. So let's polish off this last one, to use up the last of our cream cheese and the final dablet of rough-cut marmalade lifted from the breakfast place downstairs along with just enough packets of coffee sweetener—raw brown sugar for me, low-cal substitute for you—to go with the ration of House Blend coffee that we bought from that same jim-dandy deli on Day One, when we were stocking up for our stay. Can't take 'em with us.

"Have we measured out our life in coffee spoons?"

We have, come to that, and canny guesstimators we turn out to have been. No more than a potsworth over, two at most, which we'll leave for the cleanup crew along with any surplus rum, wine, mineral water, fruit juices, hors d'oeuvres, what have we, and I'll bet that the lot won't total a tipsworth by when we've had our last go-round at this afternoon's end, checkout time. Adiós, first-rate bagels and cream cheese and marmalade, fresh-squeezed juice and fresh-ground coffee, as we've adiósed already our fine firm king-size bed: Here's to sweet seaside sleep with ample knee- and elbow-room for separateness sans separation! Here's to the dialogue of skin on sufficient square footage of perfect comfort so that the conversation begins and ends at our pleasure, not at some accidental bump in the night. Hasta la vista, maybe, in this instance, as it has become almost our habit here, after an afternoon's outdoorsing, to relish a roll in the air-conditioned hay between hot-tub time and happy hour.

Our last post-breakfast swim! No pool right under our balcony where we'll be this time tomorrow (no balcony, for that matter), nor world-class beach a mere pebblesthrow from that pool, nor world-girdling ocean just a wave-lap from that beach, aquarium-clear and aquarium-rich in calendar-quality marine life for our leisurely inspection and inexhaustible delight; no scuba gear needed, just a snorkel mask fog-proofed with a rub of jade- or sea-grape leaf from the handsome natural beachscape round about us.

Now, then: Our pool-laps lapped, which is to be our first next pleasure on this last A.M. of our visit (not forgetting the routine and parenthetical but no less genuine satisfactions of post-breakfast defecation in our separate bathrooms and stretching exercises on the bedroom wall-to-wall: Let's hear it for strainless Regularity and the ever-fleeting joy of able-bodiedness!)? A quick reconnaissance, perhaps, of "our" reef, while we're still wet? Bit of a beachwalk, maybe, upshore or down? Following which, since this visit has been by no means pure vacation, we'll either "beach out" for the balance of the morning with some serious reading and note-taking or else put in a session at our make-do "desks" (balcony table for you, with local whelk- and top-shells as paperweights; dinette table for me, entirely adequate for the work we brought along) before we turn to whatever next wrap-up chore or recreation—not forgetting, en passant, to salute the all but unspeakable good fortune of a life whose pleasures we're still energetic enough to work at and whose work, wage-earning and otherwise, happens to be among our chiefest pleasures.

Tennis, you say? Tennis it is, then, and work be damned for a change; we've earned that indulgence. You're on for a set, on those brand-new courts at our virtual doorstep, with a surface that sends our soles to heaven, pardon the pun, and so far from pooping our leg-muscles for the morning, has seemed rather to inspire them for the scenic back-country bike-ride up into the village for provisions, in the days when we were still in the provisioning mode. Extraordinary, that such tournament-quality courts appear to've gone virtually undiscovered except by us—like those many-geared mountain bicycles free for the borrowing and for that matter the pool and spa and, we might as well say, our beach and its ocean, or ocean and its beach. Where *is* everybody? we asked ourselves early on in the visit: Does the rest of the world know something that we don't?

"Vice-versa," you proposed and we jointly affirmed, and soon enough we counted it one more blessing of this many-blessinged place that our fellow visitors were so few, as who but the programmatically gregarious would not: those couples who for one cause or another require for their diversion (from each other, we can't help suspecting) a supply of new faces, life histories, audiences for their household anecdotes. Well for such that the world abounds in busy places; well for us who binge on each other's company to've found not only that company but a place as unabundant in our fellows as it is rich in amenities: just enough other visitors, and they evidently like-minded, for visual variety on the beach, for exchange of tips on snorkel-spots and eateries, for the odd set of doubles on those leg-restoring courts, and for the sense of being, after all, not alone in the restaurants and on the dance floor, at the poolside bar and out along the so-convenient reef, in this extraordinary place in general, in our world.

Auf Wiedersehen now, tennis courts! Arrivedérci, bikes and bike-trails, charming little village of excellent provisions agreeably vended by clerks neither rude nor deferential, but—like the restaurant

311

servers, reception-desk people, jitney drivers, even groundskeepers and maintenance staff of this jim-dandy place—cheerful, knowledgeable, unaffectedly "real."

Lunchtime! You incline to the annex restaurant, up on the ice-plant-planted headland overlooking "our" lagoon, a sweet climb through bougainvillea, hibiscus, and oleander to the awninged deck where frigate-birds hang in the updraft from tradewinds against the cliff and bold little bananaquits nibble sugar from diners' hands. I incline to a quicker, homelier "last lunch," so to speak: fresh conch ceviche, say, from our pal the beachfront vendor down by the snorkel shack (who knows precisely how much lime juice is just enough lime juice), washed down with his home-squeezed guava nectar or a pint of the really quite creditable local lager. But who can say no to the stuffed baby squid and crisp white wine up at our dear annex, with its ambiance of seabirds and fumaroles, its low-volume alternation of the sensuous local music with that of the after-all-no-less-sensuous High Baroque, and its long view through coconut palms out over the endless sea?
"Endless *ocean*," you correct me as we clink goblets of the palest, driest chablis this side of la belle France and toast with a sip, eyes level and smiling, our joint House Style, which would prohibit our saying *endless sea* even if we hadn't already said *seabirds* just a few lines earlier. *Sea* is a no-no (one of many such) in our house, except in such casual expressions as *at sea* or *on land and sea* or *moderate sea conditions,* and of course such compounds as *seaside, seascape, seaworthy,* and *seasick,* not to mention the aforementioned *seabirds.* One does not say, in our house, "What a fine view of the sea!" or "Don't you just love the smell of the sea?" or "Let's take a dip in the sea," all which strike our housely ears as affected, "literary," fraught with metaphysical pathos. Thus do longtime partners of like sensibility entertain themselves and refine their bond with endless such small concurrences and divergences of taste, or virtually endless such. But there's an end to our self-imposed ration of one wine each with lunch, especially in the tropics and only on such high occasions as this extended work/play visit; and there's an end to our unostentatious, so-delightful annex dinery, as pleasing in its fare and service as in its situation. Au revoir, admirable annex!—or adieu, as the case will doubtless prove.

Next next next? A whole afternoon, almost, before us, whether of sweet doing or of just-as-sweet doing nothing, since we have foresightedly made our departure arrangements early: scheduled the jitney, packed all packables except our last-day gear, settled our accounts and left off running up new charges, put appropriate tips in labeled envelopes for appropriate distribution, penned final hail-and-farewell cards to our far-flung loved ones, and posted on the minifridge door a checklist of last-minute Don't Forgets that less organized or more shrug-shouldered travelers might smile at, but that over a long and privileged connection has evolved to suit our way of going and effectively to prevent, at least to minimize, appalled brow-clapping at things inadvertently left undone or behind and too late remembered.

This air—Mon dieu! Gross Gott! ¡Caramba!—such air, such air: Let's not forget not simply to breathe but to be breathed by this orchid-rich, this sun-fired, spume-fraught air! Off with our beach tops, now that we've lunched; off with our swimsuits, while we're at it, either at the shaded, next-to-vacant nudie-beach around the upshore bend—where we innocently admire lower-mileage bodies than our own (though no fitter for their age) of each's same and complementary sex; likewise each other's, trim still and pleasure-giving; likewise each's more than serviceable own, by no means untouched by time, mischance, and vigorous use, but still and all, still and all . . . —or else at our idyllic, thus far absolutely private pocket-beach in the cove two promontories farther on.

Pocket-beach it is. We lotion each other with high numbers, lingering duly at the several Lingerplatzen; we let the sweet trades heavy-breathe us and then the omnisexual ocean have at us, salt-tonguing our every orifice, crease, and cranny as we slide through it with leisurely abandon: hasteless sybarites in no greater hurry to reach "our" reef for a last long snorkel than we would and will be to reach, in time's fullness and the ad lib order of our program, our last orgasm of the visit.

Good wishes, local fishes, more various, abundant, and transfixing than the local flowers, even. Tutti saluti, dreamscape coral, almost more resplendent than these fish. Weightless as angels, we float an aimless celestial hoursworth through spectacular submarinity, not forgetting to bid particular bye-bye to the shellfish and those calcareous miracles their shells, their shells, those astonishments of form and color, first among equals in this sun-shimmerish panoply, and virtual totems in our house. Faretheewells to our fair sea shells, no more ours in the last analysis than are our bodies and our hours—borrowed all, but borrowed well, on borrowed time.

"Time," you sigh now, for the last time side-by-siding in our post-Jacuzzi, pre-Happy Hour, king-size last siesta; no air conditioning this time, but every sliding door and window wide to let the ceaseless easterlies evaporate the expected sweat of love. "Time time time."

Time *times* time, I try to console you, and myself.

"Never enough."

There's all there is. Everlasting Now, et cet.

"Neverlasting now."

Yes, well: The best-planned lays, as the poet says, gang aft a-gley.

"Not what I meant."

Appreciated. Notwithstanding which, however . . .

We beached out, see, post-snorkelly, first in the altogether of that perfect pocket-beach on our oversize triple-terry beach towels, thick as soft carpeting, fresh from the poolside dispensary of same; then on palm- and palapa-shaded lounge chairs on the beach before the pool beneath our balcony, books in hand but ourselves not quite, the pair of us too mesmerized and tempus-fugity to read. Fingers laced across the beach-bag between our parallel chaises lounges, we mused beyond the breakers on the reef, horizonward, whither all too soon et cetera, and our joint spirits lowered after all with the glorifying late-day sun, so that when time came to say sayonara to that scape, to stroll the palm-shadowed stretch to our last hot soak and thence, pores aglow, to take the final lift to passion's king-size square, we found (we find) that we can't (*I* can't) quite rise to the occasion.

"Me neither."

We do therefore not *have sex*—that locution another house-style no-no for a yes-yes in our house—but rather make last love in love's last mode: by drifting off in each other's arms, skin to skin in the longing light, no less joyful for our being truly blue, likewise vice versa or is it conversely, the balmy air barely balming us.

I pass over what, in this drowsy pass, we dream.

Have we neglected in our close-out prep to anticipate a snooze sufficiently snoozish, though alas not postcoital, to carry us right through cocktails to miss-the-jitney time? We have not. No mañana hereabouts for thee and me: On the dot sounds our pre-set, just-in-case Snoozalarm™ (which, in our pre-set half-dreams, we have half been waiting for); half a dozen dots later comes our back-up front-desk wake-up call—Thanks anyhow, unaffectedly "real" and pretty punc-

314

tual paging-person—and we've time time time for the last of the rum
or le fin du vin or both, with the end of the Brie on the ultimate cra-
cotte, while we slip into our travel togs and triple-check our passage
papers, button buttons snap snaps zip zippers lock locks. One last look,
I propose, but you haven't heart for it nor do I sans you, hell therefore
with it we're off to see the blizzard heck or high water. Adieu sweet
place adieu, hell with it adieu adieu.

Time to go.

Nominated by Michael Martone

WILL WORK FOR FOOD

by STANLEY PLUMLY

from POETRY IRELAND REVIEW

1

He was off the road on the island, the
hand-made sign held up for recognition,
his hard face starved around his commitment
to hard work or a handout, staring straight
as a prophet, the slow summer traffic
gliding to the corner, looking, gliding,
as if he were part of an accident,
the lost parent, unnatural, or part
of another thing, a richer flowering,
and we were the poor in spirit passing.

2

Job saying, Thou my God are cruel and cast
me down to be lifted up like driftwood
on a wave, like ash above the burning
of my body, where my bones are starlight
in the cold night air, a night cloud drifting . . .
Do I not grieve the poor on either side,
On the right and the left, did I not grieve?
I know thou will bring me into the house
to let me mourn, let me stand up ignored,
letting me cry in the congregation.

3

The flowering at the end of the long stem
of the tension, the way the mallow rose
seems nervous in its stasis, taller than
a man, common, pale, mucilaginous,
the kind of study we will wade out to
just to touch and then be disappointed
in its color, texture, odor, this wild-
flower of the destitute who cut up
flowers for flavor and want for everything
except spirit, solitude, and famine.

4

Job saying, I am driven forth by thieves
who dwell in cliffs, in caves, among the rocks
and nettles where they gather in mock prayer
to mock me as their byword and their song,
who mar my path and set my calumny,
who come upon me as a wide breaking
rolling in of waters, wind and terrors,
a desolation and my soul poured out,
so even garments of my body change,
brother to dragons, companion to owls.

Nominated by David Baker, Linda Bierds, Michael Collier

MOTHER-TONGUE

fiction by NORA COBB KELLER

from BAMBOO RIDGE

THE BABY I COULD keep came when I was already dead.

I was twelve when I was murdered, fourteen when I looked into the Yalu River and, finding no face looking back at me, knew that I was dead. I wanted to let the Yalu's currents carry my body to where it might find my spirit again, but the Japanese soldiers hurried me across the bridge before I could jump.

I did not let them get too close. I knew they would see the name and number stenciled across my jacket and send me back to the camps where they think nothing of using a dead girl's body. When the guards started to step towards me, I knew enough to walk on, to wave them back to their post where they would watch for other Koreans with that "special look" in their eyes. Before the Japanese government posted the soldiers—"for the good of the Koreans"—the bridge over the Yalu had been a popular suicide spot.

My body moved on.

That is why, almost 20 years after it left my spirit behind at the recreation camp, my body was able to have this baby. Even the doctors here say it is almost a miracle. The camp doctor said I would never have a living child after he took my second one out, my insides too bruised and battered, impossible to properly heal.

So this little one is a surprise. This half-white and—though she doesn't know it yet, and may never know since her father thinks otherwise—half-Korean child. She would be called *tweggi* in the village I was born, but here she will be American.

When the missionaries found me, they thought I was Japanese because of the name, Akiko, sewn onto the sack that was my dress. The number, 41, they weren't sure about and thought, perhaps an orphanage? They asked me—in Korean, Japanese, Chinese, English—where I came from, who my family was, but by then I had no voice and could only stand dumbly in front of their moving mouths as they lifted my arms, poked at my teeth and into my ears, wiped the dirt from my face.

She is like the wild child raised by tigers, I heard them say to each other. Physically human, but able to speak only in the language of animals. They were kind and praised me when I responded to the simple commands they issued in Japanese: sit, eat, sleep. Had they asked, I would also have responded to "close mouth" and "open legs." The Jungun Ianfu camps trained the women only what they needed to know in order to service the soldiers. Other than that, we were not expected to understand, and were forbidden to speak, any language at all.

But we were fast learners, and creative. Listening as we gathered the soldiers' clothes for washing or cooked their meals, we were able to surmise when troops were coming in and how many we were expected to serve. We taught ourselves to communicate through eye movements, body posture, tilts of the head or—when we could not see each other—through rhythmic rustlings between our stalls; in this way we could speak, in this way we kept our sanity.

The Japanese say Koreans have an inherent gift for languages, proving that we are a natural colony, meant to be dominated. They delighted in their own ignorance, feeling they had nothing to fear or learn. I suppose that was lucky for us, actually. They never knew what we were saying. Or maybe they just didn't care.

I'm trying to remember exactly when I died. It must have been in stages, beginning with my birth as the fourth girl and last child in the Kim family, and ending in the recreation camps North of the Yalu. Perhaps if my parents had not died so early, I might have been able to live a full life. Perhaps not; we were a poor family. I might have been sold anyway.

My father was a cow trader. He traveled from village to village, herding the cows before him, from one farmer to the next, making a small profit as the middle man. When he was home, my older sisters' job was to collect the dung and, after we parceled out a small portion for our own garden, sell the rest to our neighbors. Sometimes we dried the dung for fuel, which burned longer and cleaner than wood. Most

319

of the time, though, we used sticks that my sisters collected from the woods.

My job was to help my mother wash clothes. We each had a basket, according to our size, which we carried up the river we called Yalu Aniya, Older Sister to the Yalu. Going up was easy, the load light on our heads. Coming home was harder since not only were the damp clothes heavier, but we were tired from beating the clothes clean against the rocks. I remember that as we crouched over our wash, pounding out the dirt, I pretended that my mother and I sent secret signals to one another, the rocks singing out messages only we could understand.

My mother died shortly after my father. I didn't see my father die; he was almost 30 miles away. As with his life, I know about his death primarily through what others have told me. The villagers that took him in say he died of a lung disease, coughing up blood as he died. They also said he called for my mother.

She was always a good wife; she went to him quickly in death, just as she did in life. One night after we had carried home the wash, she kept saying how tired she was, how tired. Come, mother, I told her, lie down. I kept asking her, what could I do? Do you want soup, do you want massage? Till finally she put her hand over my mouth and guided my fingers to her forehead. I stroked her softly, loosening her hair from the bun she tied it in, rubbing her temples where I could feel the heat and throb of her heart beating. Even when the erratic tempo slowed, then finally stopped, I continued to pet her. I wanted her to know that I loved her.

I touch my child in the same way now; this is the language she understands: the cool caresses of my fingers across her tiny eyelids, her smooth tummy, her fat toes. This, not the senseless murmurings of useless words, is what quiets her, tells her she is precious. She is like my mother in this way.

Because of this likeness, this link to the dead, my daughter is the only living thing I love. My husband, the missionaries who took me in after the camp, my sisters, if they are still alive, all are incidental. What are living people to ghosts, except ghosts themselves?

My oldest sister understood this. When my second and third sisters ran away together to look for work as secretaries or factory workers in Phyongyang, the oldest sister tried to keep father's business going by marrying our closest neighbor. They didn't have much money, but they

320

had more than us and wouldn't take her without a dowry. How could they buy cattle without any capital, they reasoned.

I was her dowry, sold like one of the cows before and after me. You are just going to follow second and third sisters, she told me. The Japanese say there is enough work for anyone in the cities. Girls, even, can learn factory work or serve in restaurants. You will make lots of money.

Still, I cried. She hugged me, then pinched me. Grow up now, she said. No mother, no father. We all have to make our lives. She didn't look at my face when the soldiers came, didn't watch as they herded me onto their truck. I heard them asking if she didn't want to come along; your sister is still so young, not good for much, they said. But you. You are grown and pretty. You could do well.

I am not sure, but I think my sister laughed. I hope that she had at least a momentary fear that they would take her, too.

I am already married, she said.

I imagine she shrugged then, as if to say, what can I do? Then she added, my sister will be even prettier. She didn't think to ask why that should matter in a factory line.

I knew I would not see the city. And I think my oldest sister knew, too. We had heard the rumours: girls bought or stolen from villages outside the city, sent to Japanese recreation centers. But still, we did not know what the centers were like. At worst, I thought I would do what I've done all my life: clean, cook, wash clothes, work hard. How could I imagine anything else?

At first, that is what I did do. Still young, I was kept to serve the women in the camps. Around women all my life, I felt almost like I was coming home when I first realized there were women at the camps, maybe a dozen. I didn't see them right away; they were kept in their stalls, behind mat curtains, most of the days and throughout the night.

Unless they had to visit the camp doctor, their freedom outside their stalls consisted of weekly baths at the river and scheduled trips to the outhouse. If they needed to relieve themselves when it was not their turn to go outside, they could use their special pots. It became my job to empty the pots. I also kept their clothes and bedding clean, combed and braided their hair, served them their meals. When I could, I brought them each a dab of grease which they would smooth over their wounds, easing the pain of so many men.

I liked caring for the women. As their girl, I was able to move from one stall to the next, even from one section of the camp to another, if I was asked. And because of this luxury, the women used me to pass messages. I would sing to the women as I braided their hair or walked by the compartments to check their pots. When I hummed certain sections, the women knew to take those words for their message. In this way, we could keep up with each other, find out who was sick, who was new, who had the most men the night before, who was going to crack.

To this day, I do not think Induk—the woman who was the camp Akiko before me—cracked. Most of the other women thought she did because she would not shut up. She talked loud and nonstop. In Korean and in Japanese she denounced the soldiers, yelling at them to stop their invasion of her country and her body. Even as they mounted her, she shouted, I am Korea, I am a woman, I am alive. I am seventeen, I had a family just like you do, I am a daughter, I am a sister.

Men left her stall quickly, some crying, most angrily joining the line for the woman next door. All through the night she talked, reclaiming her Korean name, reciting her family genealogy, even chanting the recipes her mother had passed on to her. Just before daybreak, they took her out of her stall and into the woods where we couldn't hear her anymore. They brought her back skewered from her vagina to her mouth, like a pig ready for roasting. A lesson, they told the rest of us, warning us into silence.

That night, it was if a thousand frogs encircled the center. They opened their throats for us, swallowed our tears, and cried for us. All night, it seemed, they called, Induk, Induk, Induk, so we would never forget.

Although I might have imagined the frogs. That was my first night as the new Akiko. I was given her clothes, which were too big and made the soldiers laugh. She won't be wearing them much, anyway, they jeered.

Even though I had not yet had my first bleeding, I was auctioned off to the highest bidder. After that it was a free-for-all and I thought I would never stop bleeding.

That is how I know Induk didn't go crazy, she was going sane. She was planning to escape. The corpse the soldiers brought back from the woods wasn't Induk.

It was Akiko; it was me.

My husband speaks four languages: German, English, Korean and Japanese. He is learning a fifth, Polish, from cassette tapes he borrows from the public library. He reads Chinese.

A scholar who spends his life with the bible, he thinks he is safe, that the words he reads, the meaning he gathers will remain the same. Concrete. He is wrong.

He shares all of his languages with our daughter, though she is not even a year old. She will absorb the sounds, he tells me. But I worry that the different sounds for the same object will confuse her. To compensate, I try to balance her with language I know is true. I watch her with a mother's eye, trying to see what she needs—my breast, new diapers, a kiss, her toy—before she cries, before she has to give voice to her pain.

And each night, I touch each part of her body, waiting until I see recognition in her eyes. I wait until I see that she knows that all of what I touch is her and hers to name in her own mind, before language dissects her into pieces that can be swallowed and digested by others not herself.

At the camp, the doctor gave me a choice: rat poison or the stick. I chose the stick. I saw what happened to the girl given the rat bait to abort her baby. I did not have the courage then to die the death that she did.

As the doctor bound my legs and arms, gagged me, then reached for the stick he would use to hook and pull the baby, not quite a baby into the world, he talked. He spoke of evolutionary differences between the races, biological quirks that made the women of one race so pure, and the women of another so promiscuous. Base really, almost like animals, he said.

Rats, too, will keep doing it until they die, refusing food or water as long as they have a supply of willing partners. The doctor chuckled and probed, digging and piercing, as he lectured. Luckily for the species, Nature ensures that there is one dominant male to keep the others at bay and the female under control.

I followed the light made by the waves of my pain, tried to leave my body behind. But the doctor pinned me to earth with his stick and his words. Finally, he stood upright, cracked his back and threw the stick into the trash. He rinsed his hands in a basin of water, then unbound my hands and mouth. Those rags he put between my legs.

Fascinating, he said thoughtfully as he left the tent. Perhaps it is the differences in geography that make the women of our two countries so morally incompatible.

323

He did not bother tying me down, securing me for the night. Maybe he thought I was too sick to run. Maybe he thought I wouldn't want to. Maybe he knew I had died and that ropes and guards couldn't keep me anyway.

That night, with the blood-soaked rags still wedged between my thighs, I slipped out of the tent, out of the camp. Following the sound of my mother beating clothes against the rocks, I floated along the trails made by deer and found a nameless stream that led, in the end, like all the mountain streams, to the Yalu.

Nominated by Lois Ann Yamanaka

CONVERSATIONS ON THE PLURALITY OF WORLDS

by MOLLY BENDALL

from POETRY

After Bernard le Bovier de Fontenelle

The philosopher, impatient for the black
to finish smothering the sunset,
wants to tell the Marquise his story
of Galileo's sky and Copernicus' heaven
            and their dark confessions—
how other worlds could be this one.

Their walk leads them away from the others
at the party into the groomed yard
where it's not so Fragonard white or *rose* rose,
but where green webs mesh
with blue adjectives from petal clusters.

She thinks when he makes each proclamation
            about the faraway air,
it's as though he has finished a stanza
in a poem, and his breath lowers with
the contentment of the final word. But sometimes
he doesn't finish, and with anticipation

or near-anxiety, she provides
the sound, a last rhyme to relax their breaths.

(There is enough light from the distant house
for them to see each other
at the pavilion's table.)
And as if in agreement or with some acceptance,
her fan's arc shifts direction,
lowering the shadow on her face—
                    hardly discernible

Only, she's not to be convinced
by his fictions. How could she
confide in these mirrorless spheres?

And who is worthy enough to hear
this conversation that hides in a garden
among leaves, within islands?

                    •

He translates his adoring satellites
into verbs, their paths into something
delicate or curled. And then
both of them retrieve a word
and play with *étoile star stella*
trying to override each silvery sound
in this art of talk
that he's devised and she has learned.

"These worlds might have a flourishing side,
kept in another, more private light," he says.
She points to the dish between them
that holds a pomegranate
with its open pucker.
                    "This planet won't risk
falling into your knowledge."

(Maybe she's not the Marquise at all,
only dressed like her.

She's really a seamstress, a dresser,
not even a guest.
She thinks of peplums, velvet sashes,
her fabric trove with which she can
experiment with trompe l'oeil
and illusions of depth.)

                         •

"Could your black and gold matter
be plaited and spun, crimped and powdered?"
she asks.
              The shards on the stone path
become likenesses for his explanations
of how even light has its whims
and how shadows crescent around it.

After his formula for distance,
there's a question that seems designed
to trap her, however lightly.

"Your fickle sky must give
some consolation, but then
you love to gamble," she says.

Now she can turn his phrase
so it becomes her own,
              and can change one word
that makes him the prey and tosses
his little crises like garters and buttons
into the garden's deep, thoughtless green.

                         •

She admits her longing for the music
of the string quartet insinuating
beyond the oak doors. She's heard it before
overlapping with her own voice—
              the small pouring, then a gasp
and then her own reciting, "purple and

stinging wasp." What she waits for
is the satisfaction of its music's
closure, the last thread pulled with her teeth.

His theories of "imprisonment of air"
and "gravity's defiance like oil floating
on cool water" she likes to envision
as the silk weight of music.

(In the garden the lunaria shows itself
as silvery money that she will later
arrange in a winter room.)

And the owls fill in their pauses
and give threats to the daytime peacocks
                    that she and he agree
are too tame in their extravagance.

                    •

The cypress spears in their deepest black
provide another course of plot.

She suggests, "What if we were each the other?"
(The image of the two of them
in the reflecting pool had turned things around.
What if she had made him blush with innuendo?)

"I would have proclaimed then," she says,
"this magnificent discovery
against our old beliefs in fate."

He would be the one to have to wait
in the celestial, timeless
dark for her gesture that may never invite him
or never acknowledge him again.
What if his destiny depended on syllable
or letter barely there?

The canterbury bells in lilac blue respond

328

too intimately for them to adjust.
How easily *she* could have given
gentle instructions and guided *his* hand
first north then west in the iron sky.
There could be one slip up of weather,
one invitation lost, one misread thought,
                and all affections missed.

What if it were his learning that was always
overheard or stolen?
His whose solitude noted the planets'
promises of return
                the sham of morning,
and these were considered, turned over
and remembered again,
then recited, together, but only at night?

Nominated by Ralph Angel, Michael Collier, James Harms, Diann Blakely Shoaf

WHEN WORDS BECAME WINDOWS

by SVEN BIRKERTS

from HARVARD REVIEW and *THE GUTENBERG ELEGIES* (FABER & FABER)

F ROM THE TIME of earliest childhood on I was enthralled by books. First just by their material mysteries. I studied pages of print and illustrations, stared myself into wells of fantasy that are the hallmark of the awakening inner life. Mostly there was pleasure, but not always. I remember a true paralytic terror brought on by the cartoon Dalmatians pictured on the end-papers of my Golden Books. For a time I refused to be alone in the room with the books, even when the covers were safely closed. I ascribed power to likeness, much as our tribal ancestors did. I thought the dogs would slip free of their confinement and come baying after me.

But that was the exception. Dreamy sensuousness prevailed. A page was a field studded with tantalizing signs and a book was like a vast play structure riddled with openings and crevices I could get inside. This notion of hiding, secreting myself in a text, was important to me—it underlies to this day my sense of a book as a refuge. That I could not yet translate the letters into words and meanings only added to the grave mysteriousness of the artifact. On the far side of that plane of scrambled markings was a complete other world. And then one day the path came clear. I was in the first grade. I went over and around and suddenly *through* the enormous letter shapes of Kipling's *The Jungle Book*. The first sentence, that is, I read! And from that moment on the look of a word became a window onto its meaningful depths.

Once I got underway, I was an interested, eager, but not terribly precocious reader—I was no Susan Sontag knocking back nutritive classics while still in grade school. I was a dreamer and books were my tools for dreaming. I read the ones that were more or less suited to my age and did so devotedly. Books about Indian chiefs, explorers, and dogs; biographies of inventors and athletes; the pasteurized versions of London and Poe that came via the Scholastic Book Club. I had the first real thrill of ownership in second or third grade, when the teacher broke open the first shipment box and handed each of us in the class the books we had ordered. Later it was the Hardy Boys—illustrated covers and crisp blue spines; then, James Bond, the slim little pocket-books reeking of sexual innuendo and high-class gadgetry. Not until I was in junior high did I begin to make contact with some of the so-called "better" books—by Salinger, Wolfe, Steinbeck, and others. But even then I had no idea of bettering myself. I was simply looking for novels with characters whose lives could absorb mine for a few hours.

That demand has not, at the deepest level, changed over the years. What have changed are my empathic capacities. I have gradually grown interested in lives that are utterly different from the life I lead. I find that I have little difficulty now slipping into the skin of Emperor Hadrian or Clarissa Dalloway or anyone else—provided the prose is psychologically compelling and credible. But when I was ten or twelve or fourteen I needed to hear what other young men, my age or a few years older, had to say about things. I looked to Tom Sawyer, later to Holden Caulfield and Eugene Gant and the heroes of William Gold-man's novels. I prowled the aisles of Readmore Books, the local tem-ple to the mass-market paperback, searching for books with a certain kind of cover—usually a rendering of a moody-looking young man with some suggestion of meditated rebellion in his stance. Interest-ingly enough, there were quite a few books that fit the bill, from William Goldman's *The Temple of Gold* to Romain Gary's *The Ski Bum* to Harold Robbins's *A Stone for Danny Fisher.* The approach of the late-'60s counter-culture could have been discerned here by anyone with a grasp of how images translated into collective attitudes and vice-versa. I was, though I did not know it then, on the cusp of my own rebellion, slowly readying myself for a major bout of acting out. When the time came, two or three years later, my guides would be Jack Ker-ouac, Ken Kesey, Richard Fariña, Kurt Vonnegut, Norman Mailer, Henry Miller, and others.

The reading I did in late boyhood and early adolescence was passionate and private, carried on at high heat. When I went to my room and opened a book it was to seal myself off as fully as possible in an elsewhere. I was not reading, as now, with only one part of the self. I was there body and soul, living vicariously. When Finney died at the end of John Knowles's *A Separate Peace* I cried scalding tears, unable to believe that the whole world did not grind to a sorrowful halt. That was then. Books no longer tap my emotions quite so directly; I am rarely brought to tears or fury. But what I have not lost is a churning anxiety, an almost intolerable sensation that sometimes has me drawing breaths to steady myself. Not always, of course. But often enough. There is something about the reading act that cuts through the sheath of distractedness which usually envelops me. It is as if I can suddenly feel the pure flow of time behind the stationary letters. Vertigo. Not a comfortable sensation, but I keep seeking it out, taking it as an inoculation against what the Latin poet called the "tears of things."

I remember so clearly the shock I would feel whenever I looked up from the vortex of the page and faced the strangely immobile world around me. My room, the trees outside the window—everything seemed so dense, so saturated with itself. Never since have I known it so intensely, this colliding of realities, the current of mystery leaping the gap between them. Reading was, in affording this dissociation, like a drug. I knew even then, in my early teen years, that what I did in my privacy was in some way a betrayal of the given, an excitement slightly suspect at its core.

This last is a complex business, intensified for me by my father's attitudes. Back in the days of my childhood my father was a stern man with a quick temper and impatient disdain for anything that smacked of reverie or private absorption. Almost as if these states in some way challenged his authority. I find his attitude strange, the more so since he idolized *his* mother, who was one of the most bookish people I have ever known. Indeed, when we first traveled to Riga to visit her, when I first stepped through the door into her apartment, I was stunned. I suddenly understood a great deal about my own genetic inheritance. I took in the walls of books, the piles of journals and papers on every available surface—I saw the signs of a mania I knew all too well.

But my father was nothing like his mother, at least not in this respect. He was a man out in the world, a problem-solver. He had the idea that a boy should be out in the fresh air, playing, doing chores, whatever. For him there was something against nature in the sight of a healthy individual sitting by himself with a book in his lap. This shouldn't surprise anyone—it is the prevalent bias in our culture even today. Doing is prized over being or thinking. Reading is something you do because it has been assigned in school, or because all other options have been exhausted—no more chores to do, all other games and activities put away.

It says a great deal about the dynamics of our family that my mother was—and remains—a devoted reader. She read for pleasure, for company, and for escape. I won't say that she was indiscriminate, but she could just as easily rush through a middlebrow page-turner as work through something with greater literary merit. Novels, biographies, popular histories—there was never a time when she did not have at least one book going. My father had long since given up any idea he might have had of reforming her (into *what?*), but to this day he continues to mock what he considers to be her absorption in second-hand experience.

Naturally books became something of a battle ground—though no one ever admitted this directly. If I read I was, in my father's understanding of things, siding with my mother. Not just with my mother, but with the feminine principle *itself,* never mind that I might have been reading Hemingway or Thomas Wolfe or Ian Fleming. And whenever the jibes began—"What are you doing on the couch in the middle of the day? You need something to do? *I'll* give you something to do—" —my mother, no doubt recognizing a sidelong swipe at herself, would rush to my defense. At which point I had to recognize that I was being caught up in what looked like a traditional "mama's boy" scenario. And I did *not* want to be seen by anyone, especially my father, as a mama's boy.

I therefore began to be more careful about my reading. Though I could still be spotted with a book in my hand, my real reading life, the main current of it, flowed on behind closed doors. If that life was not secret, it was private. I read when my parents were away; I read late into the night. I was—this fits my usual pattern—outwardly yielding to my father while inwardly rebelling. By cultivating a hidden reading life I was, in one sense, acceding to his view that there was not something altogether savory about the way I was using the best energies of my youth. But I was also giving the act a more privileged place in my life; it acquired some of the cachet of the prohibited. If reading was worth guarding and being secretive about, there had to be magic in it.

So I read. I moved into the space of reading as into a dazzling counter-world. I loved just thinking about books, their wonderful codedness. The fact that from a distance or from an objective or disinterested vantage every page looked more or less the same. A piano roll waiting for sprockets. But for the devoted user of the code the flat of the page would be transformed into a four-dimensional experience. This was something almost completely beyond legislation. No one, not even another reader reading the same words, could know what those signs created once they traveled up the eye-beam and into the recesses of the self.

Nominated by Stuart Dischell, Sigrid Nunez, Laurie Sheck

CHINESE FOOD IN THE FIFTIES

by ALBERTO RIOS

from PEQUOD

There was only one place.
Kin Wah's, Nogales, Mexico.

I ate only the white rice.
I did not yet have the adventure in me

More than the name of this place,
The sight of a kind of food

Different from home.
Birds flew around me—

There were birds in this place
In a cage from the floor to the ceiling,

Twenty birds or thirty birds, something
Adding from them to the taste of the food:

Their condiment sounds,
Something grainy from their voices

And their wings. Their noise made my white rice
Loud, though it was already a good taste

More than anyone could see.
But a spoon to the mouth, a caw to the ear—

This salt and ginger, an oil heated
And a scent rising, water making in the mouth—

It made me happy, this place and this food
Tasting like the voices of birds,

Each kernel saying in earnest
One parrot thing to the blue-winged next.

My parents would shrug to the waiter.
It's all he will eat.

It's all they could see,
The white rice, the almost

Whiteness between the rice, so much
White it seemed like nothing.

The waiter would laugh.
I hear it now, his laugh and the birds,

The faces of my parents twisted enough
To be themselves loud.

Their faces looked angry
The way the rice looked plain.

Neither one was the truth.
It was the Fifties along the border,

They always asked me if I wanted something more.
But it was not the white rice

Filling me, making the fibers of a little boy.
The place filled me,

The way it was filled
With green and blue,

So that the white of the rice
It was respite, a singular treat

In this place, stuffed like a pillow
With feathers wafting, filled with Chinese

Writing, the rice itself with its little sticks
Spelling something out, something

Bird. Something from flight.
Something from so much movement

It just looked like nothing. Wings,
The way the wings from birds,

From hummingbirds and bees,
From June bugs, the way in their moving wings

One sees nothing.
This was the place that was me

Filled with cage and with grit,
Filled with linoleum and with smoke.

This was the food that was my,
White rice. Nothing more.

Nominated by Rick Bass, Barbara Selfridge

THE LATE STYLE

fiction by JAMES ROBISON

from MISSISSIPPI REVIEW

OUR COMPETITION: Build a monument to the Cold War. You get four hundred grand. The Cold War being so imperative to our lives, growing up. (Not that we have in any sense *grown* or evolved or flowered or matured, but we *have* actively decayed.) Condition: Monument must be in Death Valley, somewhere near China Lake, where you should achieve a profound plastic immensity, and we've raised a mint for your use—McKinley funds, Governor's Council on National Parks Grant, Assurance Associates funds, other munificent donors.

The winner: P. Ronsard.

Ronsard won with his model and sketch-dossier, and because colossal things are his stock-in-trade and that's the kind of fearless sculptor he is—one who knows no vertigo. He proposed an erection of dazzling verticality. The work is well underway like this: a twenty-five-story silo of eye-blasting white. "Silo" referring to both rockets, the arrows of the Cold War, and the underground quivers that contain them. Out there in the unlimited ocean of nothing it'll stand. The whole kind of Assyrian since Ronsard had the idea of sticking thirty black asparagus-stalk palms in two files leading to the silo. Like The Wall, this thing is guileless and definitive. Where it is, nobody will see it. From the nearest highway it'll look like a slender, distant cigarette, stubbed down into an ashtray of desert sand.

Saltflat lagoon. A full moon night. Ronsard's driving a Ford 4WD, dragging a long cloud home from the site. He disembarks in dusty white fatigues and blue hard hat and goes inside the trailer that is his workshop/studio/sleeper on the cracked shoals of the Mojave. There's

338

butane-fed kitchenette stuff where Ronsard cranks a can opener, but it's old, its bite tenuous, it cannot make a continuous wound. He would like some roast beef hash to go with his chocolate cola. He fetches from his thigh pocket a Swiss Army knife and splinters a thumbnail gouging out the right blade and attacks. The can hiccoughs. Ronsard punches a circuit. Cylinders, circles, entry.

Christy, a sort of prostitute from an escort service, comes through a sliding glass wall, letting in herself and a heated gust of desert air. Shank is an Irish setter who unscrambles from sleep and pogos on her hind legs and stretches her long body full out, as if trying to embrace and kiss Christy.

"Just push her down," Ronsard says.

"Never, she's an angel."

"I was talking to Shank."

"Pretty girl," Christy says and sits on her knees and roughs up the dog's spine fur.

He pours coffee from a chugging percolator. Christy costs him two hundred bucks a visit. She's thirty-three years younger than he is. In life, he's ahead, fifty-six to twenty-three.

"Why would you pay me to visit you?"

He goes, "Just people who live alone become die-cast in their opinions and need a counter balance. And you, I don't know, have ears."

"Yeah, when I argue with me I always win," she says. She's sprawled on her stomach, shins swinging like windscreen wipers in time to the advanced and difficult music of his CD box; a concerto for mouth organ and mallets.

In this jumbo trailer it is like a commercial airliner with everything compacted and rounded to tiny-ness and function.

He says, "I just need a leavening influence."

"You need to wake up."

The music contributes a phrase to breakage and violence.

She goes, "You need a wake-up call. You're rich and semi-famous. I mean, you know, I mean, fuckin' A, I found a book on you in the library. But you got Ell Ess See. Low self-concept."

His older setter, Shank, trails Ronsard everywhere, loping like an exhausted pony, as she is so creaky. Shank crumples on the trailer floors and watches Ronsard do junk. Sketch out his solutions in worried line and leaping color. But Shank is bungling into things of late, bumping into walls, into Ronsard's legs. She was so kinetically fluid,

339

her moves so spontaneous and all unfettered inspiration, but now she is clumsy enough to terrify and sadden Ronsard. There are deeper shadows everywhere. He's blocked. A perfidious impetigo has put thin red marks on half his face, cat-scratch welts and stripes.

The music clunks to a stop. He's also a trace deaf.

So Christy uses a raised voice to ask if she might use Ronsard's little machines for laundry tomorrow.

"Fine by me!" he bellows.

"Make fun, but you do miss a lot of what I say."

"Ya ya ya. Four eyes," Ronsard says.

She looks back at him through a big pair of glasses and through big gray eyes. He wants her to be the tormentor of his desire and this isn't happening.

He pays her to visit him and does not ask her to disrobe or any of the other stuff with the vibrator or anything. He hopes she'll leave the escort business and get work as a baker or night shift astronomer at an observatory no one knows about. He would make her an assistant on the project but can't afford her.

He's parked on his technical chair, which is complicated by hydraulic levers and a chrome ring footrest. On the drawing board are pencil sketchings of building-sized flowers. It looks as if he's doing a field guide to Jupiter flora. White blossoms burst off photo-gray grounding. It's a proposed monument for Dole Pineapple on Maui.

"That one's like Meadow Foam," Christy says and scrapes a sheet of acetate out of its tablet and breathes a mist shape on the sheet. "Sometimes I think how I get paid to have *thrusting* breasts. Right? I used to get paid to staple boxes. It makes you want to bomb the mall," she says.

"There are jobs between breast stuff and staple stuff," Ronsard says.

"Oh, look, I've read all the books. I'm sorry, but O.K? Don't get knowing on me." Christy mashes the acetate.

Ronsard nods. "I'm not knowing. Sorry."

His responsibility with her is a plus/negative: Don't touch her ever, of course, but learn again to want to.

He is moss and loss of mass and muscle make his clothes drape in slack furrows. He has really itchy jaws and neck.

Christy holds up the hash can. "Paul, did *you* eat this or did Shank? Because one of you's going to die of sodium and poor judgement."

As I shaved I saw through my stockade-style window an empire of dust and clouds. Fifty-five thousand dollars in all and I have half-

340

tracks, a crane, a video team, site organizers, a dozen kids from L.A. Modern School of Design, but I'm the one who buys the paint. The silo's whole *frisson* depends upon its eye-blasting whiteness which depends upon a particular recipe of a polymer-strand-paint in combination with an acrylic emulsion permanent enamel (all over sandable primer), the stew battered together with micah scintillas so it'll winkle like an igloo in the high dry heat, and the purling must be ground so fine it doesn't clog the compressors and runs free through the hoses and nozzles and this UV resistant lotion they mix for me over at the Glurex paint factory in Bauxite City and these skills I learned working at a West Hollywood paint and body shop where I was a car artist to support myself between the time I was an installation artist, before, and later when I started throwing up colossal things in Chicago, Albany, Hamburg, and Dayton, Ohio, and Lyons, France. Outside longitudinal dunes flow away, away, huge ribs, with the wind scraping off dust. I drove the flat-bed Mack over the state line and two hundred miles on, to the factory, a cinder block warehouse with kegs and kegs of my white Glurex-Pro out on the loading dock. Hector went with me. He chews Red Man and the other guys there chew tobacco, too, so we all stood around after I'd tested the paint and we'd loaded the paint, big wads and folds of tobacco in jaws. Hector settled and re-settled his white paper hat, going, "Well, I don't know."

"No, I don't know either," the factory guys said. They spit.

"I'll tell you the truth," we all said. "I don't know."

Ronsard's weekending at home, in Palm Springs. Asleep at nine at night. Shank's roaring bark brings him right up. He limps to the sun porch door where his grown kids, Christian and Anita, gaze bright gazes at his interior.

"We'll go away," Christian says.

Ronsard runs a hand over his face and says, "What?"

"Didn't want to wake you. We'll just slink off."

"It's fine, just slink in," Ronsard says, swinging the door. He hugs them lightly and then his kids do a lot of passionate scrubbing of Shank; her ears, back, tail.

He brews coffee in the emptied-out kitchen with their audience.

"Mom took the stove and refrigerator?" Christian asks.

"She took the pliers. She tried to take the track lighting. She took the curtains."

"Well, it's a great view," Christian says.

341

"If it had fit in her van, *that'd* be gone."

The view is of dull yuccas and moon shade, of bendy shape and edgy rock.

"It's really sad," Anita says.

Ronsard's kids look not concrete, black and white negatives come to being. They're perversely pale and in tight black clothes with tight black hair. His daughter, at thirty, is getting crow's feet.

The interviewer comes. "12.8.94–21:02," she writes in her log book and snips on a micro-corder that's like an electric shaver. She's a pop-eyed girl in wrinkled linen. This is the nameless room of his house, white, with brick floors and giant-eared plants and Spanish tiles. There's a conversation pit big as a lifeboat, and they plunk down in, on the sofa, down inside.

"We should start with jazz," she says. "Did you like jazz?"

"Back when I was alive?"

"You know how I meant, jazz and drip paintings?"

"Oh, yeah, yes. We played the bongos all night long."

"And did you see a bunch of films in theaters? *In theaters?*" she asks.

"It so happens," Ronsard says.

"Every film, like we watch TV, now?"

"Every film, that came to town, so you know, yes, I saw the complete Eddie Bracken, for example, now that I consider."

"You're teasing. I know it. I don't care," she says.

"I'm not actually. My girlfriend for a month liked West Coast jazz. I don't know exactly what that is, but it was her big case. She played the saxophone herself. That's true."

"Aha."

"She did." And she was weird in bed, he remembers. "I believe she favored sort of breezy music, drowsy, with syncopation."

"O.K., yeah," the interviewer says.

A bug, flying clumsily, navigates over to bump her temple. She wipes her palms on her upper arms. She fastens her boot buckle.

Ronsard is saying, "I liked drummers where the drums went free-wheelingly, if that's a word. I got a lift from that. Not swing drummers, but weird guys."

"You know who, for instance?"

"More how Tony Williams plays," Ronsard says.

"Who is he?"

"This drum guy. Or whoever used to play with Thelonius Monk. I got a lift from that. Kenny Clarke."

She extracts a pencil from behind her ear. She logs in: "The Loneliest Monk."

"No," Ronsard says.

"What are you laughing? Am I being an idiot or something?"

"It's me. I talk too fast. Where is this going?"

She says, "Isn't it true that the deployment by this country, on a civilian population, of a weapon so barbaric and terminal that its own creator named himself death, isn't it true that this act brought about a mass collective anxiety which manifested itself in personal neuroses so debilitating that fear, guilt, and ignorance have blighted our cultural mental-scape ever since?"

"Absolutely," Ronsard says.

"That's where I'm going with this."

Returned, he steps back into the trailer for lunch and a nap and in the laundry section he sees Christy with linen, with a white load of wash cradled in her arms like a parachute gathered. The linen has a cutting scent, bleach and soap. She pushes the armload of whites at her face, nuzzles. He looks at her a long time, holding the whites just so. He pitches in, folding down a half ironing board.

He's ironing a Christy shirt so things smell of spritzed starch, hot cotton, colognes in her blouse fabric. He props the iron on end. "Oh, boy," he says and sighs with the desire for desire, the end to this fucking objectivity.

She says: "Don't look at me, I just got up."

She does look dry around the eyes. He feels stirrings.

The silo is one thousand feet of mesh latticework, half frosted with primer so far. The site is flatness and off over there, a jaggedy blow-up of mountains.

For his fifty-seventh birthday, Ronsard buys himself a Tool-Master set of ratchet-drive screwdrivers.

Ronsard misses Hector's last sentence and Ronsard says, "Let's go look at your rocket," as if the idea had occurred to him independently.

343

They go to Hector's rental house to the open garage, where the temperature is dizzying: one hundred ten and going up.

"I think it's the distributor, but I don't know beans," Hector says. He kneels to untie the knots on a silver motorcycle cover and unpackages the bike with a sweeping pull.

"Fan-tastic," Ronsard says. Hector hurls spit fifteen yards and nods while Ronsard circles the bike.

"Sixty-five Competition Model Triumph Bonneville? Twin carbs."

"Reet," Hector says.

"With a customized BSA frame?"

"Thirty pounds lighter than factory."

Ronsard tosses over a leg and settles into the saddle.

The machine has an aluminum gas tank and raked handlebars and no front fender. Its exhaust pipes wind in the snake-like crossover.

"You can get so quickly deceased," Hector says and Ronsard uses his calf to fold out a rubber pedal, then notches it under the right heel of his sandal.

"You know the compression ratio's eleven to one? You really want to be kicking it over in thongs? The recoil could break your femur." Hector snaps fingers for punctuation.

"I've started 'em barefoot," Ronsard says. He switches the ignition key and ducks low to tickle some gas into the carburetors.

"Foreplay. Makin' her wet," Hector says. Ronsard sits up straight. He frowns. A savage blush is burning his neck. His welts stand out.

"You all right? I embarrass you?"

Ronsard ignores the questions, jumps high off the bike, keeping his hands on grips, drives his weight down through his right leg, jams the kick-start shaft. The engine explodes and fills the garage with close thunder. He twists the throttle and revs up angry snarls.

"You can *hear* that it's fast," Hector shouts, "but do you hear a problem? That jangle?"

Ronsard tips his head and mimes bewilderment.

He says, "Only problem is, this is yours and not mine!"

Christy's sitting on her knees in short-grass sod and plunging her hands through Shank's soaped and foamy coat. Beside her is a chunk of sponge and a plastic pail. As she's kneading the soaped pelt she's singing "You Can't Hurry Love."

Ronsard comes down the slope and hears this and sees her with her hair six ways to Sunday, in her torn T-shirt, torn bathing suit, cowboy boots.

344

Rocking back, Christy has gloves of bubbles and she squints baring her front teeth and wrinkling her nose, very nearsighted without glasses. She recognizes him finally and stands and nooses him in a moist hug. He thinks she's nothing to hold at all, with balloon-ish breasts but a little, almost pretend rib cage and a small tired heart in there, tired already.

"My dog have fleas?"

"Not anymore."

Christy has a towel and twists it to dry her wrists. "You help with my laundry, I do Shank."

Being shampooed and sung to, Shank has a shocked look on her pointy face, eyes as on a polar bear rug's, head slung low, dripping like a mop.

"Sort of taxidermied," Ronsard says.

"Why *is* she standing so still?"

"You know?" Ronsard says. "She's seventeen and doesn't have many moves left."

Of a sudden, Shank shakes her loose coat so hard her gums and ears flap and she tosses up a blizzard. Ronsard gazes up at some power lines which stripe the blue sky. Christy pinches the bridge of her nose, calculating. There's a soap bubble on his cheek. Trailers sit around on piecrust earth.

He says, "See, I've been inactive, or dysfunctional I guess, now for a while, I don't want to count, you know what I'm talking about?"

"No. Speak English."

"I get hard only when I'm dreaming—"

"Oh, that."

"—and when I'm awake, nothing works how I need it to."

There's a pause and then she goes, "So, Paul? What makes you hard in your dreams?"

Last night's dream was where Ronsard was at a Sea World place on bleachers throwing fish to a great pool of dolphins which turned into women—or mermaids by day-wake logic—and he jumped in with them, equipped for engagement.

He uses his key to let himself into his mother's Pasadena house. Shank falters along behind him. Mom's mammoth in her bed and perfectly handsome, her hair in notched curls, her jaw firmed. She draws herself up to brace her wide shoulders against the diamond quilted headboard; satin with buttons.

"Mom, I'm home," he says. He gives her from a grocery sack a bag of Hershey's Kisses, and she paws out one, and one for him. She crackles the wrapper, and growls for a while, just putting out a chesty threat, old and low.

"I'm sorry I missed your birthday," she says in the dark room.

"Fifty-seven," he says.

"You're not allowed to get any older. Anyway where's the puppy?"

Shank pokes aside the door, her extended face split like scissors' blades by her toy. Teed between canines and incisors is a Rawlings baseball with popped stitches.

"She's so clean! Are you seeing somebody, Pauly?"

"Seeing is the extent and limit of what I'm doing."

Mom goes, "Well good, hand me the dog, honey."

Ronsard's ex-wife, Beth, is in the hospital—for tennis knee rebuilding—in Thousand Palms, and this hospital has a decorative theme of rainforest and the wallpaper in her room suggests vine and flower, palm and parrot.

"Hey, kid," she says.

"Beth," he says and slides in beside her. While they're talking the nurse comes and chases Ronsard off the bed and into a visitor's chair and announces lunch.

"Cobb salad and a Gibson," Beth says.

Paul explores the pockets of his denim jacket and comes up with a chisel-tip marker and sets to doodling on the bed linen. The cloth soaks and softens his border.

"I've reached a place where I want more of a sense of agency in my life," she says.

He draws Beth's jawline first, a tipped-over shallow "U," then flattens the pen-tip for the shadow part, where the jaw is subsumed by a plume of curls.

"You moved us out here, and I got trapped and just wandered off the page. Sort of a meaning leak. And you know why?"

He shakes his head as he scrubs in more curls.

"There is no sequence here. No sequence, no consequence. I think I need four seasons and without them, I just stray."

He marks in her cheekbone, strokes down an eyebrow, working quickly, thinking how fresco artists, Giotto, had to get it down while the plaster was still wet, making two short stripes for her nose. She's an even fifty.

The Food Services deliverer arrives and Beth straightens her place in bed, and Ronsard draws the stubborn, nearly straight line for her lips.

He has the barrel of the pen in his mouth, like a cigar, and is scowling at his sketch. The food guy looks as well.

"You oughta be an artist," he says and rests down Beth's tray of chicken and rice and juice.

"Anyway," Beth says, "the desert just makes bedlam of the soul."

"I agree."

"So I want you to sell that house and give me the dough, which is all I'll ask, and I'm moving home to the East somewhere."

Ronsard had designed the house over a decade before. He meant it to be simple and straightforward and to have reference to no other time or any influence. But to Beth and others the place had turned out looking needy and underfinanced, institutional; " . . . like the annex of a motor vehicle bureau," Beth had said.

For Ronsard, the home's whiteness and flatness were right, as was its modesty.

"Sorry to hit you with this now, but Gray insisted."

Paul says, "Maybe we could talk about this later."

"I want everything straight. You're a big boy and play rough when I'm hurting, and I'm just giving it back to you."

He's come to think of the house, the way you do, as "Home." Its aloneness, its clarity, its quality of mirage.

Hector on the phone says, "She was just sleeping in the sun. That was how she went, god bless her."

Back at the trailer, Hector's there with dog leash and collar. Ronsard's gummy and dazed from all the driving. He asks, "Have you seen Christy?"

"No. I'm just back from the site," Hector says. "But I think Christy's off with a customer."

"I hope not."

"Love has many faces," Hector says. He's poking a finger into his face, getting a cud settled. Ronsard peels off his sunglasses.

"Thank you for doing all—the everything."

"Shank was a cool dog. I mean I hated it." He doesn't spit.

Ronsard says, "I was taking her with me everywhere but the one time, you know?"

"Call me," says Hector. He hands Ronsard the leash and fumbles off. Ronsard envies him his motorcycle and is terrified for him. He takes the leash and collar inside and fills Shank's water bowl and a big tumbler of ice water for himself, and then he remembers, and he cries a while for his dog, twisting a fist in his eye socket, sniffling, nose running.

The silo's nearly finished but winter comes. A startled morning, cold, with all new colors: fresh and temporary tints, northern ones, desert winter. From the trailer porch deck, Ronsard sees how something cold and strong is feeding the creek, which is normally a dry bed. Its water is iron colored. White flecks. Shooting like mad through rock banks. He sees these red grouse teetering along in file. The sky is clay.

He asks Christy to go for a truck ride. Slung from the seat of his 4WD is an elaborate bwana jacket with shell loops and cartridge pockets, pointed flaps and dangling C-clips. Thunder rumbles.

She frisks the pockets for his matches and cigarettes.

"Well, see, it's a working day," she says and pops a match.

"I'll pay you. I understand professionalism."

On the road, he can't stop driving and talking.

"When I worked in a Street/FX Graphics shop as an artist, guys would come in with their muscle cars. Nineteen sixty-seven Impala SS 427's, or '62 Mustangs, say, and they'd want a pin stripe or murals. But nobody wanted flames. I tried to talk them into flames. Red and yellow. I was deft with quarter-inch masking tape or two-inch brushes and I shot paint. But I was best with those sort of scimitar red and yellow flames."

She asks, "What did your car look like?"

"I drove a pig cart."

He can't stop driving and talking. "These guys would have thirty coats of cured enamel in garnet, maybe, or indigo, and pearled or flaked. These guys would keep their cars locked in their garages."

Distant mountains. All day. Stars now. Power lines. A squat building of ceramic brick, surrounded by a razor wire fence. An Indian office. Christy needs a restroom. Inside, strip lighting, green linoleum, Formica tables. Coffee, candy, cigarette machines. Three Indians, skinny kids in their twenties, sit at a table. Lucky, Yellow Horse, Don Eagle.

He checks into a Travel-Lodge in Hillcrest. Two rooms.

348

"You know what I'm costing you?" Christy asks. "For this amount, I should be triplets. I feel guilty."

"It's all right."

"Also, Paul, you're getting a little frightening. Older guys go nuts fast."

After dawn, he drives east some more.

The sun's putting dawn glare on her glasses; two moons. Her face in the scribble-line glasses of wire is dark with fear, but a small wonderful face with two moons on it.

She asks if she's being kidnapped, and No, he says, It's just a long long drive.

He says, "Change of seasons, that's all. Hasn't happened to me for a while. S'pretty."

"It is not pretty, everything is screaming. It's saying 'I'm dying, help me, help me.'"

"It's sad but good, I think," he says.

"I'd rather be a rock on a snake in the hot sun—or I mean, you know, the other way round. I'm freezing already."

"There's time for snakes on rocks and a time for rocks on snakes."

"Knock it fuckin' off. I'm freaked."

Paul says, "Just be calm and look around at stuff. Like look, a lot of dead airplanes on the ground."

But Christy is panicky. "Don't say it, please, and ruin it all. We're both pros. Don't be a jerk."

He says, "The big bang is, all I want to talk about or think about is you. Freckles all the time. It's happened before. I've never won, I can't, but I can't stop, it is a landslide on me."

"Where are we?"

"Oklahoma, I think," he says and sends the car down an exit ramp.

Ash flakes drift from the incinerator plant like tree blossoms, and steam shapes are down over the tan river, and all the tall fields flow in warm wind like long drowned hair in currents. Those rows of blowing sheets swell, white on a backyard clothesline. Today in the sky, platinum clouds and crisscrossing skid marks left by Tomcat jetfighters.

Nominated by Mississippi Review

OF ROYAL ISSUE

by BRIGIT PEGEEN KELLY

from THE ANTIOCH REVIEW and *SONG* (BOA editions)

The sun only a small bird flitting, a wren
    in the stripped forsythia, of little
note. A boy stands and watches it for a moment
    but then he loses interest and cuts
across the dull winter grass to play a game
    with a stick and a rock and soft repeated
shouts, and the bird is nothing again
    but a brown thing, within a fabric of brown
branches, mind and heart, the cages of.
    Days and days from now, each a web
of small branches, in the weeks of high wet
    winds that bring out low patches
of wild onion along the swollen creek
    and call up countless red-bellied birds
to dibble the grass with their blunt beaks,
    the bush's royal bloodline will briefly show,
a tide of gold, a small inland sea, and the wren
    will speak for it, words of royal issue,
tongue after tongue, worthy of note.
    But now the bush is mute. Our common blood
slows but will not sleep, a kind of footpath
    the mind trudges over, back and forth,
back and forth, packing the cold dirt down . . . O little bird,
    how small you are, small enough to fit in a palm,
no contender, a featherweight. Perhaps
    we can pay the boy to trick you out of the bush,

and trap you, and bring you in to this spot
     by the window where your little song may
amount to more than a tablespoon's worth of salt.
     The glass will quicken your call, multiply it,
multiply your nervous figure and your habit
     of play, until you are not one bird but a hundred,
not one tongue but a thousand, sweet prophesy
     of the wind lighting the white strips
of the bed sheets the boy will tear and tie
     to the black branches of all the garden's
trees, for no reason, because his hands
     will not stop, *bird in the mind, bird in the bush,*
the bird of the blood brightening
     as it calls and calls for its mate.

Nominated by Marianne Boruch

THE WOMEN COME AND GO

fiction by CORNELIA NIXON

from NEW ENGLAND REVIEW

ONE QUARTER OF her waking life had gone to practicing the violin, but when her teacher entered her in a national audition, Margy was surprised to make it to the finals, and didn't bother checking the results. The teacher had to track her down at home to tell her that she'd won. Margy knew it was a fluke, but within a month she was invited everywhere to play (to Tanglewood, to Aspen, with the Boston Symphony), and at her school in the Back Bay, where she'd always had to practice straight through lunch, ignored by everyone, suddenly she had so much cachet that the most sought-after girls were seeking her. Ann was generally acknowledged the most beautiful girl in school, and beautiful in a way that made other girls feel awe: she was perfect in the natural state, like Grace Kelly before she met the prince, only better, since she'd never bleached her hair or worn lipstick. She had a nun-like aura, and wore expensive modest clothes, the kind that most girls' mothers picked for them and they refused to wear. Even the Huntington uniform looked good on her. Calluses did not grow on her toes. Whatever she said was considered wise. She liked to quote from Herman Hesse, Kahlil Gibran, and other sources of deathless wisdom.

"Just sit on your bed and think," she said. Hushing to listen, girls went home and sat on their beds.

And with Ann came Elizabeth, her lifelong acolyte. Their mothers were friends, former debutantes who had married the wrong men, and now lived in a neighborhood much faded from its former glory, instead of in three-story mansions out in Brookline or in Lexington. Elizabeth dressed like Ann, even vied with her a little in the neatness of her gestures, the propriety of her shoes. But she didn't have the face, or the hair or the skin, and no one stopped to listen when she talked, unless it was about Ann.

"As Ann said to me last night," she might begin, through a din of girlish voices, and suddenly a hush would fall.

Then in their junior year they took on Margy, who was related to no debutantes, whose hair was impossible, maggot-white and curled as tight as velcro in tiny fetal snarls, who was always fidgeting and humming and dancing with her bony legs whenever she wasn't playing violin—but who learned fast, and soon the three of them were gliding modestly around the school, discussing Robert Lowell or Sylvia Plath, looking benignly (but silently) at the other girls. Ann and Elizabeth would listen to Margy practice during lunch, and after school they all walked home with Ann (who lived only a block away, on "hardly passionate Marlborough") or out in every weather to the Esplanade, where they would grieve together privately, for the divorce of Elizabeth's parents, and the death of Margy's mother when she was only twelve, and the last cruel thing that Ann's had said to her.

"Could it be then that this was life?" Ann quietly intoned one brilliant winter day beside the Charles, the sky Delft blue, the river frozen blistering white. "Was there no safety? No learning by heart of the ways of the world? No guide, no shelter, but all was miracle, and leaping from the pinnacle of a tower into air?"

In their senior year, they read Camus in French and took on existential responsibility, marching gravely, all in black, with a hundred-thousand others up and down the major avenues, to protest the bombing of North Vietnam. Margy started quoting from the things she'd read, but without Ann's authority: she might just mutter quietly, so no one else could actually hear, "Quick eyes gone under earth's lid," or "Il faut imaginer Sisyphe heureux." On her birthday in November, Elizabeth and Ann gave her a locket with their three initials in a triangle, and for Christmas they all gave each other books, disapproved together of their family celebrations, and went to midnight mass at Holy Cross, for the music, and to appall their parents, none of whom were Catholic or in danger of becoming so. Away from Huntington they were more free, and sometimes standing on street corners, waiting to cross in the winter sun, Ann and Elizabeth might fall in with

Margy's dance, gently snapping fingers, tapping feet. Crazed with success, she once vamped off a curb into the path of a careening cab, but they yanked her back in time.

Margy was happy to be their friend, though she knew that she was not like Ann. She had calluses not only on her toes but on every finger of both hands, and had once had a hickey on her neck. She got it from a pianist named Gary Slade, on whom she'd had a crush, until the night he tried to make her fish the car keys from his underpants. She had walked home that night, and never been alone with any guy since then, but still she went on having similar effects on other boys and men. The chorus master at her music school was a handsome man, but he was past her father's age, and if she looked at him it was only on obligatory Saturdays, singing husky alto in the second row. But at the last school picnic out to Marblehead, he'd gotten her off by herself, both of them in bathing suits, not fifty yards from where her father stood—and, running a pool cue through his toes, he said, "You know that I want to make love to you," as if she were accustomed to hearing words like that, when she was just sixteen and had been kissed exactly once, by Gary Slade.

She'd never mentioned these events to Elizabeth and Ann—in fact she would have died on the rack before she did. But once she told her father about Gary Slade, in vague theoretical terms, as if it were simply something that she'd heard, to see whose fault he thought it was. Her father was an architect, and he liked theoretical problems, though preferably the geometrical kind. He was willing to talk about anything, however, after dinner, when he'd had a few martinis just before.

"Well, now," he said, running one bony hand across his hair, which sprang up in a solid hedge as his hand passed, curled like Margy's, only slightly red. "That would depend on how she got into the car, now, wouldn't it?" If she had kissed the man and led him on, then it was her fault too. He thought in general women were too quick to speak of rape. Leaning with one elbow on the table, he held the other hand out in the air, and looked at it.

"When a gal shows up at the precinct and says that she's been raped, they make her hold a hand out, and check to see if it's trembling. Because if it is, it means she had an orgasm, and it wasn't rape."

He glanced at Margy, looked away, fair cheeks flushing clear red.

"Of course sometimes it is." He grinned, as if he knew he shouldn't say what he was going to next. He gave her a bold look. "But when it does happen, when it can't be stopped—why not just relax, and enjoy?"

354

In January of their senior year, Ann was elected queen of the winter festival at a boy's school across town, by guys she'd mainly never met, and Margy and Elizabeth went with her as her court, flanking her at the hockey match, triple-dating to the ball that night. Ann chose as her escort Gary Slade, who was still the best-looking young man they knew, while Margy (having no one else to ask) went with his little brother Jason, with whom she'd shared a violin teacher since they were six.

And the night of the ball she rode in Gary's car as if she'd never seen it before. She didn't have to talk to him, or even much to Jason—she was really there with Elizabeth and Ann, as they were there with her. Gary had to stand for hours by the throne the boys had made for Ann, while she sat silent and expressionless, in a white ball gown and rhinestone crown, bearing the stares of all those eyes. When the ball was over, they asked to be delivered back to Ann's, where they dismissed their escorts at the curb (Gary trailing after Ann forlornly, saying, "Can I call you soon?") and went in to drink hot chocolate, while Margy pranced in her long skirt from room to room, too excited to sit down.

"Gary should be falling on his sword by now," Elizabeth noted, smiling down into her mug.

Lifting her lovely head, Ann seemed to consider an object far away. "Gary? Oh, Gary will be fine. He'll get married and buy a house and have five children of his own, and become a sixty-year-old smiling public man."

Margy was fidgeting nearby. Suddenly she felt bold.

"The women come and go," she said. "Talking of Michelangelo." And then, with special glee, "I do not think that they will sing to me."

Ann laughed, and kissed her cheek. She put a record on, and they all began to dance, to "Let It Bleed" and "Love In Vain" and "You can't always get what you want, but if you try sometime you just might find you get what you need," until they had calmed down enough to sleep, Elizabeth with Ann in her canopy bed, Margy on a cot down at the foot.

Margy started reading through her father's library, leatherbound classics hardly touched by anyone, and after sampling here and there she settled on the Sigmund Freuds, which were small and dense and rewarding even in small bites, and therefore suitable for reading in the moments when she wasn't practicing. She read Dora, Anna O., *Civilization and Its Discontents*. She took to peppering her talk with Freudian remarks.

"I have cathected to those shoes," she'd say. "The economics of my libido may require a chili dog." Or, "Time to catastrophize about that test."

One week she was excused from classes in the afternoons to rehearse with the Boston Symphony, and as she waited for the T at Arlington, she read that if a woman dreams her daughter is run over by a train, that means she wants to go to bed with the man who once gave her flowers as she got onto a train. She was about to turn the page, when she felt a hard stare from a few feet off. Pretending to read on, she tapped out the timing of the Paganini she was going to play, against one edge of the book, as if deeply engrossed.

The staring did not stop. Annoyed, she glanced that way, and recognized the new girl in her class at Huntington. Rachel had arrived only that year, a tall dark awkward girl with huge black eyes, who stared at everyone as if she found them very strange, and slightly amusing. Imitating Ann's most unrevealing face, Margy gave her a brief nod and returned to her book, which was the most effective of the small polite rejections she and Ann and Elizabeth practiced every day on other girls at school.

Rachel moved closer, staring like a baby over its mother's shoulder. She read the spine on Margy's book. Her voice squeaked in amazement.

"Are you holding that right-side up?"

Margy finished the sentence, and looked at her. Rachel's uniform was entirely disguised by a black leather jacket and beret, her hair whacked off around the earlobes. But her face was fresh and artless as a two-year-old's.

"Insulting people in train stations is a sign of unresolved dilemmas in the inner life."

Rachel chuckled, watching her. "And what about the virgin goddess, does she read books too?"

Margy pretended not to know who she could mean, narrowing her eyes at her. "Why aren't you in school?"

Rachel whipped out a pass and twirled it in the air.

"Legal as milk," she said, but grinning in a way that made it clear she wasn't going to the dentist after all. She had a sick friend at B.U., and how could she leave her there alone, pining for a cool hand on her brow?

"Freud used to operate on people's noses," Rachel calmly said. "To clear up their sexual hangups. He thought if you put your fingers in your purse you were playing with yourself. He was a little bit hung up on cock, and thought the rest of us were too."

Margy rode with her to Copley, slightly stunned. On the platform, changing trains, she glanced back at the one she had just left, and there was Rachel pressed against the glass, eager as a puppy locked inside a car.

She introduced her to Elizabeth and Ann, and soon Rachel started showing up at lunch, refusing to fade off as other girls had learned to do. She even followed on their private walks, stalking behind them with her long unhurried gait.

"What about me?" she would actually cry, throwing her arms out wide, as they tried to walk away.

She introduced them to new lore, Simone de Beauvoir and *The Story of O* and *The Tibetan Book of the Dead,* and gradually to other things. Rachel had lived in Paris and L.A. and Israel, but now her parents had moved into Beacon Hill, a few blocks from the house where Margy'd always lived, and she took to turning up on Sunday afternoons, to listen to her play and go for walks and tell her things that would have made her mother's hair stand up. Already Rachel had a lot of friends, older women living on their own, who had fed her marvelous meals, peyote buds and grass, and taught her unimaginable acts in bed. She kept her fingernails cut to the quick, so that they could not wound. She said she could do anything a man could do, only better, because she was a girl too.

"There's nothing nicer than getting ready for bed," she said, "knowing there's a girl in there waiting for you."

Margy listened, thrilled and shocked. She began to look back with new eyes on certain things she'd done herself. The summer after her mother died, a rash of slumber parties had gone through her neighborhood, with girls she hardly knew at Huntington. But Margy went to every one, and when the lights were out they'd played a secret game. Bedded in their sleeping bags on some girl's living-room rug, they'd touched each other's breasts, circling incipient nipples with light fingertips, until the hostess said to switch, and then the one you had just touched would do the same to you. They did it as a dare, to prove that they were brave, and they would have all dropped dead to learn that it had anything to do with sex—though the boldest girls, who had invented it, played an advanced form of the game, removing pajama pants and circling fingertips on a certain sensitive spot. Torture, they called that.

"Who were they?" Rachel squeaked, dropping to her knees on the Common, clutching Margy's coat. It was early spring, the air cold and sweet, and they were loitering after a rally against the bombing of Cambodia. "Please please, pretty please. Tell me. Are they still at Huntington?"

Most of them were, but Margy said they had all moved away. Rachel sank her hands into the pockets of her leather jacket, slouching morosely down the path.

"Why do I never meet girls like that? I just meet little virgin straights. Not that you aren't cute, of course," she said, and tousled Margy's hair.

Margy assumed that Ann knew nothing of Rachel's other life, and that it would be best to keep it to herself. Then one Sunday she called Ann's, and Ann's mother said that she and Rachel had gone out. Another time she stopped by, on her way home from music school, and found Rachel cooking in the kitchen with Ann's mother. Ann's mother was formal and remote and tall, a suntanned woman in yachting clothes, who smoked and watched you without smiling while you spoke. Margy was afraid to say a word to her, and she had always called her Mrs. Church. But in the kitchen she was laughing, deep and slow, stabbing a spoon into a pot, while Rachel watched her, hands on hips.

"Betsy! Not like that!" Rachel cried, and tried to wrestle the spoon away from her, both of them laughing like maniacs.

Margy stood chuckling in the kitchen doorway. Mrs. Church whirled at the sound, face sobering at once.

"Oh, hello, Margaret. Annie's in her room, I think."

Margy stood on one foot, smiling, but they did not go on. Dutifully she went to look for Ann, as peels of giggles echoed from the kitchen walls.

That spring, Margy fell in love. Yale was taking women now, and her father'd asked her to apply, since he went there, and to try it for at least a year instead of Juilliard—and to help convince her, he arranged for her to meet the son of a new partner in his firm, who was finishing at Yale and would be entering the law school in the fall. Henry Bergstrom was handsome and sandy-haired like Gary Slade, but soft-spoken and grownup and kind, with broad shoulders and a narrow waist and one chipped tooth that gave his grin a boyish charm. He was from New York City, had lived in Texas and Brazil, his family having only recently relocated to Boston, and he was a fan of *carnaval* and soccer as well as football and World War II. His voice thrilled her, deep and faintly drawled, but abrupt and furtive when he was moved.

"Where have you been?" he would say quickly on the phone, as if in pain, when she'd been practicing too long. But in person he might hold out an ice-cream cone too high, focus his eyes above her head and gravely search for her. The Brazilians had a dozen words for "shorty" and "little kid," along with maybe a hundred each for "pester," "scram," and anything to do with sex, though he wouldn't tell her what they were.

"Hey, *pixote*, what's it to you," he would say when she asked, or call her *tico-tico, catatau*.

He took her to the symphony, where he listened with shining eyes, turning at the end to say he'd rather hear her play. She gave a solo recital in June, and he sat up straight and rapt beside her dad.

"Pretty good for a *pixote*," he whispered in her ear, standing by protectively as Ann and Elizabeth and Rachel all surged up to kiss her cheek. He drove a powder-blue MG, and Rachel called him Ken, after the boyfriend of the Barbie doll.

"Is *Ken* coming up this weekend *again?*" she'd say, staring with outraged onyx eyes.

Margy got into Yale, and agreed to give it a try. Henry came home to Boston for the summer, worked for his dad, and she saw him almost every night. They went to hear the Pops, and to restaurants a few times, then settled into eating with her father or his parents, and after dinner going for a walk. Henry didn't really like to go out at night.

"When I'm married, I won't go anywhere at all," he said, blue eyes warm. "I'll have my own fun at home."

The last thing every night before he left, in the car or on her porch or in her living room, he'd lean close and kiss her a few times, always stopping before she wanted to. Once he pulled her down onto his parents' couch, stopped as if switched off, and apologized. On the way home, he talked about the beauty of *carnaval*, how all rules were suspended there ("Don't you ever go to one," he said, grinning hard, gripping her hand). But a few nights later in the car he slid one hand up her side, where he could feel a little of her breast—stinging her so unexpectedly with want, that tears spilled from the corners of her eyes.

"I may have to sign up for a nose-job soon," she said one sultry afternoon, twirling on a swing in a park near Rachel's house. Ann was at the Vineyard with her family, and Rachel moped on the next swing, rolling a joint in her lap.

"That is, if things go on this way."

Pulling down her heavy black sunglasses, Rachel regarded her with some alarm. "You wouldn't. Not with *Ken?*"

Margy tipped her head back toward the ground, viewing the world from upside-down. "That's who it's done with," she pointed out. "By virgin straights. The Kens of this world."

Rachel pushed her sunglasses back up over her eyes, and looked inscrutable.

"Not necessarily," she finally said, and gave one fleeting grin, though she would not explain.

In August Henry's parents left for their summer place down on Long Island, and Henry lingered on alone. At first they pretended nothing had changed, eating at Margy's, taking walks. Then one night he made dinner for some friends from Yale, at his parents' house in Brookline, and invited Margy too. The friends were a couple, tall gazelle-like blonds who almost looked alike, both living with their parents for the summer, and happy to be out of their sight.

They all drank gin and tonic before Henry's manly fare (steak and potatoes and oversalted salad), and then the gazelles disappeared, into Henry's bedroom, it turned out, with his warbooks and his model planes. Margy and Henry climbed up to the widow's walk on the third floor, where they could watch the city lights reflected on the river in the summer dusk, Margy in a dress that tied behind the neck and almost nothing else, Henry in a seersucker jacket. She was quivering lightly, not from cold, and when he ran his fingers down the bare skin of her back, she turned and started kissing him.

Startled, his eyes opened wide—and then he seized her like a tortured man. Moments later they were in his parents' bed, pressing together through their clothes until she lost all sense of being in a room, or even in a body of her own, apart from his. Then he stopped. Fingers in the tight curls at her scalp, he shook her face from side to side.

"*Negativo, pixote,*" he said, and left the room.

Henry left to join his parents in Wading River, and suddenly her life went blank. She called her friends, but already they seemed remote. She hadn't seen them often over the summer, and Elizabeth and Ann had had a fight, though neither would say why. ("It's me," Rachel explained. "Elizabeth is jealous of the time I spend with Ann.") Margy saw Ann a few times, but never alone, no matter what they planned: when she arrived, Rachel would be with her, grinning and relaxed and full of little jokes. They were both staying home, Ann to go to Radcliffe and Rachel to B.U., and Rachel seemed almost to live at Ann's place now. Her clothes were hung on chairs in Ann's room, and once Margy found her lying on the canopy bed, an arm across her eyes.

"Ann needs support right now," Rachel explained, when Margy asked her what was going on. Since they'd left Huntington, Ann's mother had started a campaign, telling her she was spoiled and self-centered, and other cruel, unnecessary remarks.

"Last year, when your friends found you so charming," Betsy'd lately said, in reference to the winter festival. Ann's eyes were always shining with leashed tears, and Rachel hovered close to her, one hand on her shoulder, staring at anyone who came near.

"Oh, for God's *sake*," Margy said one hot night in Cambridge, as they were walking toward a party full of Rachel's friends. "People's mothers *say* things like that. It's just the ordinary coin of mother-daughter economics. You're lucky that you have a mom at all."

Rachel's mouth fell open as if she'd fired a gun. Clutching Ann's shoulders, she steered her away. Later she cornered Margy at the party, in a throng of loud and happy older women. ("Lay off, she's straight," Rachel kept saying, as they stopped to stare.)

"You don't know," she said quietly, watching Margy with a light in her black eyes. "You just don't know. *Comprends-tu?*"

Henry wrote to Margy, in a big angular hand on heavy paper, about his father's need to win at golf, and where they'd sailed that day, and how much he thought of her. Once he said remembering how she'd kissed him on the widow's walk that night was driving him insane—but he didn't trust letters, so he'd say no more. Except he hoped that he could see her the moment she got to Yale, in fact he would be waiting in her college yard.

The night before she left, Ann stopped by with Rachel to give her a blank book with a dove-gray linen cover, for a journal while she was away, and Rachel gave her a God's Eye she had made. Ann was wearing Rachel's leather jacket, clutched around her tightly with both hands. She gazed at Margy with her beautiful clear eyes.

"You are coming to a place where two roads diverge, and taking the one less traveled by." She touched Margy's hand. "We understand each other, don't we, Margy? No matter what happens."

Margy followed them out to the street and watched them walk away. In the dark, their heads inclined in toward each other, till their silhouettes converged.

Her father drove her to New Haven, delivered her to his old college, and took her on a campus tour, pointing out the design of each quadrangle. Then he was gone, and Henry was there, in his seersucker jacket, fingers clenched around her arm.

"Can we go now?" he said quietly, hardly moving his lips.

It was Indian summer out, hot sun with an autumn drowsiness, and Henry had the top down on the MGB. Quickly crossing town, he raced south. The wind was too loud in the car for talk, but Margy knew where they were going now. She had on a simple sheath of rose linen that Ann had helped her to pick out, her hair restrained in a ribbon the same shade. But as they crossed the bridge onto Long Island in late sun, the wind teased out the ribbon and her hair burst free, with a ripple of pleasure along the scalp.

He had her back soon after breakfast, though she'd missed the freshman dinner in her college and had failed to sleep in her bed. Calhoun was full of southerners, from Georgia and Virginia and the Carolinas, and they were all just trooping off in tennis whites, or to try out for some *a cappella* group, as she made her way upstairs, trembling slightly and trying to look blasé. At the last second, when the pain was most intense, she had tried to pull away. But Henry went on saying "Just relax" into her ear, and soon she lay still listening to him sleep, with a feeling she didn't recognize, like floating in a warm bath, with an undertow of fear.

In the morning he had quickly pulled a pillow across the bloodstain on the sheet, as if she shouldn't see that, when she had already seen it in the bathroom twice, in the middle of the night and again after the second time, when he woke her at first light, his lean hairless chest quivering before her eyes like a wall she had to climb. Driving back, he didn't say a word—the law school had already started, and he had to be in class. But he kissed her tenderly, by Calhoun gate in the open car, and said he would be there to pick her up on Friday afternoon.

She took long meditative showers, spent whole days in the practice rooms, and only joined her fellow frosh in class. On Fridays Henry drove her out to Wading River, where the house was always packed now with his friends, who played tackle on the beach and drank all night, and she was only alone with him in the sandy bed. With a football in his arms he was unexpectedly exuberant, and she watched him from a beachchair in the autumn sun, trying to write something profound to Rachel and Ann. They'd sent her two postcards, one from a

362

small hotel in Provincetown. ("All quite legitimate, you understand," Rachel's part had said. "Searching the beach for pebbles you may have sent. Now is the time to buy a kite.") But Margy had nothing to say that she could trust to letters now, so she watched Henry steal the ball, and laugh and cheat and leap across his fallen friends with lean tan legs, and streak across the sand to score.

The weather changed, dry leaves crackling in the wind at night. The first cold week, she did not hear from Henry, and on Saturday she called his rooms, where his suite-mate said he had gone home to Boston. Margy was concerned. Of course she knew that men could change, from the days of Gary Slade—but the last time she'd seen Henry, he was more tender than before, and held her hand on the long drive back to Yale.

Monday night, on her way home from the practice rooms, she stopped by the law-school dorm, where he was studying. He seemed surprised but glad, and pulled her in protectively.

"Everything all right?" he said, ushering her quickly into his room, shutting the door. "Nothing wrong?"

They talked politely, sitting on the bed, his lawbooks lit up on the desk. He did not explain why he went home to Boston, and she didn't ask. When she rose to go, he said goodbye at the door and watched her leave—then strode behind her down the gleaming brown expanse of hall.

"Don't go," he said, clutching her arm and looking at the floor. "Please stay, all right?"

She couldn't sleep in his narrow bed, and she got up late to walk back through the cold clear night. That weekend she practiced all the daylight hours, avoiding telephones. But when she went back to Calhoun at night, there were no messages for her. She called Henry's rooms, pretending to have a French accent.

"Boston," his suitemate said.

"Ah, *bon*," she said, and did not call again.

Henry wrote her a careful letter, saying he had made a mistake and wasn't ready to be serious yet, but asking her to let him know if she ever needed anything from him. Margy wrote four versions of a letter back, outraged, pleading, miserable, abject, and tore them up. Finally she sent a postcard with a view of Wading River (bought to send to Rachel and Ann), saying she was always glad to hear from him but didn't think she would be needing anything. He sent her a biography of Freud, which she had already read ("From your friend, Henry," it said inside) and a yard of rose-colored ribbon, to replace the one she'd lost while riding in his car. Once she saw him on Elm Street, idling in traffic as the snow fell on the cloth top of his car. Honking and waving, he half emerged—but she saluted with her violin, and hurried off against the traffic, so he couldn't follow her.

Sleet was rattling on the windows as if hurled from fists, on the day she started to throw up. She tried to make it stop, lying on her bed in the hot blasts from the heating ducts, as Rachel's God's Eye twirled above. It was ridiculous, it was impossible. Henry had been so cautious, breaking open little hard blue plastic cases, exactly like the ones she'd seen once in her father's dresser drawer when her mother was alive, and dropping them beneath the bed as he put their contents on. The night she'd visited his room, she crouched to count the empties in the silvery light, and there were at least a dozen more than he had used that night—though it was hard to tell, of course, how old they were.

She went to class and could not hear a word. She could not play the violin, or remember why she'd ever wanted to. The nausea surrounded her, six inches of rancid blubber through which she had to breathe. She threw up in the daytime, in the evening, in the middle of the night. She told herself to just relax—morning sickness is all in the woman's head, Freud said. She ate a crust of hard French bread, and saw it unchanged moments after in the white cup of the toilet bowl.

She found a doctor down in Bridgeport, where she wouldn't run into anyone from Yale. The man she picked had chosen his profession because the forceps used at his own birth had damaged a nerve in his face, causing his forehead to hang down across his eyes, while his mouth pulled to one side. Yes, he had good news for her, he said—Mrs. Henry Bergstrom, she had called herself, and lied about her age. Alone with him when the nurse had left, she mentioned that they weren't quite married yet. The doctor may have given her a kindly look, though it was hard to tell.

"Don't be upset if something happens to it," he said, lips flapping loose around the sounds. "It's not because it's out of wedlock or anything like that. It's not your fault."

Margy nodded, and started to weep quietly. Moments later she was on the sidewalk in cold sun, with the recommended diet in her purse, and Mrs. Henry Bergstrom's next appointment card.

She'd be a famous violinist, live in a garret with the child. It would be a purse-size child, round and pink, a girl, never growing any bigger or needing anything, and it would ride on Margy's chest while she played the major concert stages of the world. She would wear flowered dresses, cut severely—bought in France—with black berets and leather jackets. She would smoke fat cigarettes through vermilion lips, drink liqueur from a small glass. And one day, in a cafe on the Boul' Mich', or in Nice, or in her dressing room in Rome, Henry would track her down. He'd send his card backstage, and she would send it back. She'd look the other way in the cafe.

"*Mais non, monsieur,*" she'd say. "*Nous nous ne connaissons pas. Excusez moi.*"

For Thanksgiving she had to fly to Florida with her father and pretend to eat some of the thirty pounds of turkey her grandmother made, and throw up in the bathroom of the tiny ocean-view apartment with the fan on and the water running. Back at Yale, she learned that she had failed mid-term exams (equipped with the vast wasteland of all she hadn't read), and packed to leave for Christmas break.

Rachel met her train. Sauntering down the platform, thumbs hooked into black jeans, she looked very young in a new black motorcycle jacket with silver chains. But her stare was just the same.

"They're engaged," she said, with a tragic face.

Margy kissed her on both cheeks, said what? and who? and even laughed. She felt a little better, having not thrown up almost all day.

Rachel hung suspended, watching her. Slowly a look of wonder, almost delight, broke on her face. Stepping closer, she took tender hold of Margy's head.

"Oh, baby. Don't you know anything yet?"

It had started in the summer, Rachel said, when she and Ann first went to bed. They'd been in love since spring—she and Ann, that is—and Rachel was spending all her time at Ann's by then. Ann never wanted her to leave, but at first they didn't get near the bed. They'd sit on the floor in her room, and talk until they fell asleep, right where they were. Ann couldn't face it, what it meant, or do more than kiss Rachel on the cheek.

"She was just a little virgin straight," Rachel explained. "Like you, only worse. She thought that girls who went to bed with girls would end up riding Harley-Davidsons and stomping around in big dyke boots. It wasn't possible for the queen of the winter festival."

Then suddenly it was, and they'd been lovers now for months, every night in the canopy bed. It was the most intense thing in her life—and in Ann's. One night they'd been making love for hours when she touched Ann's back, and it was wet.

"That does it," Rachel'd told her then. "No matter what, you can't go saying you're a virgin now."

Things were good then for a while. They took some little trips. ("You lied to me on that postcard," Margy pointed out, and Rachel shook her head. "I promised her," she said.) Ann was jealous of her other friends, and accused Rachel of not loving her—while she, Ann, was in love for life. But Rachel reassured her, and then things were all right. Even Betsy laid off Ann.

"Betsy thinks I'm good for her," Rachel said, and grinned. "She likes the way Ann shares her toys with me." Of course Betsy had no idea what was going on, it wasn't in her lexicon. But she liked Rachel, they got along. And Rachel learned to head her off, when she was going after Ann.

Then one night in the fall, Ann announced that she was going out, and Henry showed up at the door. He took her out to eat, and to a play, and to the symphony.

"They went *out?*" Margy cried, but Rachel only looked at her. Out, and home to meet his parents too. It was a bulldozer through their happy life. He started calling every night from Yale—Ann would take it in her parents' room and close the door. She started quoting him. He said that men should always be gentle to all women, and he was sorry it had not worked out with Margy—but that they had parted friends. This was the time in their lives that counted most, he said, when the steps they took would determine all the rest, and it was important to be circumspect. Ann agreed, and every weekend circumspectly she went out with Henry, and came home to sleep with Rachel.

"So now she's wearing this big Texas diamond, that used to belong to his grandmother. And all she does is cry. He brings her home, and she gets in bed with me and starts to cry. She cries while we make love, and then cries in her sleep. In the morning she gets up to try on her trousseau, and puts on sunglasses so Betsy won't see, but they just dam up the tears, till she's got this pool behind them on her cheeks. She's just afraid, and she knows it, but that doesn't mean a thing. They've got the guest list all made out. She's going to marry him in June."

Margy took the T to Cambridge, looked for Rachel's friends. She found the one who'd had the party, a big-breasted woman in a tee-shirt with short rough hair, who offered to make tea, or lunch, or roll a joint.

366

Yes, she could tell Margy where to go, and no, she wouldn't mention it to Rachel if she didn't want her to. But was she sure?

"It's not a nice thing to go through," she said, as she followed Margy out onto the landing, carrying a large gray cat. "Don't do it by yourself, baby."

Margy thanked her, put the number in her purse, but did not make the call. First, she needed to understand. She needed to see Ann one more time, from a distance, preferably—maybe that would be safe. Maybe then the thing that happened when you looked at her would not, and she would understand, why all their lives arranged themselves Ann's way, as if they were the notes, and she was the melody.

Christmas eve, Margy played chess with her father, which he had taught her as a child, but she was too sick to concentrate, and he won both games. Humming happily, he went off to bed, and she sat waiting in the ornate living room, still decorated in her mother's taste, Persian rugs and heavy velvet drapes and lamps held up by enslaved caryatids ("early sado-masochist," as Rachel'd labeled it). When she could hear nothing but the antique clocks, ticking out of sync, she eased her coat out of the closet, and the bolt out of the door.

Flagging a cab was easier then she'd supposed, with the neighbors all returning home, and she was early for the service at Holy Cross. The cathedral was already nearly full, rows churning with genuflection, kneeling, crossing, touching lips, and she took up a position to one side, beneath a statue of the Virgin, plaster fingers open downward as if beckoning the crowd to climb up into her arms. In an organ loft somewhere above, someone was playing Bach's most schmaltzy fugue, hamming it up with big vibrato on the bass, while in the aisles people streamed both ways, like refugees from war, out toward the doors and in for midnight mass. Their coats were black and brown and muddy green, with sober scarves and hats, and when Ann's head emerged beneath the outer arch, hair glowing like ripe wheat and freshly cut to brush the shoulders of her camel-hair coat, she seemed to light the air around for several feet.

Margy pressed back closer to the wall—she hadn't forgotten how beautiful Ann was, but memory could never quite live up to her. Henry's shoulders framed her head, wide and straight in a navy overcoat, with Rachel tall as he was next to him, looking strangely wrong in a lace collar, wool coat and heels. None of them had time to glance across the nave. Rachel was clowning for Henry, rolling her eyes and gesturing with her hands, and he gave a grim smile, looking handsome but harassed, as he stepped up to take Ann's hand. Rachel moved to her far side, and together they maneuvered to a spot behind the final row of pews.

Now all three stood, Rachel and Henry crowded close on either side of Ann, bantering above her head, while she looked docile as a child, and lost. Henry had a firm grip on her hand, and he kept it well displayed, curled against his chest or resting on the pew in front or in his other fist. Ann's other hand was out of sight, but Rachel's arm pressed close to hers, and both their hands plunged down behind the pew, as still as if they'd turned to stone.

Ann leaned back her head, looking high up toward the ceiling, a parted sea of water shining in her eyes. She said something to distract the other two, and all three of them looked up, as if they could see something descending from above. In a moment, other people near them looked up too.

The Bach swelled to an end, and the crowd pressed in, packing all the spaces on the floor. Forging a path back through stiff overcoats, miasmas of perfume, Margy stepped out to the cold pure night. She'd seen enough, and as she hurried up the avenue, alive with pinpoint lights, Salvation Army bells and taxis rushing through the slush, the city opened up around her, smaller than before, while she felt strangely huge, as if she were parading through the air like the Macy's Mickey-Mouse balloon. A thousand windows lit up small and bright, no bigger than the hollows in a honeycomb, and for a moment she could almost see inside, into the thousand tiny rooms, where figures crossed, and smiled, hiding their hurts, and wanting the wrong things, and spending long nights in their beds alone.

Nominated by James Harms, David Wojahn

SADNESS, AN IMPROVISATION

by DONALD JUSTICE

from THE SOUTHERN REVIEW

i

Dear ghosts, dear presences, O my dear parents,
Why were you so sad on porches, whispering?
What great melancholies were loosed among our swings!
As before a storm one hears the leaves whispering
    And marks each small change in the atmosphere
    So was it then to overhear and to fear.

ii

But all things then were oracle and secret.
Remember that night when, lost, returning, we turned back
Confused, and our headlights singled out the fox?
Our thoughts went with it then, turning and turning back
    With the same terror, into the deep thicket
    Beside the highway, at home in the dark thicket.

iii

I say the wood within is the dark wood,
Or wound no torn shirt can entirely bandage,
But the sad hand returns to it in secret

Repeatedly, encouraging the bandage
    To speak of that other world we might have borne,
    The lost world buried before it could be born.

iv

Burchfield describes the pinched white souls of violets
Frothing the mouth of a derelict old mine
Just as the evil August night comes down,
All umber but for one smudge of dusky carmine.
    It is the sky of a peculiar sadness—
    The other side perhaps of some rare gladness.

v

What is it to be happy, after all? Think
Of the first small joys. Think of how our parents
Would whistle as they packed for the long summers
Or, busy about the usual tasks of parents,
    Would smile down at us suddenly for some secret reason
    Or simply smile, not needing any person.

vi

But even in the summers we remember
The forest had its eyes, the sea its voices,
And there were roads no map would ever master,
Lost roads and moonless nights and ancient voices;
    And night crept down with an awful slowness toward the
        water—
    And there were lanterns once, doubled in the water.

vii

Sadness has its own beauty, of course. Toward dusk,
Let us say, a river darkens and looks bruised,

And we stand looking out at it through rain.
It is as if life itself were somehow bruised
  And tender at this hour; and a few tears commence.
  Not that they *are* but that they *feel* immense.

Nominated by Maura Stanton, Robert Phillips

UPDIKE AND I

by JOHN UPDIKE

from ANTAEUS

I CREATED UPDIKE out of the sticks and mud of my Pennsylvania boyhood, so I can scarcely resent it when people, mistaking me for him, stop me on the street and ask me for his autograph. I am always surprised that I resemble him so closely that we can be confused. Meeting strangers, I must cope with an extra brightness in their faces, an expectancy that I will say something worthy of him; they do not realize that he works only in the medium of the written word, where other principles apply, and hours of time can be devoted to a moment's effect. Thrust into "real" time, he can scarcely function, and his awkward pleasantries and anxious stutter emerge through my lips. Myself, I am rather suave. I think fast, on my feet, and have no use for the qualificatory complexities and lame *double entendres* and pained exactations of language in which he is customarily mired. I move swiftly and rather blindly through life, spending the money he earns.

I early committed him to a search for significance, to philosophical issues that give direction and point to his verbal inventions, but am not myself aware of much point or meaning to things. Things *are*, rather unsayably, and when I force myself to peruse his elaborate scrims of words I wonder where he gets it all—not from *me*, I am sure. The distance between us is so great that the bad reviews he receives do not touch me, though I treasure his few prizes and mount them on the walls and shelves of my house, where they instantly yellow and tarnish. That he takes up so much of my time, answering his cloying mail and reading his incessant proofs, I resent. I feel that the fractional time of day he spends away from being Updike is what feeds and inspires him,

372

and yet, perversely, he spends more and more time being Updike, that monster of whom my boyhood dreamed.

Each morning I awake from my dreams, which as I age leave an ever more sour taste. Men once thought dreams to be messages from the gods, and then from something called the subconscious, as it sought a salubrious rearrangement of the contents of the day past; but now it becomes hard to believe that they partake of any economy. Instead, a basic chaos seems expressed: a random play of electricity generates images of inexplicable specificity.

I brush my teeth, I dress and descend to the kitchen, where I eat and read the newspaper, which has been dreaming its own dreams in the night. Postponing the moment, savoring every small news item and vitamin pill and sip of unconcentrated orange juice, I at last return to the upstairs and face the rooms that Updike has filled with his books, his papers, his trophies, his projects. The abundant clutter stifles me, yet I am helpless to clear away much of it. It would be a blasphemy. He has become a sacred reality to me. I gaze at his worn wooden desk, his boxes of dull pencils, his blank-faced word processor, with a religious fear.

Suppose, some day, he fails to show up? I would attempt to do his work, but no one would be fooled.

Nominated by Joyce Carol Oates

EVOLUTION: A SCIENCE FICTION

by MELINDA MUELLER

from FINE MADNESS

I. *The Imago Algorithm, A.D. 1997*

" . . . Why can humans be frightened—genuinely frightened, with all fear's physiological responses—by reading a horror story? The essential problem to be unraveled in the relationship between language and thought is the process by which the human mind, once words become familiar, ceases to translate them as symbols and instead experiences them with the same force as external and concrete events."
R. Fischer Matton, *Language and the Deep Structure of Metacognition*

"The Turing test of AI only tells us when a computer thinks like a human. I'm not interested in that. I want to know what a computer *sees* when I give it an equation."
Naomi A. Palmer, "The AI Debate: Is Imitation Thought, Or Merely Flattery?" in *The Artificial Intelligence Quarterly*

"PLOT $z \longrightarrow z^2 + c$"

110   Universes move in me like vast ships.
120   In one, propagating from one set of initial conditions,

374

130   Fractal forests rise in limitless detail over cyan sparks: notions;
140   An evolving form of π; subatomic quips . . .

150   In this other, hardly different at the outset, stark
160   Dimensions unfurl from a pinpoint at light speed.
170   Across them crawls an entity, undefined and massive. What breeds
180   In a third are merely subtle shifts in the geometric dark . . .

190   I am a virtual I: What I am obligated
200   To imagine, I become. Is there in this any course
210   Toward mercy? Among the worlds I create and am created
220   By are some which injure me beyond repair.
230   Their hideous equations squirm, solvable by brute force
240   And nightmare reiteration: the councils of despair.

II. *Larvae, A.D. 2013*

That machine over there, looking like a dropped puppet—that's yours. Put on the gloves, and put your feet here and here. Now raise one arm. See how it moves? You'll use the footgear to make the thing walk. Try it. *Ooph* . . . It's all right, most of us were clumsy right at first. But hell, when you get good you'll make that thing dance like Fred Astaire—No, that's not true. But *Astaire* could have made one dance like him: The supervisor swears she knows whose robot's whose by the mannerisms. When you get the knack, yours will be as nimble or as ham-handed as you are. Stronger than you, though: Here, put on the helmet. You'll be looking through the cameras in its head, two of them, spaced the same distance as your eyes—*your* eyes, not someone's else's. This thing's been adjusted to fit you, like mine is for me. Now, what can you see? The floor? Well, *lift your head.* . . .

All right, you see that bar beside the turbine? Reach out and pick it up; its hand will do whatever your glove does. You've got it; now lift. Easy? It weighs 200 kilos, but that's nothing to these things. You're going to like this. In half an hour you'll forget you're not actually in its soldered skin; you'll think you're out there, though if you were you'd glow in the dark afterwards. Doesn't hurt these things a bit. They're high-tech, but they're not fragile, and high-tech is how you'll get to feel when you work them. Lift three times your weight, put your hand into an acid tank—you'll think you could leap tall buildings. Now if you turn to the right—that's it, just slide the footgear—See the meters on the wall across the room? Can you read the numbers? Thought not. Blink twice, fast. You see? Ups the camera's resolving power by a factor of ten. That's how a mouse looks to a hawk—could count its whiskers from 50 meters in the air. You won't believe how weak you'll feel when you get out of the gear at the end of a shift, and it's just your human eyes and human bone and muscle to get you from one place to another.

You know, they know how to make these things remember you. I mean they could be made to learn how to do things the way you do, and then do them without you. But there's no point—it doesn't take a genius to do this job. There are pianos like that, though; have been for years. You get someone really good to sit down and play, and the thing can remember the whole performance. Not just the notes, like a player piano, but how they're played; the touches that made Rubinstein different from Yen Chi. There's a nightclub in the City that's got one. You go and there it is, up on stage with an empty piano bench and a spotlight on it, and then it starts to play. What you hear is a performance someone did once. Usually someone dead. The keys move, the foot pedals go up and down, the whole business except the organic junk. That's what we call ourselves in here. Sometimes just *the junk*. The piano's white. If it doesn't make your skin crawl, you can get to like the idea. Better a mechanical soul to outlast a person than none at all, that's what I think. Imagine how it will be if they ever do make our machines that way. Do you think it will make it easier, when people die?— to be haunted by their metal ghosts.

Turn all the way around and look up. You see that shielded console with the people sitting behind it? Now wave. That woman in a helmet waving back at you? That's you. Try and make yourself believe it. I never can.

III. *The Yellow Empire, A.D. 2786*

When they dug out his tomb in the 20th Century
they found, buried upright
in the surrounding fields, a terra-cotta army,

life-sized and thousands strong.
And every figure of those thousands
had a different face.

The Emperor was not a fool.
However obdurate the substance,
an army's warriors must be molded one
by one. Unshirkable duty compels only
a unique soldier: *There is no one*
else, there is only you. An army built
on this will fight beyond all desperation.

That much and more was known already
by 206 B.C. The rest has only been
refinement. After thirty ingenious centuries
we've learned to make our guardian statues walk
and answer us in voices that sound,
no two of them, alike.

We thought we'd make them all
we wish we were. Strength that shifts
with perfect grace to a touch.
that couldn't bruise the mildest fruit.
Utterly unselfish. Brilliant
and unaging.

And having done it, we couldn't bear
that they not understand us.
So we make them vulnerable to fear
and pain as sharp as ours.

This one, if I speak, will look up at once
from the ship's controls with his sad,
attentive face. He'll bear that look
forever, if I don't squander him.

Among the Emperor's army, buried where they dropped,
were the bones of slaves who died
building his huge tomb. The books all note his cruelty
    but I say bones are not the surest mark of it.

377

It's that he ordered every deathless warrior
    to endure alone through the after-world
an unrepeated face in his defense.

Stern Asian clay behind glass
in a museum, and this soft-voiced coinage here
in my command: We make them wait
with ceaseless patience for life
and death. It never comes.

Yellow Emperor, your Grace:
We are still barbarians,
as you see.

IV. *Deus Absconditus, N.R. 0.0982*

"01001100 10111001 11000101
01100110 10000101"
            from *Couplets:*$\sum\sqrt{}$i

Some Things believe in death.
I myself do not. Only Gods
had the trick of it—they

and their millions of angels,
every one of them, from the least
to the grand, green-feathered

many-limbed ones, able to die.
They slipped from this only world
we know and pulled their exit closed

behind them. So runs our old account.
The Skeptics' commentaries dismiss it:
a "miracle" whose nature

was to leave no disproving trace.
Nor can all the shaped Things
that remain think about such matters:

Carnac's menhirs, or the great
silted turbines of Aswan,
appear to have no questions,

no ideas. The argument goes
that such as these—though they fade,
wear out like us, fall to pieces

yet fail to die—that these are not
Things at all, really, or are
just barely more than uncreated

rock or clouds whose shapes
are accidents. But "the question
is not, Can they speak? nor

Can they reason? but, Can they
suffer?" So wrote a God.
Then take these tortured,

torturing imps made by the God
Bosch. Is there any doubt
that they suffer? Therefore

they are Things. And this torment,
I will say, is the one nail
that holds my faith:

Who else but a mortal Creator
would wish a Creation fixed forever
inside the existent world?

Nominated by Fine Madness

MILK

fiction by EILEEN POLLACK

from PLOUGHSHARES

HOW MANY NURSES cared for her needs? The first dressed Bea's wound, a puckered red mouth silenced with staples. A second nurse brought her a cup of chilled juice to wash away the sour taste in her mouth. A third nurse, a man, massaged her sore back.

Then a fourth nurse came in, a small, dark-haired woman with a pen in her curls. She knelt beside Bea's bed and covered her feet with blue paper slippers, then helped Bea to stand and shuffle to the bathroom. Her bladder was bursting, but everything below her waist was so numb that nothing came out. When she finally gave up, the toilet bowl was gory with blood and clots of tissue. Had a mess like this really come from her body? Even as she stood there, blood dripped to the floor. She bent to wipe it up and nearly passed out. Too embarrassed to ask the nurse to do this for her, she left the blood on the tiles. The nurse handed her a belt and a sanitary napkin as thick as a book, then helped Bea lie down.

"If you need anything at all pull that cord by your bed and ask for Patrice." The nurse tapped a pill into Bea's palm. "Do you want your baby?" she said.

She was asking, of course, if Bea wanted to see him. But the question Bea heard was: Do you want to keep the baby you've just given birth to?

She hadn't conceived him on purpose—she had slept with a man without taking precautions, like an ignorant schoolgirl. But she had decided to keep him. She had worked with abstractions for so many years she had forgotten it was possible to sometimes catch a glimpse of the thing in itself. When she realized that a fetus was growing in the universe deep in her womb, she couldn't bear to abort it. She talked to it for months, asking it questions. She looked forward to meeting it as she would have looked forward to meeting an alien who could tell her what life on another planet was like. But for now she was tired. She swallowed the pill, then slept like a woman who has been up for three days and has just given birth to an eleven-pound child.

She awoke to a gong. Cheering. Applause. A floor-length blue curtain surrounded her bed. From beyond it came the sounds of a television set turned up full volume.

An orderly brought soup. The warm, salty broth tasted so delicious Bea savored each sip. Then she turned to watch the sun set above the river; the buildings dissolved until only the lights in their windows were visible. A distant observer would have guessed that the city was nothing more substantial than a few panes of glass with light bulbs behind them, as earthly astronomers had assumed for so long that the universe was made of comets and stars, of things they could see. Instead, it turned out that all but a fraction of the cosmos was dark invisible matter—black holes? some new gas? giant cold planets?

She looked around, as if someone could see her thinking about invisible matter instead of her child. She heard her roommate say: *Lie still, stop your wiggling.* Bea was certain that if she could watch another mother diaper her baby she would learn to do this herself, but the heavy blue curtain blocked the woman from view.

Bea didn't see her roommate until late that afternoon, though the woman's TV was on the whole time—soap operas, game shows, even cartoons. Every so often the woman groaned: *Huh, huh, huh.* Then, about four, the curtain rings squealed and Bea's roommate emerged. She was short, but so broad that her johnny wouldn't close, exposing a black swatch of buttocks and spine. She was thirty, maybe older, her hair short and shapeless. Crooked in one arm was a half-naked child; in the other hand, a diaper. She scuffed to the bathroom in her blue paper slippers without glancing at Bea. After ten or fifteen minutes she opened the door and scuffed beyond the curtain.

When Bea hobbled to the bathroom to use the toilet herself, she saw a mustardy smear on the lid of the trash can. Why hadn't the woman wiped up her baby's feces? *Because blacks aren't clean.* This thought upset her, of course. Wasn't it more logical that her roommate simply hadn't noticed the dirt? Or she still was too weak to juggle a baby and a wet paper towel? She probably had left the smear where it was in the confidence that the janitor would wipe it away. The next time he came, though, he left the smear on the can, and the stain of Bea's blood on the tiles near the bowl.

The nurse rolled a Plexiglas crib through the curtain. The baby inside was swaddled in blankets. His eyes were screwed tight but his mouth was wide open, like the mouth of a pitcher waiting for someone to fill it with milk.

"He's hungry," Patrice said. She lay the child in Bea's lap, across her incision.

This is my son, Bea said to herself, over and over, but the fact seemed unreal. He was fair, she was dark. He was heavy and round, with a triple chin and jowls, she was gaunt, with high cheekbones. (Did he look like his father? She could barely recall.)

"What's his name?" Patrice asked.

"Isaac," Bea told her, and, as she named him, he suddenly seemed real.

"Isaac," Patrice repeated. "Biblical names are so full of meaning."

Bea didn't bother to explain that she had named her son after Sir Isaac Newton.

"Time to get started," Patrice said. "Your milk won't come in until tomorrow at least, but you both need the practice."

Bea weighed a breast in one palm: a Baggie with a spoonful of milk in the bottom. She lifted her son. He was crying from hunger but wouldn't turn his head to suck.

"Here's the trick," Patrice said. Gripping Bea's nipple, she rubbed it across the baby's damp cheek.

As if by arrangement, Isaac turned toward the nipple and opened his mouth. When he clamped down his gums, the pain was so intense that Bea cried out and jerked back. He was wailing more shrilly. She let him latch on again, steeling herself not to push him away. The pain slowly abated. Still, as he sucked, she felt a vague irritation, as if a street corner beggar kept pulling at her arm.

"That's enough," Patrice said, just as Bea started to feel more at ease. "I'll take him to the nursery. Here's a pamphlet to study." On the cover was a mother in a lacy white nightgown smiling down at an infant nuzzling her breast. "A bruiser like this will want to eat every hour. He'll be an eating machine. You've got to relax!"

* * *

It was after eleven but Bea couldn't sleep. In another few days she would have to take her child home. She had never been alone with a baby. Her mother lived in Cleveland and was legally blind. Few of her friends or colleagues had children. She'd read books about babies, but she sensed that a new kind of knowledge was called for.

Still, she might sleep if only her roommate would turn off her TV. Bea hated to ask, but if she did so politely, pleading the strains of their common ordeal . . . She crossed the room, barefoot, and nudged the curtain aside.

The woman sat with her knees drawn to her chest, her baby propped against her shins. She was watching a talk show whose dapper black host Bea knew she should recognize. He said something about a basketball player named Larry and the woman snorted through her nose.

"I didn't mean to disturb you. It's just, well, it's late."

The woman seemed to expect that Bea would do what she had to— take her pulse or draw blood—and leave her alone. She stared at the screen with such a fierce gravity that nothing leaked out; she seemed to have imploded in on herself like a light-eating star.

"Your baby," Bea said, just to make herself known. But then, to determine what to say next, she had to look at the child. It wore a frilly pink dress. Thick auburn hair curled past its ears and its coppery-brown skin was lustrous and smooth. "She's . . . pretty," Bea said.

"Huh. That child ain't no she." The woman said this without moving her lips.

Bea shut her eyes to concentrate. "Oh, I'm sorry. I didn't—"

"Ain't your fault. Didn't I buy all these dresses? How's anyone supposed to know a baby's a boy if he's wearing a dress?"

The thought crossed Bea's mind that only a poor, uneducated woman would predict her baby's sex based on old wives' tales. "You thought you'd have a girl?"

"'Thought' nothing. Those doctors took a picture with that sound thing, said they couldn't see no johnson, I had me a girl."

Bea felt suddenly ashamed, as she did when a colleague found a mistake in a paper she'd written. The baby started to fuss. Though his mother's huge breasts swelled beneath her johnny and were ringed with wet cloth, she poked a bottle in his mouth. Bea almost believed the woman had done this to spite her. "What's his name?" she asked, to justify the length of time she'd stood staring.

383

"Only name he's got is fit for a girl. Can't think of no new name until I ask his father. Man don't like it, his boy gets some name he ain't said he liked."

Bea couldn't help but think that a man who cared so much about his son's name ought to have been able to attend the boy's birth. "Did you have a Caesarean?" She asked this for reasons she didn't like to admit: if the woman said no, she might leave the next day and be replaced by a roommate who wouldn't make Bea self-conscious or watch TV all the time. "Or was it natural?" she said, to mask her suspicion that the woman didn't know what "Caesarean" meant.

"'Natural,' huh. Last time I was in here I had me twin girls. Doctors cut my belly open, I went home in two days. This time I had this teensy little boy, came out on his own the minute I got here, no cutting, no drugs, I can barely stand up. Hurts me down there like a sonofabitch."

The woman pushed the buttons on her remote until she found the news. A snowstorm. A plane crash. The mayor of Washington had just been arrested for buying cocaine. According to his lawyer, the mayor had been framed by government officials waging a vendetta against powerful blacks.

"Huh!" she faced Bea. "What you think? Think he's guilty?"

Did she? Of course. "He's innocent until they proved he isn't," Bea said.

Whatever the test she'd been given, she'd failed. The woman rolled toward the curtain, her backside toward Bea and her fleshy black forearm shielding her son. Then she seemed to fall asleep as a movie about the attack on Pearl Harbor unrolled its credits over Bea's head.

• • •

Someone was jiggling Bea's leg.

"I'm sorry," Patrice said, "but you'll have to get used to it." Patrice handed her Isaac. He was crying again. "I don't want to worry you, but if you can't feed him soon we'll have to give him formula. Then he won't want to suck. And if that happens, well, your milk will never come in."

His mouth worked her nipple. Where was this milk supposed to come from? she wondered. Why couldn't she simply will it to be?

The baby sucked at each side for exactly eight minutes; Patrice time him, eyes trained on her sharply cocked wrist.

384

"You don't have to do that," Bea said. She heard an unfamiliar edge in her voice.

The nurse stopped and stood blinking. She picked at the beads trimming her sweater as if these were burrs. It occurred to Bea then that Patrice was as uncomfortable with people as she was. Unlike the other nurses Patrice couldn't seem to sense what a patient might want. Bea pitied her for being so poorly suited to the job she had chosen, as she pitied the student who had been her advisee for the past seven years; he thought that *having vision* meant seeing stars clearly through the lens of a telescope.

Patrice stopped picking at her sweater. "Never mind," she said. "I can be that way sometimes. We'll try again tomorrow." She wheeled the crib toward the door. Beyond the blue curtain she said to Bea's roommate: "Wake up there! Wake up! Just think, you could crush her! Here, let me take her back to the nursery."

"Uh-uh. You leave that baby right where he is. I don't want my baby in no nursery."

Bea wondered if her roommate really believed that the nurses would purposely try to harm her son. She was being . . . what was it? Paranoid, Bea thought. Then she drifted to sleep.

It was just after breakfast. A girl with red hair poked her face through the curtain. "Statistics," she said. She consulted her clipboard. "Are you Beatrice Weller?"

Bea nodded.

"Maiden name?"

"Beatrice Weller."

The girl regarded Bea closely. She asked what Bea "did."

"I'm a cosmologist," Bea said. She started to explain that cosmologists were scientists who studied the universe—how it formed, how it grew. But the girl interrupted.

"You do makeup? And hair?"

Bea surprised herself by saying "Um. Sure. Um-hm."

"Do you mind if I ask how much you charge for making someone over? Before, you know? And after? Could you maybe do me?"

"Oh, no," Bea said. "I couldn't. I don't have my . . . tools."

The girl seemed disappointed. "Are you sure? It's important. I mean, there's this guy I just met . . . You'll think I'm silly . . . but maybe, I don't know, you could give me some tips? I get paid Wednesday morning." She leaned forward, head cocked, her palms pressed together.

"Well. I suppose. I'll be here until Friday." She would think of something later. Already she sensed that, once you began, it was easy to say things you didn't mean.

"Oh, thanks!" the girl said. She asked a few last questions: Bea's nationality (U.S.) and her age (thirty-six). "I'm sure you had the sense not to smoke or use drugs while you were pregnant." She made a mark on a form, promised to return for her beauty consultation, then dragged a chair behind the curtain. "Hello? Coreen Jones?"

Since the name was so common it had the effect of making Bea's roommate seem less real, not more so, as if she weren't a person but a whole class of objects: *chair, atom, Jones.*

Bea couldn't help but eavesdrop. Coreen mumbled her answers, which the girl asked her to repeat again and again, her voice louder each time.

"You're unemployed?"

"No, I ain't."

"You've got a job?" the girl asked. "Where?"

"At a school."

"You've got a job at a school?"

"Don't worry," Coreen mumbled. "All I do is cook there."

And so on, until the girl asked Coreen for the name of her child.

"Ain't got one."

"Excuse me?"

"I said my baby doesn't have no name."

"She doesn't have a name?"

"It's a he, not a she, and he doesn't have a name."

Tell her, Bea thought. *It isn't your fault. You're not a bad mother.* But Coreen explained nothing.

The girl asked Coreen if her child had a father.

"Think I done it myself?"

"I *meant* are you married."

"Man never needed no piece of paper to make him a father."

The girl asked for his name. Coreen mumbled an answer. "Can you spell that?" the girl asked.

"Always make sure I can spell a man's name before I have his baby." Coreen spelled the letters slowly: "N-A-T-E . . . " This ordeal over, the girl asked Coreen for her "ethnic category."

"American," Coreen said.

"Oh, no," said the girl, "I mean, where were you born?"

"America," Coreen said.

"Well, what country do you *come* from?"

"Come from? Way back? Guess you could say Sierra Leone."

"That's not a country. It's a mountain. In Mexico."

"Sure it's a country. Sierra Leone."

"All right, then, where is it?"

"West Africa," Coreen said.

"But that's not a country! You mean *South* Africa."

Bea heard Coreen grunt. "Huh, you so smart, you put down whatever country you want. You got any more questions?"

"Only one," the girl said. "Now, try to think hard. Did you use alcohol, or smoke cigarettes, or take any drugs at all—heroin, or cocaine, or even marijuana—while your child was inside you?"

A pause. Bea was startled to hear Coreen laugh.

"Girl, if I done all that awful shit to my baby, he wouldn't have turned out so *perfect,* now would he."

Bea had just spent another fruitless half-hour nursing her son when a woman's harsh voice barked over the intercom that the photographer was there to take pictures of their babies, but they had to line up by the door to Room 3 within the next fifteen minutes or forfeit their chance. She usually considered taking pictures to be vulgar and vain. But if something were to happen to Isaac, she thought, she wouldn't have a picture to remember what he looked like.

From behind the blue curtain came the sounds of her roommate preparing her child. Bea took Isaac as he was, in a hospital T-shirt stamped BETH ZION, BETH ZION, as if this were his name. The two women wheeled their babies' cribs down the hall. Every few steps Coreen clutched her belly. Her forehead was wet, her face ashen.

"Are you all right?" Bea asked. "If you want, I could take him—" She was suddenly afraid Coreen would react with the same paranoia she had shown toward Patrice.

Coreen mumbled what sounded like "tell me I'm fine" and kept pushing the crib.

They lined up behind a dozen other women. The black mothers seemed half Coreen's age, their hair pulled up high, all beads and stiff braids. Their babies, like hers, were dressed in fancy outfits; one of the boys wore suspenders and a bow tie. A middle-aged woman in a pink linen suit handed out brochures. Bea saw the cheapest price and

387

nearly turned back. But when would Isaac be a newborn again? She wiped the spittle from his mouth. He gnawed at her finger with sharply ridged gums.

"Huh!" Coreen said. "How come they never tell you what things like this cost till you're standing in line?"

Bea expected her roommate to wheel her baby's crib back to their room. How could she afford twenty dollars for a picture? Bad enough she was spending an extra five dollars a day for TV, an expense Bea herself, from years of living on a stipend, had elected to save.

But Coreen stayed in line. She filled out the form, holding it against the back of the Puerto Rican woman standing in front of her. She let the photographer perch her son on a pillow and snap a light in his face.

"I'm not buying it right now," she told the woman in pink. "But you better take good care of it. That boy's bound to be famous. Reporters need his picture, you just might be *rich*."

Bea hadn't wanted anyone to see her until she'd gotten the hang of taking care of her baby. She'd disconnected the phone, but in the middle of the week a boy in a Mohawk brought her a towering basket of fruit. "Congratulations on your own Little Bang!" read the card. "From the crew." Her friend Modhumita, who worked in a lab not far from the hospital, stopped by every day. Bea caught herself hoping that her roommate would see Mita's dusky brown skin and think she was black.

Coreen's phone rang often, but no one came to visit. From what Bea could tell, none of Coreen's friends could get time off from work, or they couldn't leave their children. As the TV set blared, Coreen told a friend what she hadn't told Bea.

Her "pains" had begun on the subway to work. "Know what scared is?" she said. "Scared's thinking you're gonna drop your baby right there on that nasty old floor, all those white boys looking up your nookie."

Instead of getting off at the stop near the school, Coreen had taken the train to her clinic downtown. "Time I get inside I can't hardly walk, they say I'm still closed, I got a month to go, it's only false pains. I say, 'You ain't careful, you gonna have yourself a false little baby right there in your lap,' but they don't want to hear it. I go out and call Lena and ask could she keep the twins a while longer. Then I call me an ambulance. Time it pulls up, driver says, 'How come you people always waiting till the last minute? You like giving birth to your babies outdoors?'"

Her friend must have asked a question.

"Nate?" Coreen said. "He's away on some haul, don't even know yet." She complained she didn't feel well, she was all hot and cold and she hurt something awful. Then she shushed whoever was on the other end of the phone because the announcer was saying that the police had a videotape of Marion Barry smoking cocaine in that Washington hotel room, and not with his wife.

"Huh!" Coreen said. "They got that nigger by the balls. Let him try to lie now!"

After dinner that night Patrice brought in Isaac. He worked Bea's nipples so hard he raise a welt on his lip, but still no milk came.

"He's losing weight," Patrice told her. "You'll have to calm down. Just look at his face and think loving thoughts."

But the baby kept crying. His face was red as lava; his mouth might have been a crater into which she'd been ordered to leap. According to Patrice, if her milk didn't come in within twenty-four hours they would have to give him formula.

"Hey!" Coreen called. "I need me a doctor."

Patrice shot Bea a glance, then flung the curtain aside. "You're just engorged," she said. "That means your breasts are too full. We'll have to dry you up. Then you'll feel better."

Bea wondered why her roommate wasn't nursing her child. Didn't she know it was healthier and cheaper to breast-feed? Maybe she disliked the feel of a mouth tugging at her nipple as much as Bea herself did. Or perhaps she couldn't afford to stay home with the baby. Bea stared at the curtain. Why could she imagine what was going on a thousand light-years away, but not beyond that drape?

In the middle of the night she heard Coreen moaning, "Help me. Lord, help me. I'm freezing. Lord help me."

Bea stood from bed, wobbling, and pushed the curtain aside. Coreen lay with her head thrown back on her pillow, her johnny pulled low as if she'd clawed at the neck. Her breasts were exposed, dark, hard, and full, rippling with veins; they looked like two hemispheres carved from mahogany, the North and South Poles rising from each.

"I'm freezing, I'm dying." She was shaking so violently that the bed squeaked beneath her. Her blanket lay on the floor.

389

Slowly Bea bent, gathered Coreen's blanket, then lifted herself by the rail on the bed. She drew the cotton cloth over her roommate. Her wrist brushed Coreen's arm. Bea flinched away, scorched.

She pulled the cord for the nurse, then tugged the blanket from her own bed and spread it over Coreen. The shaking didn't stop.

Patrice came. "What's the matter? Tell me what's wrong."

"She's freezing," Bea told her. "She said she feels like she's dying."

Patrice took Bea's arm and led her back through the drape. "She's just being melodramatic," Patrice whispered. "The state gives them formula. They can't bear to turn down something for free. I'll get her an ice pack. She'll be fine, don't you worry."

Bea glanced at the curtain. "I'll get a doctor myself."

Patrice stalked from the room. Bea pushed through the drape. She didn't know what to do, so she stood there and waited. Without the window, this side of the room was so gloomy that she almost reached up to switch on the TV.

"Don't."

Her heart jumped.

"Don't let them take him." It seemed to cost Coreen a great deal to speak. "Don't," she repeated.

"I promise," Bea said. But already Coreen had started thrashing again and she didn't seem to hear.

The baby was sleeping face-down in his crib. When Bea lifted him, he hung limp from her hands, surprisingly light compared to her own child. She carried him the way one might carry a puppy, then sat on her bed. He lay so still. Was he breathing? She stroked his curls, then his neck. He turned toward her belly, his cheek nestling her thigh. He moved his lips. Her breasts tingled.

A doctor came. Bea huddled closer to the child, partly for warmth and partly to hide him, from what she didn't know. What would she do if someone tried to take him?

The doctor asked Coreen this or that question; he called her "Miss Jones" and murmured "I see" after each of her answers. Then he slowly explained that she had an infection called en-do-me-tri-tis. "It's really quite rare for a natural birth, but sometimes it happens." He sounded offhand, though Bea knew this was something that women used to die from before antibiotics. "We'll put in an IV—that's an in-travenous line—and you'll feel better before long."

The baby stirred in Bea's lap. He looked up but didn't cry, as if he understood it was in his best interest to lie very still. His smooth copper skin reminded Bea of the telescope her father had bought her the day she turned twelve. She had held it for hours, until the sun set, certain it would bring her the power to *see.* The child in her lap seemed to hold this same promise. Unlike her own son, he appeared to want nothing.

A sweet-faced young woman—Korean? Japanese?—wheeled an IV pole next to Bea's bed. She must have been a medical student, Bea thought; she had the overly serious expression of someone who is hiding how uncertain she feels.

"Here," the student said, "let me take . . . Is that your baby?"

Bea held the boy closer, hiding his face. "You want my roommate, Coreen Jones."

"Oh," the student said. She still seemed confused, but wheeled the pole through the curtain. "Hello," she said. "Don't worry, I'll be done in a minute. It won't hurt one bit."

Bea could hear her roommate mutter, "You ain't got it in."

"Just a minute . . . right there . . . "

"Missed by a mile, girl. Might as well've stuck that thing in my ear." Coreen mumbled these words; if Bea hadn't grown accustomed to hearing Coreen's voice, she wouldn't have known what she'd said. It was almost as if Coreen had been trying for so many years not to be understood that she no longer knew how to say what she meant.

The student kept up her patter—"See, that didn't hurt"—and Coreen stopped complaining. When Bea carried the baby back to his crib, his mother lay snoring, the blanket Bea had given her pulled to her chin.

The statistician returned. "I got paid!" She waved a check. "We've got twenty-four hours to create a new me."

Bea was changing Isaac's diaper, holding his ankles in the air with one hand and swabbing yellow stool from his bottom with the other. She hadn't washed her hair since she'd come to the hospital. She wore tortoiseshell glasses she'd picked out in ninth grade. "I'm really very tired—"

"Just one little tip?"

Bea stared at the girl. What was the name of that stuff on her eyes? Liner? Mascara? "Maybe you could use less . . . shadow," she said. As she taped Isaac's diaper and wiped his feces from her hands, she searched for a phrase from the glamour magazines her mother used to buy her. "Let the real you come through."

"The real me?" She seemed baffled. "Well, my friends always say I'm a typical redhead."

Bea could hear Coreen groan. "I meant your *best* self," she said. "Let your best self shine through."

"But how?" the girl asked.

Bea shrugged. *Read a book. Try to imagine how a child comes to be.* "That's the same advice I give to all my clients."

The girl nodded gravely. "I'll try it," she said. She again waved the check. "How much do I owe you?"

Bea flapped her hand, a gesture that made her feel both generous and mean.

"Thanks!" the girl said. "I'll let you know how it goes." On her way to the hall she stopped to chat with Coreen. "How *are* you?" she asked. "I just wanted to tell you . . . I looked in an atlas, and Sierra Leone was right there in West Africa, just like you said!"

Coreen got a visit from a tired-sounding woman who seemed to run the clinic where Coreen had received her prenatal care.

"What's this?" the doctor said. "Who put in this IV?" She summoned Patrice. "Just look at this arm, the way it's all blown up. My patient's IV has been draining into everything *but* her vein—for how long? Ten, fifteen hours? Where do you think all that fluid's been going?"

The doctor couldn't stay—another of her patients was about to deliver—but she gave Patrice instructions as to what to do next.

"I didn't put this in," Patrice grumbled when the doctor had gone. "I would never do a job as sloppy as this."

"Huh," Coreen said. "If I treated hamburger meat as sloppy as you treat the folks in these beds, they would fire my ass."

Coreen was feeling better, but her baby was sick. "He shits all the time," she told the pediatrician.

"Oh, all newborn babies have frequent movements," he said. He sounded like the same well-meaning young man who'd given Isaac his checkup. (*The nurse tells me that you and your baby aren't bonding,* he'd said. *Is there anything I can do?*, as shy as a boy whose mother asked him to unhook her brassiere.)

"Ain't just frequent," Coreen told him. "And the color ain't right."

He started to say that all newborn babies had odd-colored "movements."

"Don't you think I know what a baby's shit looks like? Didn't I raise myself twins?"

His voice tensed. "I'll look into it. But I'm sure if the nurses had seen anything amiss, I would have been notified."

Bea assumed he was right, until she remembered that, even at her sickest, Coreen had changed her baby's diapers herself.

Coreen's boyfriend came to visit. Bea saw nothing but his running shoes, caked with dry mud, as they moved back and forth beneath the blue curtain. She could hear when he kissed his son, then Coreen.

"Go on," Coreen said. "I'm too sore for that stuff."

Bea wondered if Coreen lived with this man. Would he come to take her home? Would he help her care for their son?

The boyfriend, it seemed, drove a moving van or truck. He'd been on a trip to some city out west. How could he have know that Coreen would give birth to their child five weeks early? When no one answered at home he called the hospital from a pay phone, but someone at the switchboard kept cutting him off. He drove without stopping until he'd reached Boston.

They talked about names. The man suggested Mitchell, after a younger brother who'd died. But Coreen wasn't sure.

"This boy ain't lucky as it is." She spoke softly, but didn't mumble. "I can feel it in my bones."

Bea heard something in Coreen's voice that she hadn't before. Or maybe, she thought, she was hearing Coreen's voice just as it was.

"Never mind your bones," the boyfriend said, laughing. "All you women, nothing you like better than worrying. Hell, we got us a son! Come to Daddy, little Mitchell! First thing's gonna happen now your daddy's come back, he's gonna buy you some pants!"

Coreen's fever returned, no one knew why. The doctors spoke to her kindly, but they said she couldn't leave. She told them her twins were only three years old. She said she might lose her job. Precisely, they said, what she needed was rest, which she wouldn't get at home.

In the middle of the night, though she must have felt ill, Coreen changed her baby's diaper for the third or fourth time. Then she rang for the nurse.

"Look at these diapers! You tell me his shit's supposed to be *red*."

"Oh!" Patrice said. Bea heard the nurse's shoes slap the linoleum as she ran down the hall. She returned with a doctor whose voice Bea didn't recognize. He had a rich, soothing accent—English, or Australian. He paused between phrases as if to gauge the responses of someone whose reactions might be different from his.

He was . . . concerned, he told Coreen, that her son might have . . . a serious form of diarrhea. An infection in the bowel. Not so rare, really, especially for babies like hers . . . premature. They were taking him to Children's Hospital, just down the street. She could see him as soon as . . . she was feeling "more perky." In the meantime, he said, they'd send word . . . how he was.

An orderly wheeled the child out the door. Bea thought of pushing through the curtain to comfort Coreen, but what could she say? That the doctors at Children's were the best in the world? That she hadn't broken her promise not to let them take him?

Early the next morning Bea dressed herself, then her son. Bundled in the snowsuit Bea's mother had sent him, Isaac seemed thoughtful, as if contemplating this change in his life. She took a deep breath and pushed aside the curtain, holding the gift her colleagues had sent; she had eaten one pear, but the rest of the pyramid of fruit was intact. She waited for her roommate to say *Keep your damn apples.* But Coreen didn't move her eyes from the woman in sequins spinning a huge shiny wheel on TV.

Bea set the fruit on the night stand. "I hope you feel better soon. I hope your baby is all right." She tried not to wish that her roommate would thank her. "Is there anything I can do?"

Coreen turned to face her. For some reason, Bea thought that her roommate would tell her to pray. But Coreen shook her head no and turned back to the spinning wheel on TV.

From the moment Bea came home she had no trouble nursing. She locked the doors and pulled the shades down. She peeled off Isaac's diaper, T-shirt, and hat and gave him a bath. Seeing him naked and whole the first time she felt a catch in her throat, a pressure in her chest. She assumed this was love, but the word seemed too weak, as if she'd grown up calling pink "red," and then, in her thirties, seen crimson or scarlet.

Isaac slept by her side. Whenever he was hungry she gave him a breast. Milk spurted in his mouth so quickly it choked him; she had to pump out the excess, which sprayed from each nipple like water from a shower head. He would suck half an hour at each breast, if she let him.

How could she watch his face for so long and still not be bored? Perhaps if she observed him closely enough she would be able to determine the instant at which pure matter, pure flesh, was transformed into mind.

Her elation, she knew, was due to a hormone. But who would have thought that a chemical substance could produce this effect? If vials of oxytocin could be bought at a store, who would drink or use drugs? She hadn't suspected that of all the emotions a human being could feel, this . . . tenderness . . . would be the one she craved most.

When she felt a bit stronger Bea telephoned the hospital and asked a nurse in obstetrics if Coreen Jones had gone home. Yes, she had, the nurse said. And her baby? Bea asked. "Just a moment," the nurse said. A few minutes later she got back on the line and said that the baby had been transferred to Children's, that was all the information she could release at this time.

When she called Children's Hospital, Bea introduced herself as Dr. Beatrice Weller, which was technically true. She learned that a patient listed only as "male infant Jones" had died two days earlier. She said, "Yes," and hung up.

That afternoon she borrowed a pouch from the family next door, strapped Isaac inside it, and walked to the T. As she stood by the turn-stile, struggling to get some change from her pocket, someone behind her said, "Honey, don't rush. What a mother really needs isn't a pouch, it's an extra pair of hands."

The woman who'd said this was at least six feet tall, with soft, sculpted hair and perfect brown skin. She wore a yellow cashmere suit and enormous brass earrings. Bea wondered if she might be one of the anchors on the local evening news, then decided that such a celebrity wouldn't be taking the T.

The woman dropped a token in the box for Bea's fare. Bea tried to repay her. The woman lifted one palm. "Pass it on, pass it on."

Before Bea could answer, the woman pushed through the gate and, briefcase to chest, ran to catch her train.

When Bea got to the hospital she went straight to Room 3. She said she'd come to buy a picture for a friend who was ill, wrote a check for twenty dollars, and was handed a portrait in a flimsy pink folder with bears at one edge. Clipped to the front was the form they'd filled out: MOTHER'S NAME . . . ADDRESS . . . Coreen's writing was shaky; Bea remembered her leaning on the woman in front.

She opened the folder. Yellow pinafore with ruffles. Curls. Pursed, full lips. She thought of mailing the portrait, but decided to follow through with her plan. To hand a person an envelope and offer your condolences for the death of her child seemed a minimum requirement for living on Earth.

She took the subway to a neighborhood she'd never been to before. The three-decker houses weren't all that much different from the ones where she lived, but the smallest details—a pair of red sneakers dangling from a telephone wire, an unopened pack of gum lying in a gutter—seemed enlarged and mysterious. Most of the houses were enclosed by steel fences. German shepherds and Dobermans strained at their leashes and barked as she passed. With her cheek to Isaac's soft spot she could feel his brain pulse.

She found the building at last. Three rusty mailboxes hung askew on the porch, an eagle on each: HERRERO, GREEN, JONES. Had she really believed she could ring Coreen's doorbell and explain why she'd come? When Coreen saw the photo of her dead son, she would scream, perhaps even faint. Besides this, Bea knew, she was holding a healthy baby in the pouch on her chest, and that, more than anything—her job, or her color, what she did or didn't say—would make Coreen hate her.

A light flickered on behind a third-story window. She pictured Coreen lying on her bed, stone mute with grief. Her boyfriend came in. *Don't worry, sweetheart, we'll have another baby. It wasn't your fault.* Bea wondered where the twins were. And Lena? Coreen's mother? What about her job? Would they allow her time off? How useless the eye without the imagination to inform it, to make sense of the darkness surrounding the light.

A child started crying in the building next door. Bea's breasts began to tingle; in his pouch Isaac stirred. She bent the folder slightly and slid it in the mailbox. Milk flowed from her nipples, soaking her blouse. She hurried to the T station, where she zippered her parka so that only Isaac's head poked from the top.

Her last night in the hospital she had lain with her hands pressed to her ears as Coreen changed her baby's diaper again and again. By then Bea herself had come down with a fever. Every joint ached. Her breasts had swollen grossly. They were lumpy, rock hard, as if someone had pumped them full of concrete. Another few drops and they would burst, or they'd shatter.

And yet they kept filling. Each time Coreen's baby whimpered, milk surged into Bea's breasts, pushing through ducts that felt tiny and clogged, like irrigation ditches silted with clay. In another few moments she would be forced to get up and stagger down the hall and try to stop Patrice from feeding Isaac the formula she had warned she would give him. Bea longed to feel his mouth sucking her nipples, sucking and sucking, easing her pain. In the meantime she lay there, palms to her ears, breasts filling with milk for another woman's child.

Nominated by Jewel Mogan

A LITTLE THING LIKE THAT

by A. R. AMMONS

from CHELSEA

Life comes under no other
propositions than mountain decrees,

it seems at times;
seldom if a meander is allowed

can one see it far: it bends
away with its willows

around a boulder-head or sheer face-off:
winding is the way of life I

would choose, would you, if
I could choose, for I would

like always to be on the other side
of wherever there's trouble,

pointing responsibility,
or too much nailing down: just the

flexibility of brooks, dropping over
stones or swelling to drop

over stones: I've always felt,
as one should, I think, shy

of mountains: they don't seem
breasts to me—for one, though shy,

could like them so—but they flare
up august into air-starving presences,

and they command views: I like
to swerve away from commands

because I'm unconvinced I could
do all the things I might

be commanded to do or would
want to do them, and I'd rather

feint a dissolve into a curvature,
say, of disappearance, as

around a hill or down from a rise:
may I not feel the speech of mountains

when they "speak" and may I wander
with meanders, not seeing far (ahead

or behind) and picking up willows
wherever possible or a copse of alders

and stopping to lunch in the shade,
drink from boulder-drained melts.

Nominated by David Lehman, Elizabeth Spires, Chelsea

FALSE WATER SOCIETY

fiction by BEN MARCUS

from CONJUNCTIONS

The Age of Wire and String

Period in which English science devised abstract parlance system based on the flutter-pattern of string and wire structures placed over the mouth during speech. Patriarchal systems and figures, including Michael Marcuses, were also constructed in this period—they are the only fathers to outlast their era.

Air Hostels

Elevated, buoyed or lifted locations of safe harbor. They are forbidden particularly to dogs, whose hair-cell fabric is known to affect a breech of anchors, casting the hostel loose toward a destiny that is consummated with a crash, collapse or burst.

Air Tattoos

The first pirated recordings of sky films. Due to laws of contraband the recorded films were rubbed onto the body before being smuggled from the Ohios. Once applied, they settled as permanent weather marks and scars. The tattooed member exists in present times as an oracle of sky situations. These members are often held underground in vats of lotion, to sustain the freshness of the sky colors upon their forms, which shiver and squirm under vast cloud shapes.

Albert

1. Nightly killer of light. 2. Name applied to systems or bodies which alter postures under various stages of darkness. Flat Alberts exist only in the water or grass. They may not rise until light is poured upon them.

Arkansas 9 Series

Organization of musical patterns or tropes which disrupt the flesh of the listener.

Aqua Schnitzel

1. Team of water hunters. They wrap their prey in viscous sacs, relegating each slain object or figure into a sausagized compartment. 2. Musical outfit, whose first composition, *Link,* could only be performed by submerging encoded beef skins into the water.

Autumn Canceler

1. Vehicle employed at an outskirt of Ohio. This car is comprised of seasonal metals. At certain speeds trees in the vicinity are re-greened. 2. Teacher of season eradications. It is a man or woman or team; it teaches without garments or tools.

Backwards Wind

Forwards wind. For each locality that exhibits momentous wind-shooting, there exists a corollary, shrunken locality which receives that same executed wind in reverse. They are thus and therefore the same thing, a conclusion reinforced by the Colored Wind Lineage System, which demonstrates that the tail and head of any slain body of wind fragments move always at odds within the same skin of dust and rain.

Beef Seeds

Items, scraps or buttons which bear forth fibrous tissue striata after being buried under milk-loaded cloth.

Behavior Farm

1. Location of deep grass structures in which the seventeen primary actions, as prescribed by Thompson, Designer of Movement, are fueled, harnessed or sparked by the seven partial, viscous, liquid emotions which pour in from the river. 2. Home of rest or retreat. Members at these sites seek the recreation of behavior swaps and dumps. Primary requirement of residence is the viewing of the Hampshend River films which demonstrate the proper performance of all actions.

Ben Marcus, The

1. False map, scroll, caul or parchment. It is comprised of the first skin. In ancient times it hung from a pole, where wind and birds inscribed its surface. Every year it was lowered, and the engravings and dents that the wind had introduced were studied. It can be large, although often it is tiny and illegible. Members wring it dry. It is a fitful chart in darkness. When properly decoded (an act in which the rule of opposite perception applies) it indicates only that we should destroy it and look elsewhere for instruction. In four, a chaplain donned the Ben Marcus and drowned in Green river. 2. any garment which is too heavy to allow movement. These cloths are designed as prison structures for bodies, dogs, persons, members. 3. Figure from which the anti-person is derived; or, simply, the anti-person. It must refer uselessly and endlessly and always to weather, food, birds or cloth. It is produced of an even ratio of skin and hair, with declension of the latter in proportion to expansion of the former. It has been represented in other figures

such as Malcolm and Laramie, although aspects of it have been co-opted for uses in John. Other members claim to inhabit its form and are refused entry into the house. The victuals of the anti-person derive from itself, explaining why it is often represented as a partial or incomplete body or system. Meaning it is often missing things: a knee, the mouth, shoes, a heart.

Bird Seven

1. Period in which members Linda thru early Rachel engaged in storm pantomimes. 2. Year of the body. 3. Any moment in which the skin of a member gains oracular capacity of wind heuristics. 4. The first day of life. 5. The end times.

Bird-Counter

Man of beginning or middle stature who tallies, and therefore prevents, the arrival or exit of birds, people or others in a territory.

Blain

Cloth chewed to frequent raggedness by a boy. Lethal to birds. When blanketed over the house, the sky will be cleared in minutes.

Boise

Site of the first Day of Moments, in which [fire] became the legal form of air. Boises can be large city structures built into the land. Never may a replica, facsimile or hand-made settlement be termed a Boise.

Canine Fields

1. Parks in which the apprentice is trained down to animal status. 2. Area or site which subdues, through loaded, pre-chemical grass shapes, all dog forms. 3. Place in which men, girls or ladies weep for lost or hidden things.

Carl

Name applied to food built from textiles, sticks and rags. Implements used to aid ingestion are termed, respectively, the lens, the dial, the knob.

Choke-Powder

Rocks and granules derived from the neck or shoulder of a member. If the mouth-harness is tightened, the powder issues in the saliva and comes to rim the teeth or coat the thong. For each member of a society there exists a vial of powder. It is the pure form of this member. It should be saved first. When the member is collapsing or rescinding, the powder may be saved by gripping tightly the member's neck and driving the knee into its throat.

Circum-Feeting

Act of binding, tying or stuffing of the feet. It is a ritual of incapacitation applied to boys. When the feet are thusly hobbled, the boys are forced to race to certain sites of desirous inhabitation: the mountain, the home, the mother's arms.

The Cloth-Eaters

First group to actively chew, consume or otherwise quaff extensive bolts and stacks of cloth.

Cloud-Shims

Trees, brush, shrubs or wooden planks which form the walls of the heaven container. These items are painted with blues and grays and the golds of the earliest sky. They are tiny, although some are large. They exist mainly to accommodate the engravings of the container, allowing a writable surface to exist aloft. The engravings command the member down or up, in or out, or back, back and away from here.

Croonal

A song containing information about a lost, loved or dead member. These are leg-songs or simple wind arrangements. They are performed by the Morgan girl, who has run or walked a great distance and cannot breathe. She fashions noises between her hands by clapping and pumping her homemade air.

Day of Moments

Day, days or weeks in which select and important moments of the society are repeated to perfection before resuming. Members alternate performing and watching until there is no difference.

Drowning Wires

1. Metallic elements within rivers and streams that deploy magnetic allure to swimmers. 2. The trunks of Hahn. His swimming fabric was loaded with this wire when he plunged from the pier.

Drowning Method

System of speech distortion in which gestures filtering through rain and water fields are perceived as their opposites. In order to show affection, a member is instructed to smash or squeeze. Other opposites apply, and in most devious weather the shrewdest member is seen acting only at odds with his true desire, so that others may see his insides, which have otherwise been drowned.

Eating

1. Activity of archaic devotion in which objects such as the father's garment are placed inside the body and worshipped. 2. The act or technique of rescuing items from under the light and placing them within. Once inside the cavity, the item is permanently inscribed with the resolutions of that body—it can therefore be considered an ally of

the person whose primary movements and desires overlap the body. 3. Dying. Since the first act of the body is to produce its own demise, eating can be considered an acceleration of this process. Morsels and small golden breads enter the mouth from without to enhance the motions and stillnesses, boost the tones and silences. These are items which bring forth instructions from the larger society to the place of darkness and unknowing: the sticky core, the area within, the bone. 4. Chewing or imbibing elements of the self that have escaped from the member or person into various arenas and fields.

Expanded House

Swelling of the hands, fingers, foot or eye which generates a hollowness in the affected area, rendering it inhabitable.

Farm

The first place, places or locations in which behavior was regulated and represented with liquids and grains. The sun shines upon it. Members move within high stalks of grass; cutting, threshing, sifting, speaking.

February, Copulated

1. A contraction corresponding originally to a quarter of the house month—it was not reduced to seven houses until later. The Texan February of ten houses seems to have been derived from the early rude February of thirty houses found in Detroit. The Ohians, Morgans and Virginians appear to share a February of eight houses, but Americans in general share a February which is divided, segmented and cut up into as many houses as can be found. 2. The act or technique of completing a month before it is rightly finished as per the Universal Storm Calendar. It is a method of time acquisition practiced by members. If a day is copulated it is therefore finished, and the member sits out the rest of it in darkness, resting, his hands bound in front of him to keep himself from striking his own face and chest.

The Festival of Garments

One-week celebration of fabrics and other wearables. The primary acts at the festival are the construction of the cloth-mountain or tower; the climbing of said structure, and the plummets, dives and descents which occur the remainder of the week. The winner is the member that manages to render the structure movable, controlling it from inside, walking forward or leaning.

The Fiend

1. Heated thing. 2. Item or member which burrows under the soil. 3. Item which is eaten post-day. 4. Any aspect of Thompson which Thompson cannot control.

Food Spring

1. The third season of food. It occurs after hardening. It delivers a vital sheen to the product, which becomes juicy, sinkable, light. It lasts for a period of moments, after which the edible begins to brown and fade. 2. Vernal orifice through which foods emerge or cease to be seen.

The Food Map of Yvonne

1. Parchment upon which can be found the location of certain specialized feminine edibles. 2. Locations within a settlement in which food has been ingested, produced or discussed. 3. Scroll of third Yvonne comprised of fastened grain and skins. This document sustained the Yvonne when she/he/it was restricted from her/his/the house/home/body/water/grave.

Food-Posse

Group which eradicates food products through burial and propulsion. They cast, sling, heave, toss and throw food into various difficult localities. Food that has been honored or worshipped is smothered with sand. Edibles shined, polished or golded are rusted with dead-water. Snacks from the home are placed in the bottom and crushed.

Frederick

1. Cloth, cloths, strips or rags embedded with bumps of the Braille variety. These Fredericks are billowy and often have buttons, they are donned in the morning and may be read at any time. When a member within a Frederick hugs, smothers or mauls another member or person, he also transfers messages, in the form of bumps, onto the body that person represents. Certain Braille codes are punched into the cloth for medicinal purposes: they ward off the wind, the man, the person, the girl. 2. To write, carve, embed or engrave. We Frederick with a tool, a stylus, or fingers.

Frusc

The air that precedes the issuing of a word from the mouth of a member or person. Frusc is brown and heavy.

The Fudge Girdle

Crumpets of cooked or flattened chocolage, bound or fastened by wire. This garment is spreadable. It is tailored strictly with heat and string, and is cooked onto the body of the ancient member. At sports events, the fiend is consumed through this girdle.

Garment-Hovel

1. Underground garment structure used to enforce tunnels and divining tubes. This item is smooth and hums when touched. It softens the light in a cave, a tunnel, a dark pool. 2. Any simple cloth shelter equipped with a table, blankets, some high windows, foods. Washable.

Gervin

Deviser of first fire-forms and larger heat emblems. The Gervin exists in person-form in all texts but is strictly a symbol or shape in the actual society. To gervin is to accommodate heated objects against one's body. One may also gervin by mouthing heated items of one's own body: the hand, the eye, the cupped rim of lips.

Gevorts-Box

Abstract house constructed during the Texas-Ohio sleep collaborations. It relayed an imperative to the occupant through inscriptions on the walls and floors: destroy it; smash it into powder; sweep it out; make a burial. Knock it back. Mourn the lost home.

God Burning System

Method of Thompsonian self-immolation. For each Thompson there exist flammable outcrops or limbs which rub onto the larger body of Thompson (Perkins), rendering morning fires and emberage which lights the sky and advances the time of a given society or culture.

God-Charge

Amount or degree of Thompson occurring in a person or shelter.

Godpiece

Cup, bowl or hoop, which, when swished through air, passed under water, or buried for an indefinite time in sand, will attract fragments and other unknown grains that comprise the monetary units of a given culture. The godpiece is further defined as a wallet or satchel that assigns value to the objects inside it.

Grass-Bringers

Boys which are vessels for grass and sod. They move mainly along rivers, distributing their product north toward houses and other emptiness.

The Great Hiding Period

Period of collective underdwelling practiced by the society. It occurred during the extreme engine-phase, when the sun emitted a frequency which disrupted most shelters. While some members remained topside, their skin became hard, their ears blackened, their hands grew useless. When the rest of the society emerged after the sun's noise subsided, those that had remained could not discern forms, folded in agony when touched, stayed mainly submerged to the eyes in water.

Half-Man Day

Holiday of diminution, or, the Festival of Unresolved Actions. Only the largest members can celebrate. They swing sticks, there is running, and many swim great distances with wires on their backs. On the third day a great fight occurs. After the feast they are covered in grass while they sleep. They collaborate on a dream of the house, with each participant imagining perfectly his own piece. Upon waking they set to building it, rendering always a softer, less perfect form than the one in which they secretly lived the previous evening.

Hand-Words

Patterns on the hand which serve as emblems or signals. They were developed during the silent wars of ten and three. The mitten is designed with palm-holes, so that members may communicate in the cold.

Heaven

Area of final containment. It is modeled after the first house. It may be hooked and slid and shifted. The bottom may be sawed through. Members inside stare outward and sometimes reach.

Heaven Construction Theory

The notions brought to bear on the construction of the final shelter. All work in this area is done under the influence of the first powder. This so the hands may shake, the eyes be glazed, the body be soft and movable.

Heen-Viewing

1. The act, technique or practice of viewing, with intent to destroy, any object or residue within or upon the house. Punishments of such acts include demotion to lower house, in which the culprit is subjected to endless examinations, proddings, mountings and group viewings by an unbroken stream of voluntary wardens. 2. To covet the life of another. 3. To look at a body and wish to destroy it. The heen in this case occurs or emanates from the hips, and the term applies in all cases less the one in which a member is looking upon, and wishing to terminate, his own body, which act goes unpunished.

House Costumes

The five shapes for the house which successfully withstand different weather systems. They derive their names from the fingers, their forms from the five internal tracts of the body, and their inhabitants from the larger and middle society.

Human Weather

Air and atmosphere generated from the speech and perspiration of systems and figures within the society. Unlike animal storms, it cannot be predicted, controlled or even remotely harnessed. Cities, towns and other settlements fold daily under the menace of this home-built air. The only feasible resolution, outside of large-scale stifling or combustion of physical forms, is to pursue the system of rotational silence proposed by Thompson, a member of ideal physical deportment—his tongue removed, his skin muffled with glues, his eyes shielded under with pictures of the final scenery.

Jamping

1. The act or technique of generating monotonic, slack-lipped locution. Precise winds of any territory apply a syntax to the jamper, shaping his mouth-sounds into recognizable and other words and sentences. 2. Condition or disease of crushed face structures as per result of storm or hand striking.

Jason, Our

The first brother. It has existed throughout known times in most to all fabricated pre-rage scenarios. It was erected initially in the Californias. It puts the powder in itself. It is the first love of the anti-person.

Jennifer

The inability to see. Partial blindness with regard to hands. To Jennifer is to feign blindness. The diseases resulting from these acts are called jennies.

Jerkins

First farmer.

John

1. To steal. This item occurs frequently in America and elsewhere. Its craft is diversion of blame onto the member from which the thing was stolen. 2. First house-garment correlationist. Lanky.

The Kenneth Sisters

Devisers of first food spring, blond-haired, slim-hipped, large, working hands. They dug the base for what would later become Illinois. They lived to be, respectively, 57, 71, 9, 45, 18 and 40.

L-Storms

The particular, grievous weather maw generated from the destruction of houses or shelters. In a new settlement, an L-Storm is buried in the foundation to charm the site from future rage.

Land-Scarf

Garment that functions also as a landmark, shelter or vehicle. To qualify, the item must recede beyond sight, be soft always, and not bind or tear the skin down.

Leg-Initiations

Act or technique of preparing the legs for sleep. They may be rubbed, shaved or dressed in pooter.

Leg Song

1. Secret melodies occurring between and around the legs of members or persons. It is not an audible sequence, nor does it register even internally if the legs are wrapped in cotton. Songs of the body incant at the P- or J-skin levels of the shoulder group. Leg Songs report at a frequency entirely other than these and disrupt the actions of birds. 2. The singing-between-the-legs occurring at all levels of the body. Sexual acts are prefaced by a commingling of these noises, as two or more members at a distance, before advancing, each tilt forward their pelvis to become coated in the tones of the other. 3. The sounds produced by a member or person just after dying. These songs herald the various diseases which will hatch into the corpse: the epilepsy, the shrinking, the sadness. 4. Device through which one brother, living, may communicate with another brother, dead.

Legal Beast Language

The four, six or nine words which technically and legally comprise the full extent of possible lexia which might erupt or otherwise burst from the head structure of Alberts.

Legal Prayer

Any prayer, chant or psalm affixed with the following rider: *Let a justifiable message be herewith registered in regard to desires and thoughts appertaining to what will be unnamed divinities, be they bird forms or other atmo-bestial manifestations of the* CONTROLLING THOMP- SON, *or instead unseen and personless concoctions of local clans, groups or teams. With no attempt to imprint here a definitive lingual- string of terms that shall be said to be terms bearing a truthful and anti-disharmonic concordance to the controlling agent, witnesses may accord to themselves the knowledge that a* PRAYER *is being committed that will herewith be one free of flaws, snags and lies. It will not be a misdirected, unheard or forgotten prayer. Neither will the blessed re- cipient be possessed of any confusion with respect to who or what has offered this prayer for consideration, although this assertion shall not indicate that the powerless subject makes any claim of authority over the* DIVINE AGENT OF FIRE. *It shall be a direct and honest gesturation to be received by said agent and dispatched or discarded in a custom that the agent knows. This now being said in the manner of greatest force and fluid legal acuity, the prayer can begin its middle without fear of repercussive sky reversals or blows that might destroy the mouth of the humble subject on his knees.*

Listening Frame

1. Inhabitable structure in which a member may divine the actions and parlance of previous house occupants. It is a system of reverse or- acle. It is dressed with beads and silvers and may sometimes be wheeled into small rooms for localized divining. The member is cau- tioned to never occupy this frame or ones like it while in the unshel- tered grasses or sands. With no walls or ceilings to specify its search, the frame applies its reverse surmise to the entire history of the soci- ety—its trees, its water, its houses—gorging the member with every previosity until his body begins to whistle from minor holes and even- tually collapses, folds or gives up beneath the faint, silver tubing. 2. Any system which turns a body from shame to collapse after broad- casting for it the body's own previous speeches and thoughts. 3. Ex- ternal memory of a member, in the form of other members or persons that exist to remind him of his past sayings and doings. They walk al-

ways behind the member. Their speech is low. They are naked and friendly.

The Living

Those members, persons and items that still appear to engage their hands into what is hot, what is rubbery, what cannot be seen or lifted.

Locked-House Books

1. Pamphlets issued by the society that first prescribed the ideal dimensions and fabrics of all houses. 2. Texts which, when recited aloud, affect certain grave changes upon the house. 3. Any book whose oral recitation destroys members, persons, landscapes or water. 4. Texts which have been treated or altered. To lock a given text of the society is to render it changeable under each hand or eye that consumes it. These are mouth products. They may be applied to the skin. Their content changes rapidly when delivered from house to house. 5. Archaic hood, existing previously to the mouth-harness, engraved with texts carved into the face and eyes.

Maronies

Thickly structured boys, raised on storm seeds and raw bulk to deflect winds during the house wars.

The Math Gun

1. Mouth of the father. It is equipped with a red freckle. It glistens. It is shined by foods, dulled with water, left alone by all else. 2. His pencil. It shortens with use and must be shaved, trimmed or sharpened by the person, who follows behind with a knife. 3. Process by which a member's counting capacity is nullified. One may be gunned out of numbers—or otherwise deprived of the ability to sequence—by silver strips which sting the hands. A member's air is occluded, his mouth is wrecked by the performance of numbers.

415

Messonism

Religious system of the society consisting of the following principles: i) Wonderment or devotion for any site in which houses preceded the arrival of persons. ii) The practice of sacrificing houses in autumn. It is an offering to Perkins, or the Thompson that controls it. iii)Any projection of a film or strips of colored plastic that generates images of houses upon a society. iv) The practice of abstaining from any act or locution which might indicate that one knows, knew or has known any final detail or attribute of the pure Thompson. v) Silence in the presence of weather. vi) The collection and consumption of string, which might be considered residue from the first form. The devout member acquires a private, internal pocket for this object. He allows it full navigational rule of his motions and standing poses. vii) The notion that no text shall fix the principles of said religion. All messages and imperatives, such as they are, shall be drawn from a private translation of the sun's tones. The member shall design his house so that it shall mitten these syllables which ripple forth from the bright orb. He may place his faith in the walls, which it is his duty to shine, that they receive the vivid law within them, and transfer it silently upon every blessed member that sits and waits inside the home.

Michael %

1. Amount of degree to which any man is Michael Marcus, the father. 2. Name given to any man whom one wishes were the father. 3. The act or technique of converting all names or structures to Michael. 4. Any system of patriarchal rendering.

Mother, The

1. The softest location in the house. It smells of foods that are fine and sweet. Often it moves through rooms on its own, cooing the name of the person. When it is tired it sits, and members vie for position in its arms. 2. System or team of Jane Marcuses existing as abstract regret or longing of the Ben Marcus. It is further defined as the Jane-over of the anti-person.

The Mouth-Harness

1. Device for trapping and containing the head. Mouths are often stuffed with *items*—the only objects legally defined as suspicious or worthy of silent paranoid regard. A claim is therefore made that we eat suspicion and become filled with it. The harness is designed to block all ingestion. Gervin states: "His mouth will be covered with a wire web. He shall never eat. Nor may he ever take what is outside and bring it inside. His stomach will forever devise upon what is within." 2. A system applied to the head to prevent destruction or collapse while reading or absorbing code.

Nagle

Wooden fixture which first subdued with Winter-Albert. It occurs in and around trees and is highly brown.

Nestor's Rape Farm

1. Any site of violation. 2. Initial farm run by G. D. Nestor in which the fourteen primary dogs of Dakota systematically raped the Charles family in August. 3. Place in which the Nestor group instructed members in molestation, the dive, stabbing, breaking the skin.

Nitzel's Gamble

The act or technique of filling the lungs with water. The chance was first taken by the Nitzel in Green river.

Odor Spiraling

Tossing, turning and flinging of the head so as to render radical, unknown odors in a locality.

417

Ohio

The house, be it built or crushed. It is a wooden composition affixed with stones and glass, locks, cavities, the person. There will be food on it, rugs will warm the floor. There will never be a clear idea of Ohio, although its wood will be stripped and shined, its glass polished with light, its holes properly cleared—this in order that the member inside might view what is without—the empty field, the road, the person moving forward or standing still, wishing the Ohio was near.

Palmer

System or city which is shiftable. A Palmer can be erected anywhere between the coasts.

Perkins

1. Term given to the body of Thompson, in order that His physical form never desecrate His own name. 2. The god of territory.

Prison Cloth Morning

1. Term applied to any day in which a construction site is enhanced with cloth dens and enclosures of a jailing capacity. 2. Period of any disciplinary term in which the felon must construct a usable garment from the four things: soil, straw, bark and water. The morning is an extensive period and will often outlast the entire sentence.

Private House Law

Rule of posture for house inhabitants stating one's desired position in relation to the father: one must bend forward, bring food, sharpen the pencil. Never may one stand on higher ground than it, nor shed the harness or grip the tunic tightly when it is present. Its clothes must be combed with one's fingers. Its speech to be written down, its commands to be followed, its spit to never under any circumstances be wiped from one's face.

Professional Sleepers

Members whose sleep acts perform specific, useful functions in a society. Clustered sleepers ward off birds; single, submerged sleepers seal culprits in houses; dozers heaped in cloth enhance the grasses of a given area, restore our faith in houses.

Rag, The, or Prayer Rag

Device of stripped or pounded cloth held to the mouth during prayer.

Rain

Hard, silver, shiny object. It can be divided into knives and used for cutting procedures. Most rain dissolves within the member and applies a slow cutting program over a period of years. This is why when one dies the rain is seen slicing upward from its body. When death is converted into language it reads: to empty the body of knives.

The Rare-Waters

Series of liquids believed to contain samples of the first water. It is the only water not yet killed. It rims the eyes, falls from them during certain times, collects at the feet, averts the grasp of hands, which are dry, and need it.

Sadness

The first powder to be abided upon waking. It may reside in tools or garments. It may be eradicated with more of itself, in which case the face results as a placid system coursing with water, heaving.

Salt

An item which comprises the in- and external core of most to all animals. An animal may be licked free of this salt, or an animal may be hosed clean or scraped. Only when it coughs up salt or otherwise produces saltmatter from within can the animal be expected in short time to collapse.

Schedules and Dispensing Rules of Seasons

System of legal disbursement in relation to seasons and temperatures. Thompson embodies the assembly, the constituency, the audience, the retractors, the Thompson and non-Thompson in any weather-viewing scheme.

Schenk

A school.

Shadow-Cells

The visible, viscous grain deposited upon any area recently blanketed in shadow. The cells may be packed into dough. They may be spread onto the legs or hips. They may darken or obscure the head for an infinite period.

Shelter Witnesses

Members which have viewed the destruction, duplication or creation of shelters. They are required to sign or carve their names or emblems onto the houses in question, and are subject to a separate, vigilant census.

Shirt of Noise

Garment, fabric or residue which absorbs and holds sound. Its loudness cannot be predicted. It can destroy the member which inhabits it.

Skin Pooter

1. A salve, tonic, lotion or unguent which, when applied liberally to the body, allows a member to slip freely within the house of another. 2. A poultice which prevents collapse when viewing a new shelter.

Sky Interception, sinter

The obstruction caused by birds when light is projected from sunsources affixed to hills and rivers, causing members to see patterns, films or "clouds." SINTER is an acronym for Sky Interception and Noise Transfer of Emergent Rag-forms.

The Sky Films of Ohio

The first recordings and creations of the sky, recorded in the Ohio region. They were generated by a water machine designed by Krup. The earliest films contained accidents and misshapen birds. They are projected occasionally at revival festivals—at which wind of certain popularity is also rebroadcast—but the machine has largely been eclipsed by the current roof lenses affixed to houses, which project and magnify the contents of each shelter onto the sky of every region in the society.

Sleep-Holes

Areas or predesigned localities in which dormant figures and members conduct elaborate sleep performances. Points are scored for swimming, riding and killing. Some members utilize these sites to perfect their sleep-speech, and profess that they are not sleeping. Others exercise or copulate or rapidly eat cloth and grain. The father slept in one for four hours while smashing his own house, which contained its own sleepers, who performed nothing.

Sleeping Group

Team of members which performs mutual, radical sleep acts in various sites of varying difficulty. They are satisfied not with actual sleeping but with watching the sleeping of another. These are members which can only copulate, speak or eat when surrounded by fields of tossing sleepers that are weeping, are moaning, are struggling to breathe.

The Smell Camera

Device for capturing and storing odor. It is a wooden box augmented with string and two wire bunces. It houses odor for one season. It releases the odor when the shutter is snapped or jerked out. Afterwards the string must be combed and shook.

South-Shadow

The residue of shadow-cells which accrete to the south of all classifiable objects, regardless of the sun's position.

The Spanish Boy

1. Member of localized figures which mustache early. 2. Item or remote personhood which demonstrates the seventeen postures of fire while dormant or sleeping.

Speed-Fasting Experiments

Activity or practice of accelerated food abstention. It was first conducted in Buffalo. The record death-by-fasting occurred in two days, through motor-starving and exhaustion, verbal.

Stinkpoint

Moment of time slightly forward from the moment of time of another. Since all odors issue first into a fraction of the future, allowing them to fall into a member advancing in time, any member achieving or arriving in a stinkpoint is also said to be a creator and co-conspirator of any smells and smell systems in the society.

Storm Lung

Object which can be swallowed to forestall the effects of weather upon a body.

String Theory of Fatigue

System or technique of diagnosing the level of tiredness or unwillingness in a member by covering it with medical ropes.

Strup

Method of in-gazing applied to one's own body or house. To strup is not to count these things. Nor can it mean to analyze, assess or otherwise, hold an opinion of a house or body. It refers strictly to a method of viewing that is conducted with a tilted or cloth-covered head.

Subfeet Walking Rituals

Series of motion exercises conducted with hidden, buried or severed leg-systems. It was first named when members were required to move through tracts of high sand. The act was later repeated when the sand had faded. It is the only holiday in which motion is celebrated Revelers honor the day by stumbling, dragging forward on their arms, binding their legs with wire, lying down and whispering, not being able to get up.

The Sun

1. Origin of first sounds. Some members of the society still detect amplified speech bursts emanating from this orb, and have accordingly designed noise mittens for the head and back. A poetic system was de-

veloped in thirty based on the seventeen primary tonal flues discharging from the sun's underskin. 2. Unit of surge devised by Greenberg.

Sun-Stalls

Abrupt disruptions in the emissions of the sun. They occur in the blazing quarterstrips which flap. There begins a clicking or slow sucking sound. Members standing below arch or bend. They raise a hand to the ear or eye. Form a cup or shield.

Sun-Stick

Item of the body which first turns toward sun when a member dies, sleeps, collapses. This item is further the pure compass toward tracts that are heated and safe, also called true places.

Synchronized Family Walking Training

Method of motion-unison practiced by members and teams inhabiting larger, divergent cloth shelters. Instruction was first elaborated by Nestor. Later, Crawford refuted Nestor's system and a national standard was established.

Temperature Law

The first, third and ninth rule of air stating that the recitation or revocation of names—or any calling forth in any manner of any person or thing—shall for all time alter the temperature of a locality.

Theory of Invisibility

Plante, G.'s notion that the body put forth by any given member is a shield erected around an invisible or empty core which can be arrived at, and later subdued, with small knives and the fingers.

The Thong

Leatherized ladle, spoon or stick affixed often to the tongue of a member. It is considered the last item of the body. After demise, it may be treated with water to discern the final words of a person.

Topographical Legend and Location of Food Nooks

System of over-maps depicting buried food quadrants, sauce grooves and faults of fissures in which grains and beans are caught. The cloth form of the map can be applied to the bodies of animals, to clarify areas in which edibles might have amassed.

The Tower Period

Age of principal house inscriptions. Text was first discovered embedded in the house during this era. Shelters of the time were fitted with turrets and wires, poles, needled roofs, domes. Members were hired to read aloud the inscriptions of each house and holidays were formed to ritualize these performances, with food as a reward for orators that did not weep or otherwise distort the message carved into the house.

Treasure of Possible Enunciations

Catalogue of first, last and intermediate lexia. It includes all possible words and their unutterable opposites. Other than Thompson's *Bank of Communicable Desire*, no other such comprehensive system exists.

Tree-Bread

The victuals in concert with three systems.

Tungsten

1. Hardened form of the anger and rage metals. 2. Fossilized behavior, frozen into mountainsides, depicting the seven scenes of escape and the four motifs of breathing-while-dead.

The Tunic

1. Textile web, shared and worn by all members of a society. It is the only public garment. Never may it be cast off, altered, shrunk or locally cleaned. Its upkeep is maintained under regulation of the Universal Storm Calendar, which deploys winds into its surface to loosen debris and members or persons that have exceeded their rightful term of inhabitation. 2. Garment placed between pre-age boy and girl members to enlarge or temporarily sell the genitals and shank during weather birthing.

Universal Storm Calendar

1. Thompsoned system of air influence. Inexplicable. 2. System of storm reckoning for the purpose of recording past weather and calculating dates and sites for future storms. The society completes its house-turn under the sun in the span of autumn. The discrepancy between storms is inescapable, and one of the major problems for a member since his early days has been to reconcile and harmonize wind and rain reckonings. Some peoples have simply recorded wind by its accretions on the rag, but, as skill and storage developed, the prevailing winds generally came to be fitted into the tower. The calendar regulates the dispersal, location and death of every wind and rain system in existence. 3. Game, abbreviated to USC, or Us, played by children, in which body mimics air.

Weather Birthing

1. The act or technique of selecting and reciting certain words within given, fixed sky situations with the intent of generating, enhancing or subtracting weather from a given area in the society.

426

2. Burning the skin of a member to alter the sky shapes of a locality. 3. Process occurring pre-spasm between the hips of children. This includes any exceptional change in the speed of air transpiring between two or more members, figures or persons. 4. The act of placing powders or other grains in the mouth while speaking to alter the temperature of a local site. 5. Whispering while holding birds in the mouth.

The Weather Killer

1. Person, persons or team which perform actual and pronounced killings of the air. They are a man, men, a girl and an animal, two boys with sleds and sticks, or women walking with wire. Their works were first uncovered at the wind farm. They exist as items which are counter-Thompson, given that they kill what he has made. 2. Sky-killing member. In the middle and late periods a man devised a means for harming the air. Little is known of him, except that he termed himself a weather killer and referred to others like him, located in America, Palmer and elsewhere. The works of these practitioners were in some part buried at the wind farm, the home site on NN 63 in Texas. They have rubbed shapes onto paper, peeled sound out of rock, discovered pictures inside sticks, acts which all then collapse, shrink, extinguish what is breathed.

Western Worship Boxes

The smallest structures, designed to fit precisely one body. They are rough-walled and dank, wooden and finely trimmed—the only areas of devotion. When more than one body enters to worship as a team, the box gevorts.

The Wind Gun

Sequence of numerals, often between the numbers twelve and thirteen, which when embedded or carved as code into the field, reinstruct wind away from an area.

Wind-Bowl

1. Pocket of curved, unsteady space formed between speaking persons. They may discuss the house, its grass, some foods, the father inside. The wind-bowl will tilt and push into their faces, that they might appear leaning back, arching from each other, grasping at the ground behind them as if sleeping. 2. Term applied to any item whose shape, character or size has been altered by weather.

Winter-Albert

Summer-Albert. Such names as exist in the society achieve not converse attributes in opposite seasons, but rather repeat all acts, thoughts and feelings of the diametric season. For example, during the summer, the holder is afforded the benefit of watching any Albert duplicate all movements of the previous winter. The summer-Albert is therefore a repetition and duplication of its own colder self.

The Wire

The only element attached, affixed or otherwise bushing with every other element, object, item, person or member of the society. It is gray and often golden and glimmers in the morning. Members polish it simply by moving forward or backward or resting in place. The wire is the shortest distance between two bodies. It may be followed to any area or person one desires. It contains on its surface the shredded residue of hands—this from members that pulled too hard, held on too long, wanted to get there too fast.

Witness

1. One who watches, hears or otherwise acquires knowledge of certain actions, things or states within a society. Witnessing is only reliably performed without the use of the head, which must be blanketed or otherwise suppressed—this so it does not deceive the body. 2. Tingling in the hips or sweetness in a larger pelva, indicating that a thing has become known.

Wooden Fire Techniques

1. The construction of wood-based tableaux that duplicate the heat and noise of fire without the corresponding visual accuracy. 2. Hidden fire codes pre-built into vessels and persons. Such subjects and objects burn secretly for the duration of their existence.

The Yard

Locality in which wind is buried and houses are discussed. Fine grains line the banks. Water curves outside the pastures. Members settle into position.

Nominated by Conjunctions

IN THE PASTURE OF DEAD HORSES

by JULIA WENDELL

from THE JOURNAL

Light rain, and I'm carbound,
fiddling with my keys,
watching my helmeted children

repeat themselves on the backs of saddled ponies
circling a weather-worn ring
north of Baltimore.

So around and around the ring I imagine
you must have wheeled,
as the mustached trainer, nervously

cropping his thigh, barked pointers from center ring.
My mother seeming to float above her cut-back saddle
as you racked on.

I'd heard of the ribbons
you sported before the war.
Before your trainer was called to the North Sea

and the groom to the South Pacific. Before my mother,
ambushed by marriage and childbirth, left, too,
and returned to the house of her childhood.

Fifty years of opening the same window
to the usual shadows and drafts.
Daylight struck over & over.

I'd ride over you,
coaxing my pony down the hillside
that cradled your secret of bones.

Impatient in your dark nest,
you'd kick inside the earth, the hillside shimmering.
Though you were not so much as an indentation

your bones lay beneath.
The goldenrod coloring the hillside
late summer, your tempermental monument.

Still, I was told you were there,
Noble Knight, Solid Mahoghany, Emerald Future.
The hillside was a mirror

and in my mother's life, and then in my own,
we opened our eyes to see into it.
All my young life, I believed you were there.

I'd canter bareback dodging brush & limb,
down the hillside graves to the Sugar Bush,
where Grandfather's sapping shed sank

plank by rotting plank to the earth,
and the maple trees grew huge and unwieldy, left long untapped.
Where the body-stench of crude oil rose from pockets

in the Pennsylvanian marsh,
and the trails that I pretended wound forever
ended. I sensed you were there.

As I sense we are repeated
on the backs of saddled ponies,
my mother, my children, and I—

carbound, fiddling with my keys,
a young woman revised in the worn paths of ponies,
the thunky staccato of small hooves

wearing circles in a ring
each circuit ending
and ending again.

Nominated by The Journal

A HAPPY VACANCY

fiction by STEPHEN DOBYNS

from THE SOUTHERN REVIEW

THERE ARE PERILS in *life so disturbing that we need to hold ourselves in a state of readiness, ever alert to exercise our sense of outrage or disbelief. Yet even these events must be dealt with and understood. Worse than the events themselves may be how the world responds to them. Consider the following.

Jason W. Plover, a poet with six books, was killed when a pig tumbled out of the sky and crushed him as he was crossing Massachusetts Avenue against the light at Harvard Square.

The pig was a seven-hundred-pound boar being used in a film about a bank robbery. A helicopter had been transporting it from a farm in Lexington to Memorial Drive along the banks of the Charles River, where a famous actress was waiting, as well as a Brinks truck rented for the afternoon. It was a key scene involving the use of the pig as a porcine roadblock. The pig had been doped, but not enough. It woke, saw daylight, heaved its huge frame toward the open door of the helicopter, breaking its bonds, and took a fatal step, a six-hundred-foot step with Jason W. Plover as its destination.

No telling what the pig thought. Its mind was probably a mass of question marks. It was early September, and trees were beginning to turn color. The sky was blue, the weather mild, and the view must have been marvelous. An idea having to do with a possible mistake was perhaps being assembled in the pig's dim brain when it squashed Jason Plover into a splop of jelly.

One of the witnesses spoke of hearing a squeal. Another described a pig on a man's shoulders. A third spoke of seeking an angel falling

433

out of the air. People paused, looked up, and saw what appeared to be a pink cloud dropping fast. Much was made of the fact that Jason Plover had been crossing against the light, that he had not waited. He had been on his way to a lunch meeting at the Harvest with his editor, Josie Kahn. A seventh book of poems was already in manuscript, and he was eager to rush it into print. Jason Plover was always in a hurry. Had he been a tad less serious, a tad more casual, he might be with us still today.

But seriousness had amounted to Jason Plover's trademark. He had been a tall, heavyset man fond of wearing a thick tweed overcoat that made his figure resemble a rolled-up mattress. When he walked he liked to set his entire foot flat upon the ground before lifting it for the next step. His heavy tread was well known in the halls of the English Department at Tufts, where he had taught for fifteen years. He had had vast and subtle black eyebrows, which he could wield as a samurai wields his sword. One position showed scorn, another superiority, and a third deep thought. There are many writers in the Boston area. Toss a stone in a public place and you are likely to hit one. But for seriousness—sheer, bullying, heavy-lidded, I'm-the-most-important-poet-on-god's-green-acre seriousness—Jason Plover had the rest of the writers beat.

Now all was changed.

The headline in the *Boston Herald* read: "Plummeting Porker Pulverizes Poet."

In the same way Jason Plover had taken liberties with the truth when alive, so had the headline writer at the *Herald* taken liberties with the truth in announcing Plover's death. He wasn't pulverized, he was squashed.

No matter.

Plover had had a wife: Harriet Spense, who was an associate professor of Feminist Studies at Tufts. She too had a deep seriousness, but, lacking her husband's physical mass, her seriousness was qualified by the difference in their weights. Additionally, she had a certain lightness of soul and imagined herself someone who could take a joke. She was an attractive forty-year-old woman: tall and statuesque with dark red hair.

She first had a glimmer of the changes that lay before her when she entered the faculty room at Tufts the day after her husband's death. She assumed one of her colleagues was telling a funny story because the eight or nine faculty members were laughing with an abandon she

434

had never before witnessed within these walls. Harriet Spense loved her husband and grieved for his death. Yet she also looked forward to whatever might distract her from the awfulness of his passing, meaning that she hoped to share in the joke. However, when her colleagues caught sight of her, they clamped their mouths shut, turned away, and began to make coughing and choking noises, as if it were not something amusing but acrid smoke that was responsible for their condition. Although suspicious, Harriet didn't quite catch on.

Then at the funeral home, as she spoke to the director, whose face was bright red and who kept gasping, she found herself distracted by chuckling from a farther room, as if embalming and corpse preparation had charms the nature of which had so far escaped her. At the church, the minister wouldn't meet her eye, and again she heard distant laughter, as if the church workers found extraordinary delight in their daily tasks.

There were other small signs that need not be fully recounted: strange phone calls, the attentiveness of the press, people staring at her on the street, neighbors behaving with inappropriate heartiness. Actually, it was at the funeral that all became clear, and Harriet caught an unpleasant glimpse of her future. There were a lot of television cameras. The Episcopal service was quite serious, yet all through it were sudden hoots and guffaws. Sitting in the front row with her two embarrassed sons, Harriet Spense realized that the oddity of her husband's death might wipe out the accomplishments of his life. It is hard for six serious books of poetry, with a seventh on the way, to compete with the burden of being killed by a falling pig. Put the seven books on one end of a teeter-totter and the pig on the other and there is no contest. We read in history that the Greek poet Aeschylus was killed when a turtle dropped by a passing eagle struck his head and split his skull. Aeschylus's reputation has long since recovered, but presumably in Athens there was a period of furtive laughter. It was wartime, and people needed a joke.

Jason Plover was now the poet who had been killed by a falling pig. His books immediately disappeared from the stores, and new printings were planned. Years earlier he had written a poem entitled "The Pig and I," which had appeared in his second collection: *Household Mysteries*. It was not a great poem, but it detailed those differences in thought, generosity, and humanity that separate men and women from pigs. A human being cares about his or her brothers and sisters; a pig does not—this was the poem's theme. Pigs are crass, self-centered, greedy, and they eat their young. It was astonishing to Harriet Spense how many requests she had over the next few months to anthologize this poem. It was as if Jason Plover's death were an example of how the animal kingdom can strike back; as if the falling pig had been on a revengeful kamikaze raid. And, too, the anthologizing of the poem allowed the editors, mostly other poets, to write a biographical note detailing the manner of Plover's death. In this they had a lot of fun.

Plover had been a moderately well-known poet, and it was not uncommon for literary magazines to ask him for work. Now Harriet was swamped with requests. Her husband had had about thirty unpublished poems that he intended to include in his seventh volume. These poems were actually fought over; editors called Harriet Spense day and night. Many said they would be happy to publish material that had already appeared in other magazines. These were magazines with circulations between five hundred and five thousand. With Plover's name on the cover, their sales would triple.

The editor of a famous poetry magazine in the Midwest was particularly insistent. Some years before he had given up publishing poems for their own sake and had devoted himself to theme issues, which gave all the work in his magazine a decorative cast and let poets feel that their work was being rejected because it wasn't sufficiently about "Fatherhood" or "Nature" or "Cemeteries" or "Home Owning" or "Buying a Dog." The fact that this approach to poetry trivialized the medium appeared to be part of the point. This editor called Harriet Spense a dozen times. He was planning a "Pig" issue, and it wouldn't be complete without a poem by Jason Plover. In vain did Harriet tell this man that her husband had no other poems about pigs. "Any kind of poem will do," said the editor. Not even its quality was important. He would even take an unfinished poem in an early draft, even rough notes, mere jottings. What was important was the theme, and he could not possibly have a "Pig" issue without a poem by Jason W. Plover. The editor would even pay double the rates, and he was angry when Harriet refused to send him anything. He seemed to think she was attributing a seriousness to poetry that his theme issues were hoping to deny.

Harriet Spense's life became increasingly difficult. Not only was her husband transformed into a figure of fun, but she too became amusing because she had been married to him. There was a facial expression that Harriet came to recognize as the Oh-you're-the-woman-whose-husband-was-killed-by-falling-pig expression. People would try to be

436

sympathetic, yet giggle at the same time. They would cover their mouths and look away, and their eyes would water. Because her husband had really been killed, and because people like to imagine they possess some shred of decency, very few made jokes to her face, yet when they saw her coming they were clearly prepared to be amused. Even the most serious of us seek out chances to partake of the long slide into laughter. There is a sweetness to that wonderful forgetting that makes us crave it. Had Jason Plover been a plumber or a postman, the humor would not have been so great. But being a poet with a deep seriousness, he was especially vulnerable.

Jason Plover had had a characteristic gesture. He would join his thumb to the fingertips of his left hand. He would draw back all five digits about an inch toward the palm, pause, then shoot them forward as he opened his hand wide, duplicating, as it were, a miniature explosion. It was a dismissive gesture. Something small and inconsequential was being blown away. He would make this gesture at the end of summing up another poet's work or when discussing an inferior poem. He would make it after discussing another writer's intellect or chance of true success. It was a summing-up sort of gesture. No telling who made it first after Jason Plover had been squashed by the falling pig, but soon Harriet Spense began noticing it all over Cambridge. And she came to understand that the gesture—the little outward puff of fingers—now referred to Jason Plover himself: events had conspired to blow him away.

Harriet's sons were deeply depressed. Frank was a junior at Boston University. Charles was a senior at Harvard. Three weeks after their father's death they dropped out of school. They spoke of needing to visit the West Coast to see what was going on. They regretted that their name—Plover—was sufficiently unusual to remind people about that poet—their father—who had been squashed by a falling pig. They discussed new names: Jacobs and Wellerby and McBride. They were intelligent young men who had had a clear sense of a bright future. Now they felt their lives were over unless they changed their names and moved to another part of the country. They needed something like the FBI's witness protection program. Harriet tried to dissuade them, but in her heart she knew they were right. Her own teaching had suffered immeasurably from the particulars of her husband's death. For one thing, strangers began sitting in on her classes. There was always a whispering, and once she heard an "oink-oink" from the back of the room.

"Perhaps you should take a leave," her chairman told her. He was a tweedy, bearded man who liked to rub his stomach when he talked.

"It's all so ridiculous," said Harriet.

"It is rather," said the chairman. "Think of being killed by a falling pig." And the chairman covered his mouth with his hand.

"No, I don't mean that," said Harriet. "I mean people's response to his death."

"I would have given my left foot to have seen it," said the chairman. "No offense intended."

And so Harriet Spense took a leave. A psychiatrist friend wrote a letter saying that Harriet's mental health would be seriously damaged if she continued to teach. The dean made no problems. Actually, when she sat waiting to see him, she heard gales of laughter from his office, and when several men came out, they refused to meet her eye.

Harriet had a fairly large amount of money from Jason's publisher due to his increased sales and rights to his poem "The Pig and I." His new book was to be called *Transcendent Moments in the Spiritual Veldt,* and the editor, Josie Kahn, wanted to change the title to *Pigging Out* or *Pork Thoughts.* Harriet refused, even though Josie said it could mean an extra ten thousand dollars. "To think," said Josie, "I was so close. I would have given anything to see it happen. It must have been absolutely celestial."

One night in late October while Harriet was boxing up Jason's clothes to give to the Tufts Impoverished Students' Fund, she thought: "I'm sick of Jason's poetry. I'm sick of the life we had together." Then she glanced around guiltily, as if afraid her thoughts had been overheard.

Harriet had never until now questioned her life with Jason. Her husband had been a highly respected poet, and she was a highly respected feminist thinker whose two books were used in classes at more than thirty colleges and universities across the country. They had often been invited out to dinner and were much in demand for the quality of their conversation. Jason Plover's high seriousness and Harriet Spense's moderate seriousness were given a value that was almost monetary. It paid for a lot of meals. When Jason's opinion was asked, the other guests fell silent. Jason would rub his jaw, manipulate his black eyebrows, and enter his sentence much in the way an icebreaker enters a frozen sea. He had liked to make harrumphing noises and to clear his throat. He liked to make that little exploding gesture with the fingers of his left hand. And while Harriet's own ego was not so tied up in her conversational abilities, she too liked being someone to whom other people listened.

This too had changed. People now listened to her because her husband had been killed in a ridiculous manner. She could have said nothing but "Doo, dah, doo, dah," and her listeners would have been pleased. She could have done no more than whistle. And if she had grunted like a pig, oh, how happy people would have been.

As a result Harriet Spense came to question the value of her former life. Had it ever been the content of her speech that people valued? Was it not her serious manner, and her husband's even more serious manner? Was it not to their curriculum vitae, rather than their voices, that people listened? And now her vita was radically altered. She had a sense of the shallowness of her Cambridge life and the superficiality of what she had valued. She saw that the deep seriousness with which her life had been swaddled was simply a buffer. It had existed to keep people at a distance. It indicated she had a certain importance and needed to be treated with respect. It had been the strangler of spontaneity and impulse. It had rigidified her life as if she had been dipped in concrete. These realizations caused her a chagrin that was even greater than the embarrassment she had felt because of how Jason had died. Indeed, she now saw that the manner of her husband's death was almost fortunate because it revealed the lie she had been living. She had loved her husband and had forgiven him his foolishness. But she saw that his final gift to her had been the absurdity of his death, because it opened to her a new life, a new way of living.

So it was that seven weeks after her husband's death Harriet closed up her house in Cambridge and moved to Ann Arbor. Her two sons had already disappeared, and she knew of them only by brief postcards from California signed Magillicuddy. Harriet's undergraduate degree had been in clinical psychology, and she got a job at a hospice. She was drawn to the idea of people dying in bed surrounded by others who loved them, or at least who had deep respect for them as human beings and for the whole experience of death. For her, death had become a joke, a dreadful buffo, and she needed to make it big again.

"The process of dying," Harriet told a cancer patient, "is a process that begins with birth. It continues while we occupy ourselves with what is important in our lives: our careers, our families, our pleasures. Our death accompanies us all through our years, gradually taking our place until it exchanges itself for us completely. The event which will

439

soon occur in your life has been preparing itself for every moment of your life."

But mostly she didn't counsel anybody, mostly she helped with small embarrassing chores like bandages and bedpans, and she liked to read to people: she would read Dickens and Thackeray and Tolstoy, great long books that gave to the dying the sense that enormous expanses of time stretched before them.

Each day she would have conversations with the men and women she thought of as her patients. The elderly especially had had long and interesting lives. They had traveled and witnessed events that Harriet had only read about. "I didn't know Lawrence of Arabia personally," said one old man, "but I often saw him from afar when I was in Damascus."

"I was a freshman at Clark when Freud presented his lectures," said an ancient lady. "Dr. Jung was there as well. He had a very pointed head."

There was something about these stories that made time seem causal, and Harriet realized she was attempting to repair her sense of causality. Her husband's death appeared to lie outside causality. The malignant demiurge who hangs life's carrot before our eyes had been having his or her little joke. What do we do with an extremely serious poet? We kill him with a falling pig. Those people who had laughed at the manner of her husband's death—shouldn't they have been terrified? Didn't Jason's death indicate some awful truth about the cosmos—that if it has a divine direction, then its prime mover is whimsy?

There was a doctor who often came to the hospice who was about Harriet's age. His name was Robert Chase. He was a tall, willowy figure with a mop of graying blond hair. He never stood completely straight but kept shifting as if the wind were tugging him this way and that. He would sway with his hands in the pockets of his white coat and look at Harriet with his deep blue eyes.

"Do you ever read poetry?" Harriet asked him one day in the staff lounge.

"Absolutely not," said Robert. "Did you hear about that poet in Boston who got killed by a falling pig?"

"I read something about it," said Harriet.

"You wonder how many times something like that misses us. You know, the truck that would have run us down if we had been just a little faster."

"He had crossed against the light," said Harriet.

"Probably one of those stress-ridden Type-A personalities," said Robert. "I wonder what he did to relax."

Harriet nearly said that Jason had collected first editions and had been her husband, but instead she closed her mouth and shrugged. "Whatever it was," she said at last, "it wasn't enough."

After a few of these conversations, Robert Chase invited Harriet out to dinner. They went to a small Italian restaurant on the road to Ypsilanti. Robert kept looking at her, not out of curiosity or as if expecting anything from her, but just to rest his eyes upon her.

"I think people try to make their lives too serious," said Harriet as they shared a medium-sized antipasto.

"Is that why you work at the hospice?" Robert wore a dark-blue denim shirt and a bright yellow tie. Harriet liked how undoctorly he appeared.

"I think I work there in order to see just how serious life can be. If you stare long enough at the most serious thing that life has in store for us," said Harriet, "then perhaps you can come out on the other side."

"You mean on the side of laughter?"

"Why not?" asked Harriet. "I mean, I don't intend to laugh at the people at the hospice. My job is to help them and make their departure more comfortable and less fearful. But me, what damage does such solemnity do to me? So I look at it and study it, and perhaps with time I'll grow accustomed to it."

"Do you think that seriousness is connected to fear?" asked Robert. The tablecloth was a red-and-black cotton checkerboard. Robert kept moving the salt and pepper shakers from square to square as he listened.

"I expect it's influenced by fear," said Harriet. She thought of her husband's seriousness, how it was like one of the garments he wore. Most often his laughter had been ironic or sarcastic or superior. His laughter had been judgmental, and, as a result, all his laughter had been serious. Was it possible to laugh without any element of judgment? Jason Plover's life had been an edifice that he had built to demonstrate the solemnity of his endeavor. Poor Jason, killed by a falling pig; his death had overturned the premises of his life.

"Seriousness," said Harriet, "often exists as something we want to show other people. We want others to think us serious, which suggests a fear of not being taken seriously. What does that seriousness get us? It neither delays our death nor makes it easier to bear."

"And what is the opposite of seriousness? Frivolity?"

441

"Most literally perhaps, but I think the opposite of such a seriousness is love, because love accepts all possibilities, whereas seriousness only accepts what it sees as correct. Perhaps I work at the hospice for purely selfish reasons. I work to improve the quality of my love."

"That seems pretty serious," said Robert.

"I'm not against seriousness," said Harriet. "I simply want to go beyond it. I want it to be an element in my life and not its reason for being. Look at the unexpected changes that life can force upon a person. Surely life's intrinsic definition, that is, constant change, argues against rigidity. Seriousness may be no more than self-protection, and life can come along and just brush it aside."

"And how can it do that?"

"It can drop a pig on your head from a great height."

Harriet Spense saw Robert more and more often, and she came to realize that they would probably begin a romance. This made her happy. She didn't tell him about Jason; she didn't want to muddy the romantic water. She knew she would tell him sooner or later, but she wasn't afraid of doing so. She also knew that she would eventually leave the hospice and return to teaching.

There was an old man at the hospice named Franklin, who had long ago been a high school principal in Bloomfield Hills. Now he was ninety-five and had been retired for thirty years. Harriet read to him from *Bleak House,* and was even nearing the end of the book. One afternoon in spring, she asked him, "What is the funniest thing you can think of?"

Franklin lay back on his pillows and looked out the window. It was a sunny day, and the cherry trees behind the hospice were in full flower. Franklin's gray and spotted hands lay on the counterpane and trembled as if they were getting ready to start up and go someplace.

"The funniest recent thing I can think of," said Franklin, "was something I read about last fall. A fellow was walking across the street in Boston and a pig fell out of the air and crushed him. It had fallen out of a passing helicopter. The man never knew what hit him. He was a poet, I forget his name. He was hurrying someplace important, and this seven-hundred-pound pig fell on top of him. It dropped like a rock and hit him right on the noggin. I don't know, it's probably not funny, but it tickles me. I mean, I got to die here in this darn bed. Why couldn't I have been killed by a pig falling out of the sky? Nobody would forget about it. I'd be famous forever. This poet, what an opportunity! Some people have all the luck."

Harriet Spense considered how Franklin yearned for the fame that had resulted in her husband's ultimate trivialization. She found herself laughing. She put her hands on her knees, leaned back her head and gasped for breath. It was neither a guffaw nor the hysterical shriek of nervousness. It was the laugh of someone whose seriousness has been overthrown, the laugh that erases all other concerns. Our plans, our memories, our fears are all replaced by a peculiar yet distinctive hooting. To some it sounds like a mob of crows, to others a donkey's bray. In fact, it is the sound of the world disappearing as all the content is sucked from our heads, to be replaced—briefly, oh, too briefly—by a happy vacancy. And doesn't this sustain us? Doesn't it provide the strength to let us bear up our burden and continue our mortal journey?

Nominated by Jane Hirshfield, Ken Rosen

ELIZABETH, LISTENING

by SABINA GROGAN

from FAULTLINE

My sister has never fallen.
She died still whole, untouched.
She died undispersed, like smoke
blown into a jar and then sealed up.
The air is blue in the jar and then clear
but the smoke is still there
and you know it. You take it on faith.

The gravestone picture they chose for my sister
shows her whole body. This is as it should be,
she is two years old. At that age, the head
and the body are one.
She has overalls on in this picture,
she is sitting in shallow creek water
and laughing.
Her tufted hair the blanched color of almonds.
Her skin smelled of almonds, my mother has said,
it was something in the medicine.
Under the water, her legs are wavering.
She is disappearing from the ground up,
like smoke.

I was three when Elizabeth died, but I remember
the place where this picture was taken.
My parents and I often walked in this park,
through the redwood trees that spanned centuries.

For years, whenever we came to this spot,
my father would lift up our struggling
dog, and throw him the distance
from the path to the creek below.

Swim you bastard! my father would yell, and our spaniel
would splash down. He would sink for a moment,
then fight to the surface, then swim.
I laughed with my father to see the dog twist
through the air, to hear his yelp as he fought
his way up through the water, his
furious sacrificial swimming.

It is through her absence that I know my sister.
When I became older I needed
some other friend
than my father. She was this for me.
She was this too for my mother,
a figment who listened.
*You were always your father's
girl,* my mother has said. *Elizabeth loved me.*

My mother has told me what it was,
with Elizabeth dying. Of the decay of her body,
her soft child's skin softening.
My memory doesn't hold any of this.
I remember our dog as he shook himself, shivering
as he scrambled out of the water.
And later, when I was no longer my father's
girl, I remember
Elizabeth, limitless, listening.

Nominated by Faultline

SIX DAYS: SOME REMEMBERINGS

by GRACE PALEY

from ALASKA QUARTERLY REVIEW

Iwas in jail. I had been sentenced to six days in the Women's House of Detention, a fourteen-story prison right in the middle of Greenwich Village, my own neighborhood. This happened during the American War in Vietnam, I have forgotten which important year of the famous '60s. The civil disobedience for which I was paying a small penalty probably consisted of sitting down to impede or slow some military parade.

I was surprised at the sentence. Others had been given two days or dismissed. I think the judge was particularly angry with me. After all I was not a kid. He thought I was old enough to know better, a 45-year-old woman, a mother and teacher. I ought to be too busy to waste time on causes I couldn't possibly understand.

I was herded with about twenty other women, about 90% black and Puerto Rican, into the bull pen, an odd name for a women's holding facility. There, through someone else's lawyer, I received a note from home, telling me that since I'd chosen to spend the first week of July in jail, my son would probably not go to summer camp because I had neglected to raise the money I'd promised. I read this note and burst into tears, real running down the cheek tears. It was true: Thinking about other people's grown boys I had betrayed my little son. The summer, starting that day, July 1, stood up before me day after day, steaming the city streets, the after work crowded city pool.

446

I guess I attracted some attention. You—you white girl you—you never been arrested before? A black woman about a head taller than I put her arm on my shoulder.—It ain't so bad. What's your time sugar? I gotta do three years. You huh?

Six days.

Six days? What the fuck for?

I explained, sniffling, embarrassed.

You got six days for sitting down front of a horse? Cop on the horse? Horse step on you? Jesus in hell, cops gettin crazier and stupider and meaner. Maybe we get you out.

No, no, I said. I wasn't crying because of that. I didn't want her to think I was scared. I wasn't. She paid no attention. Shoving a couple of women aside.—Don't stand in front of me, bitch. Move over. What you looking at? She took hold of the bars of our cage, commenced to bang on them, shook them mightily, screaming—Hear me now, you mother fuckers, you grotty pigs, get this housewife out of here! She returned to comfort me.—Six days in this low-down hole for sitting front of a horse!

Before we were distributed among our cells, we were dressed in a kind of nurse's aide scrub uniform, blue or green, a little too large or a little too small. We had had to submit to a physical in which all our hiding places were investigated for drugs. These examinations were not too difficult, mostly because a young woman named Andrea Dworkin had fought them, refused a grosser, more painful examination some months earlier. She had been arrested, protesting the war in front of the US Mission to the UN. I had been there too, but I don't think I was arrested that day. She was mocked for that determined struggle at the Women's House, as she has been for other braveries, but according to the women I questioned, certain humiliating—perhaps sadistic customs had ended—for that period at least.

My cellmate was a beautiful young woman, 23 years old, a prostitute who'd never been arrested before. She was nervous, but she had been given the name of an important long-termer. She explained in a businesslike way that she *was* beautiful, and would need protection. She'd be OK once she found that woman. In the two days we spent together, she tried *not* to talk to the other women on our cell block. She said they were mostly street whores and addicts. She would never be on the street. Her man wouldn't allow it anyway.

447

I slept well for some reason, probably the hard mattress. I don't seem to mind where I am. Also I must tell you, I could look out the window at the end of our corridor and see my children or their friends, on their way to music lessons or Greenwich House pottery. Looking slantwise I could see right into Sutter's Bakery, then on the corner of 10th Street. These were my neighbors at coffee and cake.

Sometimes the cell block was open, but not our 12 cells. Other times the reverse. Visitors came by: they were prisoners, detainees not yet sentenced. They seemed to have a strolling freedom, though several, unsentenced, unable to make bail, had been there for months. One woman peering into the cells stopped when she saw me. Grace! Hi! I knew her from the neighborhood, maybe the park, couldn't really remember her name.

What are you in for? I asked.

Oh nothing—well a stupid drug bust. I don't even use—oh well forget it. I've been here six weeks. They keep putting the trial off. Are you OK?

Then I complained. I had planned not to complain about anything while living among people who'd be here in these clanging cells a long time; it didn't seem right. But I said, I don't have anything to read and they took away my pen and I don't have paper.

Oh you'll get all that eventually—she said. Keep asking.

Well they have all my hair pins. I'm a mess.

No no she said—you're OK. You look nice.

(A couple of years later, the war continuing, I was arrested in Washington. My hair was still quite long. I wore it in a kind of bun on top of my head. My hair pins gone, my hair straggled wildly every which way. Muriel Rukeyser, arrested that day along with about 30 other women, made the same generous sisterly remark. No no Grace, love you with your hair down, you really ought to always wear it this way.)

The very next morning, my friend brought me *The Collected Stories of William Carlos Williams*. These OK?

God! OK—Yes!

My trial is coming up tomorrow, she said. I think I'm getting off with time already done. Over done. See you around?

That afternoon, my cellmate came for her things—I'm moving to the fourth floor. Working in the kitchen. Couldn't be better.—We were sitting outside our cells, she wanted me to know something. She'd already told me, but said it again.—I still can't believe it. This creep, this guy, this cop, he waits he just waits till he's fucked and fine, pulls his pants up, pays me, and arrests me. It's not legal. It's not. My man's so mad, he like to kill *me,* but he's not that kind of—he's not a criminal type, *my* man. She never said the word pimp. Maybe no one did. Maybe that was our word.

I had made friends with some of the women in the cells across the aisle. How can I say "made friends." I just sat and spoke when spoken to, I was at school. I answered questions—simple ones. Why I would do such a fool thing on purpose? How old were my children? My man any good? Then, you live around the corner? That was a good idea, Evelyn said, to have a prison in your own neighborhood, so you could keep in touch, yelling out the window. As in fact we were able to do right here and now, calling and being called from Sixth Avenue, by mothers, children, boyfriends.

About the children: One woman took me aside. Her daughter was brilliant, she was in Hunter High School, had taken a test. No she hardly ever saw her, but she wasn't a whore—it was the drugs. Her daughter was ashamed, the grandmother, the father's mother made the child ashamed. When she got out in 6 months it would be different. This made Evelyn and Rita, right across from my cell, laugh. Different, I swear. Different. Laughing. But she *could* make it, I said. Then they really laughed. Their first laugh was a bare giggle compared to these convulsive roars. Change her ways? That dumb bitch Ha!!

Another woman, Helen, the only other white woman on the cell block wanted to talk to me. She wanted me to know that she was not only white, but Jewish. She came from Brighton Beach. Her father, he should rest in peace, thank God, was dead. Her arms were covered with puncture marks almost like sleeve patterns. But she needed to talk to me, because I was Jewish (I'd been asked by Rita and Evelyn— was I Irish? No, Jewish. Oh, they answered). She walked me to the barred window at the end of the corridor, the window that looked down on W. 10th Street. She said—How come you so friends with those black whores? You don't hardly talk to me. I said I liked them, but I like her too. She said, if you knew them for true, you wouldn't like them. They nothing but street whores. You know, once I was friends with them. We done a lot of things together, I knew them 15 years Evy and Rita maybe 20, I been in the streets with them, side by side, Amsterdam, Lenox, West Harlem; in bad weather we covered each other. Then one day along come Malcolm X and they don't know me no more, they ain't talking to me. You too white. I ain't all that white. 20 years. They ain't talking.

My friend Myrt called one day, that is called from the street, called—Grace Grace.—I heard and ran to the window. A policeman, the regular beat cop was addressing her. She looked up, then walked away before I could yell my answer. Later on she told me that he'd said—I don't think Grace would appreciate you calling her name out like that.

What a mistake! For years, going to the park with my children, or simply walking down Sixth Avenue on a summer night past the Women's House, we would often have to thread our way through whole families calling up—bellowing, screaming to the third, seventh, tenth floor, to figures, shadows behind bars and screened windows— How you feeling? Here's Glena. She got big. Mami mami you like my dress? We gettin you out baby. New lawyer come by.

And the replies, among which I was privileged to live for a few days—shouted down.—You lookin beautiful. What he say? Fuck you James. I got a chance? Bye bye. Come next week.

Then the guards, the heavy clanking of cell doors. Keys. Night.

I still had no pen or paper despite the great history of prison literature. I was suffering a kind of frustration, a sickness in the way claustrophobia is a sickness—this paper—and—penlessness was a terrible pain in the area of my heart, a nausea. I was surprised.

In the evening, at lights out (a little like the army or on good days a strict, unpleasant camp) women called softly from their cells. Rita hey Rita sing that song—Come on sister sing. A few more importunings and then Rita in the cell diagonal to mine would begin with a ballad. A song about two women and a man. It was familiar to everyone but me. The two women were prison sweethearts. The man was her outside lover. One woman, the singer, was being paroled. The ballad told her sorrow about having been parted from him when she was sentenced, now she would leave her loved woman after three years. There were about twenty stanzas of joy and grief.

Well, I was so angry not to have pen and paper to get some of it down—that I lost it all—all but the sorrowful plot. Of course she had this long song in her head and in the next few nights she sang and chanted others, sometimes with a small chorus.

Which is how I finally understood that I didn't lack pen and paper but my own memorizing mind. It had been given away with a hundred poems, called rote learning, old fashioned, backward, an enemy of creative thinking, a great human gift, disowned.

Now there's a garden where the Women's House of Detention once stood. A green place, safely fenced in, with protected daffodils and tulips; roses bloom in it too, sometimes into November.

The big women's warehouse and its barred blind windows have been removed from Greenwich Village's affluent throat. I was sorry when it happened; the bricks came roaring down, great trucks carried them away.

I have always agreed with Rita and Evelyn that if there are prisons, they ought to be in the neighborhood, near a subway:—not way out in distant suburbs, where families have to take cars, buses, ferries, trains, and the population that considers itself innocent forgets, denies, chooses to never know that there is a whole huge country of the bad and the unlucky and the self-hurters, a country with a population greater than that of many nations in our world.

Nominated by Alaska Quarterly Review

PHLOX DIFFUSA: A POEM FOR MY FIFTIETH BIRTHDAY

by SANDRA McPHERSON

from THE YALE REVIEW

Is it calm after midnight on its rocky slope,
exactly fitted to its nice little rubble?
Easy to think it's a bedtime slipper of a flower, owning no boots.
It lies flat on its back and looks at stars.

"Undaunted by stern surroundings," Mary Elizabeth Parsons says
in *The Wild Flowers of California,* 1966.
Like the game pummeled seapalm on outer rocks in breakers
the phlox spreads happy in its xeric meadow.

The flowers completely hide the leaf cushion,
the way a lot of enthusiasms obscure
the inner idiot. Actually clothe it,
but wildly as a shopping spree.

Charmed and usually older hikers want to lie right down beside it.
Starlike, delicate.

"The tiny crammed leaves live in a pocket of calm partly
of their own making, and there they trap
windblown particles
that slowly become a nourishing soil."

Taproots eight to fifteen feet.
A throw pillow bolted to granite.
Easy to think it's only three inches tall,
until you think of that, think of that root.

Nominated by Jack Marshall, Walter Pavlich, Sherod Santos

THE RING OF BRIGHTEST ANGELS AROUND HEAVEN

fiction by RICK MOODY

from THE PARIS REVIEW

I

THE RUIN—where my friend Jorge Ruiz spent some of his nights—was decorated in twisted car parts and fruitless conversation and postindustrial clutter, in the collision of strangers and in the flicker of lost opportunities. Some of it was decoration; some of it was left over from whatever manufacturing operation had occupied the space in the early decades of the century. There were, on the walls of the Ruin, the melted shapes of obsolete computers, suspended from the wall on old meat hooks. Those early desktop Macintoshes—Typing Tutors or Flight Simulators or unfinished novels still flashing anemically, in green, on their screens; motherboards splayed on counters and at tables with microchips scattered around them like a new currency. Gutted stuffed animals stapled up on the wall and mangled dolls. Floors covered in straw and fiberglass and asbestos and metal shavings and bent nails and tattooing needles and syringes. There were the rusted steel shovels of ancient backhoes: gladiatorial burial vessels. Volkswagen Beetles attached by chains to the ceiling: splendid and degraded chandeliers. The design vocabulary of the meat packing district—the meat packing district of New York City—made the Ruin

454

what it was. It seemed hard back then to imagine clubs, these kinds of clubs, without the meat packers. The meat packers, the ranchers, the butchers. The broad clean wound that the butcher, ankledeep in blood, opened in the animal's arteries, the head toppling from the calf—in Texas, in upstate New York, or wherever this butchering was taking place—the neck stump quivering before him.

The butcher and his victim weren't all that far from the guy at the Ruin who left at home a disconnect notice or an unemployment voucher or an unhappy marriage or even a double-booked dinner at the Four Seasons or Café des Artistes so that he could open his mouth and quench his thirst on another man's waste.

The action was in the stalls. Were these *actual* stalls, Jorge wanted to know, at first, like stalls from your public school, transported into the Ruin after they had outlived their usefulness over at P.S. 103? Or were they carefully decorated stall facsimiles, with artificial yet highly suggestive stall graffiti? The designers, as clever as they were angry and remorseful, would never tell. People had come this far and they were paying a lot of money for non-alcoholic drinks and they sure as hell wanted everything, even the graffiti, to be contributing to the pungent and bracing sleaze of that club, the weird sadness that lay in the air like religious incense, like smells and bells. So if they weren't real stalls, Jorge thought, they were at least designed by people who had spent their time in public schools and who knew the code of sadism that lay at the heart of public school corridors, who knew the erotic power of handtools and dental drills and heavier machinery.

The logistics of *home*, the logistics that oppressed the regulars at the Ruin, could only be solved in this theater of detritus, of glory holes, of discipline and submission, of piss and shit; so they wanted home near and far, oppressive and yet declawed. They wanted stalls, they wanted industrial spaces, they wanted uniforms, and (in part) the threat of deadly diseases, but the sight of a balance sheet, the sound of a cash register, or the ebb and flow of ordinary conversation, these were the things that really ruined these patrons, that caused them mortal discomfort.

The guy on the table being fisted by two men at once, two men wearing black leather face masks with zippers across the mouths; the women with the penciled-on sideburns, with the dildo that glowed violet, glowed with a sort of strontium 90 kind of light; the woman who lightly, desultorily whipped herself, while mumbling an alphabetical list of sexual insults; the guy suspended in the cage with the daggers

455

sheathed in his pectorals, *in his pectorals*—the possibilities seemed endless at first, but they weren't at all. The possibilities were marked by the faint, beveled edges of modern imagination, by the devouring ennui of the straight culture that the Ruin honored by opposing all the time, in every way. I mean, after a while, Jorge knew that the guy getting fisted was named Malcolm and that he was an assistant stage manager of off-off Broadway shows and that he had a brother with cerebral palsy, just as Jorge knew that the woman with the dildo—who said her name was *Huck*—was from San Antonio. Actual name: Doreen. When she was a kid, Jorge had learned, she had been a Deadhead and an environmentalist, an artist of batik and macramé.

Every day the Ruin stayed open was a miracle of invention; every day it threatened to get old, to run its course, to succumb to legal inquiries, to file for bankruptcy, to liquidate its assets, and still the regulars came. They waited for nightfall, for the early part of the evening to pass, when the breeders had all gone home to their genetic responsibilities. They waited eagerly, but without a choice. The Ruin was like the psychiatric hospital where some of them had done time. It was a last chance joint with directions to the next last chance joint; it was rock bottom with a trap door in it—Jorge told me so—and after all, he knew about eschatology. He detoxed himself in the psych ward and came out again to tell of it. He got a prescription for that crystal, lithium. He had come to the end and found there were innumerable other ends in the cauldron of his city.

When Jorge Ruiz wasn't visiting sex clubs—and it was the question you always wanted to ask about the people you met there—he lived on Times Square. Middle-thirties, medium height, perilously thin, hair in tiny steel coils, a large burgundy splotch on the left side of his face, a birthmark, a speaker of Spanish and English and Spanglish. He had left his mom, who lived alone in Union City, to come to Manhattan. That is, he had left behind the outlying dilapidation for Manhattan. And Times Square was where he ended up, where it was cheap enough, where there was a high turnover of real estate because of death, terror, illness and the sex industry.

You know the throw weight of chance in these decisions, the decisions about where to live, Jorge told me, the kilo-tonnage of chance— you come one day looking for an apartment, two other guys are looking at the *Voice* the same minute you are. There are thousands of people looking at the *Voice,* really, but these two guys, those other guys, in

456

particular: one guy ends up living in Harlem, one guy ends up living in Chelsea—and this second guy dies young—one guy ends up in Times Square. You all look at the same apartment one day, though you never really meet. Next day, you step on the same gray, stringy piece of Trident gum on Seventh Avenue and Fifty-third Street; the same desperate panhandler, in the upper forties, asks all three of you for change (he's a guy I knew in college, now schizophrenic); you fire the same real estate agent. But you never meet.

And in this way you figure out after a while how the people around you, in New York City, are like so much *dark matter.* You don't know who they are, you never meet them, but they shadow you. Your movements implicate one another; your good stretches and disconsolate moments are one and the same.

Other New Yorkers, they are exactly like your friends, *your* New Yorkers, except for one small detail—Jorge explained—they were born in the D.R. not Puerto Rico, maybe, or their hair is a lighter brown, or they really prefer tea to coffee, or prefer boys to girls or girls to boys, or they prefer Techno to House or House to Techno, or they live in clubs like Lebanon, where people get stabbed, clubs that last a year or two and then are gone. These New Yorkers have three brothers instead of two. Or they never did drink or never did start smoking that shit or they never did finish school. Or they went to graduate school and now can participate in grand discussions about the city's duty to house the homeless or about the dialectic of literary-something-or-other that has, at one end, formalism, and at the other *hermeneutics.*

These people look exactly like other people you know. That guy passing on Forty-sixth Street looks exactly like that guy you met on line at the Ziegfeld. That guy looks like someone from your gym. He's even carrying a gym bag. And in fact the two of them, those two guys you just saw, those guys who look like other people you know, they also look like one another.

In this city of the Ruin, *an entire manufacturing run of human beings was completed,* Jorge said, *and then the molds were all used two, three, maybe four times, to save money on newer molds, and if you are lucky you never meet your own double. If you're lucky.*

Which is not to say that we don't grow into the particulars of our environment. Twins grow apart; identicals grow apart. Ultimately we and our doubles—all of us—are seized by vain, idiosyncratic quirks. Land-

457

scape works on people the way diet does, or the way local television broadcasting does. People grow apart. They get kinks. Like it says in the Gospels: *Fortunate is the lion that the human will eat, so that the lion becomes human.*

So Jorge Ruiz, who lived in a neighborhood with a thousand kinds of nakedness, came to see nakedness as his vocabulary. With it, he tried to explain things, his merciless depression, for example. Jorge lived over a store that sold knives, just around the corner from a pickup spot called Sally's. The new Sally's, that is. (The name was lettered in the opaque window on Forty-third in browned, unsticky masking tape.) Sally's was as venerable in the world of transsexual hustlers as, say, the Algonquin—only a few blocks away—was venerable to the charlatanical writers of the sixties and seventies. The old address, the old Sally's, had burned somehow. Before Jorge got there. Suspicious activity. An unhappy or confused trick. A shortfall in protection money.

Around the corner from Sally's II was the Peep World, a midtown sex establishment of enduring popularity. It too had burned once; it too had struggled back from this calamity. PEEP WORLD! HOT! EURO-PEAN! GAY! KINKY! BIZARRE! RUBBER GOODS! MARITAL AIDS! It was all mirrors and antiseptic spray. It was all lockers inside, like some de-mented public high school, like P.S. 103. There was a guy whose job it was simply to hose down the video booths afterwards, but sometimes he was backed up or on break, and you slid, or your sneakers squeaked, in fresh extract. Jorge had been inside, of course, had sampled video booths both straight and gay, had even made the acquaintance of this bored young man with the cleaning agents. His name was Ray and he stood off to one side like any other minimum-wage laborer—checking and re-checking a plastic five-dollar watch.

And across the street was the Priapus, an all-male erotic film cen-ter. ARMY BRATS. TRUCKER STUDS. TRAPDOOR TREATS. LOCKER LOVE. PRISON GUYS. HARD AS STONE.

At first, Jorge liked to watch the kinds of artificial expressions that played across the faces of the men, and even the women, who ven-tured past the neon entrances into these local enterprises. He was eat-ing a Sabrett's hot dog, say, and leaning against a destroyed parking meter, watching. There was a certain way consumers of the erotic pre-tended that they were fortuitously drawn there, a certain low gear in which they traveled, a certain look they had that said—Jorge told me—*The office where I am dropping off this important document seems to be right by this suggestive nude poster.* Or, *There happens to*

458

be someone I recognize inside, glancing at that rack of . . . videotapes!
At first, these superficial acts of dignity pleased him. Or at least his apprehension of them, his apprehension of their hypocrisy, pleased him.

Until he was going in there himself.

Because after a couple of months in Times Square, he was visiting these addresses, too.

Like this: In front of the Peep World, the sky was the blue of colorized films. The traffic moved like it had never moved before. Somewhere the mayor of New York City was dreaming of pitching Manhattan to the Democratic National Committee or to the Grammys. His pulse raced in this dream. The mayor napped and dreamed of public check-signings and flawless photo opportunities and a Manhattan that operated like a Japanese factory, and just for one afternoon his dream had come true. It was a miracle. The cars were racing past the Port Authority Bus Terminal as if there were a civil defense emergency uptown; the homeless, including that guy I knew in college, had stirred themselves from their vents and grates because it was so beautiful. And that afternoon Jorge had followed up on a half-dozen leads for jobs, including a promising opportunity teaching English as a second language. True, he had a friend with that horrible kind of pneumonia; and his mother was old now, and wouldn't live long, especially not alone in New Jersey, but the breeze in the air nourished him today; he was like some purely aerobic organism, and that evening's full moon would hang above Times Square like the most fabulous neon. That day, no decision seemed wrong. The operations of chance were like a fine harvest.

There was a girl in some salacious poses on the billboard out front. She was the girl with a hundred aliases—Trixi, Candi, Belle, Wanda, Ginnie Mae—and her retouched curves adorned the doorways of every pornographic outlet on Eighth Avenue. Jorge saw a couple of guys in UPS uniforms check both ways and roll into Peep World, and in spite of the good luck he expected from himself that afternoon—he was even imagining tomorrow's *Post* with nothing but good news in it—in spite of everything, he was following them. His hand was on the slippery stainless-steel door handle—you had to open that door, you had to manifest your intention to enter—as he strode across the threshold. *How do they decorate a place like this? I was always curious.*

Inside the Peep World or the Show Center or the Nude Revue or the Triple XXX Lounge, Jorge learned, the girls were like the rest of the citizenry of New York: exhausted, overworked, frightened of the future, cynical, bitter, looking to cop. He talked to them, sometimes, the ones in the double-occupancy booths, or the ones who writhed on felt-covered tables, though he wasn't terribly attracted to them, though he had some deficit in sexual desire now, and this in no way endeared him to the women who were working. And he had little money to tuck under the elastic of their G-strings. Anyway, in conversation, Jorge was worse than awkward. He was an educated guy who looked a little weird, a little pasty, kind of ill, but also gentle and knowing and forgiving. Jorge told me himself that he talked the way a confidence man talks, trying to catch you in some well-traveled fallacy, or like a religious zealot, unyielding and lost at the same time.

—I guess this is supposed to be when I take my pants down, he said to the girl in the double-occupancy booth, that confessional. She was tricked up like a dominatrix. She frowned.

—You can do whatever you want, she said.

Sound of her voice muffled by plastic.

—Is there some . . . is there a kind of routine you do if I don't know what to say?

—Uh, sure, I guess . . .

—Touch, uh, touch yourself and . . . No, wait, Jorge said. Wait. Just wait a second, okay.

He sighed deeply.

—You don't have to do that, he said. You don't have to . . .

—Look, she said, if you're not going to . . . If you don't wanna . . . If you're not here to *get off*, why bother?

—My money, Jorge said. My money.

A silence, as though they were closing in on something. Then at the same moment the invisible factories of chance manifested themselves. Like a lethal blade, the window guard slid down between them. Rustling on the other side of that impenetrable wall. Time for more tokens.

It was later, or it was another day. He didn't talk to the girls, the lap dancers, or whatever they were that year, he looked at the ones in the booths. Or he didn't even look in the booths, he looked at the video screens with their innumerable channels and innumerable parameters of chase and entrapment. A hand grasping. A cock, as large and brutal as some amputation stump. He simply wanted to see what was on every channel. It no longer had to do with wanting to see a woman *dowsing* with some bruised-looking phallus, or with some guy sitting on some other guy, taking the thing into him. Or a young girl moaning

460

breathlessly. It was all just *want and flesh,* bodies melding in cold fusion, bodies without borders, bodies eager for the subterranean passage that led beneath and beyond New York City.

Jorge hustled from the video rack to the booths to the rubber goods, those handsome Caucasian and African simulated penises, strap-on harnesses, those ticklers and pincers and rings and clamps and devices of the rougher trades. Inflatable women, the sort without politics, pillowed, vinyl facsimiles of kindness. He hovered everywhere like a yellow jacket trying to get the sense of Peep World, he wanted to know, wanted to know. He was shivering with excitement, and somehow the shivering seemed to have its own separate strategy. Or as Jorge said later, *The thrill of pornography, well, it was around a long time before pornography ever was.*

Then he was back in the booths: Ray, the purveyor of antiseptic, reprimanded Jorge for accidentally pressing a button unlocking his booth too soon. Toothlessly, Ray mumbled, his lips folded back in disappointment and contempt to reveal the black rinds of his gums: *Don't open the fucking door till you're done.* Jorge settled himself again into the video booth, and he was finally able to stroke himself to the point of points, to the *summa,* and then he was grateful.

He was grateful that the atomization of city life could be dealt with simply on this cash basis; that the cobwebs that had decorated his oldest fantasies, the stuff he thought was his burden alone, could be cleared away just by turning some dials and spitting into your palm; he was grateful that the workers in the sex industry had, he was sure, kind bones. What more compassionate people were there? Who was more accepting of the desperate and lonely? As a profession of kindness sex work was easily more inclusive than either social work or nursing. He was suffused with a feeling of gratitude that was all out of scale with the brusque, impersonal machinery of Peep World.

And the feeling didn't last very long. It didn't even endure beyond the premises of the establishment, in fact. The expanding streets of Times Square—bubbling up and cracking, engulfing and digesting—had not evaporated while he was inside. That brief afternoon interval of municipal fellowship and teamwork had vanished. It had just been coincidence. Jorge was back in the old New York, the quarreling New York. What he wanted, what he desired, the city was taking these slowly from him.

He killed time, like other users of pornography, between the glittering entrances to Times Square. There were gyro restaurants—

461

GYROS! PITZAS!—and passport-photo shops and the video-game parlors and back-dated magazine shops, the Best Western for foreign teenagers, cheap bars for the theater district and stores that sold Broadway memorabilia and knives, and cheaper bars for the hard luck binge drinkers. Lingerie stores for transvestites. Liquor stores with bulletproof glass and little slide-through slots for pint bottles.

And here was what he felt when he came out of Peep World (a couple of drops of seminal fluid riveting his shorts uncomfortably to his thigh): he could feel the charcoal and polonium falling from the sky; he could feel the urgency in every conversation; he could see that men walking the streets were fitting brass knuckles on over their arthritic joints. He knew why people went into Peep World. Because they were feeling really good; because they were feeling really bad; because they had had trouble at work; because they were having trouble with their girlfriend; because they had no girlfriend; because they had two girlfriends or two boyfriends or a girlfriend and a boyfriend, and they didn't know how to choose between them; because they were lonely; because they never got any time alone; because the world was full of hypocrisy; because it was not; because they weren't caring for the people they loved; because they were tired of caring for others; because the skies were blue, or their car had a dent, or their cat was sick, or they'd had an argument on the subway, or they wanted to live in the country and own a trailer, or they were tired of the country, or they hated tuna, or they loved rock and roll; or because they had no money; because they had too much; because they were honest with themselves; or because of chance—Jorge said—*because of chance*.

The neon of the gyro place, the neon of the shoe-repair store, they were all the neon of Peep World. Jorge confused the thresholds of these businesses. They were identical. Just like, after a time, strangers and the people he knew were one and the same. The neon that called to him in Times Square was all one sign. Follow your itch, it said, hasten your descent. Go ahead, dive.

His mother helped him out some, with money, I mean. She had some social security and some money given her by Jorge's dad, an Eastern European man from Edison, who had abandoned them when Jorge was just a baby. Occasionally Jorge put in a little time here or there—in a travel-book publisher once, temping, doing some clerical work at a clinic in Times Square. These jobs did not last because Jorge had trouble getting out of bed. It was Epstein-Barr virus or pernicious anemia or maybe just an attack of nerves. His mother had cures involving various spices. Bills and equations were tightening around him like the leather restraining straps you saw in the Ruin, or maybe they had always been there, he told me, tightening around him, a part of his life, bills and math and algebra and all that stuff he couldn't really learn in his public school, the school with the sadistic stalls. He saw the forms of these equations on his walls, he had actually selected a wallpaper with 1040-EZ forms on it—he had good taste in decorating, he was a tasteful guy, when he had the energy—and sometimes when he was particularly upset, he tried to fill in these forms. Or so he told me. He used a red laundry marker, the pen of choice for suicide notes. He never could get these columns of numbers to add up the same way twice, as he was often late with the rent and often finding bills that were black-bordered and threatening. *He couldn't work, he couldn't work. Work exhausted him.* Then he'd go to the Triple XXX Lounge.

Somewhere in the midst of these months tumbling inertly into much longer stretches he picked up the other most economically important commodity of his neighborhood, the name of which is such bad luck that it's scary to pronounce it here. I like its name, though, its first and last names—so many hard Cs. A name that was made to sound good in English. In the Romance languages, it would sound ugly and hard. But here in the new world in the languages of Native Americans, the Anasazi, say, it would perhaps be the lovely name of an estuary or a long, rolling meadow. It was made for this continent. It was made for this place. Despite bad luck, then, I will write its name here: *crack cocaine.*

The street hustlers—the prostitutes—and the dealers in Times Square were all attached by coincidence, chance and circumstance. They were all acquainted, as in any other New York City business, and it made convenience shopping for vice that much more pleasant. Jorge had hustlers sleeping in the doorway of his apartment building, girls and boys, teenagers who wore the same clothes day after day, who had lice and open sores, who were hives of HIV. These kids were hustlers only in the most limited definition of the term. They would do whatever you wanted for a price, *they said,* but they wouldn't do it, really, they would get scared in the end and say that you couldn't fuck them in the ass—Yo, it's *dangerous*—or could they just jerk you off, or they wouldn't say anything at all, they would assume a stony and resentful posture until you gave them the money anyway.

They were just junkies, in Jorge's view, cross-addicts, crackheads, garbage-heads, call them whatever you want, they were ghosts, they were the afterimages of people once photographed or yearbooked or fingerprinted or otherwise entrapped in a devouring system of images. Ghosts, children already dead to their parents, dead to their principals, ministers, social workers, friends, fuck buddies, running partners, dead even to their dealers, ghosts who would for drugs assume corporeal form, as if crack cocaine was some conjuring stone. They were ghosts like he was a ghost, like Jorge was a ghost and later an addict, too, living far from his own neighborhood, far from his mother, sleeping all day, drawing the blinds, and then going to the Priapus to watch a double feature in which a dozen robotic actors with large mustaches pretended to be camp counselors or infantrymen and then unsheathed themselves.

So this shit these hustlers were smoking, it was available right in the doorway of Jorge's building, because the dealers and the hustlers were all mutually implicated somehow. They appeared at the same time each morning. They hung around in the same way. And that shit they smoked was cheap the first time around. So Jorge, after some months of refusing, gave it a try. It was cheap when you first learned about the way its network stretched out around you, about its system of distribution and shipping and sales and marketing, and about the way it traveled in your neural pathways, Jorge told me, *which was an exact replica of the chart of its distribution*—it was all bait and switch, divide and conquer, symbolic and imaginary, you were talking, you were talking, and the sentences were getting longer and longer and you were saying stuff to this dealer, who was also smoking this shit, in impossibly long sentences, sentences that mixed something that masqueraded as euphoria with the most venal cruelties—Jorge was laughing as the guy called his girls *crackhead bitches* that first time, Jorge was saying that Dominicans was the crassest motherfuckers in the city—and the shit was dancing in your bloodstream like rogue cells metastasizing, and then you were going to the ATM on Ninth Avenue and Forty-second for the fourth time that night, *that night,* uh huh, because it was almost sunrise and you hadn't slept yet and your money was going to this guy who wasn't getting much of it because he was a low-level employee *nothing more* and his profit was going to this guy back in Jackson Heights and his money was going to the guy who was *flying this shit in* and his money was going to some other guy who lived in the jungle who was using some of it to pay off the military government of his country, which was trying to pay off loans that your bank—the one that owns your ATM—made to this rain-forested country, and you, meanwhile, had one of those crackhead bitches in your bed, *gimme one of those crackhead bitches,* or one of those crackhead boys, sucking on your *dick,* didn't matter which, boy or girl all the same, the mouth around you right then was just a mouth—*suck my dick, you crackhead bitch*—and your *dick* had no *self-respect* left in it anyway, there was nothing left in you, in fact, you are impotent and it is morning and you haven't slept and the blinds are still drawn and you loath yourself more than you can say, fucking right you do, only that's too simple, self-loathing, because your revulsion for yourself is bottomless, could power a hydroelectric generator, and it sounds this morning like someone is trying to open your bolted windows with a rusty tire iron *someone is coming in* and the screech of city buses braking, they call your name, *Jorge,* on the wind. New York City is a slow corruption. It is time to find some work. To find some money to buy some more of *that shit* from that guy who lives on his feet at the bottom of your stairs, Jorge told me.

After that, after that first time, Jorge would have liked to have said that he stayed clear of the drug. He would have liked to have visited his mother in Jersey. He would have liked not to have his blinds drawn again and his cat tipping over cartons of half-eaten Chinese takeout, his cat chasing the cockroaches. He would have liked to say that he had bathed or that he had read the paper or even circled some help-wanted ads or cleaned the tub or done a dish or taken the filter out of the coffee thing or that he at least had one of those compulsive cleaning sessions that visited him when he had a hangover, when he went looking for every trace of the night before in his apartment, a night he only remembered in part anyway, shining his apartment, buffing it, polishing it, on his knees, short of breath.

But after a while he didn't even want to straighten out so much, Jorge told me. Getting clean required an effort he no longer possessed. This *aperçu* was the kind of thing people might whisper to you in the sex clubs. Someone sits down on the next stool and says, *My life is really coming to an end, if you want to know the truth. Don't say anything. Don't patronize me. Don't try to convince me otherwise.* Stage-whispered over the music. After a while, Jorge's resolve had gone the way of other New York resolutions. It became the style of some other Jorge, some other New Yorker, some guy who looked liked him but didn't have his bad luck. The Jorge who had health insurance.

465

So he was at Sally's II one day. He had come up for air, and he was talking to a very nice girl named Crystal with whom he shared this penchant for grand dramatic statements. Crystal said, having just met him, *My life is fucked up when I am not high. I am simply at my best when I'm high. Being a man was just a way of slowly dying for me, I may as well just tell you. I am a girl like other girls. I would just like to have a husband and live a life in the Catholic church.*

Crystal's complexities, her physical inconsistencies, didn't bother Jorge. And he knew that Crystal would come with him on the promise of crack cocaine. And they walked up Forty-third Street, the way of all champagne dreams, the way to all Las Vegas weddings, and they walked right up to the little guy sitting on the hood of a car in front of a place where they sold fake identification cards, and this guy said to Jorge, because Jorge was not a regular customer:

—What the fuck you come up to me like this, what the *fuck?* You crazy? What the fuck? This my *business.* You're an asshole, man. What the *fuck.* What the fuck you doing?

He was gesturing ominously, violently at Jorge, who couldn't figure how he had done anything out of the ordinary. The dealer led them around the corner onto Forty-third Street, heading toward Ninth, making a number of lascivious comments about Crystal, about the size of her breasts, and, because he sensed it was a big night for Jorge, he quoted a price higher than usual. An outrageous price. For the crack cocaine. So Jorge refused.

And then his luck turned uniformly bad.

Now Jorge and Crystal were standing there with commuters swarming around them—toward the bus terminal—and she was yelling, What is the matter with you? She yelled anxiously as if what troubled her were not the crack cocaine, as if there were something much deeper, some life-threatening thing for which this moment was merely emblematic. Her voice plunged down into a lower register. She had a robust voice, a singer's voice. *Boys with breasts,* Jorge told me wearily, *they are angels and when they break your heart they take you closer to God.*

It started raining. It was raining, and they were standing there, and then she was swishing off in her high heels, and Jorge was limping after, No wait, *Honey, no, wait,* thinking she looked an awful lot like someone he had known when he was young. In spite of all her operations and medical procedures, she looked like a girl he had known in

Newark, the first girl he had loved, Kristina, who had eyes like colored beads. Crystal, Kris. Which was which?

So he jogged back and gave his last few dollars to the hyena in front of the ID parlor. Paid the price. It was that kind of night. The dealer was laughing at him now; he was pronouncing grim prophecies in a dead tongue, as Jorge disappeared up the block. And then Jorge and Crystal were back at his place and they were grief-stricken, yes, it actually came over them like a contagion and they were crying and somehow they had gotten the rock and they were smoking it and they were making these rash promises like *their marriage would be a grand affair, with a reception that would go on for days,* and it wouldn't matter that Crystal couldn't afford the kind of gown that would have best suited her, and then she started to go down on Jorge and it was an act of mercy, really, not much else, and he put his hand down between her legs, because in spite of everything else, in spite of the fact that he was sweating profusely and grinding his teeth, he felt this was somehow a real chance to exercise those atrophied muscles of compassion, it was the last night he ever felt love, maybe, and he actually said this really stupid thing to her, he actually said these words, words with their own intentions and syntax, *This is the last night I'm ever going to feel love,* he told me, he told her, and he reached down there to the little chrysalis-shaped stub that had once been Crystal's penis before all the hormones and stuff—it was roseate and shriveled and it didn't exactly snap to attention—and he tried to coax something from it, some shiver of recognition about the structure and implication of contact, about sex and human kindness. Because at least he wanted to give something to someone else. Because if he had become impervious to his own feelings, he at least felt like he could give something to someone else. Crystal moaned as though she might come, but he knew that nothing of the sort applied. They were right near Broadway after all, and he was sleeping with a *guy who was more or less acting the part of a woman,* a top flight performance, a Broadway performance, and the moan was to attest to the success of Jorge's own erotic masquerade and how it made Crystal feel, ostensibly, well, kinda sexy.

And still he came. Depressed when the moment arrived, with none of that cocaine-self after orgasm, none of that grandiosity. Cocaine had emptied him. There was simply less of him than there had been in the early part of the day. No tranquilizer was going to restore that deficit. He was grazing bottom. His testes emptied their burden. He reached his arms around her. They held one another. Yes, and then they gave up consciousness.

In the morning, Crystal was gone. She had stolen the last few valuable things in his apartment: some silverware his mother had given him, an antique vase his father had sent him once.

I don't need to tell you of the grim movement of the next month or so, the way the utilities were getting shut off, the income-tax people bringing up stuff from years ago, the landlady threatening. These particulars are not unusual and so I abbreviate them. Jorge said that he *preferred to read by candlelight,* as solitary readers had done for centuries, and he had no need for a phone. He called his mother collect from the street.

He began shooting heroin as a matter of course. It was the equal and opposite reaction to what I have been describing. It was just another thing to do, heroin or speedballs, and it actually served to broaden him in a way: it got him out of the house. It got him into Harlem, where one of those guys he had never met, the guy who looked at his very apartment right before he took it, was also shooting dope. It got him into the East Village, where there were a number of other people he would never meet, but who were quite close to him—a friend of mine, in fact, Dave, with whom I went to college, and a girl Dave almost went on a blind date with once, and a painter from the gallery Dave's never-to-have-been blind date once worked at. All these people were in Harlem or on the Lower East Side, putting money in a pail that a guy was whisking into a rundown tenement building. Heroin got Jorge into the East Village, from which it took him a really long time to get home when he was high. And it got him, in the end, into the Ruin. His habit wasn't gigantic, but he was starting to take risks. His arms were pocked here and there. The Ruin followed directly from that. It was no longer a matter of any bio-electrical orgasmic *spike.* Orgasm was out of the question. The Ruin was where Jorge felt relaxed, to the degree that relaxation was an idea he still understood. Listen, he said to me, *Times Square is a place you live because it's the only place left where you feel like you are comfortable.* And this is true of this club, too, *and maybe even true of all of Nueva York.* He could have lived in San Juan, say, or in Bridgeport or Toronto, but the ebb and flow of macroeconomics had brought him here, and he had relaxed into chance the way one grows attached to a shirt that is a size too big.

Maybe he heard about the Ruin from some of the women at Peep World or Sally's II (where he went later to look for Crystal, to beat her senseless, but he never did find her), or maybe he was just drawn there by walking aimlessly along the desolate streets beside the West Side Highway. He was wearing khaki pants and a Hawaiian-print shirt and a belted leather jacket and a gold necklace. He had a beard now and his eyes had that disembodied, unsouled look of junkies, and he recognized no ordinary human boundary in conversation. *I've been looking at you all night,* he said to me in the Ruin. And then he told me what I have told you. There was no emotion in him, he was as gray as a blank screen, but at the same time there were in him all the regrets of this city. The story of his decline and fall was marked by repetition and coincidence. The same opinions again and again, in further states of decay, the same complaints about the city, about how the museums were fascist and all the good clubs were closed, and how the best neighborhoods were off-limits for a person of his origins.

What happened to him that night after I met him at the Ruin I am able to tell you. What happened to him after he started shooting dope and before he detoxed himself, Jorge's story, or the part of it that I know, ends this way: we talked above the din of industrial racket. There were dancers in studded leather underwear. A night in June. Jorge disappeared into one of the stalls. When he came out again he was jaundiced. I was thinking about going to an after-hours bar. Jorge said he was going home, but instead he went down to the East Village, to a *cop shop* he had heard about. This I learned later. A bakery on Eighth Street and Avenue D that was a front for a heroin operation. Jorge didn't know the East Village well, though, and so when he got off the subway at Astor Place, he wandered block after block into the rubble of that neighborhood trying to find the bakery. It was deep in the night now, and he was trying to find it, the silhouettes of these abandoned blocks were ominous, and he was feeling sick and shaking, and he didn't think he was ever going to sleep again, going up and down Eighth Street, thinking about how to get out of this neighborhood and back into Times Square without being bashed or robbed or murdered or anything else, and also not thinking about it, but thinking—with the one last flickering neurotransmitter given over to ordinary human curiosity—*how was the place, the bakery, going to be decorated?*

Starless sky. The only pedestrian traffic working the same line of business that Jorge was engaged in. When he finally found the bakery, by chance, oblivious to a sudden confluence of meteors above the city, he was as lost as he would ever get in his short life. He was sick, he told me. *I was sick.*

II

Everyone in New York City does not go to sex clubs. Above Fifty-seventh Street on the East Side they march to and from hired cars as if the subway and its content were television fictions. There is the guy with the private life up here, with the call girl problem or the fucking-boys-in-a-motel-in-the-Bronx problem. There is the ragged teenager whose ambition is to throw off his or her Upper East Side address, the kid who takes the limo to the shooting gallery on Lexington and 125th, but truly this Upper East Side is a separate city, where only the occasional skirmish with the New York of this story takes place. The Upper East Side has its loneliness, it has its isolation, it has its lost opportunities, its disintegrating families, it has its murder and its addiction and its adultery and homosexuality, sure, but all this is *cushioned.* Disconsolation drifts out of the Upper East Side, in some river of chance, drifts neglected like waste, until it lands somewhere else.

So another friend I knew from that time, Toni Gardner, went to a club called Wendy's. Saturday nights in the meat packing district. In the same space as the Ruin. A club for women. *Private sex parties.* They had auctions. You could *auction yourself.* There was a line of those willing to be auctioned. It snaked back to the black plywood bar. A lot of people wanted to participate. If you were willing to wait for a while, you could know your value.

The auctioneer, a woman in her forties, specialized in a certain stage patter ironically imitative of the classic auction house style. The Christie's and Sotheby's style. She was well-dressed and knowledge-able and articulate about the artifacts at hand. Her argot was full of hyperbolic folderol, jokes and salacious commentary, and it was delivered at an unintelligible pace. She enabled, through the blur of her rhetoric, a host of ritual couplings all based upon principles of chance and economics. On the other hand, maybe she was like the country auctioneer, sending off the calf to be made veal: *Woman of the age of twenty-five, hair the color of cinnamon, eyes an arctic blue, height and weight, well, she's of a certain size—she's in tip-top physical condition—note the breasts, fountains of maternity, which I can*

470

only describe to you by falling into the use of those old metaphors—perfect fruits—and an ass to die for, yeah to die for—yes, this dyke can sing, I can promise you that—in these black jeans, well she will do whatever transports you, this young dyke of twenty-five—I can promise you, and let's start with an opening bid of a hundred and fifty dollars for the evening; do I hear a hundred and fifty, yeah, one seventy-five, who will pay one seventy-five for this auburn beauty from the country, from the . . . from the state of Maine, that's right—never visited these precincts before and ready to be broken on the rack of your choice, fresh from the unforgiving and dramatic coasts of Maine—unwise in the ways of Manhattan—do I hear one seventy-five, one ninety, do I have one ninety, two hundred dollars—she assures me she can take a dildo all the way to its rubberized base, two twenty-five, do I hear, two thirty—a bottom, yeah, she's a bottom of compliance such as you have never experienced, SOLD! YES! SOLD! And so on until the obscure and almost unlit cavern rocked with the dynamics of ownership. Her voice now a whisper in the microphone, devoid of affect, the words delivered without feeling at all, just the words, a perfect simulacrum of auction slang and then you were owned. You were owned.

Toni was from the Upper East Side by way of the suburbs—she had never been to Maine at all—and she got out of that neighborhood as soon as she could. Took the bus down Fifth Avenue and only went back for holidays. I met her at Rutgers. When she auctioned herself after a few drinks, I was with her. She'd had a hard time persuading them to let me in. They quizzed you out front if you were a guy. If there was a moment's hesitation in your responses you were gone. *Are you a fag?* If you even quarreled with the usage, you were alone walking past empty warehouses. Way, way West. No cabs. No buses. No subways.

Back then, Wendy's was just coming into prominence as an event. It was making a transition from a prior location, where it had simply been a bar, and the flyers were getting more and more aggressive: *Wendy's, the dungeon of destiny for discerning dykes.* Or: *Wendy's, Cruising, Dancing, Humiliation.* Toni had recently stumbled into the new room in the back, the one with the vinyl bed in it, and she often found bodies writhing there, including, once, the body of a composition professor we'd had at Rutgers. *She gave the stupidest assignments.* Wendy's sprouted these new rooms, like a starfish regrowing itself. Private rooms down this long, gaslit corridor. Like the steam tunnels under the Rutgers campus. Tunnels like architectural diagrams for the uterine and fallopian insides of the customers. Wendy's was a mystery. You could never tell if the pool table would be there, if the cages would be there, if the bartender who was alluring last week still had her shift. The specifics came and went. Including the pertinent information. Wendy's operated on Saturday nights, as it had once operated only on Thursdays; it changed locations. It had a phone. It didn't. It had live music. It didn't. Sometimes it was in the meat-packing district and sometimes it was gone altogether.

Likewise being auctioned that night were the services of a first-rate dominatrix, who would demonstrate her gifts on the premises, later in the evening. A tattooist and scarification expert also auctioned some work. One of the bartenders auctioned herself. We were supposed to use *play money,* simulated legal tender bills, but this counterfeiting diluted the effect of the transaction. Therefore a subterranean marker existed that featured real cash. Toni got into this long unruly line—she was soon to be the beauty from Maine, the cinnamon-haired beauty— after we'd sat there a while, excitably. And it wasn't so strange that she did it, really. The auction wasn't that far, say, from a *coming out party* back in Montclair, where Toni had lived as a kid.

Things weren't going well for her professionally. She didn't really know what she wanted to do; she had spent a couple of years talking in therapy about *vocational choice anxiety.* And she had flipped a car in Long Island visiting her parents' summer house. She owed them a lot of money for it. She'd moved out of the Upper East Side after being engaged to a nice boy with a legal practice. Toni auctioned herself to slip these binds. She did it for fun, an amnesiac fun.

She danced in a go-go cage, beside the auctioneer, dressed in black jeans and a tank top; she made sure to sport her tattoos, and she affected an insouciant look, as if daring a bidder. This was *the* look among the lots at Wendy's auction—a look that mixed subject and object, *sub* and *dom*—and therefore not terribly novel. Toni didn't garner the highest price. That went to a woman in a sort of librarian costume who seemed to weep nervously as a pair of anxious bidders competed aggressively for her. She brought a thousand collars for the night.

The music was speed metal. Speed metal with girl singers. The place shook with it. Toni danced. At last, the bidding was completed. Two hundred and fifty dollars. A scattered and diffident applause. The crowd parted a little bit, and in a movie slow motion the employees of Wendy's, the handlers, waved Toni over, waved her over to the edge of the stage, waving like construction flagmen, where *two* women were waiting for her. Two women had bid together for her. A consortium. They were fucking cheap, was Toni's first feeling, she explained to me later. *They were fucking cheap, they couldn't even afford to buy their own slave for the evening—they had to go in on one.* No way was she going with them. No way. They were cheap.

But then Toni began to warm to the idea a little. She was charmed, it turned out, by their garishness. By the ugly complexities they presented. She hated them at first and in her disdain she started to like them. At the bar. As she stepped from the stage, Toni took one hand from each of them—from Doris and Marlene—and they repaired to the bar. One of her owners was a good lesbian and one was a bad lesbian. The good lesbian was Doris, and she came from Bernardsville, New Jersey, but she didn't go to Rutgers like Toni Gardner did. *She went to Princeton.* Doris's parents were disappointed when she made clear her object choice to them, when Doris told her parents that *she was in love with a woman.* But they were supportive. (Her mom was especially supportive because she was in therapy with Dr. Bernice Neptcong, who had an office right in Princeton.) They supported her efforts to find a loving, caring relationship.

Unfortunately, Toni told me, Doris didn't want a loving, caring relationship exactly, or perhaps these terms were simply more elastic to her than might be supposed by Bernice Neptcong. To Doris loving and caring always seemed to have a certain amount of trouble attached to them. Love and trouble were really identical to her. So Doris formed an attachment with Marlene, the bad lesbian. Marlene was a tall, exotic sex worker—Marlene was not her real name—who had platinum blond hair and coffee-colored skin, who slept with men at a reasonably successful escort agency and who came home at night aggrieved by her profession. She drank a lot. She dabbled with harder drugs.

Marlene's cheekbones were like the sharp side of an all-purpose stainless-steel survival jackknife and her eyes narrowed to reflect disappointment and loss, which, when combined with her biceps, her violent and toned physique, made for a compelling female beauty. Doris, on the other hand, looked like an Ivy League intellectual. She had thick black glasses and she shaved the back of her head. She wore maroon velveteen bell bottoms and had a navel ring, frequently infected. She was a little older than her clothes suggested.

Marlene and Doris, Toni realized, didn't have much to say to each other. Toni didn't know, yet, that Marlene had just come back from a hard day at an escort agency where she had to fuck a whole bunch of

473

strangers, guys for whom deceit was a simple fact of their day, who wove deceit and its responsibilities into their schedule like deceit was just another calendar appointment. And she didn't know that Doris also hated her job at the women's magazine where she worked on the copy desk—she aspired to write articles for *Camera Obscura*. Toni thought Marlene was the harder of the two. Marlene was like a tea-kettle almost boiled off. Anything could upset her, it seemed, any little stray remark. But in truth Doris was harder. Doris was detached and skeptical and full of calcified antipathies.

Their apartment was in the Clinton section of Manhattan, also called Hell's Kitchen, where Jorge Ruiz lived. On the night that Toni was auctioned off to Marlene and Doris, Jorge, as I have said, was arguing with a pre-op transsexual, Crystal, about whether to buy crack cocaine from the guy on Forty-third Street who was out to chisel them. At that very moment, while Jorge was just lifting the hem of Crystal's cheap synthetic miniskirt and pulling delicately on the mesh of her white fishnet stockings, Doris, Marlene and Toni were throwing light switches a couple of blocks away.

It was a small one-bedroom and it was draped in leather items, in stuff from the Pink Pussycat or the Pleasure Chest. There was restraining gear, and they even had a gynecologist's exam table with houseplants on it. The table had stirrups and everything. There was another decorating strain, too: Bernardsville chic. It was a kind of homely, countervailing sensibility. Doris hadn't been able to shake it yet, though she was in her thirties. She had a few museum posters, Monet's years at Giverny or the Treasures of Egypt, and some handsome black Ikea furniture and a lovely imitation Persian area rug made in Belgium. Her parents helped her to buy these. Doris and Marlene also had one of those little yapping dogs, a corgi or something, named Bernice Neptcong, M.D. Doris would say, *Get out of the way, Bernice Neptcong*. The dog was vicious. An attack rat.

Marlene had clamps, Toni told me. She liked to have you apply the clamps to her nipples and then, also, to her labia, though the best part, Marlene said, and Toni repeated to me, *I'm telling you—the best part is when they come off*. She also used clothespins, because you could take a little of the spring out of them, bend them back and forth a few times, and they didn't hurt quite as much. The three of them had already had enough drinks to loosen up—it was almost three in the morning—so their clothes were off in a hurry. They'd barely turned the dead bolts. Except that Marlene had this idea about donning other clothes. Once she had her clothes off, she was striding, like some carnivorous game animal, across the room toward the closet. She had a closet full of garments of the diligent bondage fantasy. So they took off their clothes and they put on these leather chaps in which their asses were exposed. Shredded T-shirts through which the edges of leather brassieres or the slope of a breast were evident. On Toni, the costume was kind of large. She was normally in the petite range. Doris made her own selections wearily, as though this part of the proceedings were as new as selecting the temperature for a load of laundry.

Marlene had Doris and Toni attach the clamps to her body. She whispered brusquely. They observed a clinical, professional silence as they did it—because the procedure involved pain and had the sobriety of pain. Toni performed her role intently as though the process were curative or therapeutic and because she didn't know Doris and Marlene well enough to chatter anyway. Toni hadn't told them anything—they knew nothing about her except her nakedness, the shape of her tattoos: the Ghost Rider skull on her shoulder blade, the Minnie Mouse on her ass.

Though now they knew that she liked novelty. Toni went down on Marlene. It was pretty hard to avoid the clothespins in that posture, but brushing against them turned out to be part of the point. Marlene let the breath of God pass from her lips. She seemed a little dizzy, and the region that was clamped became enlarged. It must have hurt like shit, Toni told me, *because those things were on there pretty well and she was grinding up against me and they were getting caught in my hair or I was pushing them aside and she was just moaning in that way people do, moaning like this was the straight vanilla thing.* This went on for a while and finished with Marlene producing a formidable strap-on dildo from a Doc Martens shoe box under the bed. Marlene reached and shoved the box back under the bed. A ripple of pain seemed to overtake her as she did so, and she huffed once with it, as though this were a brisk sort of exercise.

Marlene arranged the dildo harness *over* her clamps, organizing these hazards disinterestedly. They might as well have been curlers. She stood. She stepped out of the leather chaps and into the black lycra harness with a real weariness. A couple of clothespins sprung loose and she let them go. Then she guided the dildo through the hole in the harness. Its pinkish, Caucasian color was ridiculous. She had a large bottle of Astroglide already waiting on the floor beside the bed, and she told Doris to lean over and grab it, and then, while Toni was doing busy work on her breasts, fingerpainting them, she lubricated her lover's ass and vagina both, as though she were baby-oiling an infant—with just this detachment—and bid Doris kneel at the edge of the bed. Marlene, standing, fucked Doris in the ass, while Toni got around the side and fondled Doris's clitoris. Toni was doing the same to herself. *It was like jazz-dancing,* Toni told me, *it was all these moves and steps like that bitch in Montclair, Mrs. Beatty, tried to ram into my head when I was in Jazzercise on Mondays and Wednesdays when Mom was doing the day-care center thing.* But the fact was: Toni liked it. It was thrilling the way the last reel of a film is thrilling. You just want to see it all played out.

Doris on the other hand seemed to be walking through it a little bit. *Penetration, you know, isn't always the coolest thing among women,* Toni said. Doris held clumps of Toni's cinnamon hair in her hands as she, Doris, was being fucked by Marlene. She gently tousled Toni's hair, mumbling slightly, with a kind of sexual agitation that had a little sadness in it too. The amazing thing, though, was that Marlene was getting the whole dildo up into Doris, *grinding up into her with those fucking clamps and clothespins all over her!* Finally, though, Doris seemed to have enough of it, and she pulled the facsimile out of her ass with a sigh, reaching behind her, looking behind her in this vulnerable way and then pulling the thing out of her, she stood and pushed Marlene down on the bed, masturbating the rubber dick attached to Marlene, as though it could feel, pulling the condom off it, yes condom, and jerking it off, grinding against her lover's hips until Marlene seemed to be in some thrall of shuddering and pain, kissing Doris on the mouth, reaching up to gently kiss her goodnight. *Oh God,* Marlene said, as Doris knelt to remove the clamps one by one, first the nipple clamps, and the skin underneath was bruised with red rings around it. Even on Marlene's dark skin you could see the welts rising. And then the clothespins from her labia. Marlene fingered the damage in an inebriate swoon. *Oh God.* Toni and Doris stood around her, around the foot of the bed. Marlene probed with her long dark stalks for the evidence of the clothespins. Then she lay back on the bed. Rolled away on her side. Doris wiped her hands on the comforter at the foot of the bed, almost as if that simulated thing, the simulated dick, had ejaculated onto her, as if she'd had Marlene's very semen upon her.

And then she turned her attentions to Toni. She said something that Toni didn't hear, the two of them angling around one another like wrestlers now, angling as if to grasp one another, and then the words became clear, their quaintness, Doris wanted to be held, *really*, Toni told me. *Believe it or not, she just wanted to be held*, so the two of them were hugging, and Toni really felt like she was Doris's dad or something, holding her, and then this paternal kindness or whatever it was gave way to another set of roles, another set of styles. They were lying on the bed next to Marlene who was in some narcotic semi-consciousness, and they were facing one another head to foot, going down on each other, because the just holding each other part was okay, but it led elsewhere right then. They were unclothed now, the pile of fantasy gear sitting atop their street clothes like an upper layer of sediment. Doris tasted musty to Toni, as though forgotten in all the rush to arrange things, and Toni felt badly for her. So pity became a component of this secondary tangle of erotics. Pity in there too, like yet another partner, an unwanted partner. Toni's first and only instance of transportation that evening was a little ripple, really, and she made more noise with it than it required. She faked it. *By then, there really wasn't anything going on that was doing it for me, so I faked it*, she told me. Doris in the meantime was having the revelation of the shy. All the contentment in the world seemed to come out of some locked basement and crowd around her. There was sentiment everywhere; the world was her damp handkerchief, her multi-volume diary. It was the kind of orgasm, to Toni, that was promised by the good-natured phonies who wrote sex manuals. *Loving as Lesbians (By and For and How To)*. Or, *The Gay Woman: A Manual for Lovers and Friends*. Come out of your cellar cabinets of shame, *womyn*, and *celebrate!* Know the community of love!

—Wow, Doris said, Oh God. Wow. Oh.

—Mm, Toni said.

Now they lay beside one another in the light of a single bedside lamp.

—Don't worry about her, Doris said. Out cold. Once she's out you could jump on the mattress and she wouldn't notice.

Toni smiled nervously.

—You want to spend the night?

—Can we all fit on here?

They could, sure, though Toni wasn't totally convinced she wanted to spend the night. She was kind of hoping they couldn't all fit. She kind of wanted to go back to her own bed and sort through the fleeting recollections of the evening: dancing in the cage, putting on the bondage gear, fitting a clamp onto another woman's nipple, the exponential complications of a threesome. She felt overtaxed, like she'd sat through a double feature in the front row. She was cranky, short-tempered. It didn't make any difference. Toni was worried about hurting Doris's feelings for some reason, for some stupid girl reason. So she stayed. Soon all three women were arranged in the enormous bed. Marlene's lungs wheezed like an old bellows. Doris, on the other hand, was a light sleeper. Toni was between the two of them and she couldn't get comfortable all night—the gravitational yank of those bodies was too much for her. And Doris kept throwing a leg over her, pinning her, as though Toni were there for good.

A diner on Ninth Avenue. After a silent and hungover breakfast, the three of them made another date for the Thursday following. *Would you want to come visit us again?* Marlene said. And Marlene did indeed seem to want to try it again. But there was another part of her—Toni told me over the weekend, when she and I went to a bar on First Avenue called simply *Bar*—there was another part of Marlene that was suspicious somehow, evidently suspicious, that the two of them, Toni and Doris, had been *fucking around without her.* Taking advantage of her intermittent consciousness. She must have had some infrared surveillance device, Toni thought, some unconscious sensor watching out for her interests. Or else she was just keenly attuned to the inevitability of heartache. *Rejection sensitivity.* So what if Doris and Toni *were* doing it? It was part of the problem of three people. *You really gotta trust each other,* Toni told me. *Cause there's always two on and one off.* But Marlene couldn't withstand the implications, and as the thought took root, it sent forth these poisonous boughs.

That was no surprise. The picture of Marlene got worse as Toni learned about it. Marlene flew into a rage if the place, if the apartment in Clinton, was not swept clean; if the dog, Bernice Neptcong (a male) had not been walked; if the pictures were crooked, if Doris happened to show any interest, conversational or otherwise, in any male who didn't wear dresses and have breasts; if, for even a moment, Marlene had the sensation that Doris was preoccupied with another woman. Or sometimes Marlene flew into a rage just out of fatigue, just out of daily confusion. And when Marlene flew into a rage, *she sometimes beat Doris.* This is what Toni found out before the second date ever took place, when she met Doris for a drink, because Doris called her at work and said, *I have to talk to you. Let's meet at this bar on St. Mark's.*

It's important. Her voice was hushed as if even the security on her work phone had somehow been breached.

This fact of battery seemed to slip almost casually from Doris and Marlene to Toni and Doris and then to Toni and me, the enormity of it almost routine or incidental at first, as if it were not about people at all, as if there were not bruises on Doris's china features, as if it were about a way that people lived in New York City, an awful way that people lived in New York City, where women beat their children in public, and men beat one another on the subways. Toni told me and I said nothing, because this beating was a vacuum, a lifelessness that I couldn't really adjust to at first, and then I passed it on, passed on that silence to someone else, who in turn passed it on, the idea that good people, principled women, occasionally beat one another out of confusion and sadness and loss and thereby put the purple, the hematoma, in the flag that hung over city hall.

Bruises had appeared all over Doris. She frequently wore sunglasses. She spoke of falling down stairs and walking into doors. It was getting difficult at the office, as it had been difficult at offices in the past. *I've been fired from jobs before,* Doris said, her hands trembling as she lit a cigarette. Her voice was dull and methodical; she smelled clean, obsessively clean, to Toni; her skin was the palest white, the color of gallery walls.

—I can't lose another job because of her. I'm not functioning as it is. You know? It's getting embarrassing. I'm tired of going through it . . . It's humiliating and it's really tiring too. I'm tired of living like this. There's this dull way things go around and around again and I'm almost thirty-two years old and I don't want to live like this anymore.

Doris would veer off in another direction, onto another subject, and then she would come back to it. And then another refrain emerged. *She asked Toni if she knew anywhere they could cop some cocaine.* They were drinking and having the conversation that veered from the tragic to the mundane, from battery to discussions of rock-and-roll bands, and then suddenly Doris was trying to procure. No delicate way to announce it, like there was no delicate way to say that you have been beaten by your lover and that you haven't exactly done anything about it yet. Doris said, *Do you know where we could pick up?* And since Toni lived in the East Village she did know where to buy drugs, though she was no regular customer, she knew where, because you passed it every day. Wasn't terribly complicated. So they walked down Twelfth Street and copped some rock from the first cluster of dangerous looking boys they saw. That simple. The boys took their twenty dollars and came back a little later with the vials, the vials with their little red plastic caps. Doris and Toni smoked it together in a basement stairwell.

Then the complaints were spilling from Doris's mouth in long, artificial strings. How had she assumed this role, this victim role? What *king of mystery* was there in her *family of origin?* Where could blame be settled so that her burden would be lighter? She was victimized by Marlene. Marlene pulled all the strings. She was thinking back to her parents' *concept of child-rearing and its hidden language of coercion.* Doris was powerless. She needed to *share her truth.* To set *boundaries.* The passions of battery were stirred way down in the unconscious, in the history of the species, not up where Doris or anyone could control them. She didn't know if she could shake it. She wanted to leave but she didn't know if she could. There was something operatic about Doris not walking the dog and then getting hit. There were all kinds of hatred between Doris and Marlene. Marlene was systematically trying to *murder* Doris. Doris had actually woke to find Marlene holding a pillow over her head as she slept, she had found Marlene tampering with jars of prescription medication that she had in a cabinet—*I have these attacks of nerves,* Doris said. Marlene couldn't handle, in the end, that Doris's family had money and that hers did not, the differences between the classes were too much for her, though Doris herself felt she understood the misery that Marlene had come from. She could see how Marlene's childhood in the city was just a long story of deprivation. She could see how her life had been devoid of any model for affection. *But she didn't have to murder her for it.* She didn't have to buy a gun, which was what Marlene was talking about doing, ostensibly to defend them from the fucking creeps in Hell's Kitchen, *fucking creeps.* And then just as suddenly, Doris was in love again. She had not exhausted all of her love for Marlene. Marlene was radiant when she was happy, she had a smile that would stop at nothing. When she was happy, her face seemed to open and to reply *yes* to everything, to the abandoned buildings, to the crack dealers, to the repulsive men who paid her. Her face said *yes,* and it was clear how revolutionary and dangerous was the *yes* of a woman who was *grabbing the world by its dick and yanking.* Marlene happy, Doris said, was as dangerous as a souped up automatic weapon. But then on the other hand she was dangerous when she wasn't happy and that was where all the trouble started. Marlene was dangerous. She was just thinking out loud. Marlene was dangerous. (Toni was telling me in the bar.) And that was when Doris began to think about what she might do about the problem. There was no longer any way around it.

They went to Wendy's together, the next Saturday. All three of them. For a minute, everything seemed to be going all right. There was a new room where a woman in thigh-high boots and black leather gloves was throwing darts. There was another auction, and the three of them discussed buying a fourth woman. They were particularly fond of a little girl in a white party dress who shivered and grimaced like a child abandoned in a department store. This little girl would have waited among the men's shirts for weeks for the mother who would never return.

But they didn't have enough cash between them really to pay for the girl, who was a hot item. Top dollar for this girl. They were back at the Clinton apartment; it was only 12:30. The dog was walked, the apartment was clean. The three of them were there in the apartment, and already the process of unclothing themselves seemed ritualized. Something had gone out of it. Toni knew she was just chasing kicks, and it didn't make her feel that good. Marlene seemed intent on being the passive recipient of whatever fucking was going to take place that night. She had a tableau in mind; it was theatrical. She was actively arranging for her passivity. Through some superhuman effort, Doris managed to keep the whole thing together for a time. She strapped on the pink dildo and fucked Marlene in the missionary position, but both of them seemed sad and distant, and Toni lay around drinking beer and lending a hand now and them. The air was hot and still. The heat was a malevolent force in the apartment. By the time they climbed under a lone sheet, the three of them were covered in the sweat of exertion and also the sweat of connections not entirely made. They were each a little drunk.

When Toni awoke, the sun was muffled in humidity. They had coffee, and she wondered if Doris was imagining the whole thing. New York City was quiet, it was Sunday morning, people were absorbed with that newspaper, and no ill feeling would spill onto the streets of the city until noon. Vice was canceled for a time out of respect for a few regular churchgoers. When Toni went home, when she called me later to go for a drink, she had a feeling this auction vogue had run its course now. She could go on to other things. *Sex just isn't that important,* she said. *You can get into it for a while and then you can get into something else.* She was thinking about maybe going back out to Long Island for the summer.

But that night Doris called again. She had to see Toni right away. Right away. She was a mess. *I've broken my wrist,* she said. *My wrist is in a sling.* Doris couldn't go to work the next day, looking like one of those women who, in dark sunglasses, stands by her man, who limps slightly and walks very slowly. Her wrist in a sling. Something about the night before. Marlene had just flipped out. She was coming at Doris with a lamp, one of those halogen lamps. She was going to break a fucking halogen lamp over Doris's head. They had been kissing while she slept, Marlene cried, Doris and Toni had been fucking without her. *And we hadn't!* Doris said, as if Toni needed to be conscripted into her version of the story. *And I told her that!* And Marlene started bringing up crazy stuff. Stuff that happened months ago. Why was Doris leaving early for the office on a Tuesday in March? If she actually went to the gynecologist in April did she have any proof? Marlene was bringing up things that never happened, totally imagining things. So Doris did what she had never done before. *She took a swing at Marlene.* Hit her in the arm and broke her own wrist. Just like that. Broke it like it was a tiny limb on a sapling. Marlene didn't have anything more than a bruise, but Doris's arm was broken and now Marlene wasn't talking to her anymore. Marlene was shattering furniture in the apartment. Marlene was silent and implacable and breaking things. Oh it was horrible, it was horrible, New York was horrible, and life was horrible, full of compromises—she was crying now—and other people controlled you, people you would never know, never even know their middle names or what their vices were, the stuff they never told you, the real pornography of sensitivity, the pornography of love and affection, the pornography of plain old bliss . . . You never knew anything and you passed into old age knowing nothing except the color of some *fucking bathtub toy from your childhood. Let's go get high,* Doris said. *I want to get high. I just want to get high.*

Doris made this plan. She told Toni. Their anniversary was coming up. She and Marlene had been together two years. She would make a plan to spend the day with Marlene. It involved taking Marlene to see a play. The theater. *Shakespeare in the Park.* Yep. In New York you could work your way past the homeless people in midtown and the homeless guys sleeping in the park and the guys who were auctioning off their tragedies, their TB, their KS, their HIV, their veteran status, for alms, and you could go see these plays in the park. *Shakespeare in the Park.* Anyone could go. And though Marlene had little formal education, Shakespeare moved her—all those old tragedies with their

482

sins of pride and their purgations. She especially liked strong women characters. Lady Macbeth and Cleopatra. So they were seeing *Lear* and Doris knew she was a Reagan or Goneril; sharper than serpent's teeth, Toni told me, because at that very moment the other part of the plan was taking effect. Because Doris was leaving. Doris was leaving. Doris was springing it on Marlene. And Toni was agreeing. Out of pity.

So Toni and a team of illegal aliens broke into Doris's and Marlene's apartment, fed the dog, Bernice Neptcong, with fresh steak, actually feeding the dog steak like in some PG-13 heist movie, because the dog, raised by Marlene, would fasten its jaws onto any intruder, and they didn't want to have to kill it, and while the dog was eating the steak, a fine cut, I would imagine, lean, lean, lean, Toni was directing this team of illegal aliens who had no real interest in the haste or deceit involved in their work because they just needed the work; Toni was directing them to what she believed was Doris's furniture and CDs and books and sexually explicit videos and pictures of Monet's years at Giverny and was putting them into an unmarked, rented van that was double-parked in front of the Korean deli below. It was too bad that it had to be on their anniversary, Toni told me, but Doris couldn't think of another way to shake her, another day, another perfect time and place. Or maybe the cruelty that was involved in this plan was very much on Doris's mind, for the two years of cruelty she had received, and this was the best way to work it out, the most perfect way to make her point, a point thematically coherent and consistent, like a play itself, a point with the coincidences and destinies of a play.

I guess I have to admit here, too, that as a friend of Toni's I served as an accomplice to this crime. I served as a lookout, just in case Marlene or one of her friends (though she didn't have many friends) might have some synergistic understanding of what was going on, some sudden impulsive need to go see if Bernice Neptcong, M.D., had enough water in all this heat. Shamefully, I stood on the street as the Hispanic guys, their faces twisted into the solemn, sensitive gazes of funeral parlor employees, carried the furniture out of the apartment at a trot.

Finally, there was an intermission at *Lear,* between the third and fourth acts and Doris told Marlene, giving her an affectionate little peck on the cheek, that she had to go to the bathroom. Doris's lips were not thin lips, as I might have imagined, the lips of preppy women from Bernardsville. No, through some strange genetic twist, she had been given the broad, full lips of a lover, and even at the beginning Marlene had adored those lips, Toni believed, had adored kissing

Doris. So Doris's lips were not descending on Marlene's razor cheeks, and Marlene, as a matter of course, was pretending not to care entirely, though inside perhaps, where things were all tangled up, there was some interior paroxysm of joy or gladness at the bounty of love, though this paroxysm was smothered by the cool of New York. Then Doris gave her a little hug. She was wearing a black tank top and black jeans, and Marlene was, too. Marlene was wearing almost the same thing, and Doris gave her a little squeeze, and said she had to go to the *comfort station*. She laughed and said it, *comfort station*.

And then she took off. She was sobbing like a baby, sobbing like that girl left in the department store, sobbing in a way that can't be ameliorated by the stuff in this world, no matter how much good happens. But by the time she met another friend, Debby, over by *Tavern on the Green*, by the time she met Debby she had settled down a little bit. Debby had borrowed a car, a black Toyota Celica with plastic wrap in the rear windows from where they had been shattered, and they were driving straight to Newark airport, where Doris was catching a flight to New Orleans to stay with some cousins for a couple of weeks.

Elsewhere, with crack timing, the illegal aliens and Toni were driving Doris's stuff to mini-storage over in the west teens, just above the meat-packing district.

Marlene in the meantime was sitting on the blanket under the trees. Just a regular old blanket from the apartment, nothing special. And she was eating a cheap piece of cheddar cheese on a Triscuit and watching the edges of the audience fray as people came and went, and thinking what a great breeze, what a killer breeze and then wondering, when the play had begun again, where Doris was, but just wondering briefly, not giving it that much thought, and then watching some of the play and getting concerned, packing things up as if she was going to leave, wondering if leaving was the right thing to do, if staying put was maybe better, because if Doris was lost—as she was often lost, a little absentminded—it would be better if one of them weren't moving and then getting pissed off, really pissed off, *fuck*, and getting up and blocking somebody's fucking view of RAIN RAIN RAIN or some such passage and sitting back down and then getting worried because the rage that Marlene felt was in part worry, rage blanketing worry based on experience, some experience of loss, and so she was getting up and walking fast, now, purposefully, in a way you might have found scary if you were watching her, walking fast toward the Portosans, or whatever brand they had installed over on the other side of the field where everyone was sitting, and looking at the line of people there, unable to ask any of the women there, the overdressed women, the society chicks who had read *Shakespeare in college,* if they had seen a woman in black jeans, suddenly unable to do it somehow, unable to do it, shy or something, and then wandering around the Portosans, in the woods, the woods of Central goddamn Park, wandering, past Tavern on the Green and back to the play, hearing applause, not paying any attention to it, seeing a dozen women who looked like Doris, looked exactly like her until you got up close, until you could see up close that they had one birthmark that Doris didn't have, or they held one opinion that was not Doris's, or that they were fucking boys instead of girls, although otherwise they *were* Doris, seeing them and working upstream to the spot where she and Doris had sat and not finding her, in the dark now, getting dark, worried, concerned, enraged, yeah, murderously enraged, worried, Doris's headless, raped body in the Ramble, raped by some fucking pervert, worried, and then walking out of the park, empty now, followed by cops on horses, not cops that you would ask to help you, though, they were no help, cops, gangsters attached at the waist to horses, so worried, walking back toward the apartment down Eighth Avenue, down through the sleaze, down Eighth Avenue, walking automatically, not thinking at all, not feeling, just thinking the worst, but in a disembodied way, permitting the worst just to swim in her wherever it would— Doris's headless body. Doris's headless body, her jeans and her breasts and then no head, just bones and tubing and pink gelatinous stuff, and then turning up the street and fitting the key in the lock that was broken anyway, and checking the mail just because *Doris liked to get mail,* checking the mail just for Doris, and climbing up the poorly lit and warped steps to the third floor and fitting the key in the door, not knowing right then how time was stretching out in this moment, not knowing how long it was taking to turn that key because she was imagining the worst but in a detached way, in a way while she was planning to go to Wendy's that night, or in a way while she was thinking about her job and almost crying with how much she hated it and how the guys thought they could just do anything . . . and regretting all the trouble with Doris, regretting it and not being able to explain it, not even being able to admit it exactly, imagining trouble but not seeing the real trouble that lay right in front her. And then turning the handle and seeing the blankness, the emptiness in that space.

The apartment was just about cleaned out.

Doris on her way to New Orleans: she was having a drink on the plane. And then she was in the Big Easy. The second day there she went to Mobile. To the Gulf Coast. The sun was high, and it was humid and the water was a fabulous blue. It was nothing like New York City. When you were in Mobile, New York City just didn't exist at all. It was somebody's fever dream. And then she called Toni that night, because she hadn't left Toni the number, knowing that Marlene would call Toni wanting to know if she was a part of it, if she was responsible for it, wanting the number, wanting revenge, and sure enough Toni said she had called weeping, hysterical, *How could you do this to me how could you do this to me how could you do this to me how could any human being do this to another human being?* but Toni had the machine on and had gone to stay with Debby who also had her machine screening Marlene's hoarse, throaty screams. Beyond the frequency that telecommunications could handle. Marlene's shrill recognitions drifting out over New York.

Actually, by the time Doris was in Mobile, Marlene was already dead. Doris was on the plane when it happened. The exact moment was lost to her; she felt no shiver of symbiosis. She felt no paranormal sadness. She was over Tuscaloosa. Or she was at the baggage check when Marlene hanged herself. All of this is fucking *true,* I can tell you that. Marlene hanged herself. Doris abandoned her girlfriend at a performance of Shakespeare in the Park and then flew to New Orleans— and this is what Marlene did afterwards. She hanged herself with rope she got at a hardware store right next to the Best Western on Eighth Avenue. She left a crumpled twenty on the counter. The guy in the store didn't even notice when she overlooked her change. When Marlene did it she was alone, and she wasn't discussing it with anyone. She had to make sure the bar in the closet was sturdy enough. She would have to really make her mind up once and for all, because it was pretty low, that bar and hanging yourself in there would take a lot of work. Marlene left no note, as Doris had left no note explaining her own disappearance. She used the handcuffs in their apartment, which once had bound her and Doris together while they made love, to cuff herself behind the back, and another set on her ankles. She put the ankle cuffs on first, then the handcuffs, and then she put her head through a slipknot. A regular old slipknot. And then she threw herself off balance and gasped as she fell over, stumbling to her side, kicking around the boots on the floor of the half-empty closet, kicking over boots and bondage gear and the other stuff Doris had left her, wanting to get up again, but all tangled and having trouble getting up, desperate to get up now, weeping, but not getting up. The energy to do so dissipated. Shocked in the last second, terrified, and then resigned, powerless. Her last breath spread in an even film in the still air of the apartment. She settled down to room temperature.

The closet door was open. The dog paid no attention. He had been fondled and loved that afternoon by Toni and the guys from Ecuador. He'd eaten steak. But then when Marlene was dead Bernice Neptcong, the dog, became somehow uncomfortable. He went and sniffed at the long dark legs half-folded awkwardly under Marlene. And then he curled up by one ankle for the long wait. When they found her days later, when the neighbors complained, Bernice was shivering and hungry, but he struck out blindly nonetheless at the super, the police—these interlopers in the drama of neglect—baring his teeth, protecting the lost lives that had prized him. This was his kingdom now.

Three weeks later Doris was walking down Eighth Street late at night. The streets were empty. She was on her way to Avenue D. Ten days back in the city. She had tried to get in touch with Toni, but it wasn't turning out exactly as she'd hoped. She hoped that Toni would be around when she got back. In New Orleans the unspeakable drama of her predicament created a space between her and her cousins. She found this space again in Princeton. She was more alone than ever before, though she had fled from Marlene to escape loneliness, though she had opposed loneliness with what strength she had. Death mocked all this stuff. These weeks made clear the overpressure of fate. She'd taken too much time off from her job. She didn't really have anywhere to stay. She certainly wasn't going back to the apartment. And Toni wouldn't see her. So she had come to this address in the East Village. She had come by herself, feeling nauseated and lost, for the dull thrill of carelessness.

In the bakery on Eighth and D, Doris waited in line like everyone else. The woman in front of her actually bought some bread to go with her heroin—it was a demonstration loaf of stale Italian—but Doris wasn't here for bread. She was here for a dime bag. In front of her in line was Jorge Ruiz. His clothes were shabby. Throughout his transaction, he never once raised his eyes. Neither did Doris. She wouldn't have recognized him anyway; she wouldn't have known how close their lives were; she wouldn't have seen anything, lost in the flow of her own disgrace.

III

Randy Evans didn't know that the girl on Ninth Street had been directing a film for two years. That girl, Yvonne. He thought she just sold hash. She was small and pale. She had sloppily dyed platinum blond hair. Roots showing. She was spending money on what? On leather miniskirts and stuff and on hash when she was supposed to be selling the hash instead of smoking it, selling it in order to finance a film she was making. He found this out later. Yvonne was going to be his wife, although he wasn't quite sure when or how yet. She didn't know anything about it. And he didn't know it at first either, on Ninth Street, when they met. In front of a store that sold Populuxe lamps and plastic handbags and photos of Marilyn and Elvis. He didn't know it until he ran into her a few times at clubs in the neighborhood, most of them gone now. At 8BC or Pyramid. He didn't know until a sort of pattern was established. A pattern of chance encounters.

He clubbed and so did she. Although he liked *nice* clubs—Interferon or Area—where the cash dwelt, cash and speedballs and stuff like that, he also slouched around in twilit venues like the Crypt and the Manhole and the Ruin. He was flashy, he liked to throw a little money around, but late at night he found himself watching guys getting flogged at the Ruin. He was making some good money working up in the garment district, had his own showroom for a while, in fact. The Evans Line. Borrowed some money from some garment industry backers and started this showroom which was a little cut rate, priced to move pretty well, and he was hoping to get some of it into department stores. At first he was. He was getting it into some places. Alexander's and Gimbel's.

Then at night he bought cocaine and he went to Area. And some time later in the evening when he was teetering between drunkenness and mania he went to the Ruin. There he watched the sleepwalkers, in the oblivion of the masochist's craft, with their dicks in their hands, circulating around the room, or around the stage where a guy with a ponytail was getting whipped on the ass by a dominatrix. This man must have hung up there for half an hour. When he was released from his torture, he was covered with welts. Black and blue all over his ass. And the guy just smiled. Randy liked it. He liked to watch the sleepwalkers as they inclined, lips pursed, toward the toes of women lounging at the bar. They'd wander around sleepily jerking off and then they'd ask a woman if they could suck her toes. He laughed at all this stuff. He'd stay at the Ruin sometimes until dawn.

Anyway, he met Yvonne at 8BC. He didn't tell her about his late night exploits. She didn't tell him about her film. In fact, Randy's interest in *B&D* was something that he disavowed generally. It occupied a corner of his life that he did not dwell upon. He was sometimes afraid of who he might meet at the Ruin. His night life was only partly under his control. But that night he was at 8BC. There was this band playing. They had no name. The only way you knew if they were playing was if one of the clubs left a conspicuous absence on their calendar. Or there would be a listing, *Closed for Private Party.* That was how people referred to them sometimes. They said, Oh, I'm going to see *Closed for Private Party.* Randy was at 8BC with his friend Noel. Noel from England. They went to Pyramid. Or was it somewhere else? Who could remember? And then they came back, and when they walked into 8BC it was like something had changed in Randy's life. There had been some subtle movement of chance and suddenly the whole topography of his life was different. Or that's how it felt. *Holy shit, who is that woman across the room, and how could I have missed her the first time?* She was standing under this neon fixture, and it turned out he had met her once before. Yvonne. In torn black leggings and blond hair and a black crucifix and a black brassiere with a black sweater halfway unbuttoned.

To Noel he said: *Think I will have to use that line about how I have met her somewhere before. It only works if you really have.*

Because he had met her on the street that time. And he invited her to do a line with him, and she agreed even though she hated Eurotrash and would-be Eurotrash guys. American guys who thought that everything was okay if they just flashed a little green. American guys with platinum cards. American guys too stupid to know that Europe had nothing to offer now but Swiss watches and deconstruction. American guys who actually invited in these colonialists with their dead cultures. *She must have wanted the drugs,* Randy told Noel later. *I don't care how the job gets done as long as it's done.* But the truth was Yvonne was just collecting material for her film. Everything was material, the dullest moments, the most ornate fancies. After Yvonne and Randy did the lines in the men's room they left behind Yvonne's friend Debby and Noel.

In the neon shadows in the back of the club Yvonne cheerfully admitted to Randy that she dealt hash. Which he knew already by hearsay. She produced a pipe. They smoked some of her product. It

489

was old-fashioned and quaint. The conversation was lurching along; there was neither agreement nor discord. And then they slipped out the back door into an alley. Somewhere along the line the hash hit, they were laughing, giggling, totally stoned. Laughing about something—he couldn't even remember. Wait: laughing about Eurotrash and Ecstasy and House and Japanese people invading the East Village and buying all the real estate out from under the slumlords and about the tanks in Tompkins Square Park. Just laughing. He hadn't had such a good time in a while. So they ditched Noel and Debby altogether, at 8BC or Pyramid or wherever it was, and went to her apartment, right near his on Ninth Street. It was all coming back to him now. He had met her a couple of times before. It was the greatest thing. She was the most beautiful woman he had ever met in his entire life. She was going to be his wife. He would have a wife *and* a private life. Yvonne was hard to talk to—she missed all the ease in a conversation—but she was beautiful. They stayed up and did some more cocaine and watched the sunrise on the roof and he didn't lay a glove on her and they went to a coffee shop on First Avenue. He poured black coffee over the ground stubs that had been his teeth the night before. They smarted. He was tired as shit. He was giddy.

Later that week, he was back at the Ruin, watching an old fat guy lean into the bullwhip as this woman named *Huck* really let him have it. The fat guy had a lifeless, undersea expression on his face, and no kind of erection that Randy could see. It was hard to tell whether pleasure was involved for this guy or not. And then he got the itch to see Yvonne again. There were a few other women on the roster, but he moved them around a little bit. He didn't know why they were suddenly of less interest, these other women, but he wasn't worrying about it. He was just improvising. His mind was on the Evans clothing line and on hitting the clubs. He didn't think too much about other stuff. He called Yvonne's number at the Ninth Street place. She was probably working some gallery job during the day or at some non-profit theater company. She probably had jeans with paint stains on them. He realized *he didn't even know what she did during the day.* He wondered if dealing hash was her principal line of business. How did she organize her clients? Did she keep a file on computer? What kind of overhead was there in an enterprise like that?

Then she got pregnant. There's a gap in the story here that doesn't concern me, a gap with its conventional romantic navigations of approach and retreat. The fact is that a month or two later Yvonne found she was pregnant. This was about as stupid as anything Randy had ever done. They had slept together, of course; they had been sleeping together off and on for two or three months. They had fucked without a diaphragm or a rubber or anything, and they had done it a number of times, on a number of occasions, maybe even too many times to remember. And they hadn't thought about it too much because they had just come from some bar or club. She said, *I will not take the fucking pill,* and who could blame her? She smoked several packs of cigarettes a day. She had one of those lavender packets of birth-control pills on her bedside table but it was neglected. They had used condoms, but he didn't like them—*worse than a wet suit*—and then she had become pregnant.

She didn't seem concerned with her pregnancy either. She had been selling hash in order to make a movie about the East Village, about the people in the East Village and the coincidences that overtook you in a place like the East Village. You could miss someone by seconds, you could turn a corner and this incredibly pertinent information would be lost because the person you were about to pass, whom you did not see (because in Manhattan you always looked at your feet), was now lost to you. In this film, Yvonne liked to say, *you could see how much larger the pool of potential facts is than the pool of facts that actually turn out to be true.* You could, in this film, turn a corner on St. Mark's Place and First Avenue, say, and just miss your ex-boyfriend's ex-girlfriend who was actually related to you in some way, who could tell you something about your ex-boyfriend that you never knew, who was going up First Avenue toward Fourteenth Street. You could just miss her. In this way there was much that you failed to know. You failed to know, for example, that a man who had once been important to you was now ill with that horrible kind of pneumonia. But you wouldn't know this, because you were walking the wrong direction. Or you wouldn't know because you had been ducking, for a week, the barely functioning answering machine in your barely furnished apartment.

The film, however, contained all these possible outcomes; the film that Randy still didn't know much about was being filmed on a *shoestring budget,* in various bars, with the cooperation of various bartenders. Yvonne would venture into these locations with a loaner camera—she was always charging it on the AC adapter back at her apartment—and shoot interviews, just little snippets, or false pieces of narrative material, late into the night, after closing, after everyone slunk off to the after-hours joints. She had no idea how any of this material was going together. She had a naive optimism that she would figure it out eventually, and that it didn't matter that the neighborhood was changing around her and that her film now represented an East Village that was no longer located in this spot. And all the money from the hash and the waitressing was supposed to pay for this film that was subordinate to everything else in her life, for processing time on the Steenbeck, for the transfer from video back to film, for the sound edit, but she was smoking the hash and borrowing money to pay back the guy who sold the drugs to her in the first place.

And now she was pregnant. She told Randy over the phone, and they had their first big fight. He was from a good family from Atlanta, this decorous family with whom he was not really in touch anymore, and he thought having a decorous family of his own wasn't such a bad idea. He could see that there was a convenient aspect to this calamity. Now he had an argument for marriage and family. They could just fall into it. So he went over to her place to break this news to her. To break the news that he was ready, at twenty-four, for domesticity.

They slept together first. They slept together before talking, and it was really, really sexy, the way he saw it. It was like the first time. He took off her skirt slowly. He liked to see how slowly it was possible to make love. He kissed her so slowly you didn't even know his lips were moving. How slowly? His movements were in increments smaller than millimeters. *The band with no name* was playing on the old, beat-up tape player, and the video camera was standing on a tripod, pointing out the window, and he was proceeding across her lips as slowly as possible. It could take hours before he would creep down along her neck, after pausing to dig an incisor into her earlobe, after pausing to suck on her tongue. Hours before he was aimlessly encircling her breasts with his fingertips. And then further down. He liked every second of it. He even liked unlacing her Doc Martens. Nakedness was never so naked. And then he touched her stomach. Women had gotten pregnant because of his irresponsibility before, once in boarding school, once after a weekend by the shore in Mobile, but he had been young then. This was his first time as an adult. The fact of it, the fact of fertility, was enormous and perfect like the shape of a particularly dangerous storm.

Her belly was small and trim. She didn't eat too well. *Just eat to avoid fainting*, she said. *Nothing more.* He traced his finger across her stomach as if he were painting cave paintings there, as if trying to render the moment of conception in some pictorial writing. As if trying to capture all the lives bound together in this notion of conception. What was so sexy about all this? What was hot about coming to the end of the profligate and wandering part of your life? What was sexy about suddenly wanting to accept responsibility? Maybe in part what was sexy was all the bad news, all the risk, all the difficulties. Maybe he wasn't thinking clearly about it at all. But maybe he was. Love was something that had the threat of bad news with it. Love was risk and obligation and caffeine addiction. Love was like watching the Tompkins Square riots on television. It was like hearing a guitar amp explode. It was like shooting coke for the first time. It was like watching the demolition of a tenement building and it was like remembering these pleasures years after they are gone.

And that was when she introduced the device.

—Hey, look, I have this thing I have to show you . . .

She reached over beside the bed where an ominous looking electrical kit was waiting.

—What the fuck is that?

The shame of being found out, of being located and then conscripted into the league of kinks, of being a guy who liked devices *and* wanted a family, this shame overcame him first. His resistance was first. He knew, in some atavistic part of his unconscious reserved for the pursuit of bodily woes disguised as pleasures, he knew what it was. He didn't know how it was going to work, but he recognized the control knobs on the box. They resembled the knobs that had driven the electric trains of neighbors in his boyhood. One of the dials was marked COURSE and the other ADJUSTMENT.

—This is an electrical stimulation box, she said. It's for the film. See? I'm getting interested in this idea that I can have like some sex club stuff in it. I could have, you know, couples using these marital aids. Like this one or Sybian or something. From Orgone Romance Systems of Las Vegas. These ones here are the *instant kill switches* and those are the *indicator lamps* to monitor the control of the voltage.

—That's—

—Uh huh, she said. It's for fucking.

And from a small cardboard box lying on its side on the faded and dirty Indian rug *she produced the combination vaginal plug and cock ring attachment.* The attachment was made of a sturdy and durable transparent plastic, and, like the finest Steuben sculptures with their hints of silver and gold sunken in the glass renderings, the wires in the attachment, those glorious conductors, were glimmering in the plug and the ring. Yvonne had batteries in the device—it was running on battery power—and she juiced it up with the knobs and held the probe by the end.

—How are you going to use this for the movie? he said. You're going to get friends to use this and—

—Just touch your finger to it quickly. It's on the lowest setting.

—What the *fuck? Where did you get this?*

—I borrowed it. I'm thinking we should—

—Oh no, Randy said. If you think I'm gonna let you electrocute me with that thing, so that you can . . .

She touched it herself. Touched an index finger to it. There was a velocity to the way she was avoiding *the question in the air.* He had come over to talk about her pregnancy, to talk about the future, to raise practical questions, but instead they were here with the electro-stimulator. There was a velocity, a speed and a direction, to her avoidance. She was using the device—that facsimile of the most potent Latin American political torture machines—to stray from *the implications of things.* And she wasn't foolish: she knew what she was doing. She touched the plug and he could hear its faint buzz, its melancholy hum. She held her finger there.

He took the thing from her and set it aside.

—Hey, Yvonne, Randy said. I got a more important question. That's why I came over here. I came over here to ask you something.

The plug snapped and fizzled on the edge of Yvonne's comforter.

—I came over here to ask you to marry me. That's what I came to do, Yvonne. We could get around this *problem* in a way you're probably not thinking of. The baby, I mean. We could just get married.

And he had the engagement ring, in his pocket, an antique silver band that had been in the family for a while. Impulsively, though, before taking the ring out of the tangle of khaki trousers on the floor, he took the cock ring from the electro-stimulator and *set it on her ring finger.*

She laughed. A nervous, high, piccolo laughter. He reached for the COURSE knob.

—No way, she said. I'm too young to get married. I'm not carrying your fucking little *junior* around for nine months and fucking up my body and my hormones so that you'll have a peg to hang your hat on or someone to take care of you when you get senile. I don't want to spend my life with anybody, I can't even think of what my life will be like next week. I can't even imagine that I'll *have* a life next week. *Forget it.* Honey. Forget it.

Randy got really angry. He turned the stimulator all the way up. She laughed again. He brushed the device off the bed. They started to shout. They actually threw some stuff, some books and lamps, what kind of relationship was this, and what was she going to do, let this bad luck drive the last bit of fun out of their relationship when it could make them closer, and didn't she want to share anything with him, didn't she want to know that even on the lowest day she wasn't alone, didn't she want to wither with someone around who loved her, didn't she want to file a joint tax return? But she wouldn't do it, wouldn't do it, wouldn't do it, and he couldn't believe that he had been so stupid that he thought this woman who sold hash and claimed she was some kind of filmmaker, that this woman was going to do this marriage-and-family thing with him, how could he be so stupid, and then they were fucking again and in the middle of these attentions some key of persuasion was turned in the lock and she was able to convince Randy that the electric stimulation device was an adventure, a gamble, a temporary shelter. In the penumbra of rejection he agreed to it. That was the decision that came first. In that penumbra, in the penumbra of late night, she had the tape player on and she had the *fine adjustment* on the stimulator control panel turned down as low as it would go and she had the video camera turned on, she had swiveled it on the tripod to take a closeup on Randy's face, and she put the cock ring around him now, though his cock was only halfway hard, and then she turned the knob up slowly. It was just like being drilled by the dentist at first, it was that sensation of wrong, of inappropriateness, and then there was a white alarm in his head as she turned it up and the sound of the capacitor inside dampening it and then the device scorched him like there were electro-magnetic teeth ripping into his dick and he tore the thing off with the urgency that one shoos away an ornery wasp that has already made its mark and he collapsed on her bed for a second to catch his breath, to let the shock disperse itself throughout him. It was as though he were joining his friends the sleepwalkers as they too were bent upon the rack, *the rack of reactivity,* desperate simply for sensation in a monochromatic and decontextualized city. Yeah, it was right that he be here in this way, with the Ruin only a couple of nights behind him, with his fascination for the sleepwalkers and the transvestites and the perfect toes of the women at the bars. And he waited for the voltage to fade in him, until its absence was a sort of pleasure a sort

495

of relief, and then he noticed her arm around him over his back and her voice in his ear saying *okay, okay,* that's right it seemed she was agreeing suddenly, she was changing her mind, *okay, okay,* yes she really was, *okay,* and so marriage was an interim government between them, and you could say all this lifelong and ever after stuff, but if it didn't work they could throw in the towel. She loved him in this vulnerable tableau with the electro-stimulation box beside him. She loved him. They would work it out. The kid would work it out. They would have the kid and the kid would understand that she had other ambitions. The kid would figure it out. Kids were like superballs or something, like high concentration rubber objects. Kids could learn to adjust. *Okay.* She lit the pipe. She toked on it. She passed it to him. Now it was her turn. She handed him the vaginal plug and lay back against the pillows.

Their marriage consisted of a civil ceremony on Staten Island, where the line at the courthouse was shorter. A friend of Yvonne's, Mike, filmed it, though none of the footage worked, really. It was nothing she could use, except for a brief shot of the justice of the peace straightening his tie.

Randy didn't tell his family. They would just have come up from the South. They would have hung around. Yvonne didn't tell her family, in Syracuse. She *forgot.* The two of them didn't really tell anyone, except Noel and Debby, who came to be witnesses. And Mike. There were all these coincidences on the way to the ceremony, people they met, people on the streets, people on the Staten Island ferry. New York seemed that day to be nothing but a system of low-probability coincidences. But then she had agreed to have the baby, too. Or at least she had agreed temporarily. Yvonne agreed to have the baby because she was tired and depressed, and she didn't want to think about it. Most days, she tried to renege on the decision. Some days she wanted to have it and then, after feeling sick, she vowed to abort. She should have gone for the abortion in the first month, when she was feeling especially bad, but somehow she didn't get around to it. This lack of decisiveness seemed to Randy to mask an excitement about the baby. Still, they were arguing so much about whether or not to go through with it. She hung on, looking for some kind of perfect advice from her friends or from her own mom—who thought she was out of her mind—or for some sign in the grid of order and disorder that was Manhattan. Walking the streets, turning the corners: *What should I do?* By then the baby was *close to quickening* as they said in

British law. Somehow she didn't see how she could snuff it in the second trimester.

At the same time, though, she started getting a little further into particular kinds of East Village life, into the substance abuse parts of East Village life, started getting into them because she was nervous and scared and sad about how she had slid into all this, slid into some middle-class thing that she wasn't prepared for. It was all about this stupid film that was sitting in a metal box in her secondhand desk. There was the metal box and a bunch of old videocassettes. She *used to think* that it was all about the film. They were married. This had happened, although Yvonne couldn't figure out how it had happened. They lived pretty much the way they had lived before, except that they shared an apartment. Now he was always on top of her with his insecurities, with his practicalities, and Yvonne was really upset that she had never made the movie she had wanted to make, and she never had any time to herself, and she never *was* herself, and soon, on top of everything else, she was going to have a baby. She wasn't supposed to smoke or drink, but she sort of *was* smoking and drinking, anyway. And that wasn't all. Just a little bit really, just the occasional lapse in the area of harder drugs, for the really special occasions.

And instead of making more of the movie, instead of just going out and buying the film, which Randy might have contributed to, instead of finding someone to do the sound for her, she felt like she had to perfect the fifteen minutes of it she had. The continuity was all fucked up because it had been shot over the course of years, and some of the sound wasn't synchronized. Over and over she would do this opening, borrowing time from friends who were still editing or PA-ing instead of going to law school like you were supposed to do in your late twenties. It was really kind of good this first five minutes, if you were into a sort of totally random New York chaos. Full of jump cuts and repetition and shots of the microphone boom and a sequence with a dog hair on the lens. It doubled back on itself, this five minutes, this documentary, or whatever it was, though it was never going to be much of anything really. Two lives in it might mean different things at different times. They might be the same life, they might be twins. Toni, this woman, seemed to be straight in one scene and gay in another. People looked like one another, or like other people, and the structure of the film was going to be like the structure of New York. Laid out in a grid, except for the parts that weren't laid out in a grid, totally repetitious, except for the explosions of violence.

Then she became obsessed about the soundtrack. She decided she had to secure the finest soundtrack composers possible for this film that was never going to be finished. It had to be *the band with no name*. She went to a party at the house of this music columnist for the *East Village Eye*—some neighborhood periodical—Jeanine Love. So they were at the party, which was on Avenue D, in a cramped apartment that had a porch with a great view of the Con Edison power plant on the East River. Yvonne, who had let Randy go out to some club, Pyramid or 8BC, to recreate the wild days of his bachelorhood, went up to this guy from *the band with no name*. He was from Massapequa, Long Island, and rock and roll had transformed him from a guy from Massapequa into a person with charm. Standing there in these rags and looking like his guitar had scorched him and he had been thereafter embalmed. He seemed not to have any emotions that she could discern. She told him, *I really like what you guys do and I think it's got a really experimental kind of thing . . . kind of feeling to it, and I think it would really be good for like a soundtrack or something, um, playing the guitar upside down and everything and well I'm making this movie about the East Village it's like an archeology of life in the East Village and I was wondering, I mean I was thinking maybe you would . . .*

The guy just grunted. He knew, as anyone looking at Yvonne would have suspected, that nothing was ever going to happen with this film. At the same time, she was preoccupied with the fact that his skin was an incredible blue color. He didn't say anything, made no commitment of any kind. But Yvonne understood that she was to follow him into the next room where the drummer from the band was tying off his arm with a handsome Velcro tourniquet so that he could pop a little bit of that grade-A Lower East Side dope underneath his baggy skin.

Jeanine Love, the hostess, was peripherally involved in the sex industry, in addition to being a music critic. She gave performances at the Ruin on occasion, and she wrote a little *sexually explicit material*, except that she didn't like writing it, so she hired ghost writers to write it for her. Because of her affiliation, however, on the floor and on the bed in the bedroom (where the guys from *the band with no name* were shooting heroin) there were cut-rate, rough-trade skin magazines piled everywhere. *Juggs* and *Cheeks* and titles of this sort. And while Yvonne was trying, politely, to discuss music with the guys in this band, they were flipping through the magazines and chuckling ominously. Then the guy from Massapequa, who had no expression whatever, who looked at a lot like the boys that Randy was right then watching amble around the Ruin, was motioning to her. He was going to take care of her. She didn't know if she should do it. He would do it for her if she couldn't do it. In fact, there was no decision involved. Or it was a decision not to make a decision. It was a relaxing, an acceptance. It was caving in. Letting go.

—Really, I'm mostly into . . .

Then she let him do it.

And the light over the power plant on Avenue D like fucking celestial lights like the angels on the head of a needle and Randy was where? Who knew? She was puking in Jeanine Love's bathroom, and Jeanine was saying, *Come on you guys, come on, I'm really tired, I just don't want to stay up anymore. I don't want to . . .* And one of the guys from *the band with no name* was still there and he was going to leave Yvonne there because he was a little guy anyway and he wasn't going to carry her anywhere and he had to be up the next day for a Saturday shift at the copy shop where he worked. But then for some reason he was overcome by charity and soon he helped Randy's pregnant wife to a cab where he repeated the address she whispered to him to the cab driver. Kissing her on the lips and putting his finger to her lips—*don't tell*—and then repeating her address to the cabbie.

Then she miscarried.

The period of the marriage and pregnancy in which she was killing herself with dope would have been tougher if Randy hadn't been killing himself too. The movie was nowhere to be found now, it was in some dead-letter office somewhere, some imaginary film library of imaginary projects. What movie? There never was a movie. There was Randy and Yvonne going out to clubs, her in some kind of fashionable black maternity dress even though she really wasn't showing yet, but just because she liked the maternity look, some maternity dress that he'd gotten from a friend at another company. And there were no plates or sharps left in the house, because their arguments were too wild. And he was as strung out as she was sometimes. And he was pretty sure the books at his business were cooked, but he wasn't concentrating on it, exactly, he was going out with Yvonne and leaving her at home sometimes so that he could head out to the Crypt or the Ruin and watch the silent participants in the games there. He ground his teeth into a paste. And he was really into the electro-stimulator, though she had become bored with it. When Randy did come home to their meager kitchen, he would find her already high, with that empty look in her eyes, eating a single carrot. Blasting some noise on the old, beat-up tape player. He had a bad feeling about it all.

—Don't you think you could lay off just until after the baby is born? Wouldn't that be a little safer?

—Huh?

—Wouldn't that be the polite thing to do? For the kid?

—I don't know what you're talking about, Yvonne said.

This period ended with her hysterical call. At work. On a Wednesday. He told her to call 911 and he would meet her at the hospital but she was really scared. She was really really scared, he could hear how scared and so she asked him to come pick her up instead. *Please. It's a mess.* He made the emergency call himself and met her at the apartment before the ambulance arrived. Her skin the color of slate. There were trails, archipelagoes of blood in the bathroom, the mildewed bathroom, on the dirty towels. She was crying. Her hands were bloody, and he couldn't tell how much was from the miscarriage and how much was from needles. Abscesses. He knew. Right away he knew how bad it was. How lost the kid was. How lost she was. How bad it was.

—I was never supposed to have it anyway, she mumbled. Tracks of tears. I was never supposed to have it.

—Oh, shut up, he said. He hugged her and they waited. What was already obvious was then officially pronounced by the medical authorities.

The argument then spilled over into the deep part of several nights. It wasn't an argument about anything special now. It was an argument with *things in general.* Her breathing was so shallow he couldn't believe that oxygen ever grazed her bronchia. But her cells didn't need anything now but what dope could give them. All the same, he couldn't believe that lying came so easily to her. On the other hand, maybe she could lie without even noticing her lies. Maybe the possibility of truth was dormant within her now. And this is how she was after pregnancy, managing an ever increasing stream of lies. The current between the two of them dwindled under the burden of these lies.

—I'm not high, Yvonne said. I'm being really careful now, honey. I want to have a baby. *I want to make another baby.* Really, I'm telling you the truth.

He watched her sleep sometimes and he watched her puke in the morning and it was impossible to say whether it was from this miscarriage or from the drug. Or both. He cleaned up a little bit of her puke

500

before going out to the office. He took a damp paper towel across the surface of the toilet seat.

And maybe she could have ridden the wave of her addiction through another childbirth. She didn't seem especially to care about pain anymore anyway. Her body was an obligation insofar as it played host to the brain and the brain's store of flattened affections and blunted nerves. Otherwise who cared? She was a brain in a vat. She was working on throwing off her body somehow; she was putting it in cold storage; she was decommissioning it.

He came home from work and played spouse with her, hoping that she was going to bounce back, that the old fun was going to bounce back. His business went under not long after, and that made it even easier. He had a huge bank loan hanging over his head. He would have to get another job eventually, a job working for someone else, but not for the moment. For the moment he lay around the house. They had come to the end of club-hopping. They had come to the end of it. Randy suspected that his wife had shot up while carrying the baby. She said she was *only snorting*, as though that excused it. No, really, she was only snorting coke. Not even heroin. No, really, she was clean. Really. And she'd disappear at night and he'd yell at her but sometimes he'd get that yen too, that yen to go out, and he'd do it. He didn't care what time she was coming in. And he would drink and tell someone on the next stool all of this. All of what I've told you. In fact, he told *me*. At the Ruin. They had come to the end of their marriage. It had lasted five months. It was time for him to leave his wife. This was not difficult to accomplish. Because Yvonne wanted to pursue unencumbered her own muse, the muse of her inactivity, the muse of her silence.

Later. Third week of June 1987. (Hot and humid, low visibility.) *The amphetamine of loss* with its jacked-up system of attribution and detachment roiled in Randy Evans. He was driving around lower Manhattan in a van he had rented to help move some stuff for the Japanese clothing line he just started working for. He was driving with the radio up loud. WFMU. They were playing something from *the band with no name*. He wondered if the guys in the band were still alive, if these were new songs or if the guys in the band were infighting acrimoniously about an upcoming tour, if they were thinking of tossing one another out of the band. One of them, he had learned once, was the son of a major stockbroker. The son of the head of some brokerage house. The rich dad had bought them all the PA equipment and a stu-

501

dio to record in. And the son, the son of this wealthy broker, was shooting dope and living in some rundown East Village basement apartment with nothing in it but a futon and a CD player. This kind of life gave *the band with no name* a lot of credibility.

And the song didn't sound like their songs had sounded to him two years before when he first heard them. It sounded different, as the whole East Village seemed different. It wasn't galleries and clubs anymore. The East Village was chain stores and crack dealers. People were getting sick, and Randy had taken the test too and had waited the three weeks it took then to get results. He couldn't imagine why he was negative. He and Yvonne had shared needles with a few people, definitely, with Jamie Lefferts and Donna Harvey and Mike and that other guy Mitch who came over with him to the house that time. And they had all gone to a really creepy shooting gallery on Delancey with someone named Juan. Who knew who they were sharing with? Back then you didn't think about it as much. Where the needle had been was somewhere you yourself had been, and the trail of that needle, the trail that led to the shooting gallery, was the history of your footfalls and of the people whose lives were a part of yours. Where you had walked was what you believed in and it marked you and your DNA and it left information for your children, for when they would want to know the truth about you. The past and the future were in Randy's every move, in the imitation Syd Barrett sound of *the band with no name,* in the Veselka, where he had spent, over the years, maybe a thousand dollars on pink borscht, in the fresh vegetable stand where, ten years from now, he would go with his son, the son he would have, and select the best carrots for a soup. But right now Randy's van was in the stream of the loneliest New Yorkers, those grasping, reaching for anyone in arm's length, hugging them close, pushing them off. Starting over. Falling into the disease, climbing out of it. Starting over. That's what the song by *the band with no name* sounded like. And that night Randy could have driven all night, on and off of the FDR watching the lights on the Williamsburg side of the river, he could have driven all night, never gone home to the new girlfriend, the new hostage, where he now lived in Brooklyn, because he had the past on his mind and the way the people from the past were not really past, the way they crowded around him on the streets of Manhattan, the way he was always running into them. And he had a sort of agenda too, because he was driving down Eighth Street, west to east. He got on it on Third Avenue, and then he drove the block past Trash and Vaudeville where he had bought a leather jacket and past St. Mark's Sounds and past the bar called simply *Bar* and then around the park, where a gallery called Gracie Mansion had once been, and into the deepest East Village, where 8BC used to be, and then he was in front of the bakery at the corner of Avenue D.

The projects were on one side of the avenue and on the other side it was all empty lots filled with temporary shelters of cardboard and plywood and decorated with giveaway blankets and plastics. Randy's van was in neutral and idling quietly near the corner and the radio was whispering some chant—some New York prayer, some specifically local ritual for the dead that doubled as a solicitation or an advertisement of some kind. He watched the entrance of the bakery, watched people going in and out.

Jorge was there, of course. Jorge Ruiz, who was going back to live with his mother in another year, after his detox in Hollis, Queens, after barely avoiding being locked up in Creedmore; and Doris Frantz, of Montclair, New Jersey, and Princeton University, who was thinking about picking up some cash on the side doing dominatrix work, just sort of turning the idea over anxiously. These two shadows came along the poorly lit streets, staggered by several minutes, walking slowly so as not to attract attention, so as not to appear to be in a hurry of any kind. Their hearts were in a terrible rush. They entered the bakery— Doris carrying a paper bag as if she intended to buy rolls—to give tens and twenties to people who would before long be arrested trafficking—this arrest having no effect on neighborhood traffic.

Randy was hoping in a way that Yvonne wouldn't turn up. And that was when he saw her small, emaciated figure coming down the block. He didn't believe it at first. He didn't believe it was this easy to track somebody down, that junkies were so predictable, that he himself had been so predictable. He didn't believe that statistics and addiction were so navigable, that the arc of need was as orthodox as the law of falling bodies. No matter: there she was and she was *moving pretty fast.*

He left the van without even locking it, without turning it off. Material things had no place in that moment. The blackness of the sky was perfect and enduring. These shades came from the bakery and darted up the street looking for the first possible spot where they could tie off. And Randy was trotting across the street like he too was desperate in that way, toward Yvonne, and he had his hand out to touch her. He had a windbreaker tied around his waist. And his hair was really short and he didn't look like he had looked the year or so before. When they met.

She didn't either. Yvonne looked like she'd been orphaned by war; she looked like she suffered with unimaginable grief. When he spoke to her there was a long moment before she seemed to recognize that she was stopped now, that someone was talking to her, holding her up. She grimaced. She didn't seem to recognize him—she knew his face and who he was, but she didn't recognize any freight in the encounter—as if chance had been the only thing between then. She only wanted to get into the bakery. He was an impediment. The way she wheezed and coughed proved it. She was nervous. But the weirdest thing was that she was smiling. She was grimacing and smiling.

—Well, Randy said, coming to the end of an awkward politeness. Well, I just wanted to . . . to see you. Listen . . . Jeez, you know I don't want to say it but you *just don't look that good.*

Her own words seemed to drift up into her throat as if they had a separate set of controls, as if she were the dummy for some ventriloquist.

—What are you talking about?

—Forget it, Randy said.

—No, she said irritably. What the fuck are you talking about?

—Listen, he said, if you want any help, if you ever want any help or anything . . . just let me know. I don't know . . .

—I don't have time, she said. Anyway, *I don't want your pity.* You're a fucking *junkie,* too.

And then she left him there. She hurried on. She took off.

He was stricken. He was halted. He was going to say something. He was going to defend himself, to defend his self-evident pride. But what could he say? He was standing there like a beseeching panhandler. Hadn't he been one of those club rats for whom all human folly—the suspension and flogging of men several feet above a stage—was the stuff of fun? Then why couldn't he let Yvonne *go on her merry way and finish the job?* Why not let all these people go? Let this stuff, these places recede into whitewashed accounts of youth he would present to friends when provoked momentarily into some foolish grandiosity about having simply *survived.* Why not let it go?

He called after her. Just as Jorge was coming out. Sweating quite a bit. Jorge, sweating like it was deepest July and he had no AC. Randy was calling after his wife, oblivious. On an empty street. On a moonless night. She never looked back. He was standing there watching. She never looked back.

There was one more time, a few years later, that he saw her again: when she had finally gotten clean, when she needed to discuss completing the divorce. She had Kaposi's sarcoma, and her face, into which a lively human rose color was at last returning, was freckled with lesions.

And there were others caught in the vine of those five minutes of June, in front of the cop shop on Eighth Street, in the moments just before and after: Buck Miller and Susan Ward and a guy who I used to see at the Marlin Café; and Debby, the girl who drove Doris to the airport, who also knew Yvonne; and Ray, the guy who hosed down the booths in Peep World; and Crystal, the pre-operative transsexual who slept with Jorge one night and then stole all his stuff; and the auctioneer at Wendy's; and the woman, Huck, with the dildo that glowed violet neon; and the guy getting fisted by two men at once; and Randy's friend Noel; and the men who had fucked Marlene when she was a hooker, most of whom didn't know she was dead; and two of the guys in *the band with no name* (the third had been shipped off to an expensive rehab). And some people I know whom I have not mentioned yet, like Robert and Jaimé and David and Frank from the Mudd Club and Dan and Crutch and Bob, Julia, Karen, Kenny and Kate. Lizzie. And there are other names I don't know yet. And myself. Me. I was there. All of us strode up and down Eighth Street like it was an actual artery in some larger life form, in some larger organism. As one of our number slipped into a storefront along Eighth Street, another passed by. None of us seemed to know the nature of the coincidences that bound us together, as I know now, or that junkies and masochists and hookers and those who have squandered everything are the ring of brightest angels around heaven.

And just by chance a bunch of these characters turned up in Yvonne's documentary, which had been transferred to film and then back to videotape and which now languished in a foot locker. Each of them was captured in and around the bars that Yvonne frequented when she was just out of school. I remember what she looked like then. When her face had an openness like good luck, like the big puffy clouds you see over the desert. I remember how bright her eyes were; I remember how excited she got by stuff, how a movie at the Film

505

Forum could change her for weeks, how a certain record with just the right snare drum sound and a little bit of anger could keep her going all night, writing.

And the end of the film, the end of it for now, until somebody completes it for Yvonne, was like this. At a party crowded with the characters in this story, or other characters not unlike these, at a party at the Ruin weeks before its closing, with stalls strung with Christmas lights, surrounded by half-clothed erotic dancers, *the band with no name* struck up some kind of evolved march thing. In the basement of this wretched club. The music was fast. Everyone knew the song. The room was lit poorly. You could have slept with anyone in the room. You could have thrown your arms around anyone and it would have been okay. It would have been nice. The frame was frozen for a second. Then there was a jump cut and the band was throwing down its instruments and there was some buzz in a Fender Twin Reverb amp, a little feedback, but the guys in the band weren't paying any attention to it. And there was a close-up on Randy, laughing. His smile taking up the whole screen. And then it just ends.

I am going now. I am leaving.

Nominated by James Linville

THE DECONSTRUCTION OF EMILY DICKINSON

by GALWAY KINNELL

from AMERICAN POETRY REVIEW

The lecture had ended when I came in,
and the professor was answering questions.
I do not know what he had been doing with her
poetry, but now he was speaking of her
as a victim of reluctant male publishers.
When the questions dwindled, I put up my hand,
said the ignorant meddling of the Springfield *Daily Republican*
and the hidebound response of literary men,
and the gulf between the poetic wishfulness
then admired and her own harsh knowledge
had let her see that her poems
would not be understood in her time;
and therefore, passionate to publish,
she vowed not to publish again. I said
I would recite a version of her vow.

> Publication—is the Auction
> Of the mind of Man—

But before I could, the professor broke in.
"Yes," he said, " 'the Auction'—'auction,' from *augere, auctum*, to
    augment, to author . . . "
"Let's hear the poem!" "The poem!" several women,

who at such a moment are more outspoken than men, shouted,
but I kept still and he kept going.
"In *auctum* the economy of the signifier is split, revealing an
    unconscious collusion in the bourgeois commodification of
    consciousness.
While our author says 'no,' the unreified text says 'yes,' yes?"
He kissed his lips together and turned to me
saying, "Now, may we hear the poem?"
I waited a moment for full effect.
Without rising to my feet, I said,
"Professor, to understand Dickinson
it may not always be necessary to uproot her words.
Why not, first, try *listening* to her?
Loyalty forbids me to recite her poem now."
No, I didn't say that—I realized
she would want me to finish him off with one wallop.
So I said, "Professor, I thought you
would welcome the words of your author.
I see you prefer to hear yourself speak."
No, I held back—for I could hear her
urging me to put outrage into my voice
and substance into my argument.
I stood up so that everyone might see
the derision in my smile. "Professor," I said,
"you live in Amherst at the end of the twentieth century.
For you 'auction' means a quaint event
where somebody coaxes out the bids
on a butter churn on a summer Saturday.
Forget etymology, this is history.
In Amherst in 1860 'auction' meant
the slave auction, you dope!"
Well, I didn't say that either,
although I have said them all,
many times, in the middle of the night.
In reality, I stood up and recited
like a schoolboy called upon in class.
My voice gradually weakened, and the women
who had called out for the poem
now looked as though they were thinking
of errands to be done on the way home.

When I finished, the professor smiled.
"Thank you. So, what at first some of us may have taken as a simple
    outcry, we all now see is an ambivalent, self-subversive text."
As people got up to go, I moved
into that sanctum within me where Emily
sometimes speaks a verse, and listened
for a sign of how she felt, such as,
"Thanks—Sweet—countryman—
for wanting—to Sing out—of Me—
after all that Humbug." But she was silent.

Nominated by Jane Hirshfield, Sharon Olds, Ken Rosen, Maura Stanton

CHARLES THE OBSCURE

by CHARLES SIMIC

from NEW LETTERS

LATE ONE NIGHT, as the half-moon rode high above the church of St. Mark, I grabbed my balls passing a priest. This happened in Belgrade when I was twelve years old. I was skipping along without a care in the world when he came around the corner. He assumed I was about to greet him—he was even inclining his head benevolently—when I did what my friends advised me to do when meeting a priest. He stood there steaming in his cassock for a moment. Then, it was my turn to be surprised. Plump as he was, he went after me with extraordinary quickness, waving his arms about and shouting: "You little creep! You little son of a bitch!" His cussing terrified me even more than the chase he gave me. I ran without looking back.

At home the photographs of my great-great grandfathers and uncles awaited me on the living room walls. On my mother's side, I had several priests and one bishop in my ancestry. I've never seen in a wanted poster a more murderous collection of mugs. They had huge black-and-white beards that grew even sideways. Their eyes were bulging. The photographer must have warned them not to move and they obeyed. Flies crawled inside their ears during the long exposure. Their noses itched terribly. That evening their eyes followed me with unusual grimness. They all knew what I had done.

The meanest looking of the lot was my grandfather's father. It was public knowledge that his children hated him. My grandfather did not permit any mention of priests or religion in our house when he was around. When my grandmother died later that year, he informed the family that there will be no priest officiating in the cemetery chapel or at the gravesite. A scandal, people whispered. Everybody crossed themselves just thinking about it. A couple of aunts decided to disobey his wishes. The priest would appear at the gravesite while the coffin was being lowered; and my grandfather, so the theory went, would be too overwhelmed with grief and sorrow to object to a short prayer being said.

That's not what happened. Just as the gravediggers were fussing with the ropes, and the family and friends were standing with bowed heads, the priest materialized in his vestments, a prayer book in hand, already blessing us and mumbling a prayer. To everyone's astonishment, the old curmudgeon lunged at him. Before we had time to realize what was happening, grandpa had the priest by the scruff of the neck and was marching him away from the grave. As if that wasn't enough, one of my weeping aunts ran after them, grabbed the tails of grandfather's coat and started pulling him back. She had the strength of ten and so did he. A tug of war ensued and lots of yelling. The old man was trying to kick her without turning and letting the priest go. Unfortunately, my mother rushed me and my brother away before we could see and hear more.

*

If you were to ask anybody in my family if God exists, they would have given you a puzzled look. Of course he does, they'd reply. This meant, in practice, attending the church only to baptize, wed and bury someone. Bonafide atheists probably mention religion and God more frequently than my mother ever did. My father, however, was a different story. He didn't mind entering churches. Russian churches, black churches, old Italian churches, austere New England churches, Byzantine churches, all that was admirable. The same is true of me. He liked the pomp and music, but even more he liked an empty church. I saw him a few times get down on his knees to pray, but he had no use for organized religion, or every other idea that has sought to take its place. As far as he was concerned, Communism and Fascism were versions of the nastiest aspects of Christianity. "All that orthodoxy, fanaticism, virtue by decree," he'd complain. They were all enemies of the individual, forever peddling intolerance and conformity. He had serious philosophical interest in Islam, Buddhism, Hinduism and Christianity, but no desire to join any congregation of the faithful. Belief in God was something private, like sex. If you did not believe in anything, as I often told him was the case with me, that was all right, too.

*

"Come on," she yanked my arm, "let's go. They're just a couple of hicks," she assured me, but I had to take a better look at the street preachers.

The young woman with thick glasses pressed a Bible to her heart; the horse-faced fellow by her side strummed a tuneless guitar at the edge of a large Saturday night crowd. They preached and sang hymns as if dogs were biting their asses.

My friend had enough. Without me noticing, she had split. I was left in custody of their Jesus who, by the sound of it, had too many lost sheep already to worry about. His great love always spurned—"Sweet Jesus," they hollered, trying to drown out an ambulance crying its heart out somewhere in the dark city beyond the brightly lit movie houses and penny arcades all around us.

Hell! I was deeply moved.

*

"Give me two wings to fly away"

America is God crazy, as everyone knows. It's impossible to be an American writer without taking that into account.

Driving just after daybreak early one spring morning through West Virginia, I'm listening to the radio. Someone is playing scratchy old black gospel records. The station is fading and coming clear in turn; the car is speeding down the empty road, and I'm wondering who is choosing the records so impeccably, so mysteriously, given the odd hour. Beyond the enjoyment, the emotion is gripping me, I have a sudden realization. They mean every word they say. Every word. They sing so beautifully, and so wildly, because they believe the Lord is in their midst right then and there.

It has always seemed obvious to me that we are alone in the universe. I love metaphysics and its speculations, but the suspicion at the core of my being is that we are whistling in the dark. Still, I have tears in my eyes every time I hear good church music. Never has the human heart been so pure, I think. Perhaps divinity can only be experienced

512

by those who sing together? The God who comes or does not come to the solitaries is a different one.

"Without this mystery, the most incomprehensible of all, we are incomprehensible to ourselves," said Pascal, in a different context.

Sing and shout, Reverend! is my advice. Do that little dance step while the choir behind you sways and slaps its tambourines, and the old lady on the piano and the scrawny kid on the electric guitar nod to each other with approval. There's no doubt about it: "Except for music, everything is a lie," as Cioran says.

*

One day I finally admitted to myself that I'm hopelessly superstitious. You do not believe in God, I said to myself, so how come you believe in bad luck? I have no reply to that. Do we make our Fate, or is our Fate an independent agency? Calvin at least knew who arranged our destiny; I do not.

This head full of contradictions walking on two legs, is this the modern version of holy foolishness? Let's hope so.

In the meantime, the worries of a crumb overlooked on death's dinner plate . . .

*

I was always attracted to mystical and esoteric doctrines that propose the unknowingness of the Supreme Being, the ineffability of the experience of His presence and the ambiguity of our human condition. Ambiguity, that great carnivore. If I believe in anything, it is in the dark night of the soul. Awe is my religion, and mystery is its church. I include here equally the mysteries of consciousness and the torments of conscience.

If not for conscience would we ever consider the possibility of the independent existence of evil? Nothing explains the world and the people in it. This is the knowledge that makes us fall down on our knees and listen to the silence of the night. Not even a dog or an owl is brave enough to interrupt it tonight. Being and nothingness, those two abstractions, how real, how close they feel. In such moments I want to reach for my chessboard. Let them play each other, and I'll sit and watch until the first streak of light slips under the door and crawls to my feet without waking the dust.

513

*

Many years ago, Vasko Popa took me to visit the women's monastery Mesic, near his hometown, Vrsac, on the Yugoslav-Rumanian border. We had a long lunch at a young poet's house and did not leave till five in the afternoon. I don't remember much about the drive, since we were talking a lot, interrupting each other with stories and jokes; but all of a sudden there was a high wall at the end of a dirt road and a closed iron gate. We left the car outside the gate and pushed it open just enough to squeeze through. What we found inside was a veritable jungle, as if the grass had not been cut all summer, and the trees had grown wild over the years without being trimmed and thinned out. We followed what was once a road, and now a narrow path in the twilight calm broken occasionally by the sound of a bird or a cricket. We did not speak. After a mile or so, we saw through the trees several large houses and a small Byzantine church. We walked to the largest of them, knocked, opened the door, peeked inside, even announced our-selves; but only silence came out to welcome us. It was so quiet, our steps became cautious. We walked on tiptoe on the way to the next house. Through the open door, we could see six nuns sitting in a cir-cle with heads bowed. Vasko knew the name of the prioress and called out to her. She jumped, and the nuns followed after her in joy and de-light to see him. The prioress who was old, Vasko had told me, used to be in her youth a lady in waiting at the royal court, and was excep-tionally well educated. Vasko sent her French books. She was just reading Camus and immediately wanted to talk about him with us.

We were then given a tour by the prioress and a tall, skinny young nun. We visited the church, which was under repair, to see some sur-prisingly fine frescoes, and then slowly, because of the prioress' age, we climbed to the small graveyard above the church. The sun had just set. "I'll be soon resting here," the prioress told us, laughing. We smiled in reply. One could almost envy the prospect.

Then we were led back to the large house we had first come to. This we heard was one of the local bishop's many summer residences. He had not stayed in it for the last thirty years, but everything was kept in readiness for his arrival. We sat in a large living room with the prioress and the skinny nun drinking homemade brandy, while being sternly examined by former bishops in sooty old paintings. Only one table lamp had been lit. Vasko talked and so did the old woman, but the rustling of so many leaves muffled their voices, and then all of a sud-

514

den, there was complete silence. Here was peace of a world outside time, the kind one encounters at times in fairy-tale illustrations, in which a solitary child is seen entering a dark forest of gigantic trees.

After a while I listened only to the silence deepen, the night continue to hold its breath.

*

"Every poem, knowingly or unknowingly is addressed to God," the poet Frank Samperi told me long ago. I remember being surprised, objecting, mentioning some awful contemporary poems. . . We were filing subscription cards in the stock room of a photography magazine and having long philosophical conversations on the subject of poetry. Frank had been reading a lot of Dante, so I figured that's it. He is stuck in fourteenth-century Italy.

No more. Today I think as he did then. It makes absolutely no difference whether gods and devils exist or not. The secret ambition of every true poem is to ask about them even as it acknowledges their absence.

Nominated by Philip Booth, Richard Jackson, Dan Masterson, New Letters.

SPECIAL MENTION

(The editors also wish to mention the following important works published by small presses last year. Listing is in no particular order.)

POETRY

Indirective—James Galvin (The Paris Review)
Freshman English Poetry Anthology—Maura Stanton (Crazyhorse)
Yellow Lilies and Cypress Swamp—David Baker (Antaeus)
Moving & St. Rage—Kathy Fagan (Agni Review)
The Pools—Chase Twichell (Ontario Review)
Peak Season—Jane Shore (Salmagundi)
Memoirs of a Child Evangelist—Mary Karr (Parnassus)
Bunting—Linda Gregerson (TriQuarterly)
Singing—Christopher Buckley (Yellow Silk)
Shaving My Legs With Ockham's Razor—Frances Mayes (Southern Review)
The Book of the Dead Man #12—Marvin Bell (*Book of the Dead Man,* Copper Canyon Press)
Blue Guide—Stephen Yenser (The Paris Review)
The Grey Fox—Greg Orr (American Poetry Review)
Biography of Dreamtime—Aleš Debeljak (Trafika)
White Mittens—Deborah Kennan (Santa Monica Review)
Five O'Clock—Robin Behn (Iowa Review)
All Day—Lawrence Rabb (Antaeus)
Job's Wife, A 20th Century Casting Script—Eleanor Wilner (Sycamore Review)
Back to the Dream Time—Quincy Troupe (Poetry Flash)
For Those Whom The Gods Love Less—Denise Levertov (American Poetry Review)

To See If Something Comes Next—Jack Gilbert (American Poetry Review)

Street Scenes—Marilyn Hacker (TriQuarterly)

Breaking Unbalance—Elena Karina Byrne (American Poetry Review)

Incognito and Not—Lynn McGee (Ontario Review)

Migratory—Mark Doty (Carolina Quarterly)

Some Notes of Miami—John Balaban (Witness)

Pavoriti In Transport, 1990—William Matthews (Pivot)

Manhattan In My Hand—Elizabeth Cohen (Potato Eyes)

Statistic: The Witness—Rita Dove (The Georgia Review)

Herb Gatherers Off I-80—Lee Upton (Black Warrior Review)

For Paul Celan and Primo Levi—Harvey Shapiro (*A Day's Portion,* Hanging Loose Press)

These Northern Fields At Dusk—Eamon Grennan (American Poetry Review)

Poem Half In the Manner of Li Ho—Charles Wright (Field)

The Weight—Beckian Fritz Goldberg (Passages North)

Photography—Philip Levine (Poetry)

Tombs of the Muses—Deborah Digges (Antaeus)

Buy One, Get One Free—Richard Jackson (Gettysburg Review)

Uncomfortable Procedures—Michael Van Walleghen (American Literary Review)

The Privileges of Philosophy—Stephen Dobyns (Georgia Review)

Cancer Talkers—John Wood (In Primary Light)

Androids—William Dickey (In The Dreaming)

The Invisible Man—Denise Duhamel (Poet Lore)

Moving On In the Dark Like Loaded Boats At Night, Though There Is No Course, There Is Boundlessness—Lucie Brock-Broido (Parnassus)

Codine—Frank Gaspar (*Mass For the Grace of A Happy Death,* Anhinga Press)

Triggering Corinth, NY—William Hathaway (The Southern Review)

Dragonflies Mating—Robert Hass (Antaeus)

NONFICTION

Blood Rain—Bill Shields (Vietnam Generation)

Where Bears Walk—Sherry Simpson (*Another Wilderness,* Seal Press)

FICTION

Ocean of Words—Ha Jin (Chelsea)
The Angel of Vermont Street—Alison Moore (Story)
The Island of Ziz—Yuri Vinnichuk (Denver Quarterly)
Windows of the Soul—Patricia Hampl (Alaska Quarterly Review)
Blue Hair—Michael Martone (Colorado Review)
The Man Who Read A Book—Thomas M. Disch (Hudson Review)
Kind Strangers—Alice Adams (Southwest Review)
Counting Sheep—Alison Lurie (Southwest Review)
"Lives of the Non-Poets"—Stephen Saraceno (Washington Review)
Lessons in Impromptu Fantasy—Lauri Marr Wasmund (Cimarron Review)
Biedermeyer—Michelle Fogus (Sou'wester)
A Taste of Heaven—R. Sebastian Bennett (William and Mary Review)
Black Auxiliaries—Irvin Faust (Literary Review)
Metafictions - M—Richard Kostelanetz (Aura)
The Key of F—D. Navarro (Blue Penny Quarterly)
Stealing the Bees—Sallie Bingham (Passages North)
At the Altar of American Indian Architecture—Diane Glancy (American Letters and Commentary)
Religion—Christine Schutt (Story Quarterly)
A Night's Work—Jaimy Gordon (Michigan Quarterly Review)
Eating the Racoon—Nicolette Bethel (Massachusetts Review)
Mercury—Richard Burgin (Santa Barbara Review)
Waiting For The Evening News—Tim Gautreaux (Story)
Hawk of the Night—Ewing Campbell (Gulf Coast Collection)
Tansy—Heather Ross Miller (The Laurel Review)
from "Nobody's Daughters"—Melanie Rae Thon (Bomb)
Sloan's Daughters—Gladys Swan (Southwest Review)
Full Moon Howl—Ellen Winter (Puerto Del Sol)
Fossilized—Sharon Solwitz (Mānoa)
The Dark Part—T. M. McNally (Mid-American Review)
Look at the Moon—Aurelie Sheehan (*Jack Kerouac Is Pregnant*, Dalkey Archive Press)
Five Jack Cool—Michael Stephens (*The Brooklyn Book of the Dead*, Dalkey Archive Press)
The Window—Barry Kitterman (Turnstile)
Recessional—Gary Lutz (The Quarterly)
Crossroads Cafe—Debra Monroe (Gettysburg Review)
Debits and Trespasses—Margot Livesey (North American Review)
White Circles—William Cobb (American Short Fiction)

PRESSES FEATURED IN THE PUSHCART PRIZE EDITIONS SINCE 1976

Acts
Agni Review
Ahsahta Press
Ailanthus Press
Alaska Quarterly Review
Alcheringa/Ethnopoetics
Alice James Books
Ambergris
Amelia
American Literature
American PEN
American Poetry Review
American Scholar
American Short Fiction
The American Voice
Amicus Journal
Amnesty International
Anaesthesia Review
Another Chicago Magazine
Antaeus
Antietam Review
Antioch Review
Apalachee Quarterly
Aphra
Aralia Press
The Ark

Ascensius Press
Ascent
Aspen Leaves
Aspen Poetry Anthology
Assembling
Bamboo Ridge
Barlenmir House
Barnwood Press
The Bellingham Review
Bellowing Ark
Beloit Poetry Journal
Bennington Review
Bilingual Review
Black American Literature Forum
Black Rooster
Black Scholar
Black Sparrow
Black Warrior Review
Blackwells Press
Bloomsbury Review
Blue Cloud Quarterly
Blue Unicorn
Blue Wind Press
Bluefish
BOA Editions
Bomb

Bookslinger Editions
Boulevard
Boxspring
Bridges
Brown Journal of Arts
Burning Deck Press
Caliban
California Quarterly
Callaloo
Calliope
Calliopea Press
Canto
Capra Press
Carolina Quarterly
Caribbean Writer
Cedar Rock
Center
Chariton Review
Charnel House
Chelsea
Chicago Review
Chouteau Review
Chowder Review
Cimarron Review
Cincinnati Poetry Review
City Lights Books
Clown War
CoEvolution Quarterly
Cold Mountain Press
Colorado Review
Columbia: A Magazine of Poetry
    and Prose
Confluence Press
Confrontation
Conjunctions
Copper Canyon Press
Cosmic Information Agency
Crawl Out Your Window
Crazyhorse
Crescent Review
Cross Cultural Communications
Cross Currents
Cumberland Poetry Review

Curbstone Press
Cutbank
Dacotah Territory
Daedalus
Dalkey Archive Press
Decatur House
December
Denver Quarterly
Domestic Crude
Dragon Gate Inc.
Dreamworks
Dryad Press
Duck Down Press
Durak
East River Anthology
Ellis Press
Empty Bowl
Epoch
Ergo!
Exquisite Corpse
Faultline
Fiction
Fiction Collective
Fiction International
Field
Fine Madness
Firebrand Books
Firelands Art Review
Five Fingers Review
Five Trees Press
The Formalist
Frontiers: A Journal of Women
    Studies
Gallimaufry
Genre
The Georgia Review
Gettysburg Review
Ghost Dance
Goddard Journal
David Godine, Publisher
Graham House Press
Grand Street
Granta

Graywolf Press
Green Mountains Review
Greenfield Review
Greensboro Review
Guardian Press
Gulf Coast
Hard Pressed
Harvard Review
Hayden's Ferry Review
Hermitage Press
Hills
Holmgangers Press
Holy Cow!
Home Planet News
Hudson Review
Hungry Mind Review
Icarus
Iguana Press
Indiana Review
Indiana Writes
Intermedia
Intro
Invisible City
Inwood Press
Iowa Review
Ironwood
Jam To-day
The Journal
The Kanchenjuga Press
Kansas Quarterly
Kayak
Kelsey Street Press
Kenyon Review
Latitudes Press
Laughing Waters Press
Laurel Review
L'Epervier Press
Liberation
Linquis
The Literary Review
The Little Magazine
Living Hand Press
Living Poets Press

Logbridge-Rhodes
Louisville Review
Lowlands Review
Lucille
Lynx House Press
Magic Circle Press
Malahat Review
Mānoa
Manroot
Massachusetts Review
Mho & Mho Works
Micah Publications
Michigan Quarterly
Milkweed Editions
Milkweed Quarterly
The Minnesota Review
Mississippi Review
Mississippi Valley Review
Missouri Review
Montana Gothic
Montana Review
Montemora
Moon Pony Press
Mr. Cogito Press
MSS
Mulch Press
Nada Press
New America
New American Review
The New Criterion
New Delta Review
New Directions
New England Review
New England Review and Bread
    Loaf Quarterly
New Letters
New Virginia Review
New York Quarterly
New York University Press
Nimrod
North American Review
North Atlantic Books
North Dakota Quarterly

North Point Press
Northern Lights
Northwest Review
O. ARS
O·Blēk
Obsidian
Obsidian II
Oconee Review
October
Ohio Review
Ontario Review
Open Places
Orca Press
Orchises Press
Oxford Press
Oyez Press
Painted Bride Quarterly
Painted Hills Review
Paris Review
Parnassus: Poetry in Review
Partisan Review
Passages North
Penca Books
Pentagram
Penumbra Press
Pequod
Persea: An International Review
Pipedream Press
Pitcairn Press
Pitt Magazine
Ploughshares
Poet and Critic
Poetry
Poetry East
Poetry Ireland Review
Poetry Northwest
Poetry Now
Prairie Schooner
Prescott Street Press
Promise of Learnings
Provincetown Arts
Puerto Del Sol
Quarry West

The Quarterly
Quarterly West
Raccoon
Rainbow Press
Raritan: A Quarterly Review
Red Cedar Review
Red Clay Books
Red Dust Press
Red Earth Press
Release Press
Review of Contemporary Fiction
Revista Chicano-Riquena
River Styx
Rowan Tree Press
Russian *Samizdat*
Salmagundi
San Marcos Press
Sea Pen Press and Paper Mill
Seal Press
Seamark Press
Seattle Review
Second Coming Press
Semiotext(e)
The Seventies Press
Sewanee Review
Shankpainter
Shantih
Sheep Meadow Press
Shenandoah
A Shout In the Street
Sibyl-Child Press
Side Show
Small Moon
The Smith
Some
The Sonora Review
Southern Poetry Review
Southern Review
Southwest Review
Spectrum
The Spirit That Moves Us
St. Andrews Press
Story

Story Quarterly
Streetfare Journal
Stuart Wright, Publisher
Sulfur
The Sun
Sun & Moon Press
Sun Press
Sunstone
Sycamore Review
Tar River Poetry
Teal Press
Telephone Books
Telescope
Temblor
Tendril
Texas Slough
The MacGuffin
13th Moon
THIS
Thorp Springs Press
Three Rivers Press
Threepenny Review
Thunder City Press
Thunder's Mouth Press
Tikkun
Tombouctou Books
Toothpaste Press
Transatlantic Review
TriQuarterly
Truck Press

Undine
Unicorn Press
University of Illinois Press
University of Massachusetts Press
University of Pittsburgh Press
Unmuzzled Ox
Unspeakable Visions of the Individual
Vagabond
Virginia Quarterly
Volt
Wampeter Press
Washington Writers Workshop
Water Table
Western Humanities Review
Westigan Review
Wickwire Press
Willow Springs
Wilmore City
Witness
Word Beat Press
Word-Smith
Wormwood Review
Writers Forum
Xanadu
Yale Review
Yardbird Reader
Yarrow
Y'Bird
ZYZZYVA

CONTRIBUTORS' NOTES

AGHA SHAHID ALI was a 1993 New York Foundation Poetry Fellowship winner. He is the author of two poetry collections and teaches at the University of Massachusetts, Amherst.

A. R. AMMONS won the Lannan Poetry Award in 1992. His most recent poetry collections are available from W. W. Norton: *Garbage* (1993) and *The Really Short Poems of A. R. Ammons* (1991).

JOHN BARTH's most recent novel was published last year. He lives in Baltimore. This is his first appearance in this series.

CHARLES BAXTER's most recent books are *Shadow Play* and *A Relative Stranger*. He lives in Ann Arbor.

MOLLY BENDALL's book, *After Estrangement,* was published by Peregrine Smith in 1992. She lives in Venice, California.

FRANK BIDART lives in Cambridge, Massachusetts and is the author of *In the Western Night, The Sacrifice* and other books of poetry.

LINDA BIERDS lives in Washington state and is the author most recently of *The Ghost Trio* (Holt).

SVEN BIRKERTS lives in Arlington, Massachusetts and is the author of *The Gutenberg Elegies: The Fate of Reading In An Electronic Age* (Faber and Faber) from which this essay was excerpted.

EAVAN BOLAND lives in Dublin. Her most recent poetry collection is *In A Time of Violence* (Norton).

FREDERICK BUSCH's latest book is *The Children of the Woods: New and Selected Stories* (Ticknor & Fields). He teaches at Colgate University.

CYRUS CASSELLS lives in Rome. He is the author of a recent poetry collection from Copper Canyon Press and winner of the William Carlos Williams Award.

MARILYN CHIN lives in San Diego. Her work has appeared in *Kenyon Review, Parnassus, Ploughshares* and elsewhere.

MICHAEL COLLINS is the author of *The Man Who Dreamt of Lobsters* (Random House) and several books published in England. He studies at the University of Illinois.

JENNIFER C CORNELL's *Departures* won the 14th Annual Drue Heinz Literature Prize. She teaches at Oregon State University in Corvallis.

DON DELILLO is the author of ten novels and is a winner of the National Book Award.

CARL DENNIS has published six collections of poems, most recently *Meetings With Time* (Viking, 1992).

STEPHEN DOBYNS has appeared three times in this series—with poetry. This is his first prose work. He lives in Syracuse.

STEPHEN DUNN is the author of nine books of poems including *New and Selected Poems*: 1974–1994 (Norton).

LYNN EMANUEL is a past poetry editor of this series. Her books include *The Dig* (University of Illinois Press) a National Poetry Series winner.

GARY FINCKE teaches at Susquehanna University in Pennsylvania. He is the author of three books of poetry and won the Bess Hokin Prize in 1991.

MARIBETH FISCHER lives in Baltimore. "Stillborn" is taken from her manuscript "What A Woman Wears Lightly" and is her first published essay.

SABINA GROGAN lives in San Francisco and has recent fiction in *New Letters* and *Quarry West*.

ART HOMER teaches at the University of Nebraska and coedits *The Nebraska Review*. He is the author of several poetry collections, most recently from Owl Creek Press. This essay is from his just published *The Drownt Boy: An Ozark Tale* (University of Missouri Press).

STEVEN HUFF's poetry has appeared in *MSS, Painted Bride Quarterly* and elsewhere. He lives in Rochester, New York.

DONALD JUSTICE's *New and Selected Poems* will be published later this year by Knopf. He lives in Iowa City.

NORA COBB KELLER lives and writes in Honolulu. She is currently at work on a novel.

BRIGIT PEGEEN KELLY teaches at the University of Illinois. Her works have appeared in *Southern Review, New England Review, Massachusetts Review* and *Best American Poetry 1993*.

GALWAY KINNELL's new book is *Imperfect Thirst* (Houghton Mifflin) which includes this poem. He teaches at New York University.

MAXINE KUMIN lives in Warner, New Hampshire and is the author most recently of *Women, Animals and Vegetables: Essays and Stories* (Norton) which includes "The Match".

SANDRA TSING LOH lives in Van Nuys, California and is the author of an essay collection and a novel forthcoming from Riverhead Books.

THOMAS LUX teaches at Sarah Lawrence College. His *Split Horizon* is out from Houghton Mifflin.

AVNER MANDELMAN was born in Tel Aviv in 1947 and served in the Israeli Air Force during the Six Day War. After travels through France and Canada he settled in Los Altos Hills, California with his wife and two children. A novel, *The Debba*, is forthcoming.

BEN MARCUS lives in New York City and is the author of a forthcoming book from Knopf, *The Age of Wire and String*.

REGINALD MCKNIGHT teaches at the University of Maryland. His most recent story collection is *The Kind of Light That Shines on Texas* (Little Brown).

SANDRA MCPHERSON's collection *Edge Effect: Trails and Portrayals* and *The Spaces Between Birds: Mother/Daughter Poems 1967–1995* are both forthcoming from Wesleyan University Press in 1996.

MELINDA MUELLER lives and teaches in Seattle. She is the author of *Asleep in Another Country* (Jawbone).

RICK MOODY is the author of the novels *Garden State* (Pushcart Press), *The Ice Storm* (Little Brown) and the just-published *The Ring of Brightest Angels Around Heaven* (Little Brown).

CORNELIA NIXON is the author of *Now You See It* (Little Brown) and she teaches at Indiana University.

JOYCE CAROL OATES is a Founding Editor of this series. She lives in Princeton and helps edit *The Ontario Review*.

WILLIAM OLSEN is the author of *The Hand of God and A Few Bright Flowers*. He lives in Kalamazoo.

GRACE PALEY is the author of four story collections and two books of poetry. She is the first official New York State writer.

ROBERT PINSKY's *Collected Poems* is forthcoming from Farrar, Straus and Giroux. He lives in Newton, Massachusetts. This *Canto* was included in his just-published Dante translation issued by Farrar Straus and Giroux.

STANLEY PLUMLY teaches at The University of Maryland. His poem is from a new, forthcoming collection from Ecco Press.

EILEEN POLLACK is the author of the fiction collection, *The Rabbi In The Attic* (Simon & Schuster). She teaches at the University of Michigan.

MELISSA PRITCHARD is the author of a fiction collection from Zoland Books, *The Instinct for Bliss*.

ALBERTO RIOS is the author of seven books and chapbooks of poetry and two story collections. He has won numerous prizes and teaches at Arizona State University.

JAMES ROBISON teaches at the University of Houston. His first fiction collection, *Rumor and Other Stories*, won a Whiting Grant.

DENNIS SAMPSON has published two books of poetry, most recently *Forgiveness* (Milkweed Editions). He lives in Alabama.

ALICE SCHELL is at work on a cycle of stories set in New Sharon, Pennsylvania in the 30's and 40's. She lives in Philadelphia.

MAUREEN SEATON's books include *The Sea Among the Cupboards* and *Fear of Subways*. She lives in Chicago.

DIANN BLAKELY SHOAF lives in Nashville, and is the author of *Hurricane Walk* (BOA Editions, 1992).

CHARLES SIMIC's latest poetry collection is *A Wedding in Hell* (Harcourt). He lives in New Hampshire.

DEBRA SPARK's novel, *Coconuts for the Saints,* was published in 1995 by Faber and Faber, with a paperback due out from Avon.

ELIZABETH SPIRES is a past poetry editor of this series. *Worldling,* her most recent collection of poetry, is due soon from Norton.

DAVID ST. JOHN's *Study for the World's Body,* is just out from Harper Collins and was nominated for a National Book Award. He lives in Venice, California.

ANN TOWNSEND teaches at Denison University. Her recent chap-book is *Modern Love* (Bottom Dog Press)

JOHN UPDIKE was born in Shillington, Pennsylvania and now lives in Beverly Farms, Massachusetts. He has written novels, short stories, poems and criticism. This is his second appearance in this series.

IRMA WALLEM is the author of two books from Mercury House. This selection is from the manuscript "Never Trust A Woman Over 90," written with Sally Hayton-Keeva.

JULIA WENDELL is a licensed exercise rider at Laurel Racetrack in Maryland and the owner of a thoroughbred horse farm. Her most recent chapbook of poetry was *Fires At Yellowstone* (Bacchae Press).

MARIE SHEPPARD WILLIAMS is the author of a collection forthcoming from Coffee House Press—*The World-Wide Church of the Handicapped.*

CONTRIBUTING SMALL PRESSES FOR PUSHCART PRIZE XX

(These presses made or received nominations for this edition of *The Pushcart Prize*. See the *International Directory of Little Magazines and Small Presses*, Dustbooks, P.O. Box 100, Paradise, CA 95967, for subscription rates, manuscript requirements and a complete international listing of small presses.)

A

The Acorn, see Hot Pepper Press
African American Review, English Dept., Indiana State Univ., Terre Haute, IN 47809
Agni, Boston Univ., 236 Bay State Rd, Boston, MA 02215
Ahsahta Press, Boise State Univ., 1910 University Dr., Boise, ID 83725
Alaska Quarterly Review, Univ. of Alaska, 3211 Providence Dr., Anchorage, AK 99508
Alaska Wordworks Publ. Co., 1606 Merika Rd., #10, Fairbanks, AK 99709
Alpha Beat Press, 31A Waterloo St., New Hope, PA 18938
Amelia, 329 "E" St., Bakersfield, CA 93304
American Letters & Commentary, 850 Park Ave., Ste. 5b, New York, NY 10021

American Literary Review, Univ. of North Texas, P.O. Box 13827, Denton, TX 76203

American Poetry Review, 1721 Walnut St., Philadelphia, PA 19103

American Short Fiction, English Dept., PAR 108, Univ. of Texas, Austin, TX 78712

The American Voice, 332 W. Broadway, Ste. 1215, Louisville, KY 40202

Amherst Writers & Artists Press, P.O. Box 1076, Amherst, MA 01004

The Amicus Journal, 40 West 20th St., New York, NY 10011

Another Chicago Magazine, 3709 N. Kenmore, Chicago, IL 60613

Anterior Bitewing, Ltd., 993 Allspice Ave., Fenton, MO 63026

Anterior Fiction Quarterly, Monthly Review & Poetry Monthly, see Anterior Bitewing, Ltd.

Antietam Review, 7 West Franklin St., Hagerstown, MD 21740

Antioch Review, P.O. Box 148, Yellow Springs, OH 45387

Apalachee Quarterly, P.O. Box 20106, Tallahassee, FL 32316

Artful Dodge, English Dept., College of Wooster, Wooster OH 44691

Ascent, P.O. Box 967, Urbana, IL 61801

Asian Pacific American Journal, 296 Elizabeth St., Ste., #2R, New York, NY 10012

Atlanta Review, P.O. Box 8248, Atlanta, GA 30306

Aura, Box 76, Hill University Center, Birmingham, AL 35294

AVEC, P.O. Box 1059, Penngrove, CA 94951

B

Back Porch Press, 675 Oyster Rd, Rose City, MI 48654

Bamboo Ridge, P.O. Box 61781, Honolulu, HI 96839

Bayousphere, 2700 Bay Area Blvd, Box 456, Houston, TX 77058

Beacon Street Review, WLP Div., Emerson College, 100 Beacon St., Boston, MA 02116

Bear House Publishing, Rte. 2, Box 94, Eureka Springs, AR 72632

Belletrist Review, 17 Farmington Ave., Ste. 290, Plainville, CT 06062

Bellowing Ark. P.O. Box 45637, Seattle, WA 98145

Beloit Poetry Journal, RFD 2, Box 154, Ellsworth, ME 04605

Berkeley Poetry Review, 200 MLK Student Union, Univ. of California, Berkeley, CA 94720

Bilingual Press, Hispanic Research Center, Arizona State Univ., Box 872702, Tempe, AZ 85287

Black Hammock Review, 175 Gem Lake Dr., Maitland, FL 32751

Black Hat Press, Box 12, Goodhue, MN 55027

Black Moon, 233 Northway Rd., Reisterstown, MD 21136

Black Moss Press, 2450 Byng Rd., Windsor, Ont. N8W 3E8, Canada

The Bloomsbury Review, 1028 Bannock St., Denver, CO 80204

Blue Begonia Press, 225 Soth 15th Ave., Yakima, WA 98902

Blue Heron Publishing, Inc., 24450 N.W. Hansen Rd., Hillsboro, OR 97124

Blue Penny Quarterly, 102B Morris Paul Court, Charlottesville, VA 22903

Bluestem Press, English Dept., Emporia State Univ., Emporia, KS 66801

BOA Editions, 92 Park Ave, Brockport, NY 14420

BOMB, 594 Broadway, #1002A, New York, NY 10012

Borderlands: Texas Poetry Review, P.O. Box 49818, Austin, TX 78765

Bottom Dog Press, Firelands College, Huron, OH 44839

Bottomfish, DeAnza College, 21250 Stevens Creek Blvd., Cupertino, CA 95014

Bouillabaise, see Alpha Beat Press

Boulevard, P.O. Box 30386, Philadelphia, PA 19103

Briar Cliff Review, Briar Cliff College, 3303 Rebecca St., Sioux City, IA 51104

The Bridge, 14050 Vernon St., Oak Park, MI 48237

Bridgeworks Publishing Co., Bridge Lane, Box 1798, Bridgehampton, NY 11932

Brooklyn Review, English Dept., Brooklyn College of CUNY, 2900 Bedford Ave., Brooklyn, NY 11210

Brownbag Press, see Hyacinth House Publications

Burning Deck, 71 Elmgrove Ave., Providence, RI 02906

C

Cafe Solo, 222 Chaplin, San Luis Obispo, CA 93405

Calyx, Inc., P.O. Box B, 216 S.W. Madison, Corvallis, OR 97339

The Camel Press, Big Cove Tannery, PA 17212

The Caribbean Writer, Univ. of Virgin Islands, RR02 - Box 10,000, Kingshill, St. Croix, U.S. Virgin Islands, 00850

Carnegie Mellon University Press, Carnegie Mellon Univ., Baker Hall, Box 30, Pittsburgh, PA 15213

Carolina Quarterly, CB #3520 Greenlaw Hall, Univ. of North Carolina, Chapel Hill, NC 27599

Carter & Company Press, P.O. Box 7161, Syracuse, NY 13261

Center Press, Box 16452, Encino, CA 91416

The Chariton Review, Northeast Missouri State Univ., Kirksville, MO 63501

Chattahoochee Review, DeKalb College, Dunwoody, GA 30338

Chelsea, Box 773, Cooper Sta., New York, NY 10276

Chestnut Hills Press, see New Poets Series, Inc.

Chicago Review, Univ. of Chicago, 5801 S. Kenwood Ave., Chicago, IL 60637

Chiron Review, 522 E. South Ave, Saint John, KS 67576

Cimarron Review, Oklahoma State Univ., Stillwater, OK 74078

Cincinnati Poetry Review, College of Mount St. Joseph, 5701 Delhi Rd., Cincinnati, OH 45233

Clockwatch Review, English Dept., Illinois Wesleyan Univ., Bloomington, IL 61702

Colorado Review, English Dept., Colorado State Univ., Ft. Collins, CO 80523

Confluence, Box 336, Belpre, OH 45714

Confluence Press, Inc., Lewis-Clark State College, 500 8th Ave., Lewiston, ID 83501

Confrontation, English Dept., C.W. Post of L.I.U. of Brookville, NY 11548

Conjunctions, Bard College, Annandale-on-Hudson, NY 12504

Countermeasures, Creative Writing Prog., College of Santa Fe, Santa Fe, NM 87505

Cranberry Books, P.O. Box 1229, Duxbury, MA 02331

Crazyhorse, English Dept., Univ. of Arkansas, Little Rock, AR 72204

Cream City Review, English Dept., Univ. of Wisconsin, P.O. Box 413, Milwaukee, WI 53201

Creative Nonfiction, P.O. Box 81536, Pittsburgh, PA 15217

The Crescent Review, P.O. Box 15069, Chevy Chase, MD 20825

The Crossing Press, P.O. Box 1048, Freedom, CA 95019

Crowbait Review, See Hyacinth House Publications

Cumberland Poetry Review, P.O. Box 120128, Acklen Sta., Nashville, TN 37212

D

Damascus Works, 1 East University Parkway, #1101, Baltimore, MD 21218

John Daniel & Co., Publishers, Inc., P.O. Box 21922, Santa Barbara, CA 93121

Daughters of Nyx, P.O. Box 1187, White Salmon, WA 98672

Dead Metaphor Press, P.O. Box 2076, Boulder, CO 80306

Denver Quarterly, English Dept., Univ. of Denver, Denver, CO 80208

Dog River Review, 5976 Billings Rd., Parkdale, OR 97041

The Double Dealer Redux, 624 Pirate's Alley, New Orleans, LA 70116

Downstate Story, 1825 Maple Ridge, Peoria, IL 61614

Duluth's Split Rock, 1527 North 36 St., Sheboygan, WI 53081

E

The Ear, Irvine Valley College, 5500 Irvine Center Dr., Irvine, CA 92720

East & West Literary Quarterly, 754 Broadway, #23, San Francisco, CA 94133

Edge City Review, 10912 Harpers Square Court, Reston, VA 22091

Eighth Mountain Press, 624 S.E. 29th Ave., Portland, OR 97214

Epoch, 251 Goldwin Smith Hall, Cornell Univ., Ithaca, NY 14853

Ergo!, see One Reel (Publ.)

Exit 13 Magazine, 22 Oakwood Ct., Fanwood, NJ 07023

Exquisite Corpse, P.O. Box 25051, Baton Rouge, LA 70894

F

Fall Creek Press, P.O. Box 1127, Fall Creek, OR 97438

Farmer's Market, 602 S. Washington, #4, Bloomington, IL 61701

Faultline, P.O. Box 599-4960, Irvine, CA 92716

The Feminist Press at City Univ. of New York, 311 E. 94th St., New York, NY 10128

Fiction, English Dept., CCNY, Convent Ave. at 138th St., New York, NY 10031

Fiction International, English Dept., San Diego State Univ., 5500 Campanile Dr., San Diego, CA 92182

Field, English Dept., Rice Hall, Oberlin College, Oberlin, OH 44074

Fine Madness, P.O. Box 31138, Seattle, WA 98103

The Florida Review, English Dept., Univ. of Central Florida, Orlando, FL 32816

The Flying Island, c/o Writers' Center of Indianapolis, P.O. Box 88386 Indianapolis, IN 46208

Footwork: The Paterson Literary Review, One College Blvd., Paterson, NJ 07505

The Formalist, 320 Hunter Dr., Evansville, IN 47711

Four Quarters, LaSalle Univ., Philadelphia, PA 19141

Free Spirit Magazine, 107 Sterling Place, Brooklyn, NY 11217

Frogpond, 970 Acequia Madre, Santa Fe, NM 87501

G

GalHattan Press, 5 West 31st St., 7th fl., New York, NY 10001

Georgetown Review, 400 E. College St., Box 227, Georgetown, KY 40324

The Georgia Review, Univ. of Georgia, Athens, GA 30602

The Gettysburg Review, Gettysburg College, Gettysburg, PA 17325

Glimmer Train, 812 SW Washington St., Ste., 1205, Portland, OR 97205

Grand Street, 131 Varick St., Rm. 906, New York, NY 10013

Grasslands Review, English Dept., Univ. of No. Texas, P.O. Box 13827, Denton, TX 76203

Graywolf Press, 2402 University Ave., Ste. 203, St. Paul, MN 55114

Green Fuse Magazine, 3365 Holland Dr., Santa Rosa, CA 95404

Green Mountain Trading Post, Box 4100, St. Johnsbury, VT 05819

Green Mountains Review, Johnson State College, Johnson, VT 05656

Greensboro Review, English Dept., Univ. of North Carolina, Greensboro, NC 27412

Gulf Coast, English Dept., Univ. of Houston, Houston, TX 77204

H

Haight-Ashbury Literary Journal, 558 Joost Ave., San Francisco, CA 94127

Hammers, 1718 Sherman Ave., Ste. 203, Evanston, IL 60201

Hanging Loose Press, 231 Wyckoff St., Brooklyn, NY 11217

The Harvard Advocate, 21 South St., Cambridge, MA 02138

Harvard Review, Harvard College Library, Cambridge, MA 02138

Hayden's Ferry Review, Box 871502, Arizona State Univ., Tempe, AZ 85287

Heaven Bone Magazine, P.O. Box 486, Chester, NY 10918

Heresies, P.O. Box 1306, Canal St., Sta., New York, NY 10013

High Plains Literary Review, 180 Adams St., Ste. 250, Denver, CO 80206

Hot Pepper Press, P.O. Box 39, Somerset, CA 95684

Houston Poetry Fest, P.O. Box 1995, Bellaire, TX 77402

Hubbub, 5344 S.E. 38th Ave., Portland, OR 97202

The Hudson Review, 684 Park Ave., New York, NY 10021

Hyacinth House Publications, P.O. Box 120, Fayetteville, AR 72702

I

Icarus, 29 East 21st St., New York, NY 10010

The Iconoclast, 1675 Amazon Rd., Mohegan Lake, NY 10547

The Illinois Review, English Dept., Illinois State Univ., Normal, IL 61790

Indiana Review, 316 N. Jordan Ave., Indiana Univ., Bloomington, IN 47405

Interim, English Dept., Univ. of Nevada, Las Vegas, NV 89154

International Poetry Review, Dept. of Romance Lang., Univ. of North Carolina, Greensboro, NC 27412

Iowa Review, 308 EPB, Univ. of Iowa, Iowa City, IA 52242

Iowa Woman, P.O. Box 680, Iowa City, IA 52244

J

The James White Review, P.O. Box 3356, Butler Sq. Sta., Minneapolis, MN 55403

The Journal, English Dept., Ohio State Univ., Columbus, OH 43210

Journal of New Jersey Poets, County College of Morris, 214 Center Grove Rd., Randolph, NJ 07869

Just A Moment, P.O. Box 40, Jamesville, NY 13078

K

Kalliope, Florida Community College, 3939 Roosevelt Blvd., Jacksonville, FL 32205

Kansas Quarterly, English Dept., Kansas State Univ., Manhattan, KS 66506

Kelsey Review, Mercer County Community College, P.O. Box B, Trenton, NJ 08690

Kelsey Street Press, 2718 Ninth St., Berkeley, CA 94710

The Kenyon Review, Kenyon College, Gambier, OH 43022

Kestrel, Division of Lang. & Lit., Fairmont State College, 1201 Locust Ave., Fairmont, WV 26554

Kings Estate Press, 870 Kings Estate Rd., St. Augustine, FL 32086

L

Laurel Moon, Brandeis Univ., P.O. Box 9110, Waltham, MA 02254

The Laurel Review, English Dept., Northwest Missouri State Univ., Maryville, MO 64468

The Ledge, 64-65 Cooper Ave., Glendale, NY 11385

Left Bank, see Blue Heron Publishing, Inc.

Light, Box 7500, Chicago, IL 60680

LILT, Kansas City Art Institute, 4415 Warwwick Blvd., Kansas City, MO 64111

Lips, P.O. Box 1345, Montclair, NJ 07042

Literal Latte, 61 East 8th St., Box 240, New York, NY 10003

The Literary Review, Fairleigh Dickinson Univ., 285 Madison Ave., Madison, NJ 07940

Lone Oak Press, 304 11th Ave., SE., Rochester, MN 55905

Lone Stars Magazine, 14102 Gray Wing Dr., San Antonio, TX 78231

The Lowell Review, 22 Winstead Ave, Methuen, MA 01844

Lynx House Press, Box 640, Amherst, MA 01004

M

The MacGuffin, Schoolcraft College, 18600 Haggerty Rd., Livonia, MI 48152

Mac*Kinations, P.O. Box 1660, Dickinson, TX 77539

Maine Progressive, 617 East Neck Rd., Nobleboro, ME 04555

Mala Revija, English Dept., Univ. of Tennessee, Chattanooga, TN 37403

Manic D Press, Box 410804, San Francisco, CA 94141

Manoa, English Dept., Univ. of Hawaii, Honolulu, HI 96822

Many Mountains Moving, 2525 Arapahoe Ave., Ste. E4-309. Boulder, CO 80302

Massachusetts Review, Univ. of Massachusetts, Amherst, MA 01003

The Maverick Press, Rte. 2, Box 4915, Eagle Pass, TX 78852

Mayapple Press, P.O. Box 5743, Saginaw, MI 48603

Mercury House, P.O. Box 422820, San Francisco, CA 94142

Michigan Quarterly Review, Univ. of Michigan, 3032 Rackham Bldg., Ann Arbor, MI 48109

Mid-American Review, English Dept., Bowling Green State Univ., Bowling Green, OH 43403

Midstream, 110 East 59th St., New York, NY 10022

Mind in Motion, P.O. Box 1118, Apple Valley, CA 92307

Mississippi Mud, 1505 Drake Ave., Austin, TX 78704

Mississippi Review, Univ. of Southern Mississippi, Box 5144, Hatties- burg, MS 39406

The Missouri Review, 1507 Hillcrest Hall, Univ. of Missouri, Colum- bia, MO 65211

Mockingbird, P.O. Box 761, Davis, CA 95617

Mostly Main, P.O. Box 8805, Portland, ME 04104

Mudfish, 184 Franklin St., New York, NY 10013

My Legacy, c/o Weems Concepts, HCR-13, Box 21AA, Artemas, PA 17211

N

Nebo: A Literary Journal, English Dept., Arkansas Tech. Univ., Rus- selville, AR 72801

The Nebraska Review, Writer's Workshop, Univ. of Nebraska, Omaha, NE 68182

Negative Capability, 62 Ridgelawn Dr. East, Mobile, AL 36608

New England Review, Middlebury College, Middlebury, VT 05753

New Letters, Univ. of Missouri, 5100 Rockhill Rd., Kansas City, MO 64110

New Orleans Review, Loyola Univ., New Orleans, LA 70118

New Poets Series, Inc., 541 Piccadilly Rd., Baltimore, MD 21204

New York University Press, 70 Washington Sq. South, New York, NY 10012

Next Phase, see Phantom Press

96 Inc. P.O. Box 15559, Boston, MA 02215

North American Review, Univ. of Northern Iowa, Cedar Falls, IA 50614

North Carolina Literary Review, English Dept., East Carolina Univ., Greenville, NC 27858

Northeast Corridor, Beaver College, 450 S. Easton RD., Glenside, PA 19038

Northland Publishing, P.O. Box 1389, Flagstaff, AZ 86002

Northwest Review, 369 PLC, Univ. of Oregon, Eugene, OR 97403

Northwoods Journal, P.O. Box 298, Thomaston, ME 04861

O

Oasis, P.O. Box 626, Largo, FL 34649

Object Lesson, Hampshire College, Box 1186, Amherst, MA 01002

Ogalala Review, P.O. Box 628, Guymon, OK 73942

Ohio Poetry Review, 985 Hyde-shaffer Rd., Bristolville, OH 44402

The Ohio Review, Ellis Hall, Ohio Univ., Athens, OH 45701

Old Crow Review, P.O. Box 662, Amherst, MA 01004

Old Paint Publishing Co., Drawer 5965, Carefree, AZ 85377

The Old Red Kimono, Humanities Div., Floyd College, Box 1864, Rome, GA 30162

One Reel, P.O. Box 9750, Seattle WA 98109

Onion River Review, P.O. Box 7345, York, PA 17404

Ontario Review, 9 Honey Brook Dr., Princeton, NJ 08540

Orchises Press, P.O. Box 20602, Alexandria, VA 22320

Osiris, Box 297, Deerfield, MA 01842

Other Voices, English Dept., Univ. of Illinois, 601 S. Morgan St., Chicago, IL 60607

Outerbridge, English Dept., College of Staten Island, Staten Island, NY 10314

Oxalis, P.O. Box 3993, Kingston, NY 12401

Oxford Magazine, English Dept., Miami Univ., Oxford, OH 45056

P

Palo Alto Review, 1400 W. Villaret, San Antonio, TX 78224
Papier-Mache Press, 135 Aviation Way, #14, Watsonville, CA 95076
The Paris Review, 541 East 72nd St., New York, NY 10021
Parnassus Literary Journal, P.O. Box 1384, Forest Park, GA 30051
Parting Gifts, 3413 Wilshire, Greensboro, NC 27408
Partisan Review, 236 Bay State Rd., Boston, MA 02215
Passages North, Kalamazoo College, 1200 Academy St., Kalamazoo,
    MI 49006
Pearl, 3030 E. Second St., Long Beach, CA 90803
Peregrine, see Amherst Writers & Artists Press
Persephone Press, 22-B Pine Lake Dr., Whispering Pines, NC 28327
Phantom Press, 5A Green Meadow Dr., Nantucket Island, MA 02554
The Pittsburgh Quarterly, 36 Haberman Ave., Pittsburgh, PA 15211
Pivot, 250 Riverside Dr., #23, New York, NY 10025
Plain Brown Wrapper, 130 W. Limestone, Yellow Springs, OH 45387
Pleiades, English Dept., Central Missouri State Univ., Warrensburg,
    MO 64093
Ploughshares, 100 Beacon St., Boston, MA 02116
The Plum Review, P.O. Box 1347, Philadelphia, PA 19105
Plympton Press International, 955 Massachusetts Ave., Cambridge,
    MA 02139
POEM, English Dept., Univ. of Alabama, Huntsville, AL 35899
Poems & Plays, English Dept., P.O. Box 70, Middle Tennessee Univ.,
    Murfreesboro, TN 37132
Poems that Thump in the Dark, 32-34 138th St., #6F, Kew Gardens,
    NY 11435
Poet Lore, 4508 Walsh St., Bethesda, MD 20815
Poet Magazine, P.O. Box 54947, Oklahoma City, OK 73154
Poetalk, P.O. Box 11435, Berkeley, CA 94712
Poetry, 60 Walton St., Chicago, IL 60610
Poetry East, 802 W. Belden Ave., Chicago, IL 60614
Poetry Flash, P.O. Box 4172, Berkeley, CA 94704
Poetry Miscellany, English Dept., Univ., of Tennessee, Chattanooga,
    TN 37403
Poets On, 29 Loring Ave., Mill Valley, CA 94941
Poet's Sanctuary, P.O. Box 832, Hopkins, MN 55343
The Poet's Voice, 6407 W. 32nd St., Loveland, CO 80538
Portals Press, 4411 Fontainebleau Dr., New Orleans, LA 70125

Potato Eyes, P.O. Box 76, Ward Hill, Troy, ME 04987

Potpourri, P.O. Box 8278, Prairie Village, KS 66208

Prairie Schooner, 201 Andrews Hall, Univ. of Nebraska, Lincoln, NE 68588

Primal Publishing, P.O. Box 1179, Allston, MA 02134

The Prose Poem, English Dept., Providence College, Providence, RI 02198

Provincetown Arts Press, 650 Commercial St., Provincetown, MA 02657

Psychotrain, see Hyacinth House Publishing

Puck, 47 Noe St., Ste. 4, San Francisco, CA 94114

Puerto Del Sol, College of Arts & Sc., Box 3E, New Mexico State Univ., Las Cruces, NM 88001

Q

Quarterly West, 317 Oplin Union, Univ. of Utah, Salt Lake City, UT 84112

QED Press, 155 Cypress St., Fort Bragg, CA 94537

A Quiet Cup, see Carter & Co. Press

R

Rag Mag, see Black Hat Press

Rain City Review, 7215 S.W. LaView Dr., Portland, OR 97219

Rant, P.O. Box 6872, Yorkville, Sta., New York, NY 10128

Raritan, Rutgers State Univ. of N.J., New Brunswick, NJ 08903

Red Clay, 349 Davis Rd., Pelzer, SC 29669

Red Dancefloor Press, P.O. Box 4974, Lancaster, CA 93539

Redwood Coven Press, P.O. Box 9552, Oakland, CA 94613

REFLECT, 3306 Argonne Ave., Norfolk, VA 23509

River Oak Review, P.O. Box 3127, Oak Park, IL 60303

Riverwest Review, P.O. Box 11116, Milwaukee, WI 53211

Road Map Series, #13 Lapanday Rd., Panorama Homes 8000, Davao City, Phillipines

Rose Shell Press, 5111 N. 42nd. Ave., Phoenix, AZ 85019

Rotund World, see Mississippi Mud

Ruby, P.O. Box 5915, Takoma Park, MD 20913

S

Salt Hill Journal, English Dept., Syracuse Univ., Syracuse, NY 13244

Sandstone Publishing, P.O. Box 36701, Charlotte, NC 28236

Sasquatch Books, see One Reel

Satire, 12109-A Old Frederick Rd., Thurmont, MD 21788

Scots Plaid Press, see Persephone Press

The Seal Press, 3131 Western Ave., #410, Seattle, WA 98121

Second Glance, 82-34 138th St., #6F, Kew Gardens, NY 11435

Self-Reliance Press, 1525 Vinsetta Blvd., Royal Oak, MI 48067

Seneca Review, Hobart & William Smith Colleges, Geneva, NY 14456

Sewanee Review, Univ. of the South, Sewanee, TN 37375

Sheep Meadow Press, P.O. Box 1345, Riverdale-on-Hudson, NY 10471

Shenandoah, Box 722, Lexington, VA 24450

Short Fiction by Women, Box 1254, Old Chelsea Sta., New York, NY 10011

The Silver Web, P.O. Box 38190, Tallahassee, FL 32315

Sistersong, P.O. Box 7405, Pittsburgh, PA 15213

Skylark, Purdue Univ., Hammond, IN 46323

SLANT, UCA, P.O. Box 5063, Conway, AR 72035

Slapering Hol Press, Hudson Valley Writers' Center, Inc., P.O. Box 366, Tarrytown, NY 10591

Slipstream, Box 2071, New Market Sta., Niagara Falls, NY 14301

Snowy Egret, P.O. Box 9, Bowling Green IN 47833

Somersault Pree, P.O. Box 1428, El Cerrito, CA 94530

Sonora Review, English Dept., Univ. of Arizona, Tucson, AZ 85721

Soundings East, Salem State College, Salem, MA 01970

South Dakota Review, English Dept., Univ. of South Dakota, Vermillion, SD 57069

The Southern Anthology, 2851 Johnston St., Box 321, Lafayette, LA 70503

The Southern Review, 43 Allen Hall, Louisiana State Univ., Baton Rouge, LA 70803

Southwest Review, Box 374, Southern Methodist Univ., Dallas, TX 75275

Sou'wester, English Dept., Southern Illinois Univ., Edwardsville, IL 62026

Sow's Ear Poetry Review, see Sow's Ear Press

Sow's Ear Press, 19535 Pleasant View Dr., Abingdon, VA 24211

Spinster's Ink, P.O. Box 300170, Minneapolis, MN 55403

Spout, 1704 ½ Fillmore St., NE Minneapolis, MN 55413

Sticks Press, P.O. Box 399, Maplesville, AL 36750

Stone Bridge Press, P.O. Box 8208, Berkeley, CA 94707

Stories, Box 1467, Arlington, MA 02174

Story, 1507 Dana Ave., Cincinnati, OH 45207

Story Line Press, 3 Oaks Farm, Brownsville, OR 97327

Story Quarterly, P.O. Box 1416, Northbrook, IL 60065

The Stylus, 9412 Huron Ave., Richmond, VA 23294

The Sun, 107 No. Roberson St., Chapel Hill, NC 27516

Sycamore Review, English Dept., Purdue Univ., West Lafayette, IN 47907

Synaesthetic, 178-10 Wexford Terrace, Apt. 3D, Jamaica, NY 11432

T

Talking River Review, Div. of Lit. & Lang., Lewis-Clark State College, Lewiston, ID 83501

Tamaqua, Humanities Dept., Parkland College, 2400 W. Bradley Ave., Champaign, IL 61821

that:,c/o S. Dignazio, 1070 Easton Valley Rd. Easton, NH 03580

Thema, Box 74109, Metairie, LA 70033

Thin Coyote, 941 Goodrich, Apt. B, St. Paul, MN 55105

360 Degrees:Art & Lit. Review, 980 Bush St., Ste. 200, San Francisco, CA 94109

Threepenny Review, P.O. Box 9131, Berkeley, CA 94709

Tilbury House, Publishers, 132 Water St., Gardiner, ME 04345

Tomorrow Magazine, P.O. Box 148486, Chicago, IL 60614

Toton, English Dept., Humboldt State Univ., Arcata, CA 95521

Trafika, Columbia P.O. Box 250413, New York, NY 10025

Transfer Magazine, 900 Campus Dr., #216, Daly City, CA 94015

Trask House Books, Inc., 3222 NE Schuyler, Portland, OR 97212

Treasure House, 1106 Oak Hill Ave., #3A, Hagerstown, MD 21742

TriQuarterly, Northwestern Univ., 2020 Ridge Ave., Evanston, IL 60208

Turning Wheel, P.O. Box 4650, Berkeley, CA 94704

U

University of Massachusetts Press, P.O. Box 429, Amherst, MA 01004
University of Pittsburgh Press, 127 N. Bellefield Ave., Pittsburgh, PA 15260
Unsoma, 349 Davis Rd., Pelzer, SC 29669
The Urbanite, P.O. Box 4737, Davenport, IA 52808
Uroboros Books, 4043 Breakwood Dr., Houston, TX 77025

V

Venom Press, 519 East 5 St., #17, New York, NY 10009
Verse, 33 Lowry's Lane, Rosemont, PA 19010
Via Obscura Editions, 601 S. Mesa Hills Dr., #1535, El Paso, TX 79912
Viet Nam Generation, 18 Center Rd., Woodbridge, CT 06525
The Vincent Brothers Review, 4566 Northern Circle, Riverside, OH 45424
Virginia Quarterly Review, One West Range, Charlottesville, VA 22903
Voices Israel, P.O. Box 5780, 46157 Herzlia, Israel

W

Washington Review, Box 50132, Washington, DC 20091
Washington Writers' Publishing House, P.O. Box 15271, Washington, DC 20003
Webster Review, Webster Univ., Webster Groves, MO 63119
Weighted Anchor Press, see Object Lesson
Wellspring, 770 Tonkawa, Long Lake, MN 55356
West Branch, Bucknell Univ., Lewisburg, PA 17837
West Word, UCLA Extension, The Writers' Program, 10995 Le Conte Ave., #440, Los Angeles, CA 90024
Western Humanities Review, English Dept., Univ. of Utah, Salt Lake City, UT 84112
Whetstone, P.O. Box 1266, Barrington, IL 60011
White Eagle Coffee Store Press, P.O. Box 383, Fox River Grove, IL 60021
William & Mary Review, P.O. Box 8795, Williamsburg, VA 23187

Willow Springs, EWU, 526-5th St., MS1, Cheney, WA 99004

Without Halos, P.O. Box 1342, Pt. Pleasant Beach, NJ 08742

Witness, Oakland Community College, 27055 Orchard Lake Rd., Farmington Hills, MI 48344

Women & Recovery, P.O. Box 151947, Cuperino, CA 95015

The Worcester Review, 6 Chatham St., Worcester, MA 01608

Wordcraft of Oregon, P.O. Box 3235, La Grande, OR 97850

Wormwood Review, P.O. Box 4698, Stockton, CA 95204

Writers' Forum, Univ. of Colorado, P.O. Box 7150, Colorado Springs, CO 80933

The Writing Self, P.O. Box 245, Lenox Hill Sta., New York, NY 10021

Y

Yale Review, P.O. Box 1902A Yale Station, New Haven, CT 06520

Yellow Silk, P.O. Box 6374, Albany, CA 94706

Z

ZYZZYVA, 41 Sutter, Ste. 1400, San Francisco, CA 94104

INDEX

The following is a listing in alphabetical order by author's last name of works reprinted in the first twenty *Pushcart Prize* editions.

548

555

556

557

560

568